Embodied Encounters

New approaches to psychoanalysis and cinema

Edited by Agnieszka Piotrowska

Routledge
Taylor & Francis Group
LONDON AND NEW YORK

First published 2015
by Routledge
27 Church Road, Hove, East Sussex, BN3 2FA

and by Routledge
711 Third Avenue, New York, NY 10017

Routledge is an imprint of the Taylor & Francis Group, an informa business

© 2015 Agnieszka Piotrowska

The right of the editor to be identified as the author of the editorial material, and of the authors for their individual chapters, has been asserted in accordance with sections 77 and 78 of the Copyright, Designs and Patents Act 1988.

All rights reserved. No part of this book may be reprinted or reproduced or utilised in any form or by any electronic, mechanical, or other means, now known or hereafter invented, including photocopying and recording, or in any information storage or retrieval system, without permission in writing from the publishers.

Trademark notice: Product or corporate names may be trademarks or registered trademarks, and are used only for identification and explanation without intent to infringe.

British Library Cataloguing in Publication Data
A catalogue record for this book is available from the British Library

Library of Congress Cataloging in Publication Data
Embodied encounters : new approaches to psychoanalysis and cinema / edited by Agnieszka Piotrowska.
pages cm
ISBN 978-1-138-79524-2 (hardback) -- ISBN 978-1-138-79525-9 (paperback) -- ISBN 978-1-315-75854-1 (ebook) 1. Motion pictures--Psychological aspects. 2. Psychoanalysis and motion pictures. 3. Jungian psychology. I. Piotrowska, Agnieszka, editor.
PN1995.E63 2015
791.43019--dc23
2014014364

ISBN: 978-1-138-79524-2 (hbk)
ISBN: 978-1-138-79525-9 (pbk)
ISBN: 978-1-315-75854-1 (ebk)

Typeset in Times
by Saxon Graphics Ltd, Derby

Embodied Encounters

What is the role of the unconscious in our visceral approaches to cinema?

Embodied Encounters offers a unique collection of essays written by leading thinkers and writers in film studies, with a guiding principle that embodied and material existence can, and perhaps ought to, also allow for the unconscious. The contributors embrace work which has brought 'the body' back into film theory and question why psychoanalysis has been excluded from more recent interrogations.

The chapters included here engage with Jung and Freud, Lacan and Bion, and Klein and Winnicott in their interrogations of contemporary cinema and the moving image. In three parts the book presents examinations of both classic and contemporary films including *Black Swan*, *Zero Dark Thirty* and *The Dybbuk*:

Part I – The Desire, the Body and the Unconscious
Part II – Psychoanalytical Theories and the Cinema
Part III – Reflections and Destructions, Mirrors and Transgressions

Embodied Encounters is an eclectic volume which presents in one book the voices of those who work with different psychoanalytical paradigms. It will be essential reading for psychoanalysts and psychotherapists as well as scholars and students of film and culture studies and film makers.

Agnieszka Piotrowska is an internationally recognized award-winning film maker, best known for her documentary *Married to the Eiffel Tower*. She is a Reader in Film Theory and Practice at the University of Bedfordshire, UK and is the author of *Psychoanalysis and Ethics in Documentary Film* (Routledge, 2014).

To fellow travellers.

Contents

List of figures	ix
List of contributors	x
Acknowledgements	xiv
Introduction AGNIESZKA PIOTROWSKA	1

PART I
The desire, the body and the unconscious   9

1   **Catherine Breillat and Courbet's *L'origine du monde* [*The origin of the world*] (1866)**   11
EMMA WILSON

2   *Nachträglichkeit* **and** *après coup* **in documentary film: the suffering of Aileen Wuornos as told by Nick Broomfield**   22
AGNIESZKA PIOTROWSKA

3   **The ventriloquism of documentary first-person speech and the self-portrait film**   36
ELIZABETH COWIE

4   **Identification and mutual recognition in Darren Aronofsky's *Black Swan***   51
JULIE SEXENY

5   **Terrence Malick's diptych**   60
JOHN IZOD AND JOANNA DOVALIS

PART II
Psychoanalytical theories and the cinema 75

6 Therapy and cinema: making images and finding meanings 77
   LUKE HOCKLEY

7 Psychoanalytic soundings: the case of *The Dybbuk* 91
   STEPHEN FROSH

8 Process and medium in the practice of filmmaking: the work of Jayne Parker 102
   CARLA AMBRÓSIO GARCIA

9 *Zero Dark Thirty*: 'war autism' or a Lacanian ethical act? 117
   AGNIESZKA PIOTROWSKA

10 An atheist's guide to feminine jouissance: on *Black Swan* and the other satisfaction 131
    BEN TYRER

11 Documentary and psychoanalysis: putting the love back in epistephilia 147
    MICHAEL RENOV

PART III
Reflections and destructions, mirrors and transgressions 157

12 Douglas Gordon and Cory Arcangel: breaking the toy 159
    ROBERT BURGOYNE

13 *Mirror* images: D.W. Winnicott in the visual field 171
    VICKY LEBEAU

14 Pinning a tale: the screen, the donkey and the MacGuffin 183
    CAROL MACGILLIVRAY

15 The poetics of maternal loss in Tarkovsky's *The Mirror* 194
    HELENA BASSIL-MOROZOW

16 Talking about Kevin: first-, second- and third-person narratives 207
    NAOMI SEGAL

17 This book has no pictures (a visual documentary of psychoanalysis) 219
    NICHOLAS MUELLNER

Index 227

Figures

I.1	*Obscure Window 1* by Nicholas Muellner	6
2.1	Aileen Wuornos in *Aileen: Life and Death of a Serial Killer* (2003), dir. Nick Broomfield	28
2.2	Aileen Wuornos in *Aileen Wuornos: The Selling of a Serial Killer* (1992) and *Aileen: Life and Death of a Serial Killer* (2003), dir. Nick Broomfield	29
3.1	Production still showing Grotowski being filmed as he asks the elderly man about Janek	46
3.2	Grotowski leads Franciszka's cows home	47
8.1	Jayne Parker in *FILM: Tacita Dean*	106
8.2	Stills from *K.* (16mm b/w film, sound, 13 mins, 1989)	108
8.3	Stills from *Foxfire Eins* (16mm film, video, b/w, sound, 10 mins, 2000)	114
9.1	Žižek's diagram	125
13.1	*Obscure Window 2* by Nicholas Muellner	179
14.1	A simple visualisaion of the diasynchronoscope	184
14.2	The artwork 'One, Two, Three…' (2013)	186
14.3	A captured moment from Gaffer (2012)	190

Contributors

Robert Burgoyne is Chair in Film Studies at the University of St Andrews. His work centres on historical representation and film, with a particular emphasis on questions of memory and emotion in film. Currently, he is working on the representation of war in film and photography. His recent book publications include *The Hollywood Historical Film* (Wiley-Blackwell, 2008); *Film Nation: Hollywood Looks at U.S. History: Revised Edition* (Minnesota, 2010); and *The Epic Film in World Culture* (Routledge, 2011).

Helena Bassil-Morozow, Ph.D., is a cultural philosopher, film scholar and academic writer whose many publications on film include the monographs *Tim Burton: the Monster and the Crowd* (Routledge, 2010) and *The Trickster in Contemporary Film* (Routledge, 2011). Helena is currently working on two new Routledge projects, *Identity, Systems and Tricksters* and *Jungian Film Studies: the Essential Guide* (the latter co-authored with Professor Luke Hockley).

Elizabeth Cowie is Professor Emeritus in Film Studies at the University of Kent, Canterbury. She was co-founder and co-editor in the 1970s of *m/f* a journal of feminist theory, and published *Representing the Woman: Cinema and Psychoanalysis* in 1997. She has subsequently written on film noir, on the horror of the horror film, and on the cinematic dream-work. She has published extensively on documentary, including her essays on landscape and sounds in documentary and her monograph *Recording Reality, Desiring the Real* (Minnesota University Press, 2011). Forthcoming work includes essays on documentary and surveillance, on voting, and on gesture in film.

Joanna N. Dovalis, Ph.D., is a Marriage, Family Therapist in private practice in southern California. She sees therapy as grief work, holding an essential role in the individuation process and fully actualising the self. As a depth psychotherapist, she combines her passions for the natural partnership of film and psyche, and their critical impact on the contemporary culture. Joanna gives the psychological interpretations to narratives written with co-author John Izod on films they feel have a significant impact on the grieving process. Their book *Cinema as Therapy: Grief and Transformational Film* will be published in 2014.

Stephen Frosh is Pro-Vice-Master and Professor in the Department of Psychosocial Studies at Birkbeck College, University of London. He is the author of many books and papers on psychosocial studies and on psychoanalysis, including *Psychoanalysis Outside the Clinic* (Palgrave, 2010), *Hate and the Jewish Science: Anti-Semitism, Nazism and Psychoanalysis* (Palgrave, 2005), *For and Against Psychoanalysis* (Routledge, 2006), *After Words* (Palgrave, 2002) and *The Politics of Psychoanalysis* (Palgrave, 1999). His most recent books are *Hauntings: Psychoanalysis and Ghostly Transmissions* (Palgrave, 2013), *Feelings* (Routledge, 2011) and *A Brief Introduction to Psychoanalytic Theory* (Palgrave, 2012).

Carla Ambrósio Garcia completed her Ph.D. in Film Studies at King's College London in 2013, which was funded by Fundação para a Ciência e a Tecnologia in Portugal. She is interested in psychoanalytic approaches to film, the experience of film and the practice of filmmaking, and her research focuses on the work of Wilfred Bion and Donald Meltzer. Alongside her writing, she develops her artistic practice, working primarily with 16mm film. Her first film (*Film #1*, 2003) was awarded a special mention at L'Alternativa Independent Cinema Festival in Barcelona.

Luke Hockley, Ph.D., is Professor of Media Analysis, in the Research Centre for Media, Art and Performance (RIMAP) at the University of Bedfordshire. He is also an integrative psychotherapist in private practice, UKCP reg. His latest book *Somatic Cinema: The relationship between body and screen – a Jungian perspective* was published by Routledge in 2013. His previous books include: *Jung and Film II: the return* (co-edited with Christopher Hauke, Routledge, 2011); *House: the Wounded Healer on Television* (co-edited with Leslie Gardner, Routledge, 2010); *Frames of Mind* (Intellect, 2013); and *Cinematic Projections* (University of Luton Press, 2000). He is joint Editor in Chief with Lucy Huskinson of the peer reviewed *International Journal of Jungian Studies* (*IJJS*).

John Izod is Emeritus Professor of Screen Analysis in Film, Media and Journalism at the University of Stirling. A Fellow of the Royal Society for Arts, he is also a Founding Fellow of the Institute of Contemporary Scotland. He has published many books: *Reading the Screen* (York Press, 1988); *Hollywood and the Box Office, 1895–1986* (Palgrave Macmillan, 1988); *The Films of Nicolas Roeg* (Palgrave Macmillan, 1992); *Myth, Mind and the Screen: Understanding the Heroes of our Time* (Cambridge University Press, 2001); *Screen, Culture, Psyche: A Post-Jungian Approach to Working with the Audience* (Routledge, 2006) and others. He and Joanna Dovalis have co-authored *Cinema and Therapy: Grief and Transformational Film*, to be published by Routledge in 2014.

Vicky Lebeau is a Professor of English at the University of Sussex. She has published widely in the fields of psychoanalysis and visual culture. She has recently published *Childhood and Cinema* (Reaktion and Chicago University Press, 2008). In psychoanalysis, she has interests in Freud, Winnicott, Andre Green, Jean Laplanche, Serge Leclaire, Michael Eigen, Joyce McDougall and Christopher Bollas. She is currently researching the topic of the 'arts of looking' (including writing on Shane Meadows, Michael Haneke, Gerhard Richter and Don DeLillo).

Carol MacGillivray, Ph.D., worked as a practitioner in film, animation and mixed media for 20 years. She co-authored a widely used textbook, *3D for the Web: Interactive 3D Animation using 3DS Max, Flash and Director* (with Anthony Head, Focal Press, 2005). Now a practising artist and researcher, Carol has recently finished her doctorate at Goldsmiths, University of London, where she formed an artistic partnership, Trope creating an immersive and screenless system of concrete animation called the *Diasynchronoscope*. The *Diasynchronoscope* has been widely praised by academics from psychology, media and art history as well as exhibition attendees and arts and science publications.

Nicholas Muellner is an artist whose work operates at the intersection of photography and writing. Through books, exhibitions and slide lectures, his projects investigate the limits of photography as a documentary pursuit as well as literary, political and personal narratives. His recent textual and visual books include *The Photograph Commands Indifference* (A-Jump Books, 2009), and *The Amnesia Pavilions* (A-Jump Books, 2011), which was selected as a top photo book of 2011 by *Time Magazine*. Muellner's writings on photography have been published by MACK, Afterimage, Triple Canopy, Art Journal and Rutgers University Press. He teaches photography and critical studies at the Park School of Communications, Ithaca College.

Agnieszka Piotrowska, Ph.D., is an award winning documentary filmmaker and a theorist. Her work focuses on psychoanalysis and subjectivity. She is well known for her controversial film *Married to the Eiffel Tower* (2008), which has been screened in more than 40 countries. Her latest film *The Engagement Party in Harare* (2013) was nominated for the Best Documentary in the IIFF in Zimbabwe as the only non-African filmmaker granted the distinction. Piotrowska is a Reader in Film Practice and Theory at the University of Bedfordshire. Her monograph *Psychoanalysis and Ethics in Documentary Film* was published by Routledge to enthusiastic reviews. She is currently working on de-colonial representation, particularly in the arts in Zimbabwe.

Michael Renov, Professor of Critical Studies at USC, USA, is the author or editor of several books on documentary film including *The Subject of Documentary* (Minnesota, 2004), *Theorizing Documentary* (Routledge, 1993) and, with Jane

Gaines, *Collecting Visible Evidence* (Minnesota, 1999). Renov is the co-founder of the Visible Evidence conference, which celebrated its 20th anniversary edition in Stockholm in August 2013.

Naomi Segal is a Professorial Fellow at Birkbeck, University of London. In 2004 she was founding Director of the Institute of Germanic & Romance Studies. Since the 1990s, she has served on/chaired numerous national and international committees within ESF, HERA, the British Academy, AHRC and AUPHF. She has published 77 articles and 15 books, most recently *From Literature to Cultural Literacy* (2014), *Vicissitudes: Histories and Destinies of Psychoanalysis* (2013), *'When Familiar Meanings Dissolve...': Essays in French studies in memory of Malcolm Bowie* (2011), *Consensuality: Didier Anzieu, Gender and the Sense of Touch* (2009), *Indeterminate Bodies* (2003), *Le Désir à l'Œuvre* (2000) and *André Gide: Pederasty & Pedagogy* (1998).

Julie Sexeny teaches film studies and production at Wofford College, USA, where she is an Assistant Professor of English. She received her Ph.D. in interdisciplinary studies from Emory University and an M.F.A. in filmmaking from Columbia University. She is currently researching the construction of girl subjectivity in children's films.

Ben Tyrer, Ph.D., is a lecturer in Film Studies at King's College London. He is currently preparing a monograph, titled *Out of the Past: Lacan and Film Noir*, which explores a relation between the structures of Lacanian psychoanalysis and the historiography of film noir in order to examine questions of genre, ontology and narrative, with the aim of reinvigorating the field of Lacanian Film Studies. His research interests include film theory and film philosophy, Left Bank filmmakers, and art and cinema.

Emma Wilson is Professor of French Literature and the Visual Arts at the University of Cambridge and a Fellow of Corpus Christi College. She is also Course Director of the M.Phil. in Screen Media and Cultures. Her recent books include *Cinema's Missing Children* (Columbia University Press, 2003), *Alain Resnais* (Manchester Unversity Press, 2006), *Atom Egoyan* (University of Illinois Press, 2009) and *Love, Mortality and the Moving Image* (Palgrave Macmillan, 2012).

Acknowledgements

First, I must express my gratitude for the support of Professor Garry Whannel who in his capacity as the Director of the Research Institute for Media and Performance at the University of Bedfordshire funded the Embodied Encounters event on 14 October 2013 at the Freud Museum. I am also grateful for the institutional support to Bill Rammell, James Crabbe and Karen Randell.

The majority of the essays in this book are original and this volume offers the first 'outing' for them. Some material in the chapters of Robert Burgoyne, Stephen Frosh and Luke Hockley were published before in respective publications by the Columbia University Press, Palgrave Macmillan and Routledge and a specific reference is given at the end of their chapters. We are grateful for permission to republish images: to Jayne Parker and Tate Modern for the permission to include her artwork in Carla Ambrósio Garcia's chapter, to Carol MacGillivray for her artwork in her chapter and for the brilliant design of the cover of the book, to Jill Godmilow and the Grotowski Institute for the permission to reproduce dialogue and two frames of the film in Elizabeth Cowie's chapter. I am also very grateful to Nick Broomfield for the time he spent talking to me and for his permission to reproduce the words and frame captures from his film *Aileen: Life and Death of a Serial Killer* (2003) in my chapter. We would also like to acknowledge the kindness of Profile Books for their permission to reproduce the dialogue from the book *We Need to Talk About Kevin* by Lionel Shriver in Naomi Segal's chapter.

My heartfelt thanks go to our publishers Routledge and in particular to Kate Hawes who has believed in the project and rushed it through various publishing systems and to Susannah Frearson who has exceedingly efficiently dealt with a demanding volume of 16 contributors. My production editor Natalie Larkin has again been patience incarnate. Without this wonderful team the volume would not have been produced so efficiently and so beautifully.

Last but not least, I would like to say 'thank you' to my collaborators, the fabulous writers of all the chapters. The quality of the thinking and writing is quite astonishing in this book, even if I say so myself. I am grateful for your unshakable support for the project and for me personally, for the speed of your delivery, for the boldness and clarity of your vision, for the commitment and reliability that has made us into an amazing team. It has been a great learning experience for me and a privilege to be working with you all. Thank you so very much. I am deeply proud to have put this volume together and it is my hope that it will become what we have all hoped for it to be – a lasting intervention.

Introduction

Agnieszka Piotrowska

I am very tempted to begin this book by quoting from Vivian Sobchack's (2004) introduction to her book *Carnal Thoughts: Embodiment and Moving Image Culture* in which she claims that her book is 'undisciplined', drawing from different sites but that the underpinning theme in it is her belief in 'the embodied and radically material nature of human existence' (2004: 1). This of course is quite a provocative gesture in a collection that has psychoanalysis at its core. However, it is important to state at the outset that this book's guiding principle is that embodied and material existence can, and perhaps ought to, also allow for the unconscious.

This volume, *Embodied Encounters: New Approaches to Psychoanalysis and Cinema*, was born at a symposium that took place on 14 October 2013 at the Freud Museum. The event was funded by the Research Institute for Media and Performance at the University of Bedfordshire and I was its convenor. It was originally designed to be a launch of Luke Hockley's book (*Somatic Cinema*, 2014) and my first monograph (*Psychoanalysis and Ethics in Documentary Film*, 2014) but then the event grew to a day of wonderful papers thanks to the enthusiasm of the group of eminent speakers whom I approached in the spring of 2013. It became clear quite quickly that the meeting was going to be a little more than a small conference around a book launch; there was a sense amongst the speakers and the participants that the project of re-claiming psychoanalysis for film theory and Film Studies might be an important one.

When the symposium *Embodied Encounters* was being organised, I immediately felt the initiative must become a more lasting intervention and, supported enthusiastically by the symposium's presenters, I began my discussions with Routledge even before the symposium took place. The core participants of that symposium who are also contributing to this book were, in alphabetical order: Stephen Frosh, Luke Hockley, John Izod, Vicky Lebeau, Emma Wilson and myself. While some of the group do indeed work in the academy in mainstream Film Studies, at least half of us are also involved in a variety of other things besides (Stephen Frosh is a Professor of Psychology and Psychosocial Studies; Luke Hockley is also a practising psychotherapist; Vicky Lebeau is a literature specialist, as is Emma Wilson; John Izod has been collaborating with a practising psychotherapist, Joanna Dovalis and I am a filmmaker as well as a theorist). All of us would claim very serious professional interest in Film Studies and film theory, but perhaps our broad range of interests and identities has allowed us to engage with psychoanalysis without being fearful of it being such an unfashionable approach in Film Studies right now.

In this volume we are privileged to be now joined by a wonderful group of thinkers, both young, up and coming and very established: Helena Bassil-Morozow, Robert Burgoyne, Elizabeth Cowie, Carla Ambrósio Garcia, Carol MacGillivray, Nicholas Muellner, Michael Renov, Naomi Segal, Julie Sexeny and Ben Tyrer, all of whom use psychoanalysis creatively and very differently from each other, as a tool for the interrogation of the moving image but also, perhaps more importantly, to examine our identities, memories and positions in culture.

It is important perhaps to say at the outset that all of the original contributors to the symposium in our different ways embrace the work that has brought 'the body' back into film theory, in particular the work of such groundbreaking theorists as Vivian Sobchack, Laura Marks or Linda Williams, or more recently Jennifer Barker. Our question is why psychoanalysis, which has always put the body at the centre of its investigations, has been excluded from the more recent interrogations. The way I have put the question here is a little provocative of course – we do know why.

First, there is the historical issue of the post-1968 film theory with such giants as Baudry (1969), Metz (1975) and Comolli (1974) and last but not least Mulvey (1975). That theory was influenced by Lacanian thought but used it in a very particular way for very particular purposes. Language, which is crucial in the Lacanian clinic, somehow became a methodological tool used by theorists to disavow the body – a gesture that is emphatically not inherent in Lacan's work. Second, again because of the historical and political moment in time, feminists felt it was necessary to engage in a debate critiquing the psychoanalytical notion of 'sexual difference', i.e. the patriarchal ways of thinking about sex and gender, in some ways still promoted by the notion of 'penis envy' enunciated by Freud. That made psychoanalysis immediately sound like a reactionary and conservative system. It may well have been that too to start with but it has always been a radical philosophy, dislodging the accepted dominant discourses and narratives.

Also, it hardly needs stating here that in the last 60 years many efforts have been made to re-formulate and challenge the importance of the 'penis', with the work of psychoanalysts such as Melanie Klein and indeed Jacques Lacan despite the 'Phallus' being the Master signifier in his system. Feminists of course demolished the dominance of that symbol and Elizabeth Wright famously called it a 'signifier of loss'. For the record, Lacan's *Seminar XX* very clearly stresses the importance of embodiment to psychoanalysis and culture. More, it is in that seminar too that Lacan introduces the idea that gender is not biologically determined, an idea that was then picked up by Judith Butler (who at the time did define herself as a radical feminist philosopher) and re-thought in her groundbreaking *Gender Trouble* (1990). By the time Lacan was writing his Seminar on sinthome in the late 70s (*Seminar XXIII*) the body had become crucial to his thinking. Lacan defines 'sinthome' based on the case study of James Joyce's writing, and names it as a 'marriage between the body and the unconscious'.

These ideas of course are nowhere to be seen in the post-1968 film theory. One could say that partly it was because they were not yet enunciated so clearly at the time – although *The Mirror Stage*, which was certainly a key theoretical paradigm for the post-1968 theorists, deals directly with the embodiment and its misrecognition by the subject. Mostly, however, the embodiment of the spectator was not what the thinkers at the time were mostly interested in. Instead, psychoanalysis underpinned their passionate involvement in the political battles of the time. The tools offered by psychoanalysis, with some reformulations of Marx by Althusser and others, pointed to the unconscious ideological structures of the cinema in the capitalist system. It is fascinating to observe that at the same time as some feminists were accusing psychoanalysis of being too conservative, others used its emphasis on the unconscious as a revolutionary tool that would bring down the establishment globally – through the naming of the hidden and unconscious structures and signs, which related to power.

In the decades that have followed, the world has changed but not in the revolutionary way that these radical thinkers had hoped for. I wonder whether the profound disappointment connected to the failure of that imaginary revolution, which was about to take place in the 70s, in some way explains the extraordinary history of the fall of psychoanalysis in Film and Cultural Studies ever since. It is worth recalling that the 1968 issue of the *New Left Review* contained a translation of Jacques Lacan's paper on *The Mirror Stage*, lodged between a selection of texts by Antonio Gramsci and a Bolivian guerrilla fighter (see for example Burgin 1996: 10). *Screen*, arguably the most important journal of film studies and education at the time, took a decision to use psychoanalysis as the key theoretical paradigm. This was in 1975 – a year later the ecstatic march of psychoanalysis ground to a halt.

Famously, in 1976 in an unprecedented gesture, the editorial team of *Screen* resigned en masse in protest over the alleged unilateral adoption of psychoanalysis as a dominant discourse of the journal. It is possible that it was that gesture alone with its quite extraordinary hostility that has marred the development of psychoanalysis in Film Studies ever since.

Numerous volumes on psychoanalytical film theory did follow, of course. Some thinkers and writers such as Kaja Silverman, Elizabeth Cowie and later Linda Williams and others used psychoanalysis creatively in their own way, very much thinking through bodies and the unconscious. But others sometimes unhelpfully pronounced that the generation of previous scholars got everything wrong in terms of psychoanalytical theoretical paradigms and that the new interpreters of psychoanalysis and film claimed to have at last unlocked a secret cave of its meaning (see Žižek, Copjec whom we are all using in some way, and of course more disastrously David Bordwell and Noel Carrol who in 1996 declared a demise of Theory – in particular the psychoanalytically fuelled film theory).

Vivian Sobchack's intervention of *The Address of the Eye* (1992) placed itself directly in opposition to psychoanalysis, or more precisely in opposition to psychoanalytical film theory rather than psychoanalysis itself. Sobchack draws extensively from Merleau-Ponty in her descriptions of her personal subjective bodily cinematic experiences. One might be excused for thinking that phenomenology and psychoanalysis had nothing whatever in common, no converging points, no shared histories. This is emphatically not the case. It is also important to place Sobchack's intervention within the history of patriarchal ways of thinking about the academy – Sobchack's putting her subjectivity and her body into an academic discussion was, and remains, a very radical, not to say revolutionary gesture. It is interesting, and perhaps obvious, to point out that the great majority of the proponents of the phenomenological approach to cinema have been and still are women and feminists. It is interesting also to consider briefly that psychoanalysis and phenomenology were historically if not allies exactly then certainly not enemies. My contention in this volume is that there is no reason why they could not be thought of in the same space.

Lacan and Merleau-Ponty (the latter's work on 'the visible and the invisible', drawing from Husserl, has been the foundational influence in Sobchack's thinking) were friends and colleagues in the 50s and 60s in Paris, and at the time were engaged in a continuous creative debate (see for example Roudinesco 1990: 307–315). They both acknowledged the influence of each other's work. Merleau-Ponty's interest in psychoanalysis stretched over his entire career – initially it did offer a confirmation of his work on the subjective perception and its importance (see for example Pettigrew & Raffoul 1996: 68). Lacan was always clear that Freud's discovery of the unconscious represents a challenge to virtually any philosophy, because the Western philosophic tradition has been centred on consciousness, and in as much as 'philosophic reflection as such does not have access to the unconscious, philosophy is left in the position of either submitting itself to the truth of psychoanalysis or remaining superficial' (ibid.: 103). It is important, however, to bear in mind that Merleau-Ponty did allow for the unconscious – it is a somewhat different unconscious from that of Freud and Lacan (as that emerged from their work in the clinic), but the notion of the Husserlian 'other side', that is not readily available to the subject, is nonetheless present and significant in the work of Merleau-Ponty. It is also important to bear in mind that these philosophers and psychoanalysts constituted a group of thinkers and writers who were materially in continuous dialogue with each other in Paris in the 60s. They were travelling companions. Laplanche, for example, marvelled at Merleau-Ponty's ability to observe – he felt that ability was better than those of many psychoanalysts. André Green (1964) makes an excellent point that the ultimate difference between Merleau-Ponty and Freud and Lacan lies in the fact that Merleau-Ponty is always in the body as simply 'sentient' and psychoanalysis sees the body as the centre 'of conflict and desire'.

Lacan in his *Seminar XI* devoted five sessions to the subject of the gaze and l'objet petit a – both presenting Merleau-Ponty's ideas to his students and establishing his own position, which had a number of convergences with that of the work of *The Visible and the Invisible* but also had a major conceptual difficulty in terms of reconciling the two. The key disagreement in their approaches was indeed the position of the unconscious in the process of perception as well as Merleau-Ponty's too abstract approach to the matter. Ironically, Lacan preferred a more grounded and embodied approach emphasising the intersubjective encounter, with the unconscious at the heart of it. *The Mirror Stage*, one of Lacan's foundational texts as mentioned before, far from being an abstract text presenting an abstract notion, deals directly with the subject's perception of one's body. Language was for Lacan, as for Freud, a channel through which to express something of what goes on in one's body that is often evoked by the unspoken and unspeakable traumas, forgotten memories and fragments of narratives in the unconscious. Language remains that channel – for us all.

At Birkbeck, where I did my doctoral research, it is a given that psychoanalysis now more than ever has a political dimension. The notions of the unknowable, the unspoken and unspeakable, the uncanny and the un-measurable – inside and outside the academy and inside us and our relationships with other people – are in direct conflict with the current specific requirements of the neoliberal capitalist system in which everything has to be known, measurable, commodified and commodifiable, obvious, clear and profitable immediately. The very possibility that something instead could be unfamiliar, irrational, unknowable, strange and even meandering could be considered politically dangerous. It is my greatest hope that this volume could be just such a politically subversive gesture.

If there is a serious academic ambition in this book, it is to insist on the validity of different psychoanalytical thinking in the academy and elsewhere and on the belief that the notion of embodiment and the unconscious can be held together in one space. Let me also say again clearly: the theoretical paradigms of the contributors to this book are very broad, purposefully so. We have in one volume Lacanians, Jungians, new-Freudians, Bionians and others. Most of us examine particular objects, such as fiction cinema, gallery installations and documentaries, drawing theoretical conclusions that clearly can be thought through in relation to other objects too. If the volume is radical, then it is in its very insistence on the intellectual freedom that psychoanalytical thinking can offer to those who engage with it, both to writers and readers. I did think to write here a defence of the Unconscious through the very discipline that is used to discredit psychoanalysis these days, namely neuroscience, as we know very clearly now that not all information is accessible to our brains in a conscious way (see for example Greenfield 2008), but clearly there is very little point in doing that; the notion of the unconscious is more than a scientific fact, although it is that too, it is a certain attitude towards the world that allows for opacity.

The core question for me – both in this volume and clearly for years to come – is as follows: what makes a spectator feel touched by a film in such a physical way without an actual embodied touch taking place? How can it feel 'erotic' (Barker) or violent in producing affect (Marks)? How can it feel like a physical presence of another human (Sobchack) where there is no other human present? How are you touched when you are not actually physically touched? Is it not your unconscious with the archive of all these dis-remembered memories that makes us have different bodily and emotional responses to a film?

This collection attempts to make some of these ideas and possibilities clearer.

Figure I.1 Obscure Window 1 by Nicholas Muellner
Source: Reproduced with permission of the artist

References

Baudry, J. L. & Williams, A. (1974) Ideological Effects of the Basic Cinematographic Apparatus. *Film Quarterly, 28*, 39–47.

Burgin, V. (1996) *In/different Spaces: Place and Memory in Visual Culture*. Berkeley, CA: University of California Press.

Butler, J. (2006 [1990]) *Gender Trouble: Feminism and the Subversion of Identity*. New York: Routledge.

Comolli, J.-L. & Narboni, J. P. (1969) Cinema/Ideology Criticism (1) in A. Easthope (ed.) *Contemporary Film Theory*. New York: Longman, pp. 43–51.

Green, A. (1964) Du Comportement à la chair: itinéraire de Merleau Ponty. *211, Critique*, 1032.

Greenfield, S. (2008) *ID: The Quest for Meaning in the 21st Century*. London: Spectre.

Hockley, L. (2013) *Somatic Cinema: The relationship between body and screen – a Jungian perspective*. London: Routledge.

Lacan, J. (2008 [1977]) *Écrits: a Selection*. Trans. by A. Sheridan. London & New York: Routledge.

Laplanche, J. (1989) New Foundations for Psychoanalysis. Trans. David Macey. Oxford: Basil Blackwell, p. 92.

Metz, C. (1975) The Imaginary Signifier. *Screen, 16*, 14–76.

Pettigrew, D. & Raffoul, D. (eds) (1996) *Disseminating Lacan*. New York: Suny Press.

Piotrowska, A. (2013) *Psychoanalysis and Ethics in Documentary Film*. London: Routledge.

Pontalis, J. B. (1982–83) The Unconscious in Merleau Ponty's Thought in *The Review of Existential Psychology and Psychiatry XVII*, nos. 1, 2 & 3, p. 94.

Roudinesco, E. (1990) *Jacques Lacan and Company*. Trans. by Jeffrey Mehlman, Chicago, IL: University of Chicago Press.

Sobchack, V. (1992) *The Address of the Eye: A Phenomenology of the Experience*. Princeton, NJ: Princeton University Press.

Sobchack, V. (2004) *Carnal Thoughts: Embodiment and Moving Image Culture*. Berkeley, CA: University of California Press.

Part I

The desire, the body and the unconscious

Chapter 1

Catherine Breillat and Courbet's *L'origine du monde* [*The origin of the world*] (1866)

Emma Wilson

(i)

In her volume, *Catherine Breillat: Indécence et pureté*, Claire Clouzot writes that Breillat has always refused psychoanalysis. In Clouzot's argument, film itself is Breillat's couch, fiction her transference: 'Son divan est la pellicule. La fiction son transfert'.[1] For Clouzot, indeed: 'The subject of her work is her unconscious'.[2] I note that she uses here the French word 'pellicule', that signifier for film and film stock that carries with it a memory of skin, of diaphanous surface as well as filmy acetate. Sarah Cooper offers an account of this very skin-like, layered impressionability of Breillat's works, their unconscious form and force. In her brilliant article, 'Breillat's Time', she argues that in these films: '[l]inearity is dilated through the presence of memory, the imaginary and fantasy, or disrupted, in favour of cyclical movement or myth'.[3] Cooper's analysis of this wishful, dilated form in Breillat's works, their approach to a psychical reality, inspires and underlies my attempt here to understand a meeting of the sensory and the unconscious in her films. I offer a complicit response to Breillat, a sensory, imaginative investigation, as I feel my way into her works.

(ii)

Breillat's are inchoate, ravishing films. For me their wager is to touch some membrane, some limit, between the unconscious and the sensate world. Breillat dramatizes and reflects on that peculiarity of filmmaking where living others, vulnerable, luminous, opaque, are choreographed, directed, moved, exposed, held in filming.[4] The lush, impressionable surfaces of bodies, their poses, responses, colouration, inflection, are organized into moving image art, massed, stilled, treasured in fictions which reach towards an untouchable, an unspeakable.

Critics concur that this aim, pursued across ten films from the 1980s forwards, reaches its acme in *Anatomie de l'enfer* [*Anatomy of Hell*] from 2004.[5] Here an unnamed woman (Amira Casar) pays an unknown man (Rocco Siffredi) to come for four nights to look at her sex, her hair, and the lips of her vulva. In this one scenario, first developed by Breillat in the novel *Pornocratie*,[6] and borrowed in part from Marguerite Duras's *La Maladie de la mort* [*The Malady of Death*],[7] the filmmaker finds in perfect dramatic form, infinite, timeless, the compulsion of her films with the unconscious in sensory material, with an image, and viewing scenario, thick with sensuality, ravishment, opacity, unknowing.

(iii)

A precursor for this viewing scenario, this display of the female sex, comes in Gustave Courbet's 1866 *L'Origine du monde*, painted for the collector Khalil Bey (Ottoman ambassador to Athens and St Petersburg) and later owned by Jacques Lacan, apparently purchased for his wife Sylvia Bataille.[8] Speaking about meaning versus eroticism, Breillat herself has facilitated and anticipated comparison between her films and the painting, saying: 'What I love in art and in love is *The Origin of the World*'.[9] And critics have commented on the connection between the painting and Breillat's sex shots. Sarah Cooper writes:

> even when the film does fetishize body parts, it is not complicit with the ways in which this dissection has worked against the representation of women in film. Its more provocative focal points (the pubis or anus) take us to a different visual source, more resonant with Courbet's *L'Origine du monde* (1866), and this trajectory works utterly in keeping with Breillat's project to film what is usually left outside of filmic representation.[10]

Douglas Keesey continues more affirmatively:

> Breillat modeled the close-up of Amira's sex on Gustave Courbet's 1866 painting [...] which has both naturalistic detail and mythic power in its magnified view of a woman's vagina. Breillat's close-up is not the 'beaver shot' of pornography that belittles and objectifies the female sex for male consumption, but a shot of woman as goddess with awesome creative and destructive power.[11]

My reading is in line with Cooper's and Keesey's; both attend to that paradox of Breillat's filmmaking where, for Cooper, she mounts feminist critique *and* approaches what is outside representation and, for Keesey, she marries sensory realism *and* unconscious force. Both create a further imaginary gallery of pictorial reference alluding between them too to Manet's *Olympia* (1863) and Ingres's *Grande Odalisque* (1814).[12] These other images are certainly highly resonant for Breillat, in her attention to flesh and surface, but I want to pause here over what I take to be further determined significance of Courbet to Breillat, signalled most pressingly in the example of *L'Origine du monde*, but extending beyond it too.

(iv)

In his book on the painting Thierry Savatier singles out *L'Origine du monde* saying it:

> is not a painting like any other, it has a unique place in Western art because it represents without concession, or historical or mythological alibi, not only a woman's sex, but THE sex of Woman [LA Femme] and, beyond that, of every woman, lovers and mothers.[13]

At the end of his book, Savatier imagines the painting as a representation of Eve, of the eternal feminine. In a chapter about possible models for the painting, he wonders whether this may be the unseen body of Joanna Heffernan, Whistler's mistress also painted by Courbet, or indeed the dark-haired model in *Le Sommeil* [*Sleep*] (1866). He also raises the question of whether the painting may have been inspired by a photograph. He pauses over coloured photographic images taken by Auguste Belloc now held in the Bibliothèque Nationale's *enfer*; several of these represent a woman's torso, cut off, and her displayed vulva.[14]

Courbet's image *L'Origine du monde* and his realist aesthetic date from that fold of the nineteenth century where photography and painting are held in parallel, in live interaction in their aim to touch, to catch the real.[15] If Courbet's image is realized from a photograph, a new layering, a tissue of relations between imprint on light-sensitive paper and brushstroke in viscous paint, is secured. If Belloc's images are copied, and aggrandized in paint by Courbet, a token that is erotic and illicit, the pornographic photograph underlies the epochal image of hair and flesh. *L'Origine du monde* is no secret tribute to an adored woman, to the intimacy of facing her tenderest parts, but an all-but mechanical reproduction of a pre-existing image. As Savatier details, there are explicit similarities between Courbet's painting and Belloc's images: an equivalent framing, a comparable presence of cloth or petticoat hiding the model's face, an almost identical pose.[16] The photographs are made possible because a woman shows her vulva and as we look at it we know this was actual flesh and skin. Yet the register of the images, their reference points and affect seem, as Savatier points out, largely clinical rather than intimate. The photographs look out to traditions in anatomical drawing that bring with them the coolness of scientific inquiry and the morbidity of post mortem dissection. If Courbet had already lingered at that meeting point of Eros and Thanatos in his ambiguous, and repainted, *La Toilette de la morte* [*Preparation of the Dead Girl*] (1850–1855),[17] in *L'Origine du monde*, in implicit contest with the photographer, he further closes this divide. Oil, the touch of the brush, apparently conjures sentient life. For Savatier, in Courbet's painting the woman's skin seems velvety, soft and supple to the touch.[18] Yet the photographic intertext, the chop of the framing and foreshortening in both, the shadow of the cloth, a mortuary sheet drawn back, make the image grave, more gravid (pregnant) too. The pall of photography has fallen over the painting.

It is this play between photography and painting that makes Courbet's image of further interest as intertext in *Anatomie de l'enfer*. Breillat is working with moving images, created from photographic frames set in motion through optical illusion. Her visual style, the lighting and framing of her films, their stillness, is often pictorial, and her set pieces are often embellished, rendered the more resonant, through connection to painted art. In *Anatomie de l'enfer*, in her reference to *L'Origine du monde*, she takes us to the heart of issues about her medium, the moving image, and its sensory and unconscious possibilities.

(v)

An advantage of the moving image, over painting or still photography, is that it can simulate movement itself, a living trigger or ripple of feeling that reminds us of the sensation and animation of the other, of her living and breathing. This quality of cinema and its prehensile, immersive possibility, is brought out sensuously in recent work on cinema and the senses. In the chapter on 'Skin' in her book *The Tactile Eye* Jennifer Barker thinks through the eroticism of film viewing. She writes:

> In the palpable tactility of the contact between the film's skin and viewer's skin, and in the extent to which that contact challenges traditional notions of film and viewer as distant and distinct from one another, the tactile relationship between the film and the viewer is fundamentally erotic. Film and viewer come together in a mutual exchange between two bodies who communicate their desire, not only for the other but for themselves, in the act of touching.[19]

Barker's argument about film viewing emphasizes mutuality and realization. She writes of the relation between film and viewer:

> In the mutual contact of one another's skins, each recognizes the other as a perceptive, expressive, and desiring subject. Not only do we perceive the other, as we make contact with it, as a 'real' and tangible subject, but we also perceive ourselves more tangibly as well.[20]

This mutuality in film viewing, calqued from erotic exchange, offers an ideal of involved, enraptured, apprehensive, embodied spectatorship. This is mutual, for Barker, and it is blossoming, world giving; 'In some sense', she says, 'the touch of our skin upon the world and that of the world on our skin is what brings us into being'.[21] She moves on to claim: 'The erotic touch is not about ownership or complete knowledge of the other, but is truly intersubjective'.[22] The work of Barker, Beugnet, Marks, Sobchack, Quinlivan and others has done so much to attend to film viewing as a living, breathing experience, as involved in a relay of sensations across our skin, even in our viscera.[23] And this is in part in order to dismantle the theoretical apparatus that has constructed film viewing as psychic exclusively and geared towards mastery. Yet it is evident too that this embrace of fleshy viewing need not disregard some of the hesitations and uncertainties to which psychoanalysis has been so peculiarly attuned.

Indeed it is bringing these different modes of thinking about spectatorship into contact that may allow some closer, more proximate approach to the dispossession and rapture cinema such as Breillat's allows. In her preface to the screenplay of *Romance* she contends that emotion is the written texture subliminal in cinema.[24] We think we see what isn't present, because of all that we are made to feel, or we see, and deny what we are seeing, in the face of engulfing emotion. If Breillat's filmmaking is so attuned to these vicissitudes, these convulsions of viewing, it is also radical and attentive, ethical,[25] in its embrace of different investments. Her films extend very differing invitations to different viewers. In their extremism, in their approach to unconscious desires and fantasies they allow highly cathected, subjective responses, releasing different possibilities. Because the encounter with film, its touching our skin, our psyche, happens so variously (as is acknowledged in the subjective modes of some phenomenological accounts of film), thinking sensuous theory and psychoanalysis in contact may open still more sensitive ways of reckoning with these variations, with the infinite, sometimes unspeakable pleasures that Breillat's films may release.

(vi)

In her coruscating volume *Death 24x a Second: Stillness and the Moving Image*, Laura Mulvey attends to cinema in a way that registers its chimerical qualities, its stay to mutuality or unprocessed absorption. Mulvey, like Breillat, probes a relation between matter and psyche. Exploring enigma and uncertainty in cinema, only exacerbated at the digital turn, yet always a property of the cinematic, she argues that in the moving image, '[t]he blurred boundaries between the living and the not-living touch on unconscious anxieties that then circulate as fascination as well as fear in the cultures of the uncanny'.[26] She looks in particular at the effect of stillness in the moving image:

> A still frame when repeated creates an illusion of stillness, a freeze frame, a halt in time. Stillness may evoke a 'before' for the moving image as filmstrip, as a reference back to photography or to its own original moment of registration.[27]

Stillness takes us back to the originary images of the filmstrip, back to still photography preceding the moving image. While this is denied in projection, as Mulvey puts it 'the projector reconciles the opposition and the still frames come to life',[28] she continues to argue that 'this underlying stillness provides cinema with a secret, with a hidden past that might or might not find its way to the surface'.[29] This is the repressed, still, behind the flickering, labile, lifelike image on the screen. As Mulvey argues: 'The inanimate frames come to life, the unglamorous mechanics are covered over and the entrancing illusion fills the screen'.[30] Yet harking back to her image of the uncanny she nevertheless observes: 'But like the beautiful automaton, a residual trace of stillness, or the hint of stillness within movement, survives, sometimes enhancing, sometimes threatening'.[31]

In the warmth and light, the very motility of the moving image, there exists a trace of stillness, a hint that morbidity, the stilling of the image in photographic capture, the halting of time, subtends the fleshy, responsive and evolving image. Mulvey's reckoning offers us the obverse of Barker's life-giving mutuality, her embrace of an intersubjective, sensory viewing. Mulvey shows us with aching precision that the form we reach to touch, diaphanous, is rendered sensual, sensate by mechanics, illusion; it is only a dancing puppet before our eyes.

Breillat's cinema, I argue, in its origin images and choreography of sex, engages such debates, drawing us to apprehend cinema as medium of sensory capture, rapture, and yet also as arena of manipulation and illusion. The films that brought Breillat to cinema were, after all, films of spectacle, glacial eroticism and illusion, Ingmar Bergman's *Sawdust and Tinsel* (1953) and Luis Buñuel's *Viridiana* (1961).[32] *Anatomie de l'enfer* is a clearly self-reflexive film in its attention to a regime of viewing and it is to this purpose that Breillat harnesses the very energy of Courbet's painted sex.[33]

(vii)

In her own depictions of the cunt, Breillat seems certainly to appeal to the type of immersed, sensory viewing Barker describes. This is in pursuit, I would argue, of her thinking of the sensation of interiority in particular adumbrated in *Romance X* (1999). Breillat's visual experimentation in this manifesto film works to involve us in feeling the openings of the body, in contact and in insertion, as rope is tightened on the vulva of Marie (Caroline Ducey), as it is caught in her pubic hair, as Robert (François Berléand) puts his fingers in her, withdrawing them wet, and then in lavish escalation as a host of medical students put gloved hands in her vagina, and finally as a baby's head crowns full screen as she gives birth.[34] The vulva and vagina here are sensate, responsive, vulnerable, pleasure-giving, prehensile, elastic. Breillat's screen images align with sensuous theory as they appeal to embodied knowledge, our knowledge of touching and being touched. She draws in wetness in particular as one of the ways of showing the body as responsive and making her filmmaking appeal to senses other than vision.

Anatomie de l'enfer at first pursues this appeal to sensation. The first shot of the vulva full screen, the first visual echo of Courbet's *L'Origine du monde*, shows wet pubic hair and Rocco Siffredi inserting his finger, seeing it emerge slick and shining. The film plays with its apparent advantages over pictorial and photographic representation where it shows sequence, a sexual act, summoning depth, texture, dampness, response. Yet its full-frontal framing and severing of the image owes something already to Courbet's composition, realizing its starkness, it closeness still further. There is also a disquieting stillness, impassivity, to Casar's flesh throughout the film, and its dormant materiality, its stasis as object, is apprehended still more fully in the scene I want to discuss further, the second origin sequence, which begins almost 33 minutes into the film.

Amira Casar lies here like an odalisque now dormant.[35] Her stillness creates a photographic or pictorial image within the frame. The looseness of her body recalls Courbet's *Le Sommeil*, as the press of her flesh against the white bed linen looks out to Ingres's *La Baigneuse de Valpinçon* [*Valpinçon Bather*] (1808) and more generally to his interest in contact between fabric and skin.[36] My body watching feels how Amira is pressed into the pillow softly, how the sheet touches her torso and her breast. Surveying the image at a further remove I also linger on the curve of her hipbone, and the fluid pictorial design it creates as it is rimmed in light.

In this set piece, Breillat attunes me both to the bodily pleasure of cinema, and also to the stillness of the artist pose, the choreographed body. I am drawn in to the sensory textures of the images yet uncertain about control and feeling. There is something uncanny as Rocco moves around Amira and she remains completely still, as if two enchanted realms for a moment open onto each other and intersect.[37] Rocco moves her leg and its heaviness, its fall, conjure not only sleep but a deeper, more morbid torpor. Amira's lack of response appears to legitimize the investigative mode adopted. Rocco's gripping hand on her is reminiscent of Bernini's statues of rape and metamorphosis.[38] He is holding onto her skin, but the sensorium of the film is apparently with him here, as a result of her extreme passivity.

We see him rouging her sex with lipstick, gashing the hair with carmine, a crimson paint, and the film seems oblivious to her feeling.[39] I feel what it is like to draw, not to be drawn on.[40] As Rocco moves towards her mouth to paint her lips, any moves of her body seem completely involuntary, as it is submitted to him in its idleness.[41] She is like a soft marionette, a doll painted. He touches her, imprints her, paints her, and she remains impassive. The morbidity of the image is increased by the touch of pathos brought by the bandage on her previously slit wrist and the staining of her lipstick on her cheek, fissuring the perfection of the image.[42]

In a close-up I suddenly see her animation, a pulse in her neck, this heartbeat flooding the immediately previous images, for me, with retrospective feeling. But even after Amira stirs she keeps a waxy stillness, exacerbated by the pallor of her skin and the diaphanous, milky lighting achieved in the scene, until Rocco, suitably red, lusty, breathing, rigid, enters her from behind, pawing her skin, showing its cool, lovely, looseness as he holds her. And then he weeps.

(viii)

Breillat has been interested before in passivity, showing Marie in *Romance* taking pleasure in letting herself be tied, contorted, all but disarticulated like one of Hans Bellmer's dolls.[43] Amira in her contractual relations with Rocco has submitted to this and asked him to respond to her demand.[44] There is apparent pleasure for character and viewer in the achievement of such aesthetic perfection through her stillness and her stilling of response. The morbidity of her flesh here, the way it is moved, apparently unresponsive, sinks towards annihilation, the numbness and stillness of the earth, of an inanimate object. Her body is tractable, tactile, pliable, coolly close to extinction, at the border Mulvey identifies between living and still.

If this scene pursues Breillat's interest in masochism, it also opens issues about the moving image, photography and pictorial art. In this sequence Breillat questions the choreographing of the body by a film director. Rocco moving Amira with disquiet and pleasure offers a magnified image of the film director herself demanding or responding to pliability, allowing a living other to summon gestures, expose surfaces, to be fitted and responsive to the needs of the drama. This manipulation, this folding of flesh to vision, is peculiarly exacerbated in moving image art, yet Breillat seems to remind us that it is also a pursued feature of modelling for both painting and photography. Its very unnaturalness is seemingly signalled in the distortion and awkwardness of certain poses, indeed in the slight contortion, and the remove from viable anatomy, of the splayed leg in Courbet's own painting. If Breillat shows up this choreographing it is not to critique it but to take stock of its actuality, so we see what is done to make these images available.

(ix)

I suggest that Breillat reflects on the legacy for her filmic art from a sexual painting from the nineteenth century. Creating contact between Courbet's image and Breillat's film draws me to see both hesitating between surface, lush sensuality – the gesture of the painted stripes, the grease smoothness and red stridency of the markings – and a morbid stillness in the image, a disavowed pornographic or mortuary photograph, a clay coolness to the flesh propped and moved. Mulvey has let me come closer to the morbidity of the images. Against Barker, Breillat's wager is, in the thick sexual surface and subject matter of her films, to bring us to some limit in contact, in animation, a break in relationality, a pleasure in annihilation. And what is new in Breillat, I think, beyond Courbet: the intimation that this display on a butcher's slab, this quietude, may also be, for some women, a source of pleasure.[45]

Notes

1 Clouzot, C. (2004) *Catherine Breillat: Indécence et pureté*. Paris: Cahiers du cinéma/ auteurs, 11. Translations from the French are my own unless otherwise stated.
2 Ibid., 11. Translations from the French are my own unless otherwise stated.
3 Cooper, S. (January 2010) 'Breillat's Time'. In R. Rushton and L. Russell-Watts (eds.) *Catherine Breillat – Women, Sex, Violence, Cinema*, a special issue of *Journal for Cultural Research*, *14*(1), 103–116, 103.
4 This is done most explicitly in her work in *Sex is Comedy* (2002) where she explores her own filmmaking process, casting Anne Parillaud as a film director, and showing her work with actors in the filming of intimate erotic scenes. More broadly in her

work, Breillat makes the moving and placing of bodies an integral part of her exploration of power relations. This is shown particularly movingly in her recent *Abus de faiblesse* [*Abuse of Weakness*] in her examination of a differently abled body. Breillat has said in interview with Clouzot that she speaks about 'her actress' because she films the actress as *she* sees her, capturing not the actress herself but her own gaze upon her (C. Clouzot, *Catherine Breillat: Indécence et pureté*, 143). She continues to say that she has a very strong relationship with her actresses, almost like love (144).

5   See C. Clouzot, *Catherine Breillat: Indécence et pureté*, 134. Clouzot comments on the 'douleur' (pain) bound up in the word acme, reminding us of the medical usage where it represents the stage of the illness where the symptoms are at their most intense. She comments that this is apt for *Anatomie de l'enfer*.
6   Breillat, C. (2001) *Pornocratie*. Paris: Editions Denoël.
7   Duras, M. (1982) *La Maladie de la mort*. Paris: Minuit.
8   A detailed history of the ownership of the painting is offered in T. Savatier (2009 [fourth edition]) *L'Origine du monde: Histoire d'un tableau de Gustave Courbet* [*The Origin of the World: The Story of a Painting by Gustave Courbet*]. Paris: Editions Bartillat. See also B. Teyssèdre (2007 [new edition]) *Le Roman de l'Origine* [*The Novel of the Origin*]. Paris: Gallimard L'Infini.
9   Clouzot, C. (2004) *Catherine Breillat: Indécence et pureté*, 165.
10 Cooper, S. (2010) 'Breillat's Time', 110.
11 Keesey, D. (2009) *Catherine Breillat*. Manchester: Manchester University Press, 142–3.
12 See S. Cooper, 'Breillat's Time', 109–10, where she writes: 'Douglas Keesey notes that Breillat and Arvanitis [her cinematographer] were drawn particularly to Manet's *Olympia* (1863) in their desire to make the woman appear both corporeal and sublime. The painterly qualities of the film, when it refuses to fetishize fragments of the female body, at times also summon the perfection of the *Grande Odalisque* (1814) of Ingres'.
13 Savatier, T. (2009), *L'Origine du monde: Histoire d'un tableau de Gustave Courbet*, 11.
14 These images are reproduced and discussed in S. Aubenas and P. Comar (2013) *Obscénités: Photos interdites d'Auguste Belloc* [*Obscenities: Auguste Belloc's Censored Photographs*], Paris: Bibliothèque Nationale de France. They are also discussed in the catalogue to the 2008 Courbet exhibition, *Gustave Courbet*, New York: Metropolitan Museum of Art/Hatje Cantz, with essays by Dominique de Font-Réaulx, Laurence des Cars, Michel Hilaire, Bruno Mottin and Bertrand Tillier, in the section by Laurence des Cars, 'The Nude Transgressed', 336–87, 383–4.
15 This era and its interchanges is evoked well by Roberto Calasso where he discusses a daguerreotype by Désiré-François Millet found in a drawer in the desk of the painter Ingres. In it a lost nude painting by Ingres can be seen. Calasso comments: 'The painter had done away with the picture – and apparently had kept only the daguerreotype, tucked away in a drawer, out of discretion, at the time of his second marriage', R. Calasso (2012) *La Folie Baudelaire*, translated from the Italian by Alastair McEwan, London: Allen Lane/Penguin Books, 98. Calasso comments in particular on the strangeness of the woman's pose where she is both outstretched and lying on her side: 'this pose shows the largest possible surface of the body – and all with the sane delicate luminous value, where the focus of the light is concentrated transversely between the right breast and the left part of the belly', 98. Calasso's example anticipates the hesitations of the pictorial and photographic choreographing, and the exchanges between painting and photography, pursued in imaging of the nude by Breillat.
16 Savatier, T. (2009) *L'Origine du monde: Histoire d'un tableau de Gustave Courbet*, 69.

17 See my brief discussion of this painting in E. Wilson (2012) *Love, Mortality and the Moving Image*, Basingstoke: Palgrave Macmillan, 102.
18 Ibid., p. 26.
19 Barker, J. (2009) *The Tactile Eye: Touch and the Cinematic Experience*. Berkeley: University of California Press, 34.
20 Ibid., 34.
21 Ibid., 34.
22 Ibid., 34–5.
23 See, amongst other titles, M. Beugnet (2007) *Cinema and Sensation: French Film and the Art of Transgression*, Edinburgh: Edinburgh University Press; L.U. Marks (2000) *The Skin of the Film: Intercultural Cinema, Embodiment, and the Senses*, Durham and London: Duke University Press; L.U. Marks (2002) *Touch: Sensuous Theory and Multisensory Media*, Minneapolis: University of Minnesota Press; D. Quinlivan (2012) *The Place of Breath in Cinema*, Edinburgh: Edinburgh University Press; V. Sobchack (2004) *Carnal Thoughts: Embodiment and Moving Image Culture*, Berkeley and Los Angeles: University of California Press.
24 Breillat, C. (1999) *Romance: scenario*. Paris: Cahiers du cinéma, 18.
25 In this same screenplay she speaks of creating 'un cinéma morale', which should be understood not as a policing or gauging of morals but precisely as an open uncompromising ethical cinema. See ibid., 8.
26 Mulvey, L. (2006) *Death 24x a Second: Stillness and the Moving Image*. London: Reaktion Books, 32.
27 Ibid., 67.
28 Ibid., 67.
29 Ibid., 67.
30 Ibid., 67.
31 Ibid., 67.
32 See Clouzot, C. *Catherine Breillat: Indécence et pureté*, 149. Breillat recounts here how *Sawdust and Tinsel* was the first major film for her and how it made her want to become a filmmaker. She saw *Viridiana* a week later. Both films offered images of a marmoreal, mind-blowing femininity. She mentions in particular the ways in which both films supplied images of women reclining that inspired her in construction of shots of Amira Casar in *Anatomie de l'enfer*.
33 Courbet's image is also referenced in Nan Goldin's 2011 installation *Scopophilia* at the Mathew Marks Gallery in New York. Here Courbet's image is reproduced four times, in gradually changing scale. This serial representation seems itself to be moving towards the cinematic, unfixing the icon, as well as making it part of a more mobile, lush, textured exploration of pleasure in viewing. For Goldin, as for Breillat, images from the reservoir of Western European representation are appealing material for reframing, for new, politically charged erotic investment.
34 Breillat's labile moves from sex to birth look forward to the work of artist Helen Knowles, who explains her work as follows: 'Plundered from Youtube birth videos, I use screen-grab close-ups of women's faces exhaling and reclining at the moment the baby crowns, as well as wider views of this moment revealing the women's euphoria in their domestic spaces', H. Knowles (2011) 'An interview with Helen Knowles', www.helenknowles.com/images/uploads/Interview_Helen_Knowles.pdf (accessed 11 August 2013). I am grateful to Sophie Zadeh for drawing my attention to Helen Knowles's work.
35 In an online interview, Breillat says (with a possible error in transcription): 'the woman is more an example, like an obelisk or a picture', K. Murphy, 'Hell's Angels: An Interview with Catherine Breillat on *Anatomy of Hell*', http://sensesofcinema.com/2005/34/breillat_interview/ (accessed 6 August 2013). Elsewhere in the interview

Breillat says: 'I had to make the film like a sacred painting. I had to paint my Caravaggio'.

36   Breillat's own interest in fabric is glimpsed in *Pornocratie* where she describes, for example, 'un mince kimono de satin fluide et glissant comme le reflet des eaux où Ophélie est morte' ['a thin kimono in satin fluid and slippery like reflections in the water where Ophelia drowned'], 33.

37   Fairy tale is increasingly a point of reference for Breillat as realized in her adaptations for Arte, *Barbe bleue* [*Bluebeard*] (2010) and *La Belle endormie* [*Sleeping Beauty*] (2010). This interest in different realms or orders of reality coinciding also seems to recall the perspective on dilated time offered in Sarah Cooper's 'Breillat's Time' cited above.

38   I am thinking here in particular of Bernini's *The Rape of Proserpina* (1621–2) and *Apollo and Daphne* (1622–5) both in the Galleria Borghese in Rome. Bernini is an explicit point of reference for Breillat in other films such as *Une Vieille Maîtresse* [*The Last Mistress*] (2007). As Keesey writes: 'At the 2007 New York Film Festival, Breillat compared the look on Vellini's face during orgasm to the rapturous expression of Saint Teresa in Bernini's sculpture of the *Ecstasy of Saint Teresa*', D. Keesey 'Neither a Wife nor a Whore: Deconstructing Feminine Icons in Catherine Breillat's *Une Vieille Maîtresse*' in R. Rushton and L. Russell Watts (eds.) *Catherine Breillat – Women, Sex, Violence, Cinema*, 5–14, 13.

39   Breillat speaks lushly about the colour red in dialogue with Catherine Clouzot. She speaks about the overwhelming red of fresh blood. It is an alchemical colour, she says. There is nothing more beautiful than a drop of red blood on white skin. It is the colour of coral, the blood of the Medusa metamorphosed. See C. Clouzot, *Catherine Breillat: Indécence et pureté*, 176.

40   A member of the audience at the colloquium felt this differently from me.

41   Adrienne Angelo argues: 'The sparse narrative makes *Anatomie de l'enfer* a study of the gaze. The act of looking is explicitly foregrounded in this film and is aligned with the man, forcing us to see in the medium of the visual that which is ultimately unseeable', 'Sexual Cartographies: Mapping Subjectivity in the Cinema of Catherine Breillat' in R. Rushton and L. Russell Watts (eds.) *Catherine Breillat – Women, Sex, Violence, Cinema* 43–56, 50.

42   The image of the bandage allows the shot also to recall Mañuel Alvarez Bravo, *The Good Reputation, Sleeping* (1938).

43   Clouzot, too, makes a connection between Breillat and Bellmer. See C. Clouzot, *Catherine Breillat: Indécence et pureté*, 12.

44   Breillat has said that her heroines are always 'des insoumises' and always very pure, see C. Breillat (2007) *Corps amoureux: Entretiens avec Claire Vassé*. Paris: Denoël, 32. Duras writes of her own heroine in *La Maladie de la mort*: 'Elle serait toujours prête, consentante ou non' ['She would always be ready, consenting or not'], 19.

45   I am grateful to Annie Ring for comments on a draft of this paper. I would also like to record a particular debt to Agnieszka Piotrowska for her encouragement to me to speak about Breillat at Freud's house. It felt an honour and pleasure to have the chance to talk on Breillat in the museum at the time of the exhibition *Mad, Bad and Sad: Women and the Mind Doctors*, 10 October 2013–2 February 2014 (with work by Alice Andersen, Louise Bourgeois, Helen Chadwick, Tracey Emin, Anna Furse, Susan Hiller, Sarah Lucas and Francis Upritchard). I thank Agnieszka for her support of this research. Her own filmmaking and writing have been an inspiration to me.

Chapter 2

Nachträglichkeit and *après coup* in documentary film
The suffering of Aileen Wuornos as told by Nick Broomfield[1]

Agnieszka Piotrowska

In my work I have examined a difficult space in the largely untheorized embodied relationship between the documentary filmmaker and the subject of her or his film from a psychoanalytical perspective. The space is difficult, I argue, not for the reasons one might expect, i.e. concerns about the exploitation of the other in documentary film in contemporary Western culture, although the ethical dimension is an important part of my bigger project. The space is difficult because it raises fundamental questions about the role of *emotions* in an area that deals with testimony given by another person, sometimes in great pain.

I have pointed out elsewhere (Piotrowska 2011, 2012, 2014) that for a variety of reasons psychoanalysis has not been applied much to documentary film studies, in stark contrast to film theory, which focused on fiction cinema and had its heyday post 1968. At the time the work of Metz and Baudry in France, inspired by Jacques Lacan, and Mulvey and McCabe in the United Kingdom, laid the foundations for psychoanalytically informed film theory. It explored the relationship between cinematic systems such as the apparatus and the screen on the one hand and the spectator on the other. The objects of these examinations were exclusively fictional texts.

In documentary film, as elsewhere, the stated purpose of giving testimony is to further knowledge rather than to engage in an emotional dialogue with the other. In film studies documentary film has been thought to be within the 'discourse of sobriety' as Bill Nichols puts it (1991: 4; 2010: 36), which is similar to science and hence ought to be detached and objective. My claim has been that, instead, intra-filmic documentary encounter often becomes a spectral space of desire and even love. That claim, even in the post-modernist landscape of contemporary academy, is still profoundly controversial. In the unstable world we live in, we all long for something that we can declare 'objective' and true. My view, both as a filmmaker and a scholar, is that the longing for the 'objective', while understandable, is but a fantasy at best and a delusion at worst. In documentary project deep emotions and attachments might flow between the filmmaker and her subjects. These hidden emotions are often not named or disavowed, perhaps because of the fear of possible misunderstandings, transgressions, economic considerations and rules of conduct. In addition, if a filmmaker represents a broadcaster or a funder with a different agenda, the whole project can become hopelessly complicated, despite the advances of technology. There is something colonial too in the project of documentary films. Robert Flaherty, named a father of documentary by another patriarchal figure in the history of the genre, John Grierson, made his name on his exploits to the far flung countries, imagining that his relationships with his exotic subjects somehow excused the in-excusable exploitation of the very people who made his films possible (I discussed this issue elsewhere: Piotrowska 2014). There is something unavoidably difficult and perhaps seductive in the asymmetrical encounter between the filmmaker and the subject of his/her film: conscious aspirations and unconscious narcissistic wants and desires of both will come into play. A strong bond might develop not dissimilar to love.

From a psychoanalytical perspective, that love could be called 'transference-love' as described by Freud (1915) and Lacan (1999: 77): it belongs mostly to the Imaginary register but its actual effect functions in the Symbolic as it impacts upon the spectators of the film and thus, in some ways, our culture. In a later paper, Freud does talk about other impossible professions apart from psychoanalysts, such as politicians and teachers; in their work unconscious mechanisms take place too and the result cannot be predicted and is often unsatisfactory (Freud 1937: 248). I venture that documentary filmmakers too belong to that group.

The difficulty of interrogating transference in documentary other than one's own is that there are often only traces of it left in a way that is legible to the viewer but it is my contention that the strong attachments, which are formed during the documentary filmmaking project, are ubiquitous even if not spoken about. It is important to name these mechanisms because they will affect the spectator's relationship to the presented text, consciously or otherwise.

In this paper I focus on another concept from the clinic, a term named by Freud as *Nachträglichkeit* – 'a delayed or deferred effect' of an early trauma or rather a memory of it, the full weight of which becomes significant only later in the patient's life. I will look at the way Lacan reformulated it as 'après coup' suggesting a possibility of 'un-doing' of a (repressed) memory of a past trauma through the speech exchanged *in transference* between the analyst and the analysand. In essence, Lacan believed that if the traumatic signifiers of the past can be shifted, the analysand's past *and* future will be changed too. To put it simply, through the analyst's questioning, punctuations, Lacanian 'cuts', an analysand begins to talk about her/his memory differently and thus think about it differently. In documentary too, the whole project of re-telling the past in fragments that are then re-organized can be seen as offering a different interpretation to the contributor to the film, thus potentially dislodging her/his accepted ways of thinking about the past (again I touch upon it elsewhere: Piotrowska 2014).

If transference exists between documentary filmmaker and the subject of her film and if the speech is exchanged in an embodied encounter, might that have a curative effect too? What is the role of time and speech in documentary film?

How are we as spectators affected by our own unconscious archive of infantile and other unconscious traumas in having affective reactions to a film, be it a documentary or a drama? These are the questions, which this short paper will not attempt to answer. Rather I want to re-ask them and bring them to light again.

Here I look at a specific example of Nick Broomfield's work in two films on serial killer Aileen Wuornos; one made in 1991 (*Aileen Wuornos: The Selling of a Serial Killer*) and the other 12 years later (*Aileen: Life and Death of a Serial Killer* (2003)). The films offer an intriguing example of *Nachträglichkeit* – in some way unfortunately demonstrating how hard it is to affect any change in documentary encounter. First I look at some psychoanalytic definitions of the 'deferred effect'.

Nachträglichkeit, après coup, afterwardness or 'deferred effect' suggests that a *memory* of an event, rather than the event itself, might have traumatic significance for the patient (for the analysand), beyond what that patient might recognize or be aware of. Conceived by Freud as early as 1895 in the 'Project for a scientific psychology', the concept remains in his work without official status (see also Eickhoff 2006). In Freud's original text, *Nachträglichkeit* was linked to early trauma to do with early sexual phantasmatic experiences. Freud says there: 'it is not the experiences themselves which act traumatically but their revival as a memory after the subject has entered sexual maturity' (Freud 1991 [1950]: 64). Freud later re-introduced in a number of texts, in particular in the discussion of the case of the Wolf Man in which it becomes clear that it is not even the memory of it that is traumatic but rather *the repression of it*. The deferred effect of a trauma can be thus far greater than the event itself. The basic assumption is that the experiences of the past preserved in the unconscious can acquire new meaning and greater strength in the context of later events.

Nachträglichkeit – the deferred effect of a trauma – has strong links with 'repetition'. Freud says famously that what cannot be remembered is repeated, meaning that his patients sometimes obsessively would repeat a sequence of events, relationships or circumstances even if it was perfectly clear from personal history that a disaster and destruction would follow.

Freud's paper 'Notes upon a case of obsessional neurosis' contains a footnote with the implicit reference to *Nachträglichkeit*, in which he talks of a 'complicated process of remodelling' which childhood memories undergo, so that the adolescent 'just as a real *historian* will view the past in the light of the present' (1909: 206, note 1, my emphasis). This reference to history is crucial here and it is crucial to the documentary project, which in some way (even if it is shot and presented in present time in the 'fly on the wall mode') always deals with the past and hence with history. Psychoanalyst Roger Kennedy's book, *Psychoanalysis, History and Subjectivity* (Kennedy 2002) points out that history itself is perhaps a little more subjective than some historians might like us to believe. Kennedy evokes Freud's *Nachträglichkeit* as a process in which memories and experiences are *revised and rearranged* to fit in with our experiences or new ideas. 'The constant rearrangement of memories creates history', he says (Kennedy 2002: 20). It is the issue of different temporalities, moments in time of the past, present and future that are linked in a particular way. That connection is often neither obvious nor linear.

Nachträglichkeit as a concept was near forgotten in the clinic until the work of the French psychoanalyst and thinker Jacques Lacan, whose 1953 intervention published in *Écrits, The Function and Field of Speech and Language in Psychoanalysis* (1953 [2008/1977])) and subsequent publications (Seminar XI [1998/1981]) mentions the notion of the *Nachträglich* as a way of thinking of what goes on in the clinic through *speech*, through *the embodied encounter* between the psychoanalyst and the analysand. He makes a point of differentiating between *acting out* – in which the unconscious and forgotten early trauma is repeated in a serious of failed unconscious dramatic re-enactments of it – just as Freud suggested it – as opposed to *working through* it in the psychoanalytic encounter – through 'the talking cure'.

But Lacan takes the notion further – or rather is more explicit and perhaps optimistic in his reformulation of Freud's *Nachträglichkeit*. Lacan claims that the early repressed trauma can perhaps be *dispelled* through the embodied clinical encounter – through talking *in transference* and thus through 'transference love' that springs between the analyst and the analysand. The speech exchanged by them offers a potentially transformative re-positioning of the original trauma's signification in the analysand's psyche. Through a slow and painful process, by a laborious bringing to light signifiers of the original trauma (which might not have even have seemed traumatic at the time), there is a possibility of changing *the meaning* of that original experience. It is that dazzling transformative possibility, which is almost a mysterious time travel of the body and mind, that Lacan calls *après coup*.

This is what he says (Lacan 2006 [1966]): 246):

> For the function of language in speech is not to inform but to evoke.
> What I seek in speech is a response from the other. [...] I identify myself in language, but only by losing myself in it as an object. What is realized in my history is neither the past definite as what was, since it is no more, nor even the past perfect as what has been is what I am, but *the future anterior* as what I will have been, given what I am in the process of becoming.

Lacan suggests therefore that through a psychoanalytical encounter in transference and through the re-examining of the sometimes unknowingly traumatic past, as perceived by the suffering person, that past can be *changed*. For psychoanalysis is concerned less with facts and more with how they have impacted the patient/the analysand. Once the signifiers have been shifted, *the future* therefore can be influenced and changed too. *Nachträglichkeit* or *après coup* therefore carries with it always a change of temporality.

In film in general and documentary in particular that curious spectral relationship to time and death is always present (mentioned by Derrida (Derrida & Stiegler 2002); Mulvey (2006) and more recently touched upon by Cowie (2011) and

Wilson (2012)) echoing relationship to time in photography enunciated first by Benjamin and Barthes. But the Lacanian notion of *après coup* has an agency in it, which is not just spectral; it is actual, it operates in the Symbolic. It changes perceptions and lives.

Is it too optimistic to hope that a documentary encounter too might sometimes give a chance for these transformative mechanisms to be initiated? Also, if we were to suggest that the encounter between the spectator and the film is an embodied encounter in which transference takes place, can that encounter perhaps too produce this kind of an *après coup*, a lasting change? And finally what about the documentary filmmaker? To what extent can the process of making a film have a transformative effect on them too?

Nick Broomfield and Aileen Wuornos

Nick Broomfield's two films about the serial killer Aileen Wuornos (released 1992 and 2003) offer a different take on the same story. There is some 12 years in between the making of the two films and the tonality of the work as well as its temporality is very different. The second film marks a significant stylistic departure for its director, Broomfield. In the first film, his access to Aileen is fragmentary and controlled by her various unreliable and in the end possibly exploitative helpers. It is still in part a comedy of errors with a carnival of colourful and bizarre American characters. Through Broomfield's first film we as viewers have a vague sense even then that Aileen was deeply disturbed and possibly abused in her childhood. At the time however Broomfield does not explore that story. Instead, in his usual semi-jocular way, he exposes her lawyer as incompetent, thus making us question the court proceedings and their validity. Eleven years after the original film, Broomfield is subpoenaed to take a stand in court proceedings that attempt to re-open Aileen Wuornos's case, in part at least thanks to his first film. There is a new lawyer employed and Nick's film is used as evidence against the original lawyer. The chances of getting Aileen off the electric chair appear good or at least possible.

But then, in the intervening years, something happened to Aileen. The *Nachträglichkeit*, the deferred effect of her original trauma, which may have triggered her murders in the first place, appeared devastating by the time the second film was being made. What the film manages to demonstrate strikingly is the painful deterioration of Wuornos's mental state. Her defences, dismantled by the isolated life in prison and a complete absence of any embodied encounter with anybody who might listen to her testimonies and the total abandonment by those who declared their commitment to her, Aileen does not only lose her agency, energy and confidence, she appears to have lost her will to live and apparently loses her mind. During her time in prison on death row she is *not* given any chance to 're-model' her past – perhaps it was felt that it would have been a waste of resources to offer her 'a talking cure'. The authorities, it appeared, just wanted

Aileen to die. By the time Nick met her again, Aileen did not want any appeals either – she too just wanted the pain to cease.

During the first court case Aileen maintained throughout that her seven murders of her male clients were a self-defence. Psychoanalytically of course this might have meant a number of things apart from the concrete act of defending herself. Nobody was interested in Aileen's version of the sequence of events or any psychoanalytical interpretations of her deeply disturbed state of mind.

Twelve years later, with a real chance of a re-trial, Aileen Wuornos changed her story completely – acting against herself. In his second film Nick Broomfield makes a painful point of stressing different temporalities and the changes in Aileen's speech during these different historical moments. Broomfield juxtaposes the footage from the original trial with his new footage shot for the second film. The montage, the editing, as we know from Eisenstein and from film practice, can alter the meaning of what is being presented. Here Broomfield uses it boldly, almost brutally, and the effect it has on the viewer, at least on this viewer, is a bodily visceral traumatic realization that we are witnessing here a tragic victim of a brutal abuse, as much as a murderer. Somehow the deferred effect of her original trauma, the incarceration with no possibility of exchanging speech, has broken her down completely. In addition, a sense of incredulity sweeps the viewer as we witness the utter brutality of what is presented to us. This is a different kind of 'body genre' borrowing Linda Williams's term (1991), which refers mostly to horror movies and pornography – this documentary produces a real sense of horror in the viewer because s/he knows that this is not a fantasy or fiction created for our benefit, this actually took place.

In this section I want to focus in particular on a sequence of the 2003 film. In it Aileen walks into a prison visit room to meet the crew. Her hands are tied behind her back. She smiles at the crew and Nick, who then unexpectedly for the viewer, puts his hand down Aileen's bra in order to place a microphone there. Then what follows is an exchange in which Aileen states categorically that she lied in her previous interviews and court statements 12 years ago, that she did not kill the men in self-defence; that she killed them in cold blood, because she had wanted to rob them and then she wanted to get rid of the witness.

This whole sequence is almost unbearable. It presents the reverse of the ideal of Lacanian *après coup*: any hope is extinguished, there is no future anterior, there is no future simply – there is just pain, madness and death.

There are a number of striking things to consider here: first, the extraordinary, familiar and even intimate gesture on the part of the director at the beginning of the scene. Broomfield is placing a radio mic on Aileen's bust – he probably *has* to do it as her hands are handcuffed – and yet I find it disturbing that he does not ask, he does not explain anything prior to this gesture. He is a man and she is a former prostitute charged with murdering punters who wanted to buy sex from her, but who also wanted to hurt her and to humiliate her. There is something peculiar about this moment – Aileen is smiling, slightly taken aback but not in a bad way, she appears to be almost enjoying the moment, but at the same time the filmmaker's

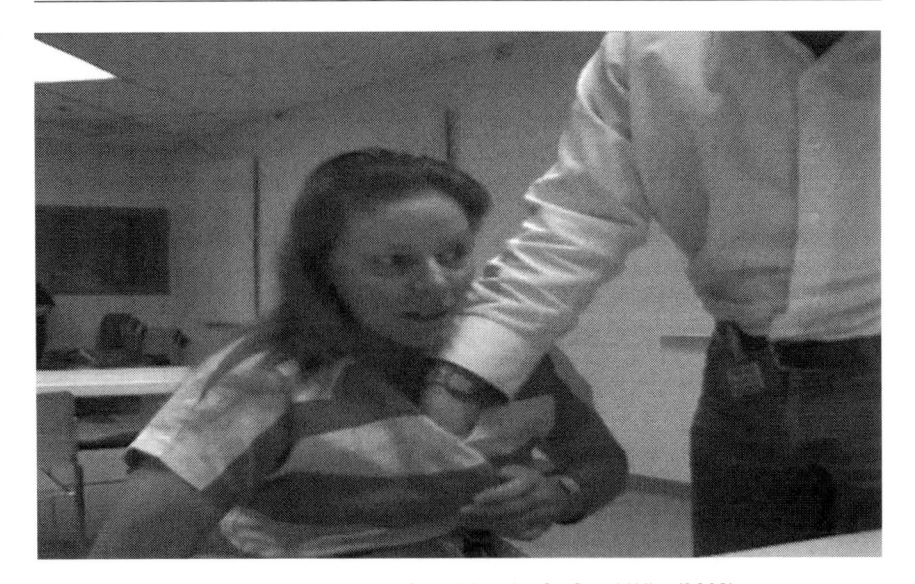

Figure 2.1 Aileen Wuornos in *Aileen: Life and Death of a Serial Killer* (2003)
Source: Director: Nick Broomfield. Reproduced with the permission of the filmmaker

gesture is curiously violating. Doesn't Broomfield, unconsciously, adopt the position of the powerful male, who has the right to interfere with Aileen's body as he pleases?

Aileen clearly has an agenda for the meeting and she does not waste any time to make her point clear: she wants to take back all she said previously about her alleged self-defence. Below are the excerpts from the scene:

AILEEN WUORNOS: I cannot go into the execution chamber and die as a liar and under the devil [...] I got to come clean and cleanse my spirit in the name of Jesus Christ ... I have got to come clean that I killed these men ...
NICK BROOMFIELD: That you killed these men ... in cold blood?
AW: Yes in first degree murder in robbery [...] I was into the robbing ... but I am coming clean before I get to the execution chamber and be executed ...
NB: So when you met them from the beginning did you know you would kill them?
AW: Pretty much ...
NB: What about the testimony ... you gave in court?
AW: I was just trying to beat the system Nick ...
NB: Really? None of it was true?

(Aileen smiles sadly, almost apologetically, and shakes her head ...)

(Cut to Aileen 12 years earlier in court, giving here spirited and emotional testimony defending herself and presenting a case of her being attacked and severely assaulted by Robert Mallorty.)

Figure 2.2 Aileen Wuornos in *Aileen Wuornos: The Selling of a Serial Killer* (1992) and *Aileen: Life and Death of a Serial Killer* (2003)

Source: Director: Nick Broomfield. Reproduced with the permission of the filmmaker

AW: ... and he said it doesn't matter to me [if you die before I have sex with you again], your body will still be warm from my huge cock ... and he was choking me ... and he said 'do you want to die slut' and I nodded no and ... he lifts my legs and he puts ... and he is rubbing the alcohol on bottle and sticks in my rectum area ... and that really hurt really bad because he tore me really bad ... and then he put it in my vagina and that really hurt ... and then he pulled my nose up. And started driving the alcohol in my nose and said 'I am saving your eyes for the grand finale'...

Aileen Wuornos's testimony above, which she gives attempting to be composed, with tears streaming down her face, her voice breaking up repeatedly, is in itself a horrific spectacle. To have it juxtaposed with the broken Aileen 12 years later, in which she just wants her execution quickened, is shocking. Her face, the symbolic face of the Other as written about by Lévinas (1981), the face that demands the Infinite Responsibility, is here recorded as a perpetual accusation to anybody who watches this film, and in particular it is a painful indictment of the conservative judicial patriarchal system, which allows for a mentally ill victim of extreme abuse to be executed by the State. Nick Broomfield later in the film keeps the sound running during his interview and Aileen admits in it that the murders were in self-defence, but that she just wanted it all to be over. She could fight no more, her brain being controlled by the radio sound waves, she said. She was very unwell, suffered a clear psychotic breakdown, and yet she was pronounced fit and sane by the three psychiatrists allowed in by the Bush administration. Broomfield did his best to stall the execution and his film, very different from his previous work, is a testimony to his efforts to uncover Aileen's deeply traumatic past.

One could argue that Aileen Wuornos, in her previous encounters, including the murders, was in some way responding to her early childhood trauma – that of her grandfather (who was probably her father) abusing her sexually, the same treatment he meted out on her mother (and his daughter – so her mother was also her half-sister), her years of using her sexuality to survive at school, and then being homeless, raped repeatedly. That much we do know now, thanks to Broomfield's work. What he uncovered or alleged to, he was able to do precisely because he was a documentary filmmaker and the level of proof is less stringent in films – for better or worse. Here it was clearly a valiant attempt to show her viewpoint – finally. When her mother left home, Aileen became everybody's sexual toy, raped and re-raped by men in the neighbourhood, sometimes given scraps of food and shelter in return. She went along with it until she could do so no more.

Throughout her life, there was no chance of the restorative *après coup*, or *le mur du langage* as Lacan would say (the wall of speech, which in French sounds a little like love), to offer a different future for her. Apart from anything else, nobody was that interested in listening to what she had to say – nobody, apart from Broomfield, that is. The filmmaker's arrival in Wuornos's life, imperfect as it was in the world of horrific abuse, abandonment and violence, was the only respite that her destiny offered to her. He listened – for his film, but nonetheless he did listen.

In this sketch about the connection between trauma and *Nachträglichkeit* in documentary it is worth perhaps mentioning the trauma of the spectator who is presented with often unbearable cases, like this one, with no easy solutions or cures. My personal trauma of watching the whole spectacle of Nick Broomfield's film will have no easy resolution either. When I delivered an earlier version of this paper at the UCL conference on Psychoanalysis and Documentary in May 2013, I played the clip that I describe above. I realized that this particular piece had the sensory effect on me but as I knew it so well, I was confident that I could just play it and proceed with my presentation in a scholarly manner. I was wrong. I watched the unbearable juxtaposition of the two temporalities: one in court in 1991, in which Aileen Wuornos was still ready to fight on, and the other one, 12 years later, in which all her energy was taken out of her, and I was profoundly, bodily moved. In front of 250 people, as the clip I had chosen to play ended, I was nearly in tears and could not speak easily. It is both easy to know why (this really was a barbaric event at the beginning of the twenty-first century in a leading world democracy) and impossible to say (my bodily reaction clearly was not just an intellectual response). Isn't it the unconscious, unknown and unknowable reaction to the material that, in the end, is not really easily analysable in an academic way, but is important to register? Isn't it important to stress that the film can be not just an intimate erotic gesture, to paraphrase Barker (2009: 34), but instead could feel like an unwelcome penetrating thrust, that one has to deal with somehow, against perhaps one's desire – but rather because it feels like an obligation, a dispensing of one's responsibility.

There is more to say. Despite the shock and horror of the story, I cannot leave it be in respectful silence. I am writing about it here and I will perhaps return to it yet. I teach it to my students. There is nothing wrong with this – in fact one could argue (and I will), it is very important to discuss it and show it, as the film does re-focus the debate of the insanity and inhumanity of capital punishment. Nonetheless, this alone does not take care of all the ethical issues surrounding this film. We are familiar with these issues – this is the debate of what is ethical to show and tell, as Cathy Caruth (1996) put it. We are familiar with the controversies surrounded the images of *Night and Fog* (1955) vis-à-vis the more austere allegedly *Shoah* (1985), which still allowed for some manipulations of the witnesses (particularly the famous Abraham Bomba scene). These are not new controversies and they remain.

However, it is important to be aware of the fact that by discussing and showing this particular clip from the film, and indeed others which deal with the unbearable aspects of human condition, by opening a dialogue with my own students about this and through it about the difficulties of documentary filmmaking, this particular *après coup* necessarily *does commodify* Aileen's pain, in a way which the photographs of the nineteenth-century hysterics presented at the Salpêtrière hospital commodified them too. Or let me say this more clearly still, by analysing a filmed trauma of the Other, I do personally commodify it and in some way by writing about it here, I invite you to commodify it too.

However, the question of the image and the words vis-à-vis the transformative nature of the *après coup* and in opposition to the voyeurism it undoubtedly invites also is something to consider here. I have written extensively about the dangers of the society of spectacle and the ethical aspects of documentary filmmaking elsewhere (2014), so let me put forward a different proposition here: sometimes perhaps a commodification of the pain in a film might be worth it as it perhaps does produce something akin to a transformative *après coup* in those who are left behind – in short, in the spectator. After a screening of *Night and Fog* (*Nuit et Brouillard*, 1955) for my students, one of them came up to me and said: 'So you are saying this is really true? This really happened?' We must not assume that the knowledge we have is somehow ubiquitously available to everybody, without the evidence, which sometimes a documentary film can provide. The usual tension between the epistemological drive to know and an ethical stance against the Lévinasian Infinite responsibility for the Other, meaning the immediate other who is in the film, is also accompanied by a hope that the work presented, the image and the words together, can produce an opening for a change that will impact the future by transforming the meaning of the past – in the case of Aileen Wuornos, a totally meaningless death of a deeply disturbed and traumatized woman at the hands of a conservative patriarchal system, can be transformed to an important gesture created by the filmmaker and as such it becomes a lasting and impactful protest against capital punishment.

Before I finish this essay, I want to get back to Nick's other gesture, namely the placing of the radio mic on Aileen's bra. That inappropriate over-familiar move is left in the film for us, the viewers, to consider despite the fact that it would have been so very easy to simply edit it out. I consider the decision to leave it in the film a highly ethical one, a bold move even, which exposes Broomfield's own vulnerability and perhaps a sense of responsibility. It is perhaps left as a trace, conscious or otherwise, of the perils of the filmmaking process, and a signal for the viewer to think of Broomfield's own intrusion into this woman's life, and through his – ours, the spectators, too.

The deferred effect of this scene on us can be challenging in a generative way: we too as spectators are invited by the filmmaker to question our own motives in watching the film in the first place; we question the filmmaker and the nature of our transference to the whole film.

After I gave the paper in May 2013, I decided I should contact the filmmaker, Nick Broomfield, to ask him about the film. I emailed him in May 2013 but he did not respond. I then emailed again and again and eventually sent an impatient email to his agent. Broomfield then got in touch and we exchanged some emails over the summer, attempting to meet but somehow never quite making it. We were both away so much. I did begin to wonder though: were we both a little reluctant to have a painful conversation about Aileen Wuornos? I know I stopped working on the paper for a while, not really wanting to re-visit its subject matter. Weeks and months flew by and with my own deadline looming eventually we managed to Skype; Broomfield in the States and me in London on 24 January 2014. I had researched what Broomfield says about the film. I was hoping he could expand on his previous statements and let me know whether that experience had affected his work in some way. Has he changed because of it in the deferred effect kind of way? On his website one can read the following:

> This is the most personal and most disturbing film I have made. I knew Aileen over the course of 12 years, and the barbaric nature of her death had a profound effect on me, and months of nightmares. [...] The violence of taking a life remains the same whether it is legally sanctioned or not.
> http://nickbroomfield.com (last accessed 2 February 2014)

When it finally happened, our Skype conversation was strange because it was so very ordinary. I said I read what he said on the website and he said 'good' and didn't really want to discuss it further. I asked again about the making of the film and the effects it had on him, and of course he talked about the authorities' revenge aspect of it, and how things were very different the second time around, and that the whole thing was very upsetting for him. 'Upsetting?' I asked, hoping for more insights. I asked about the gesture, of his hand going into her bra to put the radio mic on her – and he didn't remember it. 'Really?' I said. 'Yes, it was all such a long time ago'. I asked if the experience had influenced his work afterwards, and he said he wasn't sure.

Broomfield was not going to be emotional here in a Skype interview with me – he was going to be the detached jocular Broomfield we know from his films. Perhaps it was naive on my part to expect more.

And so we talked a little more and then said 'goodbye' and then, literally a moment before I pressed the little red button on Skype, Nick stopped smiling very briefly and said: 'Just before you go …':

> You know it was really, really hard. I didn't think Aileen's execution would hit me as much as it did … it was … I can't really talk about it at all, still. … I went away, to an island, a small island … afterwards. We went, that is … Joan [Churchill] and I … and I do remember that it was so grey, almost black, that it felt like the sun would never come … for weeks and months. … Only recently did I realize it wasn't really about the weather … it was very lucky I was not on my own … it took me years to do another film.

Broomfield has made some very serious films since his 2003 film about Aileen, all arguably featuring unfair power relationships in some way, for example *Ghosts*, a drama documentary about immigrant workers coming from China, focusing on women's suffering in particular. His latest (2013) film *Sex: My British Job* was perhaps the least successful, but it did attempt to cover the landscape of (immigrant) women being exploited by men and other women too.

'Do you think the Aileen film affected the way you see the world and make your films?' I asked again. 'I really don't know', he answered.

I thought that in the end it was perhaps my fantasy that the experience of making the Aileen film changed Nick Broomfield enough to want to make different films now, films that will address the issues of gender and power relationships in society, somehow as an evidence of a transforming *après coup* effect of the trauma of the making of the Aileen film. But then I asked: 'and the film you are working on now?'

'I am working on a story of a male serial killer in LA – but really it is a story of a horrendous complicity of silence, and the community in some way allowing these shocking abuses perpetrated by men against women. It has to be told'.

Perhaps it is not too optimistic to hope that the dialogue with Aileen Wuornos through the making of *Aileen: The Life and Death of a Serial Killer* (2003) did have some *après coup* transformative effects on the filmmaker after all.

Note

1   Dialogue and stills from *Aileen: The Selling of a Serial Killer* (1992) and *Aileen: Life and Death of a Serial Killer* (2003) appear here by kind permission of Nick Broomfield, director.

References

Barker, J. (2009) *The Tactile Eye: Touch and the Cinematic Experience*. Berkeley: University of California Press, p. 34.

Caruth, C. (1996) *Unclaimed Experience: Trauma and the Possibility of History*. Washington: The Johns Hopkins University Press.

Cowie, E. (2011) *Recording Reality: Desiring the Real*. Minnesota: University of Minnesota Press.

Derrida, J. & Stiegler, B. (2002) *Echographies of Television: Filmed Interviews*. Trans. by J. Bajre. London: Wiley.

Eickhoff, F. (2006) On *Nachträglichkeit*: The Modernity of an Old Concept. *International Journal of Psychoanalysis*, 87, 1453–1469.

Freud, S. (1937) *Analysis Terminable and Interminable* in *Standard Edition of the Complete Psychological Works of Sigmund Freud*. Volume XXIII. Trans. by J. Strachey. London: Hogarth Press and the Institute of Psychoanalysis, pp. 211–253.

Freud, S. (1991 (1950 [1895])) *Project for a Scientific Psychology* in *Standard Edition of the Complete Psychological Works of Sigmund Freud. Volume I*. James Strachey, ed. and trans. London: The Hogarth Press.

Freud, S. (1909) *Notes Upon a Case of Obsessional Neurosis* in *Standard Edition of the Complete Works of Sigmund Freud. Volume X*. Trans. by J. Strachey. London: Hogarth Press and the Institute of Psychoanalysis, pp. 53–249.

Freud, S. (1915) *Observations on Transference-Love (Further Recommendations on the Technique of Psycho-Analysis III)* in *Standard Edition of the Complete Psychological Works of Sigmund Freud. Volume XII*. Trans. by J. Strachey. London: Hogarth Press and the Institute of Psychoanalysis, pp. 157–217.

Kennedy, R. (2002) *Psychoanalysis, History and Subjectivity: Now of the Past*. Hove and New York: Brunner-Routledge.

Lacan, Jacques (1991) *The Seminar of Jacques Lacan, Book I: Freud's Papers on Technique 1953–1954*. Jacques-Alain Miller, ed., John Forrester, trans. London: Norton.

Lacan, Jacques (1997) *The Seminar of Jacques Lacan, Book III: The Psychoses 1955–1956*. Jacques-Alain Miller, ed., Russell Grigg, trans. London: Norton.

Lacan, Jacques (1998 [1981]) Seminar XI. *The Four Fundamental Concepts of Psychoanalysis*. Miller, J-A. (ed.) Trans. by A. Sheridan. London and New York: W. W. Norton.

Lacan, Jacques (1998) *Le Seminaire Livre V: Les Formations de l'inconscient*. Jacques-Alain Miller, ed. Paris: Seuil.

Lacan, Jacques (1999 [1975]) Seminar XX. *On Feminine Sexuality, the Limits of Love and Knowledge*. Miller, J-A. (ed.) Trans. by B. Fink. London and New York: W. W. Norton.

Lacan, Jacques (2006 [2002, 1999, 1971, 1970, 1966]). *Écrits*. Trans. by B. Fink. New York: W.W. Norton.

Lacan, Jacques (2008 [1977]) *Écrits: A Selection*. Trans. by A. Sheridan. London and New York: Routledge.

Laplanche, Jean (1999) 'Notes on Afterwardsness' in *Essays on Otherness*. John Fletcher, ed. and trans. London: Routledge, pp. 260–265.

Lévinas, E. (1981) *Otherwise than Being*. Trans. by A. Lingis. The Hague: Martinus Nijhoff Publishers.

Mulvey, L. (2006) *Death 24x a Second*. London: Reaktion Books.

Mulvey, L. (2007) Compilation Film as 'Deferred Action': Vincent Monnikendam's *Mother Dao, the Turtle-like* in *Projected Shadows. Psychoanalytic Reflections on the Representation of Loss in European Cinema*. A. Sabbadini (ed.). London: Routledge.

Nichols, B. (1991). *Representing Reality: Issues and Concepts in Documentary*. Bloomington: Indiana University Press.

Piotrowska, A. (2011) Animating the Real – A Case Study. *Animation: An Interdisciplinary Journal*, 6(3) (November 2011), 335–353.

Piotrowska, A. (2012) Conman and I: A Case Study in Transference in Documentary. *Studies in Documentary Film*, 6(1), 15–29.

Piotrowska, A. (2014) *Psychoanalysis and Ethics in Documentary Film*. London and New York: Routledge.

Sobchack, V. (2004) *Carnal Thoughts: Embodiment and Moving Image Culture*. Berkeley: University of California Press.

Williams, L. (1991) Film Bodies: Gender, Genre and Excess. *Film Quarterly*, 44(4), 2–13.

Wilson, E. (2012) *Love, Mortality and the Moving Image*. Basingstoke: Palgrave Macmillan.

Web resources

www.imdb.com/title/tt0364930/reviews (last accessed 26 January 2014).
http://nickbroomfield.com/ (last accessed 7 February 2014).

Filmography

Broomfield, N. (1993) USA. *Aileen Wuornos: The Selling of a Serial Killer*. USA (DVD. Lafayette Films).

Broomfield, N. (2003) *Aileen: Life and Death of a Serial Killer USA* (DVD. Lafayette Films).

Broomfield, N. (2006) *Ghosts* (DVD: Beyond Films).

Broomfield, N. (2013) *Sex: My British Job* (Channel 4).

Lanzmann, C. (1985) *Shoah*. France. Les Films Aleph (DVD: IFC Films).

Resnais, A. (1955) *Nuit et Brouillard* (Night and Fog). France. Como Films, Argos Films, Cocinor and Janus Films (DVD: The Criterion Collection).

Chapter 3

The ventriloquism of documentary first-person speech and the self-portrait film*

Elizabeth Cowie

In documentary film we encounter the stories of others who speak themselves through their words. We *listen* to them. How do we hear, and what do we learn, and is this what they intend us to know and hear? In this essay I explore the place of the voice and its speech in relation to the body in documentary film through *With Jerzy Grotowski, Nienadówka, 1980,* made with Grotowski by Jill Godmilow.[1] Jerzy Grotowski (1933–1999) was a Polish experimental theatre director and major innovator through his idea of the theatre as laboratory and his concept of 'poor theatre'. He is, with Artaud and Brecht, Stanislavski and Mayerhold, a figure of central importance to twentieth-century theatre developments. *With Jerzy Grotowski* is therefore an important audio-visual document for understanding Grotowski, while as a key innovator of theatrical methods that focus on the actor's body, Grotowski's presentation of himself in this film is especially relevant to this volume. The film follows Grotowski's journey of exploration of 'who he is', as Peter Brook explains in his voice-over introduction, in filming Grotowski's return to the village of Nienadówka for the first time since he left at the end of the Second World War, some 35 years earlier. It is a performance of remembering and identity that Grotowski enacts for there, Grotowski says 'I was born in some way the second time, in this village. All essential motives in my life started here.'

Godmilow is an acclaimed documentary film-maker but she has acknowledged that this film was very much Grotowski's, writing that:

> Nothing was spoken about it at the time, but somehow, at that first breakfast, I understood that Jerzy would be in some way directing the film and it would be my job to make it possible for him to do that, by arranging the camera and sound to record wherever, whenever, and whatever he wanted to do and say. ... So this film is a real documentary ... a document of what happened in that place when Jerzy went to find something.
>
> (Godmilow, 2008)[2]

And indeed, we see him in the film giving directions to Godmilow and the crew, as well as their difficulties in simply following him, when, as Godmilow explains, Grotowski is standing in a grove of trees, searching for something that he can't seem to find. Then he approaches the camera and explains that somewhere here ... just there – he points ... was his 'sacred tree'. The camera swings over to where he is pointing – there is nothing there but grass – as Jerzy continues, 'But it is no longer here'. We are staring at just grass ... Jerzy, me, Chiquita, the crew, the camera, and now you.

(ibid.)

Of her role in the film's making, Godmilow comments that, 'In essence, I abdicated as director, and followed Jerzy's lead. This was hard for a moment, and then it wasn't. This, therefore, is the film Jerzy wanted to make' (ibid.).

Grotowski wrote little, and the film is his only sustained account of his personal formation and ideas, as such it seems to answer the question that Jacques Derrida posed, shortly before he died: 'How do you finally respond to your life and your name?'[3] Judith Butler, citing Derrida's question, continues,

One cannot, he [Derrida] remarks, come to terms with one's life without trying to apprehend one's death, asking, in effect, how a human learns to live and to die ... he tries to come to terms with the deaths of other writers and thinkers through reckoning his debt to their words, indeed, their texts; his own writing constitutes an act of mourning.

(Butler, 2004: 32)

In *With Jerzy Grotowski*, Grotowski's return to Nienadówka is an act of rediscovery that is also a mourning, not only for his late mother, of whom he speaks, but also for his father who disappeared in 1940, and his much-loved teacher, whom he thought was dead, and the place of a way of life with others still living through whom he learned. Derrida asks, 'To keep alive, within oneself: is this the best sign of fidelity?' (2001: 36). 'For', he writes, 'ever since psychoanalysis came to mark this discourse, the image commonly used to characterize mourning is that of an interiorization (an idealizing incorporation, introjection, consumption of the other)' (2001: 158–159).[4] Yet it is the 'unbearable paradox of fidelity' for such interiorization not to be possible and completed (ibid.).

The film is not, however, autobiographical; rather it is a self-portrait in an exploration of what made Grotowski what he is rather than telling the story of what he has done. Laura Rascaroli in her study of the genre of the self-portrait suggests that 'the lack of continuous narrative is, indeed, a defining characteristic' (2012: 57), and she cites Raymond Bellour's comment of the self-portrait that it 'is distinguished from autobiography by the absence of a story one is obliged to follow' (Bellour, 1989: 8; Rascaroli, 2012: 58). Further, as she notes, 'Bellour was prompted to write that the self-portrait is perhaps the only form of autobiography truly achievable in film' (ibid.).[5]

In *With Jerzy Grotowski* it is a portrait performed by Grotowski as a speaking and embodied subject through a journey of discovery of his remembered past in a 'now' experienced by him in the places and with the people from that past that we see in Godmilow's documentary filming. The camera follows Grotowski, who has arrived in the village without arranging any meetings, but with a clear agenda for his return to both Nienadówka and for his visit with his paternal aunt at her apartment in a nearby town where he talks directly to Godmilow and the camera. For it is a carefully choreographed presentation by Grotowski of his time in Nienadówka and its role in enabling his philosophy of life and theatre.

We hear Grotowski not only as an embodied voice within the film speaking Polish and English, but also as a disembodied or, to use Michel Chion's term, 'acousmatic' voice off-screen over the images we see, so that what emerges is a complex interrelation of voice embodied and voice off-screen (Chion, 1994: 29–34).[6] On-screen, we overhear the conversations he has with the people he meets in the village, and hear his direct address to camera in English translating the Polish of those he speaks with, or describing what he feels as he re-encounters there the places and people of his childhood while he tells us of his memories of what had been. We hear him talking to the film crew on-screen and, in his aunt's apartment, directly to camera. Grotowski's acousmatic voice-over explains that what we see and hear is from another space and time, for it was recorded much later in New York, and he speaks to spaces beyond the village, and to the time of the viewer, in particular, to the community of theatre practitioners.

Voice in the film therefore embodies different temporalities that are in play for Grotowski on the one hand, and for the viewer on the other hand. And it is temporality that is also Grotowski's concern in this film, and in his theatre work at this time, of finding 'our way towards the source of what we are' (Grotowski in the film), and thereby of what we can be.

Godmilow's own films are not conventional documentaries for her view is, she writes, that:

> the documentary filmmaker should always, somehow, as Buñuel did [in *Land Without Bread*, 1933], be setting into operation a second track of meaning, a track about ourselves, so that we, watching the film, don't melt into pure disembodied spectators, spectators who seem to have no designs of our own upon the world, no personal interests, no class interests, no national interests. My own strategy for making the second track – and it means something different in every case – is to reframe the footage somehow. To reframe the footage means to renegotiate it, and in the renegotiating, to raise all possible questions about representation.
>
> (Godmilow, 2002: 9)

Godmilow's concern here is with the spectator's experience,

> I want not just information, or intimacy, or pathos, but a cinema experience strong enough to change consciousness, that is, to make it impossible to think in old ways, so that I am no longer who I was before I saw the film.
>
> (ibid.)

Grotowski had a similar project in relation to his work with actors through which he sought to enable the actor:

> to reveal one after the other the different layers of his personality, from the biological-instinctive source via the channel of consciousness and thought, to that summit which is so difficult to define and in which all becomes unity. This act of the total unveiling of one's being becomes a gift of the self which borders on the transgression of barriers and love. I call this a total act. If the actor performs in such a way, he becomes a kind of provocation for the spectator.
>
> (1968: 99)

The actor does this not 'for the spectator', Grotowski argues, 'One should rather say "In relation to" the spectator or, perhaps, instead of him. It is precisely here that the provocation lies' (ibid.). It is such an 'acting' that Grotowski himself performs in Godmilow's film, one that gives the actor

> a maximum of suggestive power on condition, of course, that he avoids chaos, hysteria, exaltation. It must be an objective act: that is to say articulated, disciplined. But above and beyond methodical efficacy, a new perspective also opens up for the spectator ... I am talking about method, I am speaking of the surpassing of limits, of a confrontation, of a process of self-knowledge and, in a certain sense, of therapy. Such a method must remain open – its very life depends on this condition – and is different for each individual.
>
> (ibid.)

For Godmilow, in her filmmaking, 'This new relationship would be based on a contract that goes something like this: "I, the filmmaker, will propose some ideas. You can listen and watch and see what you think"' (ibid.). In *With Jerzy Grotowski*, however, it is Grotowski who is proposing the ideas, his voice frames all that we see and hear. A 'second track' nevertheless emerges 'that interrogates the performance of the first, the reality footage' (Godmilow, ibid.), through the temporal and spatial dislocations of both the editing, and the off-screen, 'acousmatic', disembodied voice-over of Grotowski. This might also be called the allegorical, in the sense that Walter Benjamin develops when he writes:

> Every present day is determined by the images that are synchronic with it: each 'now' is the now of a particular recognizability. ... It is not that what is past casts its light on what is present, or what is present its light on what is past; rather, image is that wherein what has been comes together in a flash with the now to form a constellation. ... For while the relation of the present to the past is purely temporal, the relation of what-has-been to the now is dialectical: not temporal in nature but figural (*bildlich*).
>
> (1999: 463–464)

It is in the break of temporal unfolding in the film that such a dialectical – or figural, that is, allegorical – imaging emerges, which arises in the gap between documentary's time-now of telling/showing and the time-past of the told/shown. This produces a temporality that is a certain fiction, notwithstanding the indexicality – the documentary 'truth' – of the recorded seen and heard. For we are engaged by the film's time, and its organisation of its sounds and images. This gap is also documentary's ventriloquism, namely, its art of producing its voice as another's, for while the documentary film enables us to hear its participants it also organises their voices through selecting from recorded interviews and by juxtaposing them with other material or other voices not present to or heard by the interviewee, and it thus 'speaks' them. As Jonathan Kahana has observed, in documentary we experience 'the magical power of the testimonial voice, its capacity to (re)cover great distances in space and time and to spirit the viewer to another place and time than the one seen in the present image' (Kahana, 2006: 22). An uncanny ventriloquism arises, however, in the gap introduced between the voice off-screen, acousmatic, and voice on-screen embodied. For while the person whose voice we hear but who is off-screen may have been seen on-screen earlier, or is shown later, enabling us to place the voice in a body, such 'de-acousmatisation' (Chion, 1994: 131) remains uncanny for an uncertainty or hesitation is introduced by the difference – the gap – that splits the authorship of the speaker between embodied and disembodied speech.

The recorded voices body forth as material sounds such that, whether heard off- or on-screen, they each introduce a certain irreality: they are spectral. Jacques Derrida observes in the film *Ghost Dance* (1983) that

> A specter is ... a trace that marks the present with its absence in advance. The spectral logic is de facto a deconstructive logic. ... Film plus psychoanalysis equals a science of ghosts ... a trace that marks the present with its absence in advance.
> (cited in Derrida and Stiegler, 2002: 117, 115)

For Slavoj Žižek, 'Specters belong to the Real, they are the price we pay for the gap that separates reality from the Real' (1994: 194). Here Žižek is referring to Jacques Lacan's tripartite distinction of the real as the felt of an unrepresentable, of an unsymbolised, and thus of a lack that arises retrospectively as the child comes to have an image of itself – in the mirror stage – and to fantasise the absent object of its demand, the breast it has cried for, in an imaginary relation to satisfaction, which then through language and the alterity of the Other can be symbolised. The gap between the real and reality arises as well in relation to the voice such that, Žižek suggests, it too is spectral:

> An unbridgeable gap separates forever a human body from 'its' voice. The voice displays a spectral autonomy, it never quite belongs to the body we see, so that even when we see a living person talking, there is always a minimum

of ventriloquism at work: it is as if the speaker's own voice hollows him out and in a sense speaks 'by itself', through him.

(Žižek, 2001: 58, cited in Dolar, 2006: 70)

Mladen Dolar, drawing on Žižek, goes on to argue that,

> Ventriloquism pertains to voice as such, to its inherently acousmatic character: the voice comes from inside the body, the belly, the stomach – from something incompatible with and irreducible to the activity of the mouth. The fact that we see the aperture does not demystify the voice: on the contrary, it enhances the enigma.
>
> (2006: 70)

Dolar explores the voice not as a vehicle of meaning or as a source of aesthetic admiration, however, but as an object cause of desire – in the sense that Jacques Lacan gives this, drawing on Freud, of little object other, *objet petit a*, that stands in for what is felt as lost, and thereby itself signifies lack. Dolar suggests that the voice as *objet petit a* can be seen as the lever of thought for the subject who speaks. For to speak is first of all to desire to be heard by an other, to engage an encounter with an other. The voice itself, however, '*is what does not contribute to making sense*. It is the material element recalcitrant to meaning, and if we speak in order to say something, then the voice is precisely that which cannot be said' (Dolar, 2006: 15; italics in original). And, '*it is precisely the voice that holds bodies and language together*' (ibid.: 60, italics in original).

Derrida, too, posits a gap that language institutes,

> this pure difference, which constitutes the self-presence of the living present, introduces into self-presence from the beginning all the impurity putatively excluded from it. The living present springs forth out of its nonidentity with itself and from the possibility of a retentional trace. It is always already a trace.
>
> (1973: 85)

This is a subject divided, as the one who speaks, but who also hears her own words as if another. Žižek emphasises that 'gaze and voice are *objects*, that is, they do not belong on the side of the looking/seeing subject but on the side of what the subject sees or hears' (1996: 90). Moreover, Alice Lagaay notes,

> it is not a particular person's gaze, and not a particular sounding voice, that these objects refer to. Instead, gaze and voice have a quasi-transcendental status in Lacan's theory insofar as they refer to the fundamental relation from outside (the other) to inside (the self), which in constituting the subject at the same time defines it as lack.[7]

In the film Grotowski's voice explains what we see and hear, but also introduces a 'voicing' as 'object cause of desire' and thus a relation to the other, and to lack. Derrida writes, 'Hearing oneself speak is not the inwardness of an inside that is closed in on itself; it is the irreducible openness in the inside; it is the eye and the world within speech' (1973: 86). It is this openness to the other and to the voice's address as object and as speech for both the speaker, Grotowski, and the listener, that I will explore in *With Jerzy Grotowski*.

In film there are two different times of address: the present of the recorded past, and the future of the encounter with this speech by – unknown – listeners. The temporality of voiced speech, however, is always experienced as a 'now' time of address, a present tense of communication, overturning the pastness of the documentary record in the moment by moment of the present listening. At the same time sound and voice, Chion notes, are 'characteristically vectorised in time … with an irreversible beginning, middle and end' (1994: 19). This now time of hearing is duration, a continuing to hear the next, and the next, thus it is unlike the image – and the written word – that are seen entire, in a flash. Time as duration, in Henri Bergson's distinction, 'is not merely one instant replacing another; if it were, there would never be anything but the present – no prolonging of the past into the actual, no evolution'[8] (Bergson, 1911/2008: 7–8). Instead, 'Real duration is that in which each form flows out of previous forms, while adding to them something new, and is explained by them as much as it explains them, producing a cognisance of a past before our present, and a future that is after' (ibid.: 141).

It is the voice that provides continuity over editing's discontinuous images, but while recorded moving images can be viewed frame by frame, whether digital or analogue, speech cannot. We are held to the channel of communication, the speech is 'imposed to hear' rather than merely given to listen to (Chion, 1994: 33). 'Real time', 'historical time', 'actuality', 'event' are all terms that we use to mark out the temporal difference between the experienced present, the 'now' time, and its later encounter in remembering – through our own memories and through prosthetic devices of audio-visual recording.

Is the said that is heard more on the side of the actual, more rooted in the contingent and tied to the instance of utterance – a duration – as a passing present such that, re-heard it bespeaks absence as loss, not as made present again? For untied to a body, the acousmatic voice-over is both part of the image and more than the seen, so that it is encountered as well as *objet petit a*, as uncanny, for the voice is experienced in a seeming immediacy that penetrates our interiority and implies a gaze and body unseen. The gap between heard and seen persists, such that, Dolar suggests, '*the visible as such can start to function as the veil of the voice*' (Dolar, 2006: 78; emphasis in the original), introducing a possible indeterminacy of the voice from elsewhere that can haunt documentary. In film, the person whose voice we hear but who is off-screen may have been seen on-screen earlier, or is shown later, enabling us to place the voice in a body. Such 'de-acousmatisation' is always uncanny, however, for an uncertainty or hesitation is introduced by the difference – the gap – that splits the authorship of the speaker between embodied and disembodied speech.

What then is the relation of seeing to hearing? The face and the voice each address us, but we are engaged at one and the same time in two distinct bodily experiences with different affectual and cognitive implications. The heard is experienced as sensual in an embodied voicing of tone, cadence and rhythm, and as cognitive, in relation to the accent or dialect, or whether it is a child's voice or an adult's, and finally, it is heard as language. The face engages us with a question, of the nature of the other, but it can also engage us with the other's address as a gaze and voice, and thereby a different question, of who I am for the other.

It is this openness to the other, and the voice's address as object and as first-person speech, that engages us to identify, which I want to consider now in *With Jerzy Grotowski*. In returning to Nienadówka, Grotowski is not simply seeking the truth of 'who he is', but to perform that truth such that it informs – transforms – his audience. He has something to tell us, but he does so through enacting a journey of discovery that is a staging of truths about knowledge and identity. I am struck here by the parallel with Michel de Certeau's description of Lacan's way of speaking when delivering his famous *Séminaires*, 'the actor is at work. In this commedia dell'arte, where the art of the analyst takes the stage, a starring role is assumed by the speaking body, and especially by this body's throat' (1983: 23). There is an array of *disturbances* of the voice, 'as if what he said was always on the brink of dissolving, of retreating or regressing, into a kind of incomprehensible physicality' (Certeau, 2002: 243; Lagaay, 2008: 57). Such disturbances 'punctuate the chain of words and indicate all their secret of being "for the other" and of producing for the listeners the effects of meaning, of the signified. The signifiers are all the more understood in so far as there is misunderstanding about what they designate' (de Certeau, 1983: 23). Lagaay suggests:

> Lacan's eccentric style of talking can thus be seen as a kind of performative enactment of his theory of listening and of voice: it is not about understanding but about letting one's unconscious take in and react to what is heard; the voice brings to the foreground, *but in a movement of suspension, of retreat*, that of which the speaker has no knowledge.
> (2008: 57, 58, italics in original)[9]

De Certeau makes a further reference to the body in theatre, writing:

> In fact, this mimicry is only part of the repertory of a theatrical art which consists of the loss of the body in order to speak and which holds a place close to the art of Artaud. Like his 'patient', the analyst [Lacan] lets his discourse recount that part of his story which 'escapes' him and which 'flushes' (like a hare is flushed) all Lacan's 'anonymous and scattered listeners'.
> (de Certeau, 1983: 23)

For Grotowski, it is the anticipated diverse and scattered viewers of this film that he addresses but unlike Lacan, he discouraged note-taking, for he is reported to have said,

> 'If during our meeting you take notes or record on tape, you preserve from this meeting only some formulas. If you search for formulas, you search for revered truths. Just listen and somehow participate in this event. You can forget all the formulas. By themselves, they mean nothing.
> (cited by Salata, 2013: 38)[10]

Grotowski, like Lacan, spoke both as the master-teacher, as the one who knows, a guru,[11] and as not-knowing but enabling others to come to know about themselves, in the position of the analyst, as *objet a*, cause of desire, in Lacan's schema of the four discourses (Lacan, 2007: 79; 146–147).

With Jerzy Grotowski provides in moving images and sounds something comparable to Roland Barthes' in *Roland Barthes by Roland Barthes*, where Barthes presents a photo-album of still images that he captions, like his subsequent meditations, both in the direct first-person, 'But I never looked like that', addressing his image in photographs in 1942 and 1970 (1977: 38, 39), and in the indirect third-person, 'He is troubled by an *image* of himself' (1977: 43; italics in original). In *With Jerzy Grotowski*, however, it is the image-track that addresses us indirectly, while Grotowski – speaking directly – performs himself for us. Derrida writes of *Roland Barthes by Roland Barthes* that,

> I cannot tear myself away from the photographs and the handwriting. I do not know what I am still looking for, but I'm looking for it in the direction of his body, in what he shows and says of it, in what he hides of it perhaps – like something he could not *see* in his writing ... for something that regards me, or has me in view, without seeing me.
> ('The Deaths of Roland Barthes', Derrida, 2001: 63)

In exploring Grotowski's voice in *With Jerzy Grotowski* I, too, am searching in his performance not only for how he articulates 'who am I?', but also what he has not yet seen or known within what he comes to show and say. In de Certeau's words, cited above, his voice also tells 'that part of his story which "escapes" him'.

In the following I examine the misremembered in Grotowski's encounters, as well as his remembered heard, read or seen that he voices as he re-encounters the places and people of those memories. Intercut with these scenes are discussions at his paternal aunt's apartment, and where Grotowski concludes the film with an account to camera of his central idea of the body stilled, placed after his journey of remembrance, a philosophy that, as he had explained to a questioner following his course on acting in 1966, 'always comes after a technique! Tell me: do you walk home with your legs or your ideas?' (Grotowski, 1968: 169).

Speaking in often awkward English directly to camera on-screen, Grotowski's voice is hesitant as he tries to find the right word, sometimes repeating a point using slightly different words. The film opens with Grotowski introducing us to the village that he and his mother and brother fled to after the German invasion and his father's disappearance in the war, emphasising that they arrived 'without having nothing, with just empty hands, with the very big poverty'. His voice-over was recorded two years later with Godmilow in New York. She explains that 'he speaks as someone who is watching the footage of what happened there in Nienadówka and explaining it to viewers who might not understand Polish, but also at times for those who do'.[12] Yet we may hear it as if he were speaking in the time of the filming, explaining what we see, and what he thinks, heard both when he is off-screen, and when we see him on-screen. This produces a ventriloquism as Grotowski speaks himself of himself from another time and space as another remembrance, but which he doesn't comment upon. How then do we hear, and understand, his misremembering?

We next see Grotowski with an elderly man whom he asks about Janek, 'Who I have in my memory as a teacher at my school ... but in my memory he was killed'. The old man, whom Grotowski explains is rather deaf, finally recognises the name and says that he is still living, gesturing screen right, and Grotowski turns to look in the same direction. In voice-over, however, he says he doesn't believe the man, whom he thinks is speaking of 'another Janek'. Approaching the church, Grotowski examines the wall plaque that commemorates those who died in the war, saying in voice-over, 'It is some kind of memory place with the names of the killed people so I am looking for the name of "Janek", but there is none, so probably he should be living'. Another misremembering that is again a reversal arises as he views the church, now locked, and says in voice-over, 'normally in the childhood, memories, all things are bigger because the child is small, but what is strange for me is that it is opposite, I have the impression that now it is bigger'. At the school that he attended as a child and where his mother worked Grotowski meets a teacher who remembers them and, Grotowski tells us in voice-over, she confirms that Janek is still living just across the river. In the next shot, at Janek's farm, the delighted Grotowski greets Janek who finally recognises him. Grotowski explains in voice-over that yes, Janek was arrested but was not killed because it was so late in the war, and now he is the elected 'chief of the village'. They converse in Polish as Grotowski tells us, 'I said to him, before, that I very loved him when he was my teacher' and we hear him laugh – perhaps embarrassed – in voice-over.

Grotowski does not explain how he came to make his mistake so we are left to speculate possible reasons. In Nienadówka as a child, after having lost his father, Grotowski found a loved figure whom he much later came to characterise as important to his 're-birth' there, but whom he believed had died and was thereby also lost to him. Grotowski's joy on discovering that Janek is still living, in the present time of filming, cannot displace the affect of that memory, namely the unrepresentable, the real, of loss. Grotowski's father, too, had not died but chose not to return to his family in Poland.

46   Elizabeth Cowie

Figure 3.1 Production still showing Grotowski being filmed as he asks the elderly man about Janek

Source: Reproduced by permission of the Grotowski Institute ©

The uncertainty of memory figures again as Grotowski searches for the house where he had lived, but the village is now so changed. Walking into another farmyard he says in voice-over, 'I'm not sure ... but I think this it is my old home', though there is now a new extension, but when he steps through the old traditional door, he affirms 'I think it was here', but as no one is there, he leaves with the film crew, saying to camera that, 'In this place was my sacred tree, but it no more exists', as the camera pans around looking for it. Meeting a neighbour, Grotowski asks about the family he had lived with and learns that, while the head of the family had died, his wife Franciszka is still living and is out in the fields looking after the cows, 'I ask if it was in the normal place', and is told yes of course, and Grotowski walks away up a hill, to find her. He tells us that the head of the family is now the daughter, Veronka, and we see him talk to a woman working the field whom he seems to ask for directions, and he walks on, while his voice-over explains that the woman is Veronka, 'in reality she is here, but I don't recognise her'. He continues that, when they arrived in the village, 'everything was broken ... and we was waiting for a place for life' but Veronka made him welcome, he says in voice-over, '... it was really the new beginning' as we see him turn back and call to her on-screen 'Veronka'. She had already recognised him, and greets him as 'Jurek', small Jerzy, and Grotowski tells us in voice-over that there is 'Something very warm in the way of speaking of her, its absolutely impossible to translate', and that she says 'we was formed together'. This moment of recognition might be thought of as the *anagnorisis* in Greek theatre, but which is not only a recognition of the person, but also what the person stands for. Yet here, performed

The ventriloquism of documentary first-person speech 47

by Veronka, her words introduce a disjuncture that is not irony, for while 'formed together' their paths have nevertheless taken each of them to very different futures. The poignancy of this here, in 1980s Poland, is made clear when Grotowski goes on to meet Franciszka and learns that, at 82 years old, she is still working, because 'it is needed'. Grotowski now plunges into an action of remembering as he walks with her, guiding her cows, as he had done so often as a child, making jokes with Franciszka who says 'Ah, now I have my shepherd'. Memory here is a doing, engaging the experience of the being of remembering, but that can only be realised – articulated – in language and thereby becomes fixed as the 'remembered'.

Returning to the farm and its buildings, Grotowski uses these as a *mise en scène* for the telling of significant remembrances, which are then intercut with his aunt's apartment where he speaks to camera, imbricating these two spaces and their different temporalities with the remembered past. Here, Grotowski enacts 'who he became' in the performance of the film's cross-cutting. Beside the pig shed he tells of reading in its attic the Gospels, whose stories of a compassionate Christ so strongly influenced him, while in the apartment he explains how his mother, though Catholic, introduced him to Hinduism and Buddhism for she felt other religions were not in error, but connected, each being different ways of looking for 'the essential, the grain of light'. In Nienadówka Grotowski explains how he helped with the bull's insemination of the cows, and that this represented a relation to the natural, 'what I call senses of the object ... meaning the big mother world'

Figure 3.2 Grotowski leads Franciszka's cows home
Source: Reproduced by permission of the Grotowski Institute ©

that gives both fecundity and death. Grotowski, in the apartment, says 'it flows from the middle as from the source ... something inside us ... it is not myself, in the sense of the ego', but it is felt 'along with one's physical senses'.

Seated on the farmhouse steps beside Franciszka, Grotowski describes being under the table when his mother was playing a game of cards with others and hearing 'the grain of something really important', for the way they talked was not a true conversation but a kind of 'associations game', where one person responds to another's comment with a new story only vaguely connected. Their conversation, Grotowski says, was without purpose or 'reality', which he calls 'a life dreaming state'. By contrast, in the film's final scene at his aunt's apartment, Grotowski speaks of 'the movement which is the repose' within many religions, realised in the image of the Buddha lying down observed by his mother. There is movement on the outside, an involvement in the senses, in the world, but inside is repose through which, he says, instead of the conflict experienced in the fragmentation of the 'social game', of work and activity, 'in this life, which we have ... in this reality ... we should to find this meaning, fulfillment ... some kind of original joy ... original happiness ... which is our property but we lose this, just. It is in us and we lose this. It was given to us but we lose this. We lose this ... which we continue to look for, the original ... the true.'

In the juxtaposition of times then, remembered, and the filmic seen and heard 'now' both in Nienadówka and, cross-cut, in his aunt's apartment, with the voice-over 'now' recorded in New York, a 'second track' arises. In the film Grotowski has travelled back in memory to 1940 when he arrived in Nienadówka as a small boy having 'nothing' except the loss of all that was before, to give voice through a certain ventriloquism to what enabled his 'second birth' through his mother, his beloved teacher, as well as Franciszka and Veronka and the places and spaces of Nienadówka, which made him who he is, a seeker for the true that is lost. The film, through this 'second track', may lead us to think in new ways for the spectre of loss remains, not overcome but urging us on in the journey that for Grotowski is towards the source 'of what we are'.

Notes

*   Dialogue from With Jerzy Grotowski, Nienadówka, 1980, appears here by kind permission of Jill Godmilow, director. Stills from the same film appear by permission of the Grotowski Institute.
1   After the declaration in 1982 of Martial Law in Poland Grotowski left to work in the United States, first at Columbia University in New York, then in 1983 at the University of California, where he developed Objective Drama. In 1986 Grotowski moved to Italy and created the Work Centre of Jerzy Grotowski – Centro di Lavoro di Jerzy Grotowski with Thomas Richards, Pablo Jimenez and Julius Slowiacki, his collaborators from Objective Drama. He was appointed Professor of Theatre at the College de France in 1997, where Lacan, Barthes and Derrida had taught. Grotowski read very widely in philosophy and anthropology, and was influenced by the writings of Carl Jung, whom he refers to in the film, and drew on psychoanalytical terms, for example, his references to the unconscious, and to therapy, and his use of a term such

as 'individuation', which Jung used to define mental development, in his letter referring to his work on *The Constant Prince*, see Barba (1999: 31), as well as by Tibetan Buddhism and Hinduism.
2. *With Jerzy Grotowski, Nienadówka, 1980* was shot on 3/4" video.
3. Derrida made this statement in his final interview with *Le Monde*, published on 18 August 2004 shortly before he died, and thus was perhaps also speaking of himself.
4. See Sigmund Freud's *Mourning and Melancholia*.
5. I have drawn here on Laura Rascaroli's lucid and subtle discussion of the self-portrait in film.
6. Michel Chion developed Pierre Shaeffer's use of the term 'acousmatic' to refer to listening where the sound is heard without seeing its cause and which 'allows sound to reveal itself in all its dimensions' (1994: 32).
7. The letter '*a*' refers on the one hand to the *a* of l'*autre* (other); on the other hand, as the first letter of the alphabet, it stands for both the beginning of a symbolic system as well as for the algebraic place-holder, meaningless in itself, but essentially open to take on significance in a particular context.
8. Henri Bergson, *Creative Evolution*, The Project Gutenberg eBook, www.gutenberg.org/files/26163/26163-h/26163-h.htm, pp. 7–8 and p. 141.
9. In fact, Lagaay points out, 'Lacan was not a keen writer. The texts of the *séminaires* are for the most part reconstructions put together and edited by one of the students who attended them (between 1975 and 1995 nine of the 25 seminars were "reconstructed" and published by Lacan's son-in-law, Jacques-Alain Miller)' (2008: 58).
10. Kris Salata's reference for this quote, which he translated, cites Stanislaw Rosiek who presents testimonies of three people who attended the same meeting with Grotowski and took notes but who presented quite different accounts of it (Salata, 2013: 188 note 89; Rosiek, 1986: 369). See also Fumaroli (2009: 198), who explains that Grotowski was fearful, having lived in a police state, that his words that might be used against him.
11. Marc Fumaroli (2009: 199), describing the revolt young Americans attending his exercises in 1968 who accused Grotowski of being 'a dictator', comments 'Grotowski listened to this hysterical outburst very calmly and then explained that any legal equality between *teacher* and *student* should give way during the teaching to a purely functional and practical inequality'.
12. Email correspondence from Jill Godmilow, March 2014. I am very grateful to Jill for her comments and suggestions on an earlier version of this essay. I have not worked with a translation of the Polish spoken in the film, but only with Grotowski's address and speech in English. Paul Allain gave invaluable help in correcting my errors of understanding. Professor Allain has been central to the new work currently emerging in English on the importance of Grotowski's contribution to theatre.

References

Barba, Eugenio (1999) *Land of Ashes and Diamond: My Apprenticeship in Poland*, Aberystwyth: Black Mountain Press.

Bellour, Raymond (1989) *Eye for I: Video Self-Portraits*, trans. Lynne Kirby. New York: New York University Press.

Benjamin, Walter (1999) *The Arcades Project*, trans. Howard Eiland and Kevin McLaughlin. Cambridge, MA: Harvard University Press.

Bergson, Henri (1911; 2008) trans. Mitchell, Arthur [EBook #26163] www.gutenberg.org/files/26163/26163-h/26163-h.htm

Butler, Judith (2004) Jacques Derrida. *London Review of Books*, *26*(21), 32. www.lrb.co.uk/v26/n21/judith-butler/jacques-derrida, downloaded 21/2/2014.

Chion, Michel (1994) *Audio-Vision: Sound on Screen*, ed. and trans. Claudia Gorbman. New York: Columbia University Press.

——(1999) *The Voice in Cinema*, ed. and trans. Claudia Gorbman. New York: Columbia University Press.

de Certeau, Michel (1983) Lacan: An Ethics of Speech. *Representations*, 3, Summer, 21–39.

——(2002) *Histoire et psychanalyse entre science et fiction*. Paris: Gallimard.

Derrida, Jacques (1973) *Speech and Phenomena*. Evanston: North Western University Press.

——(2001) *The Work of Mourning*. Chicago: University of Chicago Press, pp. 34–67.

——(1983) *Ghost Dance*, directed by McMullen, Ken.

——(2002) With Stiegler, Bernard. *Echographies of Television: Filmed Interviews*. Cambridge: Polity Press.

Dolar, Mladen (2006) *A Voice and Nothing More*. Cambridge, MA: MIT Press.

Freud, Sigmund (1951) Mourning and Melancholia (1915 [1917]), in *The Standard Edition of the Complete Works of Sigmund Freud*. London: The Holgarth Press, pp. 237–258.

Fumaroli, Marc (2009) Grotowski, or the Border Ferryman, in *Grotowski's Empty Room*, ed. Paul Allain. London: Seagull Books, pp. 195–215.

Godmilow, Jill (2002) Kill the Documentary as We Know It. *Journal of Film and Video*, *54*/2–3, Summer/Fall, pp. 3–10.

——(2008) 'An Account of How this Nienadówka Film First Came Into Being, and Where it Has Been For the Last 28 Years, And Why it's Best To Watch the Film First Before Reading this Story'. Facets, DVD booklet, accessed 23/02/2014 at: www3.nd.edu/~jgodmilo/grotowski.html

Grotowski, Jerzy (1968) *Towards a Poor Theatre*, ed. Barba, Eugenio, preface by Brook, Peter, London: Methuen.

Kahana, Jonathan (2006) Cinema and The Ethics of Listening: Isaac Julien's *Frantz Fanon*. *Film Quarterly*, *59*(2), 19–31.

Lacan, Jacques (2007) *The Other Side of Psychoanalysis*: *The Seminar of Jacques Lacan Book XVII*, New York: Norton.

Lagaay, Alice (2008) Between Sound and Silence: Voice in the History of Psychoanalysis. *e-pisteme*, *1*(1).

Rascaroli, Laura (2012) The Self-Portrait Film: Michelangelo's *Last Gaze*, in *The Cinema of Me: The Self and Subjectivity in First Person Documentary*, ed. Alisa Lebow. London: Wallflower Press.

Rosiek, Stanislaw (1986) *Maski*. Gdansk: Wydawnictwo Morskie.

Salata, Kris (2013) *The Unwritten Grotowski: Theory and Practice of the Encounter*. London and New York: Routledge.

Žižek, Slavoj (1994) *The Metastases of Enjoyment: Six Essays on Woman and Causality*. London: Verso.

——(1996) 'I Hear You With My Eyes'; or, The Invisible Master, in *Gaze and Voice As Love Objects*, Žižek, Slavoj and Salecl, Renata eds. Durham: Duke University Press, pp. 90–128.

——(2001) *On Belief*. London: Routledge.

Chapter 4

Identification and mutual recognition in Darren Aronofsky's *Black Swan*

Julie Sexeny

In a conversation about *Black Swan* in *Film Quarterly*, Tim Fisher reads the film as feminist critique—"Irigarayan horror," as he puts it, "to the degree that it could almost be seen as dramatizing some of Irigaray's ideas" (Fisher and Jacobs 2011, 59). In contrast, Amber Jacobs execrates the film, reading the scene on the subway in which an old man masturbates while staring at the female protagonist as "disclosing (unwittingly) the film's metanarrative about its own production, the— male, masturbating—position from which the film was made" (Fisher and Jacobs 2011, 60). After I delivered a talk on the film, I found the first comment had to do not with my argument but the film itself: "I'm sorry, but this film is a bad object for me. It's filled with sexist stereotypes. And the reason the female protagonist can't survive at the end is because the entire film is Aronofsky's adolescent male fantasy of a woman!" The flurry of responses that followed either came to the film's defense or denigrated it. What in the film engenders this intense love it-or-hate it split?

Black Swan takes as its central preoccupation the struggle to differentiate one's fantasy of the other from the real other out there. It forces viewers into an unsettling identification with the professional ballerina, Nina Sayers (Natalie Portman), who in turn identifies with others, at times literally splitting in two, as she sees her self become the other. The story begins with her desire for integration—to play the roles of *both* White Swan *and* Black Swan in her dance company's upcoming performance of Tchaikovsky's *Swan Lake*. A crisis ensues when it becomes evident that her character, a prototypical White Swan, sweet, self-conscious, and frigid, must tap into her (repressed) fears of separation, destructiveness, and sexuality if she is to succeed in playing the role of the Black Swan. The film itself is structured by splits: black/white, love/hate, fantasy/reality, mind/body, frigid/sexual, sanity/insanity. Considering the reactions to the film, which I enjoyed and my viewing companion despised, we might surmise that the dramatization of splitting in the film produces an enactment of splitting in its viewers. Drawing from the work of Jessica Benjamin, I'll explore how the distinction between identification as objectification and identification as mutual recognition is central to Nina's attempts to individuate from her mother and integrate both good and bad aspects of her self. In so doing, I'll aim to offer some insight into the film's representation of the tension between splitting and integration. More broadly, I hope to understand at a theoretical level how the fantasies within the film and those within the viewer can combine to produce a new dynamic between them.

I'd like to begin, oddly enough, with my experience of writing about *Black Swan*, when I spent a summer working on the essay and found myself unable to complete a single draft. I would start with an exciting idea, go somewhere with it, then suddenly get lost or overly critical of it. I started again. And again I would abandon the draft partway through. After repeated starts and stops, it occurred to me that in my efforts to write *about the film*, I was unconsciously mirroring the experience of the protagonist *in the film*. Just as she repeats her dance moves, I was repeatedly writing drafts of the essay; just as she overidentifies with characters in the diegesis, I overidentified with her, enacting her desire for mastery and perfection. The experience was maddening, but also fascinating; indeed, it was parallel process. If what is going on unconsciously with an analysand is mirrored by what's happening in the analyst, this inevitably prevents the analyst from seeing the situation clearly. And so it was, I was identifying with Nina and the film's complicated play of fantasy/reality. Once I was able to recognize this, I had a point of departure, and Benjamin helped pave the way.

What makes Benjamin useful for film analysis is her recognition, following D.W. Winnicott (1971), that we experience the other in *both* fantasy *and* reality, that is, we relate to "the other as an object of identification/projection," what she calls intrapsychic fantasy, and "as an independent outside subject," or intersubjective reality (1995, 7).

Benjamin draws on Hegel's formulation to point out a fundamental paradox with respect to the problem of recognition, that is, the moment one asserts oneself as an independent subject, one necessarily becomes dependent upon the other to be recognized as such. In the following analysis, I therefore consider questions of identification: with whom does Nina identify? What are the psychological and political implications of such identifications? Are the identifications accepted, denied, or reciprocated? How and under what circumstances does she achieve or fail to achieve recognition—a validation of who she is and what she wants— through processes of identification?

Early on in the film, Nina overhears her fellow soloists in a conversation about Beth McIntyre (Winona Ryder), the lead dancer of her company who is being forced into early retirement. Unlike her peers who dismiss Beth as beyond her prime and a nuisance, Nina comes to her defense, identifying with Beth not only as a consummate dancer, but also as the artist she would like to become. Shortly thereafter, however, Nina witnesses Beth destroy her dressing room in a narcissistic rage. One might think this behavior would give Nina pause, cause her to re-evaluate her high opinion of Beth, but instead she sneaks into Beth's dressing room to gaze at her things and steal her red lipstick. Is Nina's identification with Beth fostering "empathy and the bridging of difference" (Benjamin 1995, 8)? According to Benjamin (1995, 8), identification can equally serve as an obstacle to recognition:

The self engaged in identification takes the other as fantasy object, not as an equivalent center of being. In this sense, recognizing the other as like subject constitutes the opposite of identification, which incorporates or assimilates what is other to self. By this logic, in loving the other as an ideal "love object" the self may take a position quite inimical to intersubjective recognition.

Nina idealizes and thus objectifies Beth. Her inability to see Beth, acknowledge her anger and destructiveness, and for Beth to see her specificity in turn, suggests their relationship to each other is more internal than real. Nina's act of stealing the lipstick points to a desire to incorporate what is other to the self, as opposed to recognizing the uniqueness of the person out there.

The film presents Nina's obsessive self-control as an obstacle to her want; it inhibits her relationships with others as well as her ability to dance the Black Swan. Nina's control of her own self—especially her body—is reflected in the control her mother (Barbara Hershey) exerts over her. Even though she is a young adult, her mother wakes her and puts her to bed, feeds and dresses her, cuts her nails and surveys her body for any signs that she has cut or scratched herself. Her mother's incessant gaze is a constant source of anxiety as Nina's body, literally, transforms into a swan, replete with markings on her back where her wings will appear, mottled skin, webbed feet, and crooked swan legs. Her mother appears to make all decisions with respect to what she does and whom she sees. There are no locks on the doors and her mother often sleeps in her room. Nina's status quo at home conveys a feeling of suffocating, mirroring oneness and dependency. This relationship makes clear that dancing the Black Swan entails separating from her mother, with whom she is only allowed to be a White Swan.

Benjamin (1995, 57) proposes that during early separation, "identificatory love" conventionally appears "first in relation to the rapprochement father (Benjamin 1986, 1988, 1991)." She (1995, 57) explains that at this time, "the mother has represented holding, attachment, and caretaking while father has represented the outside world, exploration, freedom." So, if mother represents security and self-monitoring, Thomas Leroy (Vincent Cassel), the director of the dance company and the film's paternal authority, encourages Nina to get outside of her self and just be. At the audition, he pushes her to not be so controlled and seduce her audience. Even though at this point she's unable to do what he's asking her to do, Thomas is the one who recognizes Nina's desire for greatness; he sees in her the dancer she wishes to become.

After her failed audition, Nina goes to see Thomas to convince him to give her the part. Thomas acknowledges both her desire to be the Swan Queen and her limitations, the fact that she embodies the qualities of the White Swan, not the Black. He reframes her notion of perfection to include letting go and the value of surprise. But when he suddenly kisses her and she bites him in return, it is unclear what to make of this. Is this an abuse of authority? Is he, like her mother, crossing boundaries in order to control her? Or does he cross a boundary with her precisely in order to test her ability to draw a line between them? If we think about it in relation to identification and recognition, we might read it as an invitation for her to do as he does, to practice what he has been preaching. In kissing her, he models what he means by losing control and surprising the other. And in biting him, Nina not only loses her self in the moment, but she also offers Thomas and herself a glimpse into the aspects of her self that she consistently negates, her aggression, spontaneity, and destructiveness, the very qualities needed to dance the Black Swan.

The film hints that Nina's ability to dance the Black Swan relates to her sexuality. After an event introducing Nina as the company's new star to all its investors, Thomas invites Nina back to his apartment where he tells her he wants to talk about the role—he wants there to be no boundaries between them. Once again, we associate Thomas with Nina's mother and sense in Nina the fear of the other's desire to fuse with her. He pelts her with personal questions about her sex life and then gives her an assignment: he wants her to go home and touch herself, "live a little," he says. The next morning, she begins to masturbate, but just as she is about to climax, we cut to a POV shot of her mother sleeping on a chair beside her bed. A conflict thus emerges between Nina's lack of differentiation from her mother and Thomas's invitation for her to differentiate from mother so that she may explore her own body and sexuality. The relationship with Thomas is not a sexual one, however. His motive in asking her to touch herself is not a come on, but rather an attempt to get her to feel, to be her own subject of desire because he knows this is the key to becoming a great artist.

Thomas plays a key role for Nina, but it is Lily (Mila Kunis) who most closely resembles the "identificatory love" relationship, as Benjamin would have it. Lily represents separation and desire, and Nina experiences her as *both* like *and* different. For example, when Nina first spots her from behind on the subway, she appears agitated. Lily has a similar hairdo, scarf, and coat, and then mirrors her gesture of putting her hair behind her ear. However, when Lily interrupts Nina's audition, she is confronted with her difference. As Nina strives for perfection in the audition, Lily's lateness suggests her comfort with imperfection. Lily is an outsider, a new arrival hailing from the West Coast, who is sexual, unself-conscious, and assertive. So, even though this identificatory role is often played by an older male, we see that "[w]hat appears consciously to be hetero or homo may not be so in unconscious fantasy: whether one seeks likeness or difference is not determined simply by the nominal gender of one's partner (Harris 1991)" (Benjamin 1995, 18). Even though Lily is the same age and gender as Nina, she functions here as the one who can be both like and different, who can represent a separate subject of desire. Benjamin further complicates the play of identifications: "Nor do others appear to us simply as like or different; rather, they appear in complex combinations that reflect the multiplicity of our and their gendered positions" (Benjamin 1995, 18). In this way, Lily represents that perfect storm of all that Nina fears and desires, and Nina's identification with her offers her the possibility of exploring those repressed parts of her self.

When she is cast as the Swan Queen, Nina struggles to unleash the bad feelings that the Black Swan embodies. After rehearsal one day, she hears the sound of laughter and drifts to a studio where Lily performs. Lily's long hair is down and she moves with abandon. Thomas comes up behind Nina and claims that Lily isn't faking it when she dances. The implication, of course, is that Nina *is* faking it: her preoccupation with perfection prevents her from an authentic expression of her feelings, something that is central to dance. When Thomas leaves, Nina lingers, watching as Lily messes up and falls into the chest of a male dancer. They both laugh at her mistake. Lily models the ability to fail, laugh at herself with others, and move on. Failure isn't the end of the world; rather, it's part of the process. This also applies to the work of individuation. As Benjamin (1995, 23) explains:

> Examining the early struggle for recognition—which includes failure, destruction, aggression, even when it is working—ought to show us something about our relation to ideals: mutual recognition as the basis for struggle and negotiation of conflict, when its impossibility and the striving to attain it are adequately included in the concept.

Lily opens up a symbolic space for Nina to envision what it is like to discover who she is and what she wants to be. Indeed, Nina's identification with Lily is itself an act of creativity, an authentic gesture of sorts, for "the acts of creating the ideal, forming an identificatory bond and actively pursuing the relationship with the beloved figure are, in effect, the subject's own" (Benjamin 1995, 59).

A key turning point for Nina is when Lily unexpectedly arrives at her apartment, proposing to take her out. Before long, Lily has given Nina a black lingerie top to wear and offers her some ecstasy to help her relax. As Nina declines and prepares to go, Lily challenges her to "live a little"; echoing Thomas here, the words suddenly change Nina's mind and convince her to stay, drink alcohol, take the drug, and dance. As Nina begins to feel the effects of the drug, she dances, but not with control; her body moves this way and that, with Lily and others. When they return home high and giggling, Nina for the first time stands up to her mother and refuses to be treated like a child. She and Lily make love, but the skin on Nina's legs becomes mottled like a swan's, and Lily suddenly turns into her self. Nina sits up, in a panic, but then, she turns back into Lily again, who reassures her. After Nina climaxes, Lily then turns into her mother. The implication is that just as she lets her guard down and allows herself to feel pleasure and intimacy, she is immediately assaulted with the conflation of her self with *both* Lily *and* her mother.

Following Benjamin's description of identificatory love as both inside as well as a loving tie to another—we see how the shifting realms between self and other play out most powerfully with Lily. Her character is the only one to bridge the divide between Nina's home and professional life, thus literally moving her from inside to outside and back again. By identifying with Lily, Nina tests out her sexuality, confidence, and autonomy; she's able—finally—to let go and dance with abandon rather than precision; she draws a boundary between her and her mother; she even lets herself have an orgasm. All of these things are emotionally satisfying and suggest huge psychic strides, but suddenly then, the tables turn. When Nina awakes the next morning, she is alone and late for rehearsal. When she arrives at rehearsal, Lily dances the Swan Queen, *her role*. The persecutory fantasies set in: was this all a ploy? Is she trying to sabotage her career? Is she trying to replace and become her? When she and Lily talk, Nina almost accuses Lily for her own actions—sleeping late and taking drugs—indicating her confusion of self and other. When she questions Lily about leaving her in the morning, Lily mocks Nina for having a lesbian fantasy about her.

The film pulls us in opposite directions here. On the one hand, Nina covers so much psychological ground, with respect to trust, sexuality, and letting go. On the other hand, the film undermines these achievements by troubling what in fact happened. Instead of newfound intimacy and recognition, Nina feels betrayed. Instead of connection and shared feeling, she feels more alone and alienated. Instead of feeling like she laughed with Lily, she feels laughed at by her, again, just as she did in the beginning. Paranoia sets in and Nina now feels that Lily is her enemy, out to get her. At this most egregious example of Nina's confusion of fantasy and reality, the film calls into question her sanity.

This uncertainty is exacerbated by Nina's anxiety during the night of the performance. After her dance partner drops Nina on stage, she cries and retreats to her dress room only to find Lily there, proposing that she dance the Black Swan instead. Just as she says this, however, she turns from facing the mirror, to facing Nina, and as she does so, she becomes Nina. Nina attacks her, throwing her against the mirror and strangling her, seething that the role is hers. Finally, she stabs her self/other with a shard of the mirror, and she turns back into Lily. With the crashing of the mirror and the subsequent murder, there is a rush of relief at her destruction of this mirroring relationship to the other. But is the killing of the self/other an act of integration or disintegration? Is the act of killing evidence of her ownership of her desire and destructiveness? Or is it suggestive of the destruction of her former self, the one who crippled her with self-doubt? Or finally, is it a metaphor for the way in which any performer must fully become the other in order to inhabit the role one wishes to play? That is, in order to effect a change in one's self, to become more than we were, must we also experience a kind of death or loss of the self we once were?

These questions are further complicated by the fact that Nina realizes—after her powerful, thrilling, bodily transformation into the Black Swan—that she didn't stab Lily after all; she had stabbed her self. Benjamin is particularly useful for unpacking this finale. For Nina's ultimate expression of aggression was what she was most afraid of in fantasy. As sometimes happens with many of us, her inability to distinguish intrapsychic fantasy from intersubjective reality meant that the anger and aggression she felt toward Lily was too powerful, overwhelming, indeed could have real consequences. Benjamin (1995, 91) explains:

The problem that often occurs in the process of differentiation is that if the other retaliates or caves in and withdraws, we don't really experience the other as outside us; instead of surviving and becoming real, she or he is subsumed by (seems to *be*) our persecutory fantasy.

So, instead of successfully integrating the good and bad into her self, the film presents Nina's intrapsychic fantasy *as reality*. Initially, the other doesn't survive her fantasy; then, she doesn't survive her fantasy. In this way, because *she* doesn't survive, spectators who identify with her are then forced, with her, to experience the power of intrapsychic fantasy, indeed to experience fantasy as reality. Benjamin (1995, 90), channeling Winnicott, explains the power of this dynamic:

In the course of development we do a rather paradoxical thing: we try to destroy the other person in order to discover that they survive. The paradox is that only by asserting omnipotence may we discover the other as an outside center of experience. By destroying the other, not literally but in fantasy, by absolutely asserting the self and negating the other's separateness in our minds, we discover that the other is outside our mental powers.

The film does the opposite. It legitimates the fear that somehow our thoughts are omnipotent—they can destroy others and the self—rather than the reality that our destructive fantasies are just that.

In my initial viewing of the film, I focused on Nina's exhilarating performance of the Black Swan, her success as an artist, and her achievement of perfection, while putting in abeyance her death. This was my own intrapsychic fantasy at work, wishing it had instead offered up what Benjamin sees as the best-case scenario, that is, a realization of the *constant tension* between both intrapsychic fantasy and intersubjective reality rather than an either/or. That would have been my preferred reading. But in the end, I had to contend with intersubjective reality, the text out there. And according to the text, Nina, just like the swan in the performance *Swan Lake*, commits suicide, albeit unwittingly. And so, "When mutual recognition is not restored, when shared reality does not survive destruction, then complementarity structures and 'relating' to the inner object predominate" (Benjamin 1995, 43). This retreat into intrapsychic fantasy in part explains the defensive reactions on the part of viewers who must then experience this collapse of fantasy and reality, this ultimate privileging of relating to the other as fantasy object. The fact that her self as other doesn't survive her destructive impulses finally undermines her achievement of desire, separation, and recognition. When the self/other does not survive, there is no confirmation that the other has a separate center of existence. And since we are dependent upon the other to recognize the self, there is no recognition of Nina either.

With this conclusion, the story of the ballet and the film diegesis become one; her performance of the White Swan's suicide becomes her reality. She overidentifies to the point where she is not merely acting, where a space remains between one's self and the role one plays, with a maintenance of symbolic space, but she becomes the Black/White Swan she performs. Even her body becomes part human, part swan. Benjamin explains: "In the symbolic equation (She *is* that thing) the verb 'to be' closes space opened by the verbs 'seem' or 'feel'—by the action of play and just-pretend" (Benjamin 1995, 94). In so doing, what seems, is, and the symbolic equation reigns. There is no longer any room to interpret or play the role; the space has collapsed, and we are left with, on the one hand, her achievement of perfection, on the other, with self-annihilation, another form of splitting.

And yet, in the end, it is still worth asking why Nina couldn't have survived. If she had attempted to destroy the other in fantasy and the real self/other survived, how would that have signified differently? If Nina had survived, would the film then posit that females like Nina can achieve greatness, be recognized, and integrate both good and bad aspects of their selves? Perhaps it would then be possible for all of us to sustain a tension between being empathic and aggressive, to express our anger but also be able to contain bad feelings, to own our power and agency without feeling like such efforts will end in self-destruction (or destruction of the other). Had Nina's character survived, would the film have made a rather radical move, advancing a "like subject" that diverts from the traditional Western narrative we see in the ballet *Swan Lake*? What kind of new ideal, what kind of transformation of self and other, might have been made possible for—and by—Aronofsky and his viewers? I'm reminded of films like *Thelma and Louise* (1991) and *Crouching Tiger, Hidden Dragon* (2000), in which we witness female protagonists struggle for recognition and achieve independence, only to see them fly/fall to their inevitable deaths, as in *Black Swan*. Why is it that we need to be reminded every ten years or so that women can't be allowed to express and survive their destructiveness? A simple answer is the persistence of the male fantasy of the female. And if so, perhaps it will require some psychic introspection and effort, and a bit of advice from Benjamin, to become more cognizant of how intrapsychic fantasy can and will tend to dominate and fix our relationships. Instead of simply enabling this, we might work instead to establish a shared reality, an ongoing tension between our fantasy of the other and the real other out there, both in our films and relationships.

References

Benjamin, Jessica (1986), 'The alienation of desire: Woman's masochism and ideal love', in J. Alpert (ed.) *Psychoanalysis and women: Contemporary reappraisals*, G. K. Hall, Boston.

Benjamin, Jessica (1988), *The Bonds of Love: Psychoanalysis, Feminism, and the Problem of Domination*, Pantheon, New York, NY.

Benjamin, Jessica (1995), *Like Subjects, Love Objects: Essays on Recognition and Sexual Difference*, Yale University Press, New Haven, CT.

Benjamin, Jessica (1991), 'Father and daughter: Identification with difference—a contribution to gender heterodoxy', *Psychoanalytic Dialogues*, 1, 277–299.

Benjamin, Jessica (1997), *Shadow of the Other: Intersubjectivity and Gender in Psychoanalysis*, Routledge, New York, NY.

Fisher, Tim, and Amber Jacobs, Fall (2011), 'Debating *Black Swan*: Gender and Horror', *Film Quarterly*, 65(1), 58–62.

Harris, A. (1991), 'Gender as contradiction: A discussion of Freud's "The psychogenesis of a case of homosexuality in a woman,"' *Psychoanalytic Dialogues*, 2, 197–224.

Mahler, Margaret S., Fred Pine, and Anni Bergman (1975), *The Psychological Birth of the Human Infant: Symbiosis and Individuation*, Basic Books, New York, NY.

Phillips, Adam (1988), *Winnicott*, Harvard University Press, Cambridge, MA.

Winnicott, D.W. (1965), *The Maturational Processes and the Facilitating Environment: Studies in the Theory of Emotional Development*, International Universities Press, Inc., Madison, WI.

Winnicott, D.W. (1971), *Playing and Reality*. Routledge, London, UK.

Filmography

Aronofsky, D. (2010) *Black Swan*. United States. Cross Creek Picture, Phoenix Pictures, Dune Entertainment (DVD: Fox Searchlight Pictures).

Lee, A. (2000) *Crouching Tiger, Hidden Dragon*. Taiwan, Hong Kong, United States, China (DVD: Sony Pictures Classics).

Scott, R. (1991) *Thelma and Louise*. United States. Pathé Entertainment, Percy Main, Star Partners III Ltd (DVD: Metro-Goldwyn-Mayer).

Chapter 5

Terrence Malick's diptych[1]

John Izod and Joanna Dovalis

Psyche and world, the material and spiritual are inseparable. As Robert Romanyshyn reminds us, 'the body is a hinge around which consciousness and unconsciousness revolve' (1982: 150). The present chapter investigates the embodiment of this nexus in two films directed by Terrence Malick. It deploys Vivian Sobchack's and Jennifer Barker's theories of embodiment and relates them to the sensuous impact on their audiences of the films' sounds and images. It then deepens the work by linking Post-Jungian theory to concepts of embodiment. This produces an account of the psychological lives of principal characters as individuals. Beyond that, our recourse to this blend of theoretical approaches encourages deep, emotionally driven reflection on the way these films engender a twenty-first century understanding of what humankind can know of the world's spiritual nature.

When *To the Wonder* was released in 2013, some reviewers identified stylistic resemblances between this film and *The Tree of Life* (2011). But it fell to Peter Bradshaw and David Jenkins to take a further step and recognise that they are also thematically linked. Bradshaw read the new film as a B-side companion piece or coda to *The Tree of Life* (Bradshaw, 2012, 2013). Jenkins valued the two films equally (2013). What, then, are the grounds for seeing them as a diptych?

It was widely remarked that, being set in the present day, *To the Wonder* was unparalleled in Malick's filmography; but this is inaccurate. *The Tree of Life* concludes in 2010 with Jack O'Brien (Sean Penn) in late middle age. That film can be read as largely comprising the memories, visions and reflections that thrust themselves upon him at that date. The fact that his memories reach back to the 1950s and provide a significant core to *The Tree of Life* makes it particularly interesting to consider the two films as companion pieces. We shall first investigate how the characters' lives are bound in with the times and places in which they are set and conclude by considering the degree to which each film draws the audience into participating in an embodied encounter.

Both films feature a male character who assumes the traditional role of breadwinner. Mr O'Brien (Brad Pitt) in *The Tree of Life* and Neil (Ben Affleck) in *To the Wonder* have similar personalities, being first and foremost practical men. O'Brien is a lower-middle factory manager, ambitious to design machinery. Neil is an environmental inspector who measures land contamination caused by industrial exploitation. Both men are thinking types, and both have a wounded feeling function, the most common and painful wound in Western culture. Feelings bring a sense of value and worth: deficient in them, both men have difficulty connecting with the anima (the contrasexual archetype, which, according to Jung, is experienced by men and represents the hidden feminine aspect of their personality). Mr O'Brien acts as lawgiver to his family; Neil cannot sustain a relationship with either of the women who love him. That said, they are not identical: O'Brien finds a shelter for his passions in classical music, but Neil shows little outward sign of experiencing any passion other than sexual delight.

Employed as a lower-middle manager in an industrial plant, O'Brien works a tough six-day week. Except when anger breaks out, his emotions and physical movements are, like Neil's, those of a stolid man who walks foursquare upon his yard but resents the boundaries (topographical and cultural) that separate him from richer neighbours. It is as though O'Brien has internalised the disciplined confines of his psychically unrewarding work life and projected them onto the world outside the factory gates. When the patent applications for his designs fail, he comes to believe that those who command power and wealth have not granted him his due. His inability to cross this borderline eventually brings awareness of his limitations, with envy swiftly following. His hyper focus on limits and boundaries arises from a one-sided masculine identity and repressed anima.

One day O'Brien finds himself facing a brick wall, literally and metaphorically. The plant is closing, and he must either uproot the family and accept a job nobody wants or face unemployment. The ruthlessness of capitalist enterprise signalled by its dereliction of this loyal employee finds a counterpart in *To the Wonder* in the careless exploitation for profit of the environment. Malick shows all but palpably that, to borrow David Simon's words, 'Capitalism is not a blueprint for building a society' (2013: 13). Both films present prosperous communities that have with indifference relegated their poor to social exclusion. The unemployed are the towns' human debris, their number and desperation greatly increased in the sixty years between the O'Briens' life in Waco, Texas and Neil's in Bartlesville, Oklahoma. When, as with O'Brien and Neil, thinking is the superior function, the inferior feeling function lives in the unconscious realm. Societies led by the thinking function risk losing their core values. The generative and creative energies are connected to the feeling function of the male and his anima, and will therefore heavily influence their value judgments and core psychological structure.

The sudden annihilation of O'Brien's persona drops him into midlife crisis. Loss and defeat open him to an elusive, confessional moment of grace. He cries out that he had wanted to be loved like a great man but now he is nothing. In the agony of failure he notices, as if for the first time, the glory of the natural world around him. This short-lived moment of revelation will have clear links with similarly fleeting glimpses of wonder that Neil and his lovers will be vouchsafed.

Mr O'Brien and his counterpart in *To the Wonder* habitually stand apart from others. Neil has no friends (in this like O'Brien), is accustomed to being alone and, when with a lover, soon distances himself from her, unable to hold emotional connection. His confidence lies in his profession in which he comprehends and operates on the objective world. On one tour of inspection he probes the soil around a nodding donkey. Its base has decayed so temporary barricades have been erected round it to protect by-passers from danger. Nonetheless it has not been switched off but still pumps oil night and day. Elsewhere he works around heavy equipment lifting away polluted soil that flanks the very housing project where he has lately bought a property. Later he reports finding lead and cadmium leaking from local industrial plants. He appears, as Bradshaw (2013) observes, to be investigating 'some kind of toxic poisoning of the water table' – a vivid metaphor for the debris that lives in the unconscious soil.

> Despite the vivid gorgeousness that Malick discovers everywhere, there is a fundamental problem with the American soil itself – a real crisis of faith … (Bradshaw, 2012).[2]

Although physically vigorous and healthy, Neil suffers, except when exhilarated by new love, from an inner torpor. As Andrew O'Hehir (2013) comments, the film reveals under the surface how the transcendent, spiritual beauty of the Oklahoma landscape 'has been betrayed, undermined and literally poisoned' by those who have come to live in it. Facing every day the corrosive damage that indifferent corporate enterprises inflict on the landscape where he lives and works, Neil suffers psychic injury, a spiritual depression that he is ill-equipped to recognise in himself. Nor will his lover Marina (Olga Kurylenko) escape the despoliation.

Whereas Neil and O'Brien feel separate from other people, the films' three leading female characters, Mrs O'Brien, Marina and Jane, seek relationship and connection. In *To the Wonder* Marina is a beautiful spirit who acts as if she were free but also has a wounded feeling function, expressed by her inability to act, which demonstrates lack of connection to her animus (here the contrasexual archetype that reveals the concealed masculine in women). She and Neil meet when he is holidaying in France. Their affair, as Bradshaw says, 'plays out in the gorgeous parks and avenues of Paris and achieves a transcendental quality when they visit Saint-Michel in Normandy, and are overwhelmed by its beauty and mysterious grandeur, and their own growing sense of romantic destiny' (2013). The sweetness of Wagner's Prelude to *Parsifal* draws the audience into sharing their joy as the lovers explore the abbey's cloisters. Quiet orchestral chords ascend gently but surely. Strings blend with woodwind and soft golden horns broaden the tapestry before the music fades to silence. *Parsifal's* theme, the quest to recover the Grail, is perfectly apposite. The opera juxtaposes the dualities of nature measured as, on one side, material and social progress, against the healing feminine (the feeling function). The ambiguities inherent in the elusive Grail reveal that the repellent shadow side must be integrated to achieve wholeness. In the film the music encapsulates the lovers' wonder, yet touches it with melancholy. Marina's eyes light on the cloister's roses blasted by autumn winds and sleet and (unlike Neil who misses it) she feels the omen.

In scenes where Marina is happy, Malick's director of photography Emmanuel Lubezki and his editorial team replicate a pattern of shooting and cutting they innovated in *The New World* (2005) and revisited in some sequences of *The Tree of Life*. Bernard Aspe summarises this process as one of deduction from cinematic continuity until only the minimal elements are retained that make the action just comprehensible (2011: 20). In *To the Wonder* this style is deployed when Marina, an intensely sensual woman, performs her exhilaration for Neil through extempore dancing. Some reviewers charged Kurylenko with 'twirling', missing the evidence that Marina has experienced ballet training. They also failed to notice that her ecstatic displays dwindle and stop when Neil's increasing coldness suffocates her playfulness. Dancing enacts movement, and in the cycle of nature, movement (the stages of life) must be gone through.

There is nevertheless a basis for audiences feeling discomfort with the character. Some viewers may displace their unease onto Marina's idiosyncratic *pas seul*, sensing that it seduces all too effectively Neil's adolescent yearnings. Others may have felt their desire to see a physically beautiful couple surrender to romantic bliss frustrated by Neil and Marina remaining stuck in patterns of thought and behaviour that block them from resolving their differences.

Marina's frequent voice-over meditations on her love for Neil reveal a voracious need to find her animus or soul-image through him. But her lack of maturity inhibits her capacity for relating to and judging external circumstances. Her impulsive decision to leave France and uproot her child the moment Neil invites her to Oklahoma reveals it, as does her frenzied inability to adapt back to life in Paris when she returns there.

Neil, incapable of dealing with relationship issues except when overwhelmed by desire, skirts around the major practical problem that lies between himself and Marina – that she has entered the USA on a tourist visa. They both know that the matter could be resolved if they married, but his intuitive side cannot be pressed by time, ensuring that Marina and her daughter Tatiana (Tatiana Chiline) must return to Paris. After they leave, Neil finds the child has left him a glass bird dipping its beak into water. Her affectionate gift of a toy that will run for hours after she has gone without requiring a power source rhymes poignantly with the nodding-donkey oil pump.[3] It is a gift appropriate for a child and for Neil and her mother too. Tatiana's uncanny attunement to the couple's unconscious inner life contains the knowing that they both need to dip into the waters of the unconscious life to move from being in love to being loving.

Marina, lacking work because of her own unactualised animus, loses connection to her daughter (who has moved in with her father), finds Paris intolerable and comes back to Oklahoma. She and Neil marry in court, securing her American citizenship, and move into a pretty clapboard house on one of Bartlesville's older streets. We are not told what lies behind this change of abode, nor why they subsequently return to their first home. Probably Neil has moved into temporary accommodation while the soil problems afflicting the new housing estate are rectified beneath his property. Once again, the quality of the characters' lives and the community's reverence (or lack thereof) for its natural environs are bound together. Neil and Marina's relationship comfortably regresses back to the honeymoon stage while they reside on the tree-lined avenue. Neil's tenderness is awakened when Marina has to seek medical help to resolve a gynaecological problem, a metaphor for her wounded feminine or feeling function. They now marry in church and gradually find comfort and trust in each other, becoming lovers again, passionately and quietly. However, when they return to the original house in the tract where architectural dreariness has been planned in on an industrial scale, their marriage chills toward estrangement, anger and divorce.

While Marina was in Paris, Neil chanced on a local friend, Jane (Rachel McAdams) who, like Neil, had lately exited a broken relationship. There are several resemblances between Jane and Marina. Both are physically as well as emotionally stirred by their love for Neil (Marina more recklessly). Both are anima figures and carry the otherness of Neil's shadow, the aspect of his personality that is hidden from himself (see Beebe, 2008: 10). The resemblances are aesthetically comparable in the sequences covering each woman falling in love with him; but the camera moves less flightily on Jane than Marina, a stylistic trait that helps configure the American woman as the more grounded personality. Nevertheless, when she and Neil become lovers, she too at first runs and whirls in delight like Marina.

During their first days together in France, Marina and Neil had travelled to Mont Saint-Michel, the magnificent medieval abbey and destination of pilgrims on the Normandy coast (French, 2013). As we mentioned, it became an emblem of the wonder that at the time seemed to fuse their personal love with the world. Now, opening her heart to Neil, Jane takes him to her ranch. Although in the flowering of joy Jane dances across the grassland like Marina, the prairie is also a place of work for this skilled horse wrangler. She treats the land and its creatures with loving respect, acting in the opposite way to the corporations that literally undermine it. She and Neil renew their sense of wonder when, allowing bison to surround their vehicle, they step down and let the great beasts move peacefully around them.

Marina and Jane both have a history of projecting on their lovers the image of a numinous soul-image that no mortal, let alone one such as Neil, can sustain for the life of the relationship. Marina tells Neil that if he loves her there is nothing else she needs. The delusory nature of that claim puts pressure on him, all the heavier given his limited capacity to access and articulate his feeling function (Jung, 1921). Later, as Neil and Jane become lovers, she asks him whether he knows what he wants because she can't afford to make another mistake. But Neil knows himself no better now than he did with Marina; and Jane, anxiously attempting to win Neil before Marina flies in from France, does make a risky mistake. She binds her hands together and presents Neil the rope's end, offering herself as a gift. Neil saves her from ill-judged willingness to give herself away prematurely when his insentient libido draws him back to Marina.

Taking it as self-evident that Neil is once again seeking a woman on whom to project his anima, why does he revert to Marina in preference to Jane? Perhaps he is simply dodging commitment again; but maybe the European fascinates him as steeped in an older culture that differs from American pragmatism. If Marina holds his shadow, the sensuous, spontaneous woman may offer a potent counterbalance to his extraverted rationality. By comparison, the pragmatic Jane is less 'foreign' to him. Behind Neil's personal, largely unconscious choice lies Malick's reversal of the usual Europe-as-corrupt, America-as-hope stereotypes. In *To the Wonder*, the new culture is coming to its knees while the old culture is the place where nature and civilization live side-by-side in rhythm (Branch, 2013).

According to Murray Stein, successful navigation through the mid-life transition (which faces all three characters) involves making a crucial three-stage shift from a persona orientation to a Self orientation. Taking an intrapsychic perspective, the first phase is separation from an earlier identity, the persona. The ego needs to let go of this attachment before it can float through the necessary second stage of liminality. This is a period preliminary to the third stage, deeper discovery of the Self (Stein, 1983: 27–8). The Self for Jungians is an archetypal image that contains the full potential of an individual, encompassing the unity of the personality as a whole. To complete the shift thoroughly and decisively, Stein says that a person needs to identify the source of pain and put the past to rest by grieving, mourning and burying it. But the nature of the loss needs to be understood and worked through before a person can go on (ibid.). Becoming stuck psychologically is significant because it defends against something deeper and larger. Something more must be asked of the Self, which has to come from withdrawing one's projections in order to assimilate shadow into consciousness. We do not know what happens to Jane who disappears from sight after Neil rejects her; but following the divorce, Marina does make a mid-life transition; and so eventually does Neil.

In *The Tree of Life*, Mrs O'Brien, unlike the characters in *To the Wonder*, knows love. She exists in a state of grace and wholeness of body and spirit. When preparing Jessica Chastain for the role, Malick encouraged her to adopt unusual methods to signal the character's inner being, suggesting that the actress would profit from 'studying the hands of Raphael's Madonnas in the Metropolitan Museum of Art, reading, watching old Lauren Bacall films (to learn about grace). Not to mention learning reams of Malick's lines, which he'd then ask her to say *in her head*' (Rose, 2011).

Ryan Gilbey noted how few complete scenes there are in *The Tree of Life*, most being foreshortened or distilled. He added that with many shots of Mrs O'Brien, her arms and hands slip swiftly into and out of frame (2011). As we said earlier, *To the Wonder* revisits this style in some scenes. In contrast to Marina, Mrs O'Brien is thoroughly grounded, a homemaker who lives in harmony with her often ill-tempered husband, accepting the patriarchal mode of marriage except when he behaves brutally toward their sons. Malick emphasises her numinous existence in many ways. These include the simple and attractive dresses she wears and her ecstatic, free movements that respond as much to the currents running through her soul as the breezes passing across the yard and the light held in net curtains. Throughout her life from her childhood (when we see her marvelling at the cattle and sunflowers on her father's farm) to her walking in woods to seek comfort as she grieves the death of her second son, her physical and spiritual attachment to nature remains constant. Her fidelity to the way of grace, her self-awareness and insight into others sustain her through hard times in the marriage, for she knows intuitively that the animus – her soul image – does not reside exclusively in her husband but partakes of the world around her.

Mrs O'Brien's confidence is grounded in her belief that there are only two ways through life. One is the way of nature, which wants to have its own way, please itself and have others please it too. Nature, she says, finds reasons to be unhappy when all the world is shining around it and love is smiling on all things. She contrasts this to the way of grace to which she dedicates herself, and that does not try to please itself, accepts being divided, forgotten or disliked, accepting too insults and injury.

Mrs O'Brien, Jane and Marina have all been put to the test, all having borne children and endured loss. Mrs O'Brien and her husband suffer the death of their second son. Sustained, despite everything, by the way of grace, she comes to accept the loss, though her husband and son Jack have not navigated the grieving cycle successfully. We shall discuss later the impact of unresolved grief on Jack. Jane bore a daughter in an earlier relationship, but the little girl died a toddler. Jane, like Mrs O'Brien, has worked through her grief and is reconciled to the loss. Although a Christian, her faith is not dogmatic; rather she has inherited from her father the belief (comparable to Mrs O'Brien's way of grace) that all things work together for good. After telling Neil this history she asks him to pray with her, but he replies that he has no faith. We live and we are afraid, he murmurs – the fullest account he ever gives of himself.

Marina's loss is different because Tatiana is alive. Yet she has lost her daughter to her first husband and appears to be in a disturbing stage of denial. Back in Oklahoma, she Skypes Tatiana and the girl says that life with her dad is fun. When her new stepmother calls her to dinner, Tatiana puts up only token resistance, seeming relieved to have an excuse to end the call. The stability of her father's new family unit appears to have grounded her emotionally as she finds connection to him and the masculine. Marina has betrayed her not only by leaving Oklahoma but now Paris as well. In order to be the mother the growing Tatiana needs – not only the nurturing mother she once was, but a mature guiding mother – Marina must find relationship with her own lost masculine side, her animus.

At this stage in her life, Marina, despite her beauty and yearning for love, cannot (unlike Mrs O'Brien) accept the suffering that grace requires, in particular the injury of not being loved with a fervour to match her own. Although nominally a Catholic, that faith does not pierce her soul. Yet her passionate yearning for union with Neil does sometimes deliver moments that receive light from something more than that diamond point of her deeply personal animus – glimpsed openings onto the way of grace. What, she wonders then, is the nature of the love that comes from all around, from the sky and clouds? Much later, shortly before she leaves Neil forever, she gazes at birds weaving across the dawn sky, opens her hands and lets sunlight shine through them. Momentarily, in a time of despair, she has again found the wonder, a glimpse of numinous beauty beyond her own troubles.

Neil's parish priest Father Quintana (Javier Bardem) preaches to a well-heeled congregation in a fine modern church. But these prosperous Christians have no contact with the people among whom the priest spends long hours listening to incoherent litanies of pain and dereliction. These, the desperately poor, barely survive in rotting houses and junk-filled yards, their suffering a heavy burden on Father Quintana. Yet a far worse spiritual sorrow blights his existence: he has lost the experience of God he once had, mourning that his heart is cold and hard. Father Quintana's grief is of a piece with Marina's loss of ecstasy with Neil. Were Neil and Marina self-aware like the unhappy priest, the latter's cry for help could be theirs. And if the couple were able to locate what was missing in both of them, the relationship might be rescued.

The long-suffering Father is offered an epiphany but fails to grasp it. An elderly African-American who cleans the church's stained glass windows shows the priest a different way of experiencing numinous energy. When there's no one around, the priest should let the power hit him and feel the excitement. The old man demonstrates what he means, opening himself to the spirit by speaking in tongues. Holding his hand against the richly coloured windowpanes, he says he feels in the light's warmth more than just natural light: it is spiritual. The sun renders his hand translucent like the coloured glass; touched, the priest copies him and light illuminates both hands in a sweet moment of union. Attuned to the energy around him, the cleaner (!) shows the cleric that opening himself to it will supply his spiritual needs. The wise old man has offered the priest an epiphany (and by implication an escape from dogma that time and the Church's ossified symbolism have exhausted). He (like Marina with the birds) has no need to anchor the revelation to a Christian icon dressed in quasi-human form but rather to the numinous clad in energy.

This, the priest's moment to rediscover the wonder, is overrun by external demands. Before the scene ends, dialogue bridges to a prosperous community leader lobbying him for access to more rooms. Father Quintana's rich private moment is extinguished, not so that he can assist the devotions of the faithful, nor to help ease the suffering of the needy, nor even to reinvigorate his soul, but to facilitate plays, dinners and parties, an entire calendar of secular activities.

Marina's life runs parallel to the way of nature when passions colour her perception of the world. The irony is that her misery has roots in yearning to attain grace through deeply requited love; and eventually, long after breaking from Neil, she does achieve it. To recognise this, we need to appreciate that in *To the Wonder* Malick deploys a device like the one which helps us understand that Mrs O'Brien's individuation has deepened. Marina's voice is often heard, but seldom in dialogue with other characters. Most of both women's words represent their thoughts and reflections via internal monologue.

Commenting on *The Tree of Life*, Aspe argues that the whispering voices over of Mrs O'Brien and Jack are structurally retrospective. They do not so much express what those characters are thinking as let us understand what they ought to have thought but do not realise until much later (Aspe, 2011: 20–1). Marina's monologues are not exactly the same as Mrs O'Brien's since they do express what she is thinking, albeit some of her thoughts reflect on the past and others do not directly follow the events that stimulated them. Nevertheless the key factor is that in both films these characters' internal monologues demonstrate the prerequisite imperative to becoming a psychologically individuated being: self-reflection. An instance early in *To the Wonder* occurs when Neil gathers samples of contaminated material from a riverbed. Marina, not a part of the scene, is heard in ironically juxtaposed voiceover asking herself what is the nature of the love that loves us and comes from nowhere. The astounding rush of passion she feels for her lover draws her to thoughts of the numinous; but when she meditates on sexual ecstasy she cannot understand how the emotions it arouses fall away when lovemaking is done. Her bewilderment tells that she has made a start toward self-awareness. This developmental journey will heal the split from her authentic nature, the fissure from which all psychological and emotional problems originate.

After her divorce, Marina flies back to Paris. Leaving Neil's side, she goes to the aircraft down a dark walkway toward the light at its far end. The screen fades to black for five seconds. There follows a coda that in Bradshaw's opinion makes the entire film into 'a kind of unframed flashback' (2013). It opens on a sequence comprising long takes of the great gardens, statues and fountains at Versailles. There the camera focuses momentarily on a large urn, which brings the Grail back to mind. The elegant static framing of pristine scenes devoid of people contrasts with the volatile coverage of Marina and Neil's courtship. Along a deep vista, the tranquil waters of a grand formal lake reflect an autumnal sky and encourage meditation.

As we have written elsewhere, the beauty of films invokes us. It entices us to transcend ordinary reality, creating a more capacious regard for the self and the world. Beauty forms the bridge between reality and fantasy that crosses into the infinite – conveying what is more than we can know. That bridge is what makes rapture possible (Izod and Dovalis, 2014: Chapter 9). Gilberto Perez's observations on the persuasive nature of beauty in film add to this idea.

> Beauty ... acts on the beholder. It is not, as some suppose, an object passively sitting there to be looked at. The art critic Dave Hickey talks about beauty as rhetoric, as an agency that sways and moves us. Beauty has a manifold capacity for suasion. ... Film is an art of images, of appearances, an art that works on us through the look of things ... and we must attend to the specifics of beauty on the screen.
>
> (Perez, 2005: 38)

Marina's final thoughts are voiced over those images of Versailles – art and nature in harmony. She offers thanks to what she calls the love that loves us. Her words reveal that she has drawn wisdom from the failure of this second marriage and now knows that the ecstasy and pain of human passions can open the mind to the numinous. In effect she now perceives (to borrow Mrs O'Brien's phrase from *The Tree of Life*) that the whole world is shining, and love is smiling on all things.

The coda cuts from Versailles to a pleasant enclosed garden with a small pond where a boy and girl play on an autumn morning. The camera glimpses the children's mother supervising her offspring in an extreme long shot lasting two seconds – time only to see that she is not Marina. Neil, not fully awake, comes out of the house. His wife has been coping with their children since breakfast: he appears a less engaged parent than she, his hesitancy in connecting making us wonder whether he has made the necessary changes to create a relationship with his feeling life and his family.

We cut to Marina dancing across an autumnal wood, flirting with the camera. She wears the long grey skirt (now wet from the damp earth) that she sported in the days of courtship with Neil in France, where we appear to have returned with the elegiac reprise of Wagner's Prelude to *Parsifal*.[4] However, this is not Neil's footage of his lover from their first dates for, after tasting rain drops on an ancient tree, she turns toward a wide horizon where ponies roam – the Oklahoma prairie. Late autumn sun flares in her face and, as if alarmed, she turns to see in the distance along the shoreline Mont Saint-Michel, symbol of the wonder she and Neil had shared. These final images of Marina at her most joyous and seductive seem to be memories, steeped in fantasy and breaking into consciousness, of their incomplete relationship – sad reminders of the missed chance to touch the Grail.

Late in life, Jack O'Brien in *The Tree of Life* also experiences the irruption of long-forgotten memories and fantasies. As a boy, Jack (Hunter McCracken) carries the heavy weight of expectation that can fall on the firstborn who enters the world as a miracle receiving undiluted devotion from both parents. Jack becomes the prime focus of his father who passionately wants the boy to achieve the success that, as the years pass, the pained man accepts has eluded him. In dealing with Jack, Mr O'Brien unconsciously requires the lad to carry the burden of his shadow – the archetype that represents the 'other' person in the dark side of the personality. And although 'the way of Nature' does not wholly define Mr O'Brien, it does dominate his personality. He lords it over all three sons, but governs Jack with special severity, demanding both obedience and love.

Ultimately the rage born from his father's suffocating love burdens the boy with what Jung said is the greatest price a child may have to pay: living the unlived life of the parent. Troubled by his desire to defy the paternal logos, the boy's libido is disorganised; but in adulthood it forces an outlet in his embodiment of the very imago that dominates him. Stein offers a pertinent gloss on libido and heroism that enables us to anticipate ways in which Jack years later turns his midlife crisis into the depths of a midlife transition.

> The 'hero' represents a specific configuration and movement of [psychic energy], *libido*, moving dynamically forward – into sometimes adaptive and often defensive directions – but essentially in an expansive motion outward and forward. Even in defense the hero is expansionistic and offensive: taking the initiative, catching the enemy by surprise, overwhelming him with superior force and aggressive strategy. The heroic pattern is the 'progression of libido' ... in a phallic, expansionistic modality, taking charge and winning glory.
>
> (Stein, 1983: 33)

When Mr O'Brien fails in both his first passion to be a great musician and his second ambition to bring a patented engineering design to market, he vents his frustrations only on the family. By contrast, Jack hones his anger into an implement of will that helps him achieve his goals. First seen in his leadership of a gang of neighbourhood boys, his matured will does not wholly ease his embattled inner life; but it drives his ambition as the architect of soaring twenty-first century office towers.

The film leaps forward from Jack's early teens, omitting more than fifty years of his life. We re-join him exactly forty years after the death of his younger brother, a morose figure (Sean Penn) in his late sixties, loath to face the anniversary. It plunges him into grief, which he has neither worked through nor escaped, halting his tongue and deadening his soul. Stein, reminding us that Jung called the midlife transition a 'confrontation with the unconscious' (1961: 194–225), describes what Jack seems to be experiencing. 'As the midlife transition begins, whether it begins gradually or abruptly, persons generally feel gripped by a sense of loss and all of its emotional attendants. ... The fundamental cause of this distress is ... a type of separation anxiety' (Stein, 1983: 24–5). What has been released are

> two hitherto repressed and otherwise unconscious elements of the personality: the rejected and inferior person one has always fought becoming (the *shadow*), and behind that the contrasexual 'other,' [the *anima*] whose power one has always, for good reason, denied and evaded.
>
> (ibid.: 26)

Jack's mind suddenly loses focus on diurnal time. Bewildering images break in on him. Some recur to his father disparaging his half-hearted attempts at weeding. Others bring his mother to mind, the anima evaded in repressing the taboo desires of early puberty. Such memories from the personal unconscious are juxtaposed to archetypal images whose surreal nature signals that his psyche teeters on a split between madness and numinous revelation. There come unbidden crazy glimpses of himself in his business suit walking hesitantly through gullies and over sand toward an old doorway where an anima figure beckons him forward. Standing on the beach, the door connects to nothing, surreal in its apparent lack of function; nor can he tell where the anima mother will lead him.

The questions that these incursions into his consciousness arouse cue a vision of the universe's birth, an efflorescence of light and energy as great clouds of supernovas and plasma erupt. In rending ecstasy, thunderous galaxies rumble into existence and die; a glorious soprano (Elzbieta Towarnicka) sings Zbigniew Preisner's searing *Lacrimosa*; music and light soar in a rip tide of saturated colours as, in a seamless circle, we celebrate *and* grieve for the birth and destruction of countless forms of existence, evanescent across the fleeting aeons. Jack's whispered questions seeking spiritual understanding stitch his – humanity's – bewildered suffering into the immeasurable paroxysms of a myriad worlds as they form and re-form, sometimes like lacy fabric evolving beautifully in opening blossoms, sometimes evocative of cancerous tumours, hideously elephantine. The scene focuses in from the universal to our galaxy, thence to our rumbustious planet in flaming meltdown and eventually the present century's volcanic eruptions, so furious they silence other music.

Jack's unsteady psyche is, of course, not the only vantage point available, Malick having the primary authorial claim to the vision. However, the nature of the cosmic perspective demands that something more, in terms of its socio-cultural dimension, cannot be ignored. *The Tree of Life* is mythmaking and, even when it draws on stories cherished by the ancients, renders myth for and of our time. What we see is knowable only through astrophysics, the related sciences and digital technologies. In *The Tree of Life* those scientists, technicians, other specialists *and* artists who recorded, generated, wrote plots and composed sounds, images and music were essential co-creators and myth-makers who rendered the knowledge of 2010 into truth as best they could tell it (albeit provisionally) in story form. The audience too (as members of a complex, technologically oriented culture) co-create with Jack O'Brien and Malick what they take from the film. Alan Mack (2011) wrote that the film is deeply personal to Malick and feels 'torn from the heart'. That, scarcely less elementally, is true for the engaged audience too.

In significant ways *The Tree of Life* resembles Kubrick's *2001: A Space Odyssey*. Both centre on quests to discover and share understanding of what we can humanly know of our place in the always-evolving time and space of the universe. In this respect, both films deal with the sacred, the numinous. But Jack O'Brien has not set out on a conscious quest. Buffeted by emotional forces that he cannot reconcile, his character metamorphoses *in extremis* into a type of Hermes – an unconscious hero on the dangerous journey of individuation. Archetypally he becomes for the audience a messenger of the gods. And this becomes true for his personal psyche as well as the collective when, in the vision, he meets his parental family and reconciles with them, accepting at last the death of his brother, learning to do so via the resolution of his mother's grief and bringing together the ways of nature and of grace in hard-won recognition of the Self.

In *Answer to Job* (a quotation from which opens the film and sets up this theme) Jung reworks the story of Job into the story of God's self-discovery through the agency of humanity. We experience a comparable urge toward reforming the numen as the organising drive expressed throughout *The Tree of Life*. Half a century after Jung chose Job to challenge an angry but ossified deity as humanity's agent, Malick and his creative team use Jack as their agent, creating in him an unexceptional man (albeit a leading professional member of his society) for whom the Church's stern dogmatism has killed religion (as Nietzsche foretold). Through Jack – his ageing body that goes tremulously walkabout, his intelligence that grasps so well the elegant dynamics of physical structures, his emotions (so hauntingly needful of release), and his discovery of a creation mythology fitting for the twenty-first century and consonant with every facet of his existence – through Jack's whole being, then, we experience nothing less than the necessary re-creation of the numen. Representation of the divine in *The Tree of Life* takes a form that no longer mirrors humankind's face back at itself but integrates humanity into the universal order – an order that, unlike the rigid medieval structures of so many of the world's orthodox religions, assures us not of stasis but unending metamorphosis.

It is possible to consider embodiment in the cinema in relation to three groups: actors, characters and the audience. Just as music performed is embodied first by singers and instrumentalists, acting is embodied first in the players' performances. By definition actors embody characters, their capabilities being a main consideration in casting them. We touched in passing on Jennifer Chastain's approach to playing Mrs O'Brien. We paid more attention to the way that stance, movement and gesture embody the experiences of psyche in some of the characters. To that end we singled out the O'Briens in the earlier film, Neil, Marina and the janitor in the later one. But audiences themselves, as Vivian Sobchack (2004) and Jennifer Barker (2009) have argued, respond in an embodied way to the film as it runs, albeit constrained by socially acceptable forms of conduct. They flinch and gasp confronted by fearsome attack, stretch their muscles in moments of relief, weep when sorrow is evoked and share too the pleasure of laughing out loud in the unseen community of their fellows. For the psyche to approach completion in its movement toward individuation, the hardships of transition and release into wellbeing must be felt in the emotions, and affect the body of the engaged spectator. To repeat: psyche and body, the material and spiritual world are inseparable.

For the present writers the psychosomatic impact of each of these films differed. With only two exceptions, psychologically and spiritually the principal characters in *To the Wonder* are more or less stuck through most of the narrative. They are either denied sight, or vouchsafed no more than glimpses of the wonder. Only the janitor appears able to touch and be touched by the numen whenever he opens himself. Marina is the other character who finally attains experience of what she calls the love all around humanity: the images of Versailles function as emblems for the tranquil resting point of an ordered self. However, her life journey prior to achieving her current state of integration was predominantly stuck in psychological and spiritual confusion with only momentary revelations of the divine in nature that she had not then internalised. All these signs indicate that the director's intention lies elsewhere, with the suffering for those who have no expectation of revelation (Neil), others who yearn for it but either cannot reach it, or having touched it (like Marina and Father Quintana), cannot keep hold of it. In this film, to cite Roger Ebert, Malick attempted primarily 'to reach beneath the surface, and find the soul in need' (2013).

The Tree of Life does not refuse that objective, as illustrated by Mr O'Brien who, like Marina in *To the Wonder*, finds himself thrust from deep misery into momentary awareness of what he calls the glory. But a core thematic concern in *The Tree of Life* is an extended exploration of epiphany achieved, not through Mrs O'Brien (who has no need for it), but Jack's agency. Prolonged sequences feature revelations that reorient his psyche. The engaged audience cannot escape the embodied experience that those scenes give us because the film immerses the spectator with Jack in experiencing the numinous, the glory, the wonder as, in a vision, he witnesses the birth of the universe and evolution of life on Earth that fuses with his own life.

Jung wrote to a clergyman 'God is light *and* darkness, the *auctor rerum* is love *and* wrath' (*Letters* 2, 17 December 1958). The light and darkness of the long journey undertaken in *The Tree of Life* reach into the theatre. To cite Jung again, 'the light which shines in the darkness is not only comprehended by the darkness, but comprehends it' (1954e: §756). Light and music involve reciprocal embodiment – grace experienced in the cinema stalls. Gazing at and listening to *The Tree of Life* and *To the Wonder*, many will feel light and music draw the eyes, sway moving feet, hands or head – physical expressions of the dancing, soaring heart moving the mind. The intensity and duration of aural, visual and narrative experience involve the audience in the attainment of transformation by epiphany.

Notes

1   The authors thank Jana Branch and Ken Friedenrich for contributions that shaped our thinking about these films.
2   Three hundred miles southeast of one of the principal locations for *To The Wonder*, Bartlesville, OK, and a month before the film's release in the UK, 'an ExxonMobil pipeline carrying tar-sands oil burst beneath a suburban neighborhood in Arkansas. The exact size of the spill hasn't yet been determined, but ExxonMobil says it's preparing to be able to clean up 420,000 gallons, though it doesn't believe the spill is that large. The oil flooded yards and streets and led to the evacuation of 22 homes in Mayflower' (Upton, 2013).
3   This is not the only pair of dissonant rhyming images in *To The Wonder*. Beneath Mont Saint-Michel as the tide comes in across the mudflats, Neil and Marina stomp joyfully on the jellylike surface as if defying quicksand – Neil's only dance. Back in Oklahoma he appraises a contaminated quarry where treacherous chalk slurry sucks at his boots.
4   Kyle Smith notes a 'startling moment of vicious clarity' when Marina walks up a staircase to a sleazy motel room for sex with a casual lover whom she takes as her marriage to Neil collapses. It reprises her ascent with Neil up the very different steps to Mont Saint-Michel where they had found their wonder in love (2013).

References

Aspe, B. (2011) De l'origine radicale des choses. *Cahiers du Cinéma* (December) 20–3.
Barker, J. M. (2009) *The Tactile Eye*. Berkeley and London: University of California Press.
Beebe, J. (2008) Evolving the Eight-function Model. *C. G. Jung Society of Atlanta* (Winter) 9–13. Available: www.jungatlanta.com/articles/winter08-evolving-the-eight-function-model.pdf (accessed 26 September 2013).
Bradshaw, P. (2012) *To the Wonder* – Review. *The Guardian* (2 September). Available: www.theguardian.com/film/2012/sep/02/to-the-wonder-review (accessed 17 August 2013).
——(2013) *To the Wonder* – Review. *The Guardian* (21 February). Available: www.theguardian.com/film/2013/feb/21/to-the-wonder-review (accessed 17 August 2013).
Branch, J. (2013) Personal communication.
Ebert, R. (2013) *To The Wonder*. *Roger Ebert.com* (6 April). Available: www.rogerebert.com/reviews/to-the-wonder-2013 (accessed 15 August 2013).
French, P. (2013) *To the Wonder* – Review. *The Observer* (24 February). Available: www.theguardian.com/film/2013/feb/24/to-the-wonder-review-malick (accessed 17 August 2013).
Gilbey, R. (2011) Review of *The Tree of Life*. *New Statesman* (7 July). Available: www.newstatesman.com/film/2011/07/1950s-america-tree-film-life (accessed 18 July 2011).
Izod, J. and Dovalis, J. (2014 forthcoming) *Cinema as Therapy: Grief and Transformational Film*. London and New York: Routledge.
Jenkins, D. (2013) *To the Wonder*. *Little White Lies* (21 February). Available: www.littlewhitelies.co.uk/theatrical-reviews/to-the-wonder-23238 (accessed 16 August 2013).
Jung, C. G. (1921) Psychological Types in *The Collected Works, Vol. 6*. Princeton, NJ: Princeton University Press, paras. 723–29.
Jung, C. G. (1961) *Memories, Dreams, Reflections*. London: Fontana (1995).
Mack, A. (2011) Review of *The Tree of Life*, *Little White Lies* (7 July). Available: www.littlewhitelies.co.uk/theatrical-reviews/the-tree-of-life-15546 (accessed 18 July 2011).
O'Hehir, A. (2013) Pick of the week: Terrence Malick's rapturous, religious love story. *Salon* (12 April). Available: www.salon.com/2013/04/11/pick_of_the_week_terrence_malicks_rapturous_religious_love_story/ (accessed 15 August 2013).
Perez, G. (2005) Loretta Young. *Sight and Sound*, 15, *10* (October) 38–41.
Romanyshyn, R. D. (1982) *Psychological Life: From Science to Metaphor*. Austin TX: University of Texas Press.
Rose, S. (2011) Jessica Chastain: Ascent of a woman. *The Guardian* (27 September). Available: www.guardian.co.uk/film/2011/sep/27/jessica-chastain-interview (accessed 28 September 2011).
Simon, D. (2013) There are now two Americas. *The Observer* (8 December), 30–1.
Sobchack, V. (2004) *Carnal Knowledge: Embodiment and Moving Image Culture*. Berkeley, CA: University of California Press.
Stein, M. (1983) *In MidLife*. Putnam, CT: Spring Publications.
Upton, J. (2013) Tar-sands oil spills in Arkansas and Minnesota. *Grist* (1 April). Available: http://grist.org/news/tar-sands-oil-spills-in-arkansas-and-minnesota/ (accessed 27 August 2013).

Part II
Psychoanalytical theories and the cinema

Chapter 6

Therapy and cinema
Making images and finding meanings*

Luke Hockley

This article focuses on the therapeutic dyad and how meaning is co-constructed between, and in-between, client and therapist. It does so as a way to understand the viewer–screen relationship. It is by no means self-evident that ideas that relate to one discipline, in this case psychotherapy, have value and utility to another, namely film theory. While keeping this in mind, this article is going explore whether the way in which Jungian-orientated psychotherapy understands the idea of image, and also the meanings of those images, can be used to illuminate the emotional responses we have when viewing films. The intention is to reflect on how our bodies encode those emotions. In psychotherapy the intellect, feelings and bodies are all used to help in understanding the psychology of a given situation. Central to this is the idea of the intersubjective field which is an imaginal space that is constellated between client and therapist and which contains meaning at an unconscious and bodily level. As a paradigm for the viewer–screen relationship, the intersubjective field suggests that far from meaning residing solely on the screen, or just in the mind of the viewer, it is possible that meaning exists in a space somewhere between the two. This, and the space where it resides, I refer to as the 'third image'. It is characterized by apperceptive responses to films in which collective, inscribed, narrative meanings are subsumed in unexpected personal and emotional reactions.

To a greater and lesser extent, the third image is always present when we view a film. At times it is palpable, and when this is the case the result is a special and personal relationship with films. This is one of the reasons why a film might enthrall one person and bore another; psychologically, these two people have not seen the same film – they have not had the same experience. It is also why someone can become obsessed with a film, quite literally in love with it, while everyone else is mystified about its appeal. This is the apperceptive response to film in which personal meanings are created even though such meanings are often at odds with more consensual views. I think of this as 'losing the plot'. Of course, it is losing the plot that lets us gain an insight into ourselves.

The client and therapist relationship and the intersubjective field

One of the cornerstones of psychodynamic psychotherapy theory is the curious process of transference and countertransference. The two terms are similar: transference is an attempt to understand how the client's emotions can be felt by the therapist, while countertransference is a way of distinguishing the therapist's emotions from those of the client. As we will see, this is not always as easy as it might first appear.

Quite often when the theory of transference and countertransference is taught to trainee psychotherapists they are encouraged to 'tune in', or to gain therapeutic attunement to the client as a way of enabling the process of the transference to take place in an optimal manner. They are told to 'work in the transference' or sometimes to work in the 'negative transference'. This way of working therapeutically is often referred to as the 'blank screen approach', though the term is something of a misnomer. At one level it is respectful of the client as it attempts to gain the fullest possible understanding of what the client is trying to communicate. The role of the therapist is to help the client locate the sessions' narratives in the context of broader life narratives. This act of interpretation is not unlike the process of consciously engaging and understanding the narrative of a film. This should not be taken to suggest that interpretation of the transference is only an intellectual process. Clearly, the feelings of the therapist (or viewer) have a role to play in understanding what is happening.

The problem with the theory is that it downplays the role of the therapist in creating meaning with the client. It tends to impose an interpretative scheme onto what the client is saying. Transference interpretations focus on the way two people appear to transmit emotions and thoughts in the therapeutic relationship. However, rather than seeing this as a process of transmission it is more helpful to imagine the relationship as a matrix, or field, of conscious and unconscious interactions. Here I do not mean to evoke Kurt Lewin's ideas from the 1940s in which he emphasizes social and cultural factors and behaviour. Instead what I am suggesting is that in the consulting room communication between therapist and client constitutes a psychological field in which meaning is constellated or co-created. The 'presence' of the therapist is crucial to the way that these meanings are made in therapy. Here I am going beyond the often stated claim that 'it is the relationship that heals', which, leaving aside the question of whether therapy is about healing, has a certain truth to it. Instead I am suggesting that the same client with a different therapist will arrive at a different understanding of their life. This is not just a question of theoretical orientation on the part of the therapist (an existential therapist seeing things differently to a Rogerian, for example) though that does play a role. Rather, it is the 'being' of the therapist which interacts with the 'being' of the client as together they create and understand what the client is talking about. This is going to prove important, as I want to suggest that something remarkably similar happens when we view films.

To these psychotherapeutic ideas of transference and countertransference I want to add the specifically Jungian notion of 'apperception' as it takes us closer to the idea of a psychological field. Apperception is a way of understanding how psychological changes happen. *The Critical Dictionary of Analytical Psychology* defines it as follows:

> A process by which a new psychic content (recognition, evaluation, intuition, sense perception) is articulated in such a way that it becomes understood, apprehended or 'clear'. It is an inner faculty which represents external things as perceived by the registering, responding psyche: therefore, the result is always a mixture of reality and fantasy.
>
> (Samuels *et al.*, 1986, p. 25)

Jung identified two different types of apperception that arise as the result of conscious self-reflection: active and passive. Active apperceptions require the purposeful and deliberate engagement of the senses and also of our critical faculties. By contrast, passive apperception arises from the unconscious, or is forced on the senses. In the first instance the activity comes from the ego and in the second, with the self-enforcing content, from the unconscious. The cinema, then, provides an interesting situation where visual and auditory information is 'forced' on the viewer and where the viewer also has the opportunity to engage with the process in an imaginative manner. The result is a mixture of reality and fantasy in which the role of fantasy is to make a psychological reality available in ways that consciousness, thinking and the rational part of the psyche is not able to. In this way, the 'fantasy-image' connects us to an image that encapsulates our inner psychological reality.

The third image

In psychotherapy the physical space between client and therapist is part of an intersubjective field. I think that it is helpful to think of this field as including the physical boundaries of the consulting room, the arrangement of furniture and other objects, even the temperature and lighting. It also includes the social boundaries that form part of the 'therapeutic contract' which is established with the client: non-disclosure by the therapist, the client not asking direct questions about the private life of the therapist, a non-judgmental attitude on the part of the therapist are common parts of such agreements. All these elements play their role in the creation of the intersubjective field. However, what I want to explore is the ways in which psychological meaning is experienced in this somewhat boundaried/ framed space. This is actually quite difficult to put into words because such meaning is fleeting, difficult to grasp and hard to sense. It is a meaning that is encoded in the body of both client and therapist, it is almost as though something that is both conscious and unconscious at the same time comes into being as both parties meet psychologically. This is why the metaphor of the field is more appropriate than one of transmission. It is not that emotions are being broadcast, it is more that new understandings are being created. It has to be said, this is not always a pleasant experience. There can be a palpable sense of shame, envy, jealousy, anger and sadness, as well as more uplifting emotions. When we transfer this idea to the cinema at first it does not seem to make much sense to think about an intersubjective field. Despite the claims of some phenomenological film theorists (Sobchack 1992) film does not possess a subjectivity, a consciousness nor a body, other than in the most abstract sense. Quite simply, film is not alive. However, what is very much alive is the relationship that viewers have with films and it is this relationship that animates the film and derives meaning from it.

There are numerous ways to view a film and each involves forming a different type of relationship. The following description explores three different ways of finding meaning in films. They are presented as somewhat separate but in fact they overlap and the question is really which aspect of the viewer–screen relationship is emphasized at any given moment. The most obvious way to watch a film is to let its images and sounds unfold in front of us. When we do this the locus of meaning is predominantly on screen and in the representational qualities of what it is that we see and hear. In this mode of film viewing we go along with the narrative of the film. This is the 'first image'. Even here, in the first image, meanings other than those of the narrative can arise, yet the focus of meaning remains on the representational aspects of the image and the narrative of the film. Of course, there is an unconscious aspect to this mode of viewing too. Typically in the first image, viewers are not consciously aware of how the film is communicating; they do not consciously register lighting, framing, editing music and so forth and yet this cinematic apparatus is clearly central to how the narrative of the film is created and conveyed. It is through these conventions as they combine diegetically that the viewer understands the film is a constructed fiction.

A second way to watch a film involves consciously trying to understand and interpret it. This is an intellectual and intuitive activity that incorporates an aesthetic sensibility, and it follows that is both conscious and unconscious. Here we engage with the film conceptually and are also sensitive to what it is that we feel when we watch the film. In so doing we form an understanding of the film, its narrative and the way meaning is encoded in its structure – shot, editing, lighting etc. The object of understanding is the film and the approach is one of conscious hermeneutic activity which deconstructs the film's diegetic and representational aspects. I call this the second image as it is the image that we create in our mind of what the film is about, of what the film is trying to explore and how we understand it. Here we draw on our own subjectivity, our intuitive capacity and our ability to empathize with the on-screen characters to help in understanding the film. In the creation of the second image we pay particular attention to use of formal narrative devices such as metaphor, symbol, allegory in the film. We interpret the meaning behind the editing, the framing and lighting etc. For example, we might notice how music in the film reinforces the emotions of the scene, or subverts them, or how it alludes to emotions and characters other than those on the screen, to other genres, and makes extra-textual references.

A third way to watch a film involves becoming aware of the ways in which viewing a film is a whole-body experience; in other words, that it is both a conscious and an unconscious process. Arguably, in this mode we are not viewing the film at all. Instead we are entering into a cinematic experience where meaning does not reside in the narrative of the film, nor its audio-visual structure, but instead rests in the experience of the film. As in the therapy, and with the intersubjective field, this type of relationship emphasizes those meanings that are intensely personal and deeply felt. This is a response to film that bypasses the intellect and in which the viewer is momentarily overwhelmed. This is the third image. It should not be confused with suture or diegesis. Diegesis is a term that is used to refer to the cinematic techniques that make the on-screen world coherent and believable. These techniques are used by filmmakers in order that viewers do not notice edits, the change of scene, the auditory enhancements of the soundtrack and so forth. They are the 'tricks of the trade' and they belong to the first and second images. By contrast, suture refers to the way in which the unconscious of the viewer can be 'stitched' into the structure of the film. This somewhat complicated theory suggests that the structure of film replicates intrapsychic structures and that is why we identify with films and their characters. These intrapsychic structures (ego-ideal for example) are inherently unstable; so too the structure of films is unstable as it offers a potential unity (of the body) which framing and editing cannot allow as they dissect the body into separate parts. Seen in that light, film replicates our own search for wholeness while at the same time it negates that possibility.

In the third image, what we experience is not a direct result of the techniques of cinema, though they might well be a contributing factor. What we experience is a personal affect as our unconscious temporarily invades consciousness. We no longer know why we are reacting in the ways we are. We do not understand where these tears have come from, why we are so afraid, why we are embarrassed or ashamed. Meaning comes from the intermingling of our individual psychology with the film, its narrative, images and sounds, in order to create a new meaning. This new meaning does not come directly from the screen, nor does it come from the intellectual investigations of consciousness. To repeat, this is the third image and it takes the form of an unlooked for and unexpected powerful emotional response, almost as though we have lost our mind and have been taken over by something else. We are losing the plot, yet as the narrative of the film fades into the background, so the narrative of our life comes to the fore.

One of the ideas that runs throughout Jung's work is the desirability of holding together competing thoughts or feelings at the same time. So it is not surprising that while he wants to comprehend the unconscious, at the same time he proclaims its fundamentally unknowable qualities. An interesting facet of this is the way in which Jung often constructs the unconscious as an autonomous entity that behaves in a manner that is independent of the ego. Of course, this is reminiscent of the way in which Sobchack (1992) thinks about the film as something that has an identity, perception and a body of its own. However, it is important to resist the notion that the psychological qualities of cinema are predicated solely on their replication of internal psychic structures. The reason films have a certain proximity to the unconscious is largely because they operate at the level of metaphor and allusion, of feeling and affect, which are qualities cinema shares with the psychological image of the intrapsychic field. As Jung comments:

> We have no knowledge of how this unconscious functions, but since it is conjectured to be a psychic system it may possibly have everything that consciousness has, including perception, apperception, memory, imagination, will, affectivity, feeling, reflection, judgment, etc., all in subliminal form.
> (Jung, 1947/55: para. 362)

Cinema has the capacity to trigger these responses in viewers as it brings back forgotten emotions. It helps us to imagine our life experiences laden with affect and it offers viewers opportunities for reflection and judgment, 'all in subliminal form'. Such subliminal qualities are experienced as a result of the passage of the film's images and sounds and are encoded in our bodily response to this unconscious material.

One way in which to understand what is happening in such a situation is to regard the experience as the failure of the psyche's mechanisms to repress some unpalatable contents. If this is right, then what appears to happen is that the sheer intensity of the audio-visual experience overwhelms the psyche, and as the systems of repression breakdown, the unconscious contents find their way into consciousness. This is not so unlike the mechanism of parapraxis, where evading the control of consciousness, some inner fantasy, thought or fear 'slips' unwittingly into the light of day. It might also be reasonably argued that this process is facilitated by the physical conditions of cinema, which are particularly well suited to the experience of unconscious affect. Let us allow for this possible explanation but it might be that something else is happening as well. Here, it is important to remember that for Jung the psyche is teleological, which is to say that the innate tendency in the psyche is towards a greater awareness of its unconscious contents. Theoretically this can be formulated as the movement towards an expansion of ego-consciousness; alternatively, we might say that when the ego is strong enough to assimilate the contents of the unconscious, the unconscious enables a move into consciousness. This is marked by an affective shift. It is important to remember that these unconscious contents were kept in the unconscious for a reason, namely because they were too painful or unpalatable for the conscious part of ourselves to deal with. It therefore follows that sometimes the affective shift is typified by unpleasant and seemingly unwanted emotions but their appearance also offers the opportunity for their integration into consciousness.

When we watch films there is a complicated psychological process at work in the way the unconscious finds meaning. The idea of the first image suggested that we need a sense of recognition and that what we hear and see in the cinema can be taken as a depiction of events which we accept through the diegetic as in some way believable. These events adhere to an established mode of representation which is close enough to our experience of reality to allow us to accept them as 'believable' but in which they are also codified as different. The second image suggests that we then interrogate these representations in an effort to understand their aesthetic and emotional meanings. This is a conscious attempt to use our life experiences and our intellectual and aesthetic sensibilities to understand the narrative of the film. The third image is where the unconscious parts of ourselves, memories, experiences we have tried to forget are brought to the fore by the passage of the images and sounds of the film. Equally, the reality of our current psychological situation of which we might not be consciously aware is activated. When this happens a highly personal and individual meaning is experienced as an outpouring of affect.

The experience of these affects can be so powerful that it appears as though temporarily we are not ourselves. Such affects can be strong and, if experienced outside the confines of the cinema or some other psychologically contained environment, they are also quite frightening. Nevertheless, in the safety of the cinema we have little difficulty in witnessing murder, death, violence and such like. These affects can also take the form of love, romance, erotic attraction, and other fantasies. What seems to happen is that emotions which we normally repress are able to find an acceptable outlet in the cinema. Our first psychological and defensive strategy is to displace these unconscious contents onto the characters and narrative of the film. In such cases we feel a strong sense of identification with the characters as we let them experience 'our' emotions. However, sometimes the affects are too strong and so intensely personal that displacement is not possible. When this happens we experience them in a powerful somatic manner and our body encodes the experience and, without thinking, it responds.

There is something immediate, visceral and earthy in cinema that speaks to the darker aspects of the unconscious. In particular popular cinema seems strikingly direct in its psychological affect as viewers experience a temporary state in which consciousness is eclipsed in which what might be characterized as pathological states outside the cinema can be experienced in relative safety and in a potentially psychologically beneficial manner. Much as our dreams can express the psychological reality of our lives, so too these moments when the cinematic experience invades us offer opportunities to experience what we do not know about ourselves. These momentary and affective cinematic invasions have a psychological relevance when the meaning we find in them comes from the narrative of our own lives and not the narrative of the film. While intensely personal, such moments are also archetypal, as the affect connects us to the inner workings of the objective psyche, which Jung conceived of as the foundation of the unconscious.

This interplay between the individual and the collective, and the unconscious and conscious parts of ourselves, is at the core of psychodynamic psychotherapy, and it is also at the core of the cinematic experience. Clearly, psychotherapy and viewing a film are not the same. Nor are dreams the same as films. However, a

Jungian understanding of image reveals how psychological images are the result of intellectual engagement and experience. Importantly, they also arise from dialogue. In therapy, it is an actual dialogue between therapist and client, with all the complexities of conscious and unconscious interactions that situation suggests and, indeed, requires. In dreams, the dialogue with the unconscious is mediated through images and sounds, while in the cinema the dialogue is facilitated through our bodies and the way they encode our conscious and unconscious engagement with the film. In this immersive environment we simultaneously experience the cinematic as body, concept, feeling and intellect.

Images are formed in the psyche partly as a result of structure and agency, but also as independent and semi-autonomous entities. As such, images are both the object of knowledge and the object of knowing and they serve as the fulcrum between past and future. To be clear, there is nothing mystical in this statement. Indeed, we can observe the same structure at work in the narrative of films where at any moment the viewer is aware of how the current situation has arisen, what is happening in the present, and what the future might hold. This is what Jung means when he writes that the psyche is Janus faced – any image, visual or otherwise, holds the competing needs of the individual and collective, the desire to be in the present right here and right now, and the pull of the past along side the call of the future. In microcosm, this is what occurs whenever we view a film as our own being intersects with the narrative of the film and in so doing it is diverted and becomes intertwined with our personal story. When this happens we create a new image, a new narrative and a new way of feeling what it means to 'be'. The impossibility of reconciling our personal narratives with the realities of life is temporally transcended and in these moments we also experience a greater sense of imminence. This is a type of enantiodromia in which, contrary to expectation, opposites do not pull away from each other but instead run together. It helps to explain why the cinematic experience as a fiction has the capacity to connect us physically to our bodies and psychologically to our whole selves: it is the ability of the cinematic to contain contradictory qualities which makes it such a profoundly psychological medium.

Cinema is sufficiently like reality for us to recognize what we are seeing and yet it is also quite unlike reality. This discrepancy gives us permission to fantasize and to imagine. It is also to experience cinema as liminal, as both real and unreal, as both individual and collective, as having a shared meaning and a personal meaning, and as both psychological and mundane. The cinematic experience is an experience of profound tensions yet one of its most remarkable qualities is that, unless we pause, it appears unremarkable.

The non-rational and psychological reading

The following is an account of an episode from psychotherapy. It is included here as an example of how in psychotherapy the imagery of films can have a meaning that is quite divorced from the narrative of the film. Here I will describe how my own experiences of watching films have directly informed my practice as a psychotherapist. The following example demonstrates how one of my own third images related to the psychological situation in which the client found herself. It illustrates how I evolved a non-rational understanding of the imagery of the film and how it also provided me with a way to connect to the client's unconscious anxieties.

I do not want to suggest that there is a direct causal relationship between the particular film I was watching and what the client was experiencing. The idea of the psychological field clarifies this point as it offers a metaphorical way to understand how the unconscious aspects of a situation arise in therapy from the client–therapist relationship, and subsequently how they take the form of an image. Like therapy, films provide a particularly fertile ground for this type of apperceptive response which, as we noted, is partly based in reality (the life of the client) and partly in the illusion that is the world of film. As such, the apperceptive response is a psychological fantasy and it is an image that captures a reality. Such images are akin to dream images, whose meanings are not fixed but which are negotiated, felt and embodied. These images might be felt in the room, or they might be found in art, drama, literature, or in some other fortuitous manner. What matters is not the site of the original image but the way in which the context of therapy both inflects the meaning of the image, and the way the image can inform the therapy. This is what forms the field of influences in which client, therapist, external image and internal image are all bound together.

Rebecca's entrance was remarkable as in her first session she announced, 'I can seduce any man!' It was one of those memorable starts to therapy in which an initial claim provided the basis for the next couple of years of work. Despite the power and bravado of her statement, Rebecca was in a highly distraught state and she believed that her marriage was in crisis. She no longer felt erotically attracted to her husband as she once had and whom she described as stable, solid and dependable. She was also upset by the loss of close male friend, Richard, with whom she had formed a bond. She would describe Richard as exactly like herself – effervescent and full of life. There was a powerful 'buzz' about their time together that felt intoxicating and joyous, even as she was retelling the evenings of dancing, the beautiful meals and cocktails.

When I met her, Rebecca was a somewhat unselfconsciously self-absorbed person. Her self-love took the form of a glow, and the ability to animate people round about her as they quite literally fell under her spell. While she did not recognize this as a narcissistic quality, she did know how to quite consciously use and manipulate relationships. She once described to me her 'tools of seduction' and they were well honed.

Our work together developed quickly. A few months later Rebecca's distress had quite considerably alleviated. As we explored her upbringing and childhood, so too her tendency to binge-eat subsided. The sessions did have a tendency to get a little academic and as Rebecca is exceedingly bright she unsurprisingly showed a considerable appetite for psychological self-examination. She also took to praising me, to thanking me for my insights, expressing gratitude for the work we were doing and such like. She was highly resistant to my suggestion that this was a type of seduction, and indeed that some of the ways she was with me were a type of intellectual eroticism.

Around a year, Rebecca had something of a transformative experience. While travelling abroad she discovered personal meditation, a practice that became an important part of her life although she remains somewhat surprised by this development. Meditative practice did not fit with her self-image which was of a highly polished professional and well-educated woman and not, as she would put it, 'a tree hugging charity worker'. During one guided meditation in which she imagined sending out love and kindness into the world, she astonished herself. Out of the blue she had an image of a large ball of glowing power that she was holding and then released, as she watched, it floated out across the countryside and into the sky. For Rebecca, this was not an act of imagination, as she actually saw and felt the warmth that emanated from this ball of light. Interestingly, she was not perturbed by the experience but instead internalized this glowing sensation. It left her feeling uplifted for quite some time.

As if this image and the experience were not striking enough, as Rebecca recounted her experience an image from a film that I had watched the previous day leapt into my mind. The film was *Burnt by the Sun* (Утомлённые солнцем or transliterated *Utomlyonnye solntsem*) (Dir. Nikita Mikhalkov, 1994). Outside Russia and people with a particular interest in Russian film it is not particularly well known. The film is set in a dacha near Moscow in 1936 and is shot in a fairly naturalistic style with high production values, and it emulates something of the style of contemporary American films of the nineties. On closer inspection, *Burnt by the Sun* turns out to be more ironic, self-knowing and critical of Russian society than it first appears. While most of the film is realist in style, there are two moments when a large fireball appears and it is these that I want to concentrate on.

During its first appearance the fireball emerges over a river, then collides with a falcon and finally burns down a single tree. All this takes place while the character of Dimitri or Mitia (Oleg Menshikov) tells a fairytale to a little girl Nadia (Nadezhda Mikhalkova). The story he tells concerns a good singer and musician called Yatim and his adopted father, a magician called Sirob. Sirob also has a daughter Yasum, and they all live happily until the outbreak of war when Yatim has to leave for the front. He is subsequently injured and stays abroad. Nadia claims to know the end of the story – Yatim and Yasum will marry. However, Mitia has another ending in which Yatim returns home but an important man arrives (a sort of bogeyman or ogre) and he sends Yatim away. While Yatim wants to be happy he knows that he is not allowed such bourgeois thoughts. Yasum cries, and ends up marrying the important man whose name Yatim cannot remember. In this story Mitia is actually describing the complexities of the triangular relationship between himself, Kotov (Nikita Mikhalkov) and Marusia (Ingeborga Dapkunaite). The second and final time the fireball appears is at the end of the film when it coincides with Mitia's suicide. On both occasions the fireball goes unnoticed, although near the start of the film its appearance is reported in a newspaper article read by Philippe (André Umansky).

Now it has probably struck you that the fireball in *Burnt by the Sun* has a somewhat destructive quality to it that seems at odds with how Rebecca described her experience. Even so, as she was talking, the image from the film stuck in my mind along with its somewhat jarring associations. Gradually I discerned very clearly that Rebecca's narcissistic glow had both a positive and negative quality to it. To put it another way, I became aware of how life-affirming she could be to both herself and to others, and yet also how this had the potential to be destructive, especially as her affirmation was frequently built in and around her manipulation of other people. It seemed to me that this was something we were going to explore in the work and I wondered whether Rebecca would be able to acknowledge this contradiction in her behaviour. It also crossed my mind that identifying this quality in her might mean that its grip on her would be weakened, and I wondered whether this would be entirely welcome.

A few weeks later I was talking to a Russian friend about the film *Burnt by the Sun*. She pointed out to me that the translation of the title was not accurate and that in Russian Утомлённые (utomlyonneye – burnt) actually means 'tired'. So a more precise translation of the film's title would be 'Tired by the Sun' – I checked with her to see if this had a particular meaning in Russian and was clearly told that it meant just the same as the English – 'The Sun was responsible for us being tired'. This made me wonder just how much energy Rebecca might use up in fueling her own iridescent qualities and in igniting that glow in others. I find that a useful way of thinking about psychological energy (what Jung called libido) is to imagine it as a fixed quantity. All psychological activity requires energy, be it anxiety, anger, depression, worry, an escape into fantasy and so forth. If any one of these elements is lessened, the affect becomes less intense and it is then possible to redirect the libidinal energy. In so doing, the natural tendency we have towards health means that this redeployed energy is now used more fruitfully as we feel more content and able to cope with life. This seems to fit rather well with Jung's view of the mind–body system as something which is homeostatic, teleological and behaves in compensatory manner as a dynamic system which strives for balance, but which attains it only momentarily.

What then would it mean for Rebecca if my associations to the image from 'Tired by the Sun' were indeed right? The initial phases of withdrawing energy from a psychological fantasy are often characterized by a feeling of weariness or fatigue. This was something I also occasionally felt in the sessions and I had shared this sensation with Rebecca. At first she found the idea that anyone could sense or embody the feelings of someone else rather curious. Yet as time progressed Rebecca gradually came to realize that her capacity for compassion and empathy were much greater than she had expected and that she too was capable of understanding how other people felt. It was interesting that as she became more aware of her feelings and her desire to care for others, the glow of her narcissistic aura dimmed, and it surprised her just how visible this change in her was to other people. Gradually she found the personal strength to question the core values around which she had come to build her life. Some remained, others altered in their importance, while some disappeared completely.

Here we have my associations with a film and what a client was telling me. It would be possible to take this material and go back to the film to see if its meaning has changed for me but I have not done so. Instead, I have chosen to focus on the curious coincidence of a fireball appearing in an otherwise naturalistic film and Rebecca's unusual experience of a glow of warm loving energy appearing, unlooked for and unbidden, in the midst of her everyday life. From a Jungian perspective it might be tempting to see this, an example of synchronicity, which Jung thought of, as an acausal but significant coincidence. In other words, such events are coincidences that have a psychological meaning for the client and therapist. It would be perfectly possible just to notice that I had seen a film with a fireball in it the day before my client wanted to talk about her experience. On the other hand, there is an unlooked for opportunity to engage in a creative and imaginative way with these 'found' images and in therapy I like to use whatever presents itself. My own way of thinking about this is simply to notice what has happened. I also take time to pause and wonder about the imagery. Why was I attracted to this film at this time? What was happening for me in my life that drew me to this film? Does it raise in terms of countertransference anything that needs to be kept in mind about the work? Is my reaction alerting me to something I had not previously noticed in the consulting room, and so forth? I do not find the idea of a formal mechanism, such a synchronicity, necessary here. Nor do I find that it adds much to my understanding of my experiences and those of my client. Instead I prefer to just note the psychological experience that I am having, and to be as aware of it as possible.

As I began to work with the story which Mitia tells Nadia I watched the extract (not the whole film) numerous times and I gradually discovered all sorts of other meanings that seemed relevant to Rebecca. The fairytale has three central characters, Yatim, Sirob and Yasum. To help his storytelling, Mitia uses three dolls: Yatim, whose doll is small and naked; Yasum's doll is taller and clothed; while Sirob's doll is an old disfigured male, who also looks somewhat primitive and archaic. There were a couple of points about Mita's story that particularly struck me. First, it is Yasum's father, Sirob, who is ill. Secondly Yatim does not initially recognize the now beautiful Yasum, and asks if she is the same person who 'used to pee in your pants and fall asleep on your father's knee while he was teaching me music?' She affirms it is indeed her. Finally, Nadia thinks she knows the ending of the story which is that Yatim will marry Yasum but Mitia has a different ending in which Yatim is banished from the country with the threat that if he remains he will be beheaded.

As mentioned, in the film the fairytale is an allegory of the relationships of the key characters in the room. To ensure the viewer does not miss this point the shot cuts to each person when his or her character appears in the fairytale. For example, at one point Nadia enquires if Yatim has been summoned by Koschei (translated in the subtitles as a Bogeyman) and the shot cuts to Kotov. Importantly, Koschei is not really a bogeyman at all but a well-known character in Russian folklore with an indestructible soul who abducts, or steals, the hero's wife.

Prompted by these associations it was a short step to thinking about the characters in the film and in the fairytale in relation to Rebecca and myself. I do not intend at this point to offer a whole clinical picture, rather what I want to show is how my own personal associations with the imagery of the film were closely related to the work that Rebecca and I were engaged in. For example, I found myself wondering if the sick old Sirob who gets pushed to one side was reminiscent of Jung. In the film the doll looks primitive and old, as though it might have been fashioned in a remote Russian village. It seemed a fitting figurine for Jung. The questions kept coming: did I think there was something sick (wrong) with Jung, or did Rebecca? Why did he need to be banished? Why did he need to be out of the picture, so to speak? Was he the man whom through his physical absence she could never seduce? Was it significant that the doll of Yasum is somewhat taller than the naked doll of Yatim? Did Rebecca see herself as in some way towering over a naked version of me with nowhere for me to hide in this story? Did I feel exposed before her, or was I perhaps the purveyor of the 'naked truth'?

The neat inversion of the character of the adulterous Koschei and Rebecca's boast that she could seduce any man was of course ringing in my ears. What I want to stress is how all this is at odds with what the film is mostly about. It is important to remember that the fireball and the fairytale form only a tiny part of the film, indeed so tiny that film theorists have not paid them much attention. This might be because there is a wealth of ideological and political material that is so much more accessible in the film. Yet it is precisely the oddity of the fireball and Mitia's story that I find appealing. Certainly it activated for me a series of associations and personal meanings that would not be available to any other viewer. In a very real way I negotiated my own set of meanings with at least this portion of the film. Even now the affect of those sequences stays with me and colours my understanding of the psychology of the film's characters. Similarly, my associations from the film inflected my understanding of what was happening for Rebecca.

The interaction between personal meanings and the narrative of films is a central problematic for film theory. The unconscious mechanisms of projections, identifications and complexes are always at work when we watch film. Central to this is the way that the cinematic experience offers an excellent environment in which to experience feelings that are otherwise repressed in everyday life. No doubt other art forms can offer something similar. But I want to suggest that the opportunities provided by the cinematic experience for these types of psychological process are actually greater than those afforded by other media. Occasionally clients will want to talk about theatre, television programmes, or current events in politics, the news and so forth. But without any doubt the desire to talk about emotional experiences that take place while watching films and during subsequent reflections is more common.

This takes us closer to one of Rebecca's central beliefs, namely that the glow of her narcissistic energy was necessary for her life, yet it was also destructive. She thought that if it were withdrawn then she, and those close to her, would be harmed. More particularly, if I really got to know her, it would be intolerable to me – perhaps I would not have the energy to live: coping with her would be too exhausting and I simply would have been 'tired by the sun'. So too in the film the final appearance of the fireball occurs as Mitia ends his life. To be clear, I do not mean this to be taken literally, rather the destruction that took place for Rebecca was a metaphorical destruction. My challenge was to be strong enough to hold these energies and to provide a space where Rebecca was safe and contained.

It would be possible to reflect in much greater detail about how the symbolic qualities of these extracts are relevant to the therapy. But the central point I want to make is that my film-going practices were helpful in providing a new understanding of Rebecca. The interpretations I made acted as a kind of amplification of her experiences. Significantly, my psychological relationship with the film formed a type of third image which came from a highly personal experience of the film in which the meanings I found were somewhat (though not completely) at odds with the film's narrative.

Note

* A previous version of this article was published as 'Feeling the Image' in *Somatic Cinema: The relationship between body and screen – a Jungian perspective* (2014, London: Routledge).

References

Hockley, L. (2014) *Somatic Cinema: The relationship between body and screen – a Jungian perspective*. London: Routledge.
Jung, C. G. trans. Hull, R. F. C. (1953–79) *The Collected Works* [CW], ed. H. Read, M. Fordham and G. Adler: London: Routledge.
Jung, C. G. (1947/55) *On the Nature of the Psyche*. In CW, 8.
Samuels, A. *et al.* (1986) *A Critical Dictionary of Jungian Analysis*. London: Routledge and Kegan Paul.
Sobchack, V. (1992) *The Address of the Eye: A Phenomenology of Film Experience*. Princeton: Princeton University Press.

Chapter 7

Psychoanalytic soundings
The case of *The Dybbuk*

Stephen Frosh

The gaze and the voice

It hardly needs to be said that there is a complex relationship between gaze and voice both in psychoanalysis and in cinema; but perhaps it is slightly more controversial to assert that the former, gaze, has always won out over the latter, voice, in both domains. Even for Lacan this might be true, despite his assertion of the centrality of gaze *and* voice as objects, as Mladen Dolar (2006) points out, in *A Voice and Nothing More*. 'To the list of objects inherited from Freud,' writes Dolar (2006: 127), 'Lacan notoriously added two new ones, the gaze and the voice, and it looked as if the two newcomers suddenly took precedence and came to serve as model objects.' But, he goes on (ibid.), 'although a new slogan, "the gaze and the voice," was quickly coined, it seems that all gazes were fixed on the gaze, both in Lacan's own work and in a host of commentaries, while not all ears were open to the voice, which failed to get a proper hearing.' Why should the gaze triumph; why should the voice not be heard? Perhaps this is just about comprehensible in cinema, although the importance of soundtracks is clearly critical. It is precariously arguable that what is distinctive about film is that we *see* an image; sound can come from anywhere, and in a darkened cinema, with people coughing and snoring and snaffling at their popcorn, it can be as much a distraction as a focus. But in psychoanalysis it is unimaginable that the voice could be discounted, because much of the time all that happens there is that one person speaks and another, out of sight and hidden away, is silent, very occasionally punctuating that silence with an utterance. Why should the eye dominate over the ear and mouth when it is sound that makes a difference, not vision? If a person wears spectacles, she or he will generally put them on for the cinema in order to see, and take them off for psychoanalysis in order to hear.

Some of the explanation no doubt lies, as always, in anxiety and defensiveness. For Freud, vision dominates – his supposed aversion to music is relevant here, a defence against not understanding, against the lack of content in sound, its relative indecipherability and indescribability. With regard to music, he writes (Freud 1914: 211), 'I am almost incapable of obtaining any pleasure. Some rationalistic, or perhaps analytic, turn of mind in me rebels against being moved by a thing without knowing why I am thus affected and what it is that affects me.' That this is belied by Freud's clear enjoyment of music at various times is transparent, and is engagingly debated by Dolar (2006: 128–9). 'We cannot quite take his word for it, for his musical references, if not abundant, are still curiously numerous enough, and show no lack of acquaintance,' he writes. 'Can we discern in these lines,' Dolar wonders (ibid.: 129), referring to Freud's disavowal of musical enjoyment, 'a certain anguish, or even panic, in front of something which threatens to enthrall him, flood him, make him lose his analytic stance and distance?'

It is always to sight that Freud grants primacy, and perhaps this is paradigmatic of a general tendency, not confined to psychoanalysis, to be reassured by distance, by the possibility of rational discourse and the reasoned perception of an external reality. Not that this is unemotional: the boy and girl, after all, are precipitated into their various modes of castration and Oedipus complexes by sight, and they feel these modes strongly enough. Girls, 'notice the penis of a brother or playmate, strikingly visible and of large proportions, at once recognize it as the superior counterpart of their own small and inconspicuous organ' and boys catch 'sight of a girl's genital region' (Freud 1925: 252), and from these two accidental viewings sexual difference follows with all the anxieties and desires incumbent upon it. Yet this is accompanied by relief: at last, or at least, the boy and girl know what is going on, and can relax from striving to have it all – the narcissism of absorption in the body of the other – to find themselves in the safe haven of limitation. Alternatively, sight might be a binding action, in which the unbearableness of an inner state of fragmentation is dealt with by projecting it outwards so that it takes a manageable bodily form, so that borders can be delimited and boundaries become markers of psychic integrity. This is the dynamic theorised in Lacan's most famous contribution, essential to the modern psychoanalytic encounter with cinema, the mirror phase: looking, seeing a surface, taking it for something other than what it is, a channel for identifications, bringing relief from the burden of psychic irresolution and fragmentation.

And the analyst's gaze itself: disembodied, fantasised, unreciprocal, avoidant – whose analyst does not look at the ground when it is time to say hello and goodbye? And is it just Freud amongst the analysts who resists being looked at? It is no accident that while analysts might be willing to sit 'face to face' with their clients from time to time, what they think of as 'real' analysis requires a couch, a seat behind it, and, as Slavoj Žižek (2005: 148) puts it, a relation constituted by '*no* face-to-face between the subject-patient and the analyst; instead, the subject lying and the analyst sitting behind him, both staring into the same void in front of them.' While vision produces its own anxious effects, it also saves us from too much of an encounter with them and, for that matter, with other people. And when this goes wrong, it is because vision has ceased to operate in this distancing way. John Steiner (2006) takes the line that the 'proximity senses', by which he seems to mean touch and smell, are absorbing and in a way *too close* to the object. Reading this negatively, he argues (p. 947) that 'A reliance on the proximity senses favours a part object relationship because a degree of separateness and distance is necessary for both object and self to be seen as a whole.' Vision allows this sense of distance, and is reverted to with some relief even though the proximity senses remain important 'especially in our relationship with basic elements of life such as food, faeces, illness, death and sex.' So vision is protective; touch and smell dangerously incorporative. It is precisely this distinction that goes awry when vision fails to sustain the necessary limitations, becoming blurred and destroying the separateness that it was made to engender.

Freud himself tells us something of what might happen next in his paper on *Psychogenic Disturbance of Vision*. Wrapped up in a guilty voyeurism that makes looking equivalent to sensual touching, repression acts not only on the sexual gaze, but on all sight in a kind of 'talion' punishment. 'The beautiful legend of Lady Godiva,' Freud writes (1910: 217), 'tells how all the town's inhabitants hid behind their shuttered windows, so as to make easier the lady's task of riding naked through the streets in broad daylight, and how the only man who peeped through the shutters at her revealed loveliness was punished by going blind.' This is the realm of gaze as something compulsive and material; distance is lost and the subject and object are linked by sight, binding and blinding them to one another. And then there is the vision that becomes a kind of scopophilia, as Fenichel (1937) calls it in his classic paper on the subject, where looking becomes equivalent to devouring and the history of medusas and turning to stone comes into play. So vision has its ailments, but they are precisely that: they derive from the *breakdown* of the distance that the gaze offers, a distance that is maximised in psychoanalysis, with its aversion to any kind of physical contact, however brutally intertwined the intercourse between patient and analyst might be.

If the distancing of vision is a protection, the envelopment and distraction of sound is a disturbance. The question here is one of location. There is a considerable amount of psychoanalytic work on the sound environment of the womb and its possible association to music; and indeed on the rhythmicity of music and sound in general, and its unconscious impact (e.g. Schwarz 1997; Nagel 2013). But there is also something else about sound, and specifically about the disturbing nature of the human voice, which Dolar (2006) references when he discusses its 'acousmatic' nature. What does this mean? Dolar adopts a longstanding musical idea of acousmatic sound, referring to a sound without an identifiable cause, and builds on the cinematic theorising of Michel Chion (1994) to describe the acousmatic voice as,

> simply a voice whose source one cannot see, a voice whose origin cannot be identified, a voice one cannot place. It is a voice in search of an origin, in search of a body, but even when it finds its body, it turns out that this doesn't quite work, the voice doesn't stick to the body, it is an excrescence which doesn't match the body – if you want a quick but vivid example of this, think of Hitchcock's *Psycho*, which revolves entirely around the question 'Where does the mother's voice come from? To which body can it be assigned?' We

> can immediately see that the voice without a body is inherently uncanny, and that the body to which it is assigned does not dissipate its haunting effect.
>
> (Dolar 2006: 60–1)

There are some useful terms here. The voice without the body is 'uncanny'; well, we know from Freud (1919) that the uncanny is a repetition of something familiar but out of place, and also that it is an augury, a reminder of what is to come. This 'what is to come' is a universal phenomenon: the awareness of death that shadows life from the beginning, accentuated by certain circumstances and gathering momentum tangibly as we age. The uncanny presages the death drive both chronologically in the sense that the paper *The Uncanny* was written shortly before *Beyond the Pleasure Principle* (Freud 1919, 1920) and conceptually: what is shown to us is often not what we have been, but what we will or might become; the power of the 'double', for example, is that it both cheats and reminds us of death. As indeed do cinematic and aural recordings: the potential enjoyment of the possibility that something of us will survive after we have gone is matched by the melancholic appreciation that this is *all* that will be left, and that as we listen or view we may be seeing or hearing the material remains of those who have already died. Embodiment does not completely resolve things: 'the body to which [the voice] is assigned does not dissipate its haunting effect.' I hope to demonstrate this shortly, but Dolar gives his own convincing *Psycho* example: 'the voice without a body is inherently uncanny.' Moreover, here is Žižek, who is also quoted by Dolar, and whose version of this kind of haunting is a universalising one:

> An unbridgeable gap separates forever a human body from 'its' voice. The voice displays a spectral autonomy, it never quite belongs to the body we see, so that even when we see a living person talking, there is always a minimum of ventriloquism at work: it is as if the speaker's own voice hollows him out and in a sense speaks 'by itself,' through him.
>
> (Žižek 2001: 58)

Ventriloquism, speaking by itself, the uncanny location of the voice in a body to which it does not belong, the voice as some kind of 'foreign body' (Dolar 2006: 131); we are, surely, talking here about a deep anxiety, that goes under the name of 'possession'. It is to a filmic example of how this might operate that the rest of this chapter is devoted.

The Dybbuk[1]

Possession comes in different forms across differing cultures and times. However, one common variety is what in Jewish folklore is known as a 'dybbuk': a dead soul that enters the body of a living person and takes it over, 'cleaving' to it (the Hebrew origin of the term) and speaking through it. Such dybbuks are usually the unsettled ghosts of people who have died without fulfilling their responsibilities or promises, leaving something broken and unattended to that has to be put right. Usually, they are male souls that enter a female body, gaining access either because the victim is a sinful girl or because she is particularly sexually 'pure' (Roskies, 1992). In the twentieth century, the established traditions of the dybbuk myth were eclipsed by one modern rendering that substitutes a love story for that of arbitrary, pernicious possession: S. An-Sky's *The Dybbuk*. This *Dybbuk*, subtitled *Between Two Worlds*, is a strange and powerful meditation on how welcome and necessary possession can be. It was first a play, written by An-sky between 1916 and 1920 and heavily influenced by his ethnographic recordings of folk stories in the Jewish Pale of settlement between 1912 and 1914. Indeed, to make the first acoustic link, Gabriella Safran (2010: 221) speculates that An-Sky may have been fascinated by dybbuk stories because they echoed his use of the gramophone to record the stories and songs he heard on his travels. 'The fantasy of conquering death was prominent in the early history of sound recording,' she writes, 'and An-Sky recorded the people of the shtetl sometimes willingly and sometimes against their will, preserving their voices so that they could be heard long after their death.' The preservation of voice is one important element in any dybbuk story, and in *The Dybbuk* it is of central significance, as we shall see. This naturalistic reading is, however, just one layer of the multiple ghostly resonances of *The Dybbuk*. An-Sky, who died in 1920, never saw his play performed. It was written in Russian, translated into Yiddish and then by the famous poet Chaim Nachman Bialik into Hebrew, then by An-Sky back into Yiddish after he had lost the Yiddish manuscript when he fled Russia following the Bolshevik revolution. From the start it was a multiple palimpsestic piece resonant with the terms of old (Yiddish) and new (Hebrew) languages and uncertain as to its exact linguistic and mythical grounding. *The Dybbuk* was first performed in 1920 to enormous acclaim as well as critical controversy (even then it was seen by some as romanticising an outdated myth) as part of the commemoration of An-Sky's death, was revived several times, and became the subject of the greatest Yiddish film of all time, Michał Waszyński's (1937) version, shot in Warsaw and on location in the Polish village of Kazimierz.

Watching this film is an irrevocably haunting experience. The world it conjures up had already largely gone by the 1930s; but the faces and voices were real enough, as many of them belonged to the actual inhabitants of Kazimierz, most of whom died in the Nazi terror. Indeed, we could say that not only the people, but voice itself was murdered and returns only as a ghostly presence, a haunting figure, in this film and others like it. *Language* was massacred: the Yiddish language died soon after the film was made, at least as a means of secular, everyday discourse, and its speakers were wiped out. Consequently, almost everyone nowadays interprets the film through English subtitles, which are themselves meaningfully if not intentionally inadequate, even absent in important places, leaving the viewer to guess what might be going on. As with many dead voices, whose tone is all that remains, most viewers are left listening to the timbre of the language, but understanding it only through the overlay of another tongue. Just as poignantly, there is the soundscape of the film, which centres on the miraculous singing of Gershon Sirota, one of the great pre-war cantors. Sirota's voice is heard in the penitential synagogue service at the start of the film, raising immediately the key question of the relationship between song, suffering and forgiveness; and his singing haunts the film through the recurrent theme of the *Song of Songs*, a Biblical poem that traditionally signifies both human and divine love and that is used in *The Dybbuk* to communicate an intense but unspoken erotic charge between lovers and across generations. Sirota was killed in the Warsaw Ghetto in 1943. Reading or watching the play, but particularly viewing the film, is thus itself an act of memory and resurrection, laced unbearably with the knowledge of what came next; haunted, that is, by the future as much as by the past. 'What was to come' is the temporality of viewing; the viewer's body is itself inhabited by the dybbuk of those whose lives were cut short, and perhaps have nowhere to go.

There is much to say about this film (see Frosh 2013), but I want to focus here briefly on one feature. The story of *The Dybbuk* is quite a complex one. The key players are Sender and Nissen, two devoted friends at the court of their Hassidic master, and their respective children, Leah and Khonon. At the start of the film, Nissen and Sender, enraptured with each other, promise that their unborn children will marry; various eventualities occur, including the death of Nissen, but Khonon finds his way to Leah, only for her to be betrothed to someone else. Dabbling in Jewish mysticism and trying to summon the power of Satan to make him rich enough to displace this groom, Khonon dies. Before the marriage ceremony, Leah visits the cemetery, ostensibly to invite her mother to her wedding. However, she actually invites Khonon. The film then offers one of its most famous sequences: a set of dances that the bride has with the sick, the poor and with a figure of death, who she mistakes for Khonon; what is then dramatised is the active desire of the girl for this figure, a death drive in the most literal sense. At the wedding, Leah casts herself on the grave that stands in the middle of her village, the grave of a young couple murdered on their own wedding day by an antisemitic mob centuries before. When she looks up, she is speaking with the voice of Khonon: 'You have buried me! But I have returned to my promised bride and will not leave her!' (p. 29). The Messenger – the closest representation of an analyst in the play – announces, 'A dybbuk has entered the body of the bride' (Ibid.) and this declaration is clearly a performative act: subsequently, everyone behaves as if it is true.

The final acts of the play centre on Reb Azriel from Miropolye, the Hassidic sage at whose court Nissen and Sender had originally met, who reluctantly agrees to excommunicate the dybbuk in order to free Leah. He carries out a trial to hear the accusations against Sender by Nissen, that is, by the dead against the living, and then when the dybbuk refuses to leave he is forced into an excommunication ceremony. He invokes all his power whilst still pleading with the dybbuk to leave on its own accord, but it is only when the shofar, the ram's horn, is blown that the dybbuk gives in. The Rebbe then releases him from the excommunication and calls for the planned wedding to take place immediately. But whilst the whole party is out greeting the approved groom and his family, who have been called urgently to them, Leah wakes up to find the dybbuk leaving her, and enters into a desperate and romantic dialogue with this lost soul. Finally, in a heartbreaking moment of lament, she steps outside the magic circle that the Rebbe has drawn around her and unites with Khonon, who says that he has left her body to enter her soul. The play and film end with the formula on discovering a death, 'Blessed be the true Judge.'

There are two fundamental aural phenomena to note here. The first is a curiosity of the staging of the film: the dybbuk does not actually speak with Khonon's voice, but with Leah's, albeit in an obviously lowered register. This decision of the filmmaker's was not a necessary one for technical or artistic reasons: Khonon's voice could easily have been dubbed in, and various stagings of the dybbuk have used simple devices to do this. In the opera of *The Dybbuk* by David and Alex Tamkin, for example, the soprano playing the possessed Leah mouths the words which are sung from behind a screen by the tenor playing Khonon, producing a very disconcerting effect that has its own alienating and ventriloquistic elements and in some ways even more effectively draws out the gender issues that are prominent in the story: how is it that a woman can only speak her desire through the voice of a man? But the film dramatises what is both a traditional and a modern representation of dybbuk possession: the woman is hysterical, surely, she *imagines* herself possessed and speaks in her *own* voice; but what is extraordinary is that the society around her, from her father to the wonderworking Rebbe, believe her and act as if she is actually inhabited by a real spirit. Is this the only way that she can be heard? There is a trial in the film, involving the living and the dead (the ghost of Nissen), and the dead speak, but the film shows only the wind rushing through the court room and the report of the Rebbe has to stand in for the voice of the dead; that is, we do not hear the ghost's voice, any more than we hear the dybbuk's. Indeed, it is only at the very end, when the dybbuk has left Leah's body and is now literally disembodied, that we hear it again; and now it is truly not clear whether this is her imagination, her death wish, her death *drive*, or whether we should take it as real.

A simple interpretation would place all this in the realm of superstition and sorcery, the eagerness with which a moribund culture will believe in spirits even when it is obvious that a fraud, intended or unconscious, is at work. Certainly the lack of any supernatural component to the film, with the possible exception of the Messenger's capacity to appear out of the blue, encourages a psychological reading. The Messenger declares the girl possessed, and in a suggestible society that is enough for everyone to behave as if this is so. But this naturalistic rendering is not sufficient, because the presentation in the story is of a girl who is *truly* possessed and the culture is *truly* haunted, albeit not necessarily by something outside it, but by its own desire. To return to Dolar (2006: 80), commenting on voice in general,

> The voice comes from some unfathomable invisible interior and brings it out, lays it bare, discloses, uncovers, reveals that interior. By so doing it produces an effect which has both an obscene side (disclosing something hidden,

intimate, revealing too much, structurally too much) and an uncanny side – this is how Freud, following Schelling, described the uncanny: something that 'ought to have remained ... secret and hidden but has come to light'.

Of course it is the girl's desire that is on display and that troubles the culture; secondly, it is the fathers' desire, the love pact between Nissen and Sender that is doomed from the start; and thirdly, it is the despair of a social order that finds itself degenerated, losing its way, and speeding towards an abyss that it can sense, but at this moment – recall again it is 1937 – it cannot imagine. The dybbuk is real enough; we all speak with the voice of something that has gone before and should have been laid to rest; yet it is also our own voice, the one that 'comes from some unfathomable invisible interior.' What can we say to that? Once the thing that 'ought to have remained secret and hidden' is severed from us, expelled, there is only the dance of death.

The second aural phenomenon is how the dybbuk 'resolutely' (ibid.: 45) refuses to leave the girl's body even under the threat of excommunication until the shofar, the ram's horn, is blown – in fact, until seven are blown together. For Lacanian commentators (Wolfe 2010), this is because the 'dead' letter of the law needs the 'supplement' of the Real (the shofar) to bring it to life and give it potency. But this shofar has its own background and resonance. The ram's horn is chosen as the instrument of religious force, used as an awakening to penitence, because of the Biblical ram which replaces Isaac as the sacrifice in the story of the binding of Isaac in Genesis chapter 22. We even know what happened to that ram: 'as to its horns, with the left one the Holy One, blessed be He, sounded the alarum at Mount Sinai; and with the right one, which is larger than the left, He will in future sound the alarum at the Ingathering of the Exiles in the Age to come' (Spiegel 1967: 39). The shofar is therefore a call to repentance, a reminder of the covenant between Abraham and God, and a window into another world, a direct channel to the source of the Symbolic itself, to revelation and messianic salvation. It is also a reminder of violence, both the threatened sacrifice of his son by Abraham and the actual killing of the ram – 'He comes and in his eye/ is the cold glint of murder', as Ruth Brin (1999) expresses it in her *'Poem by a Ram to God'*. It is in these different ways a mark of the Real, in which what *lies behind* the Symbolic is allowed to break through as the strange voice that resonates across generational differences to make them all present at the same time. All Jews, living and to come, were supposedly present at the Revelation on Mount Sinai, when the shofar blew; similarly, the Ingathering involves the resurrection of the dead, so all will be present at that future time as well. Experienced in this way, the shofar destroys temporality and along with it the organised structures of law and Symbolic order. It announces judgement and awe, which is why the dybbuk flees from it; it also supplants the natural order of things, creating a world in which everything is possible all at once – which is perhaps why it also allows the lovers to escape the bounds of their bodies and become united as souls. And finally, it has a maternal element: the sound of the shofar is terrifying, but it is also all-embracing; it surrounds the people at Mount Sinai and will do so again 'at the Ingathering of the Exiles'. Through the sound of the shofar, the people will be *ingathered*, gathered together, taken up in a nurturing hold, brought out of their lonely graves where they are separate from one another, and united again with their source. There is a powerfully 'matrixial' feel about this. Bracha Ettinger's (2006: 100) insight into the Akedah as an exemplary instance of *compassion*, comes to mind: 'This compassion is primary; it starts before, and always also beyond, any possibility of empathy that entails understanding, before any economy of exchange, before any cognition or recognition, before any reactive forgiveness or integrative reparation.' The Rebbe certainly has compassion on the dybbuk even as he drives it out; he says as much (An-Sky 1920: 36): 'Wandering soul! I cannot help but feel deep pity for you and will do everything in my power to release you from the angels of destruction.' It is in the womb that the infant is surrounded by sound, an auditory environment that supports it and, one can only guess, gradually differentiates out, perhaps in the separate-but-together way that Ettinger proposes. The total immersion in the sound of the shofar does something similar. It terrifies, for sure, as an announcement of the presence and power of God, of the Real that can destroy all Symbolic relations. However, it is also a return of sorts; it offers a total environment of compassionate holding, into which the lost soul flows, to be joined almost immediately by the other that has been promised to it.

I have argued elsewhere (Frosh 2013) that *The Dybbuk* can be understood as both an instance of transgenerational haunting and as an attempt to recognise and repair the fabric of a society in decline, a social order that cannot deliver on its promises. Both the content and form of the film compress time, so that one generation and the next are contemporaneous, trauma recurs and memories are projected inwards and outwards. The 1937 film stands on a precipice; within eight years, most of its presences became literally ghostly, wiped out in the cataclysm of the Holocaust. Their visual image remains; but most hauntingly of all, the aural resonance of the musical soundtrack, dominated by Gershon Sirota's singing of the prayers, stays behind in its own all-embracing time-warp. What we have in *The Dybbuk* is an instance of haunting as *witnessing and as aural reverberation.* Within the film this is expressed in the way the lovers live out the repressed traumatic bond between their fathers, putting right the social order's failure to meet the terms of their pledge. They reconstitute the order that has missed its mark, and in so doing also reveal the haunting presence of something that causes this rift in the first place. But there is a more material element to this ghostliness as the film *becomes* the ghost that haunts its viewers into future generations. One cannot watch it without shivering with memory, nostalgia and loss. There are no doubt other such archives, both Jewish and non-Jewish; in some ways they are the common stuff of melancholia in the face of communal destruction as well as colonialism. This particular one is no different, but it is especially resonant; *within eight years* everything had gone.

Conclusion

There is an argument that the psychoanalytic focus on vision, which is contradicted by its utter reliance on voice, derives from the fear of possession. What I mean here is that while a respectable degree of visual distance can be maintained, there is separation between subject and other; this is why it is so disturbing when sight breaks down, when looking causes problems, either through the scare of what one sees or through the effects of the Evil Eye on what one loves. In the case of the aural, the barrier of reason is much more fragile: the aesthetics of sound enter into and envelop the listener at the same time; possession is a routine phenomenon, and the insistence of voices and of music in the mind is such that it can drive one to despair. *The Dybbuk* can perhaps be allowed to claim something else as well. As Roger Luckhurst (2008) and others have shown, the visual imagery of the cinema has fed into contemporary experiences and conceptualisations of trauma, for example in relation to the insistence of the 'flashback' as a restaging of an original event that is both unsymbolisable and relentlessly visually intrusive. Perhaps in a more diffuse way, the cinematic voice can also repeat the unfinished business of the past, whispering its secrets at times, but also demonstrating how noisy they can be. This noisiness is both embodied and disembodied: on the one hand, it appears manifested in the hystericised body of the desiring girl; on the other, it is a displaced voice from a soul wandering 'between two worlds'. It hardly seems to matter whether this is the soul of a girl who cannot express her desire, or that of a lover who cannot find his place of rest and relinquishment, or a combination of the two; or whether it is the soul of a society that cannot come to terms with its internal tensions or that of a culture that has been murdered. In all these instances, which may turn out to be rolled together in one, 'the voice doesn't stick to the body' (Dolar 2006: 60). It becomes 'acousmatic' in that something speaks, but this is not simply the person whose body the voice inhabits and it does not necessarily reflect agency. Rather, the voice comes from somewhere else, perhaps representing a historical trauma, maybe a mystical connection or possibly a psychological debt. This suggests that there are conditions under which we all speak with the voices of others who are seeking expression for these modes of unfinished business. Given how each generation is chained by memory and hope to the previous one and the next, gathering things up that have been secreted away, passing them on down in an altered form, then maybe it is the acousmatic voice that has primacy over the subject, and the disembodied that is closest to the real.

Note

1 This section is developed from material in Chapter 7 of S. Frosh (2013) *Hauntings: Psychoanalysis and Ghostly Transmissions*. London: Palgrave Macmillan.

References

An-Sky, S. (1920) The Dybbuk. In S. An-Sky, *The Dybbuk and Other Writings* (edited by D. Roskies). New York: Schocken, 1992.

Brin, R. (1999) Poem by a Ram to God. In R. Brin, *Harvest: Collected Poems and Prayers*. Minnesota: Holy Cow Press.

Chion, M. (1994) *Audio-Vision: Sound on Screen*. New York: Columbia University Press.

Dolar, M. (2006) *A Voice and Nothing More*. Cambridge: MIT Press.

Ettinger, B. (2006) From Proto-Ethical Compassion to Responsibility: Besideness and the Three Primal Mother Phantasies of Not-Enoughness, Devouring and Abandonment. *Athena*, 2, 100–154.

Fenichel, O. (1937) The Scopophilic Instinct and Identification. *International Journal of Psychoanalysis*, 18, 6–34.

Freud, S. (1910) The Psycho-Analytic View of Psychogenic Disturbance of Vision. *The Standard Edition of the Complete Psychological Works of Sigmund Freud, Volume XI (1910): Five Lectures on Psycho-Analysis, Leonardo da Vinci and Other Works*, 209–218.

Freud, S. (1914) The Moses of Michelangelo. *The Standard Edition of the Complete Psychological Works of Sigmund Freud, Volume XIII (1913–1914): Totem and Taboo and Other Works*, 209–238.

Freud, S. (1919) The 'Uncanny'. *The Standard Edition of the Complete Psychological Works of Sigmund Freud, Volume XVII (1917–1919): An Infantile Neurosis and Other Works*, 217–256.

Freud, S. (1920) Beyond the Pleasure Principle. *The Standard Edition of the Complete Psychological Works of Sigmund Freud, Volume XVIII (1920–1922): Beyond the Pleasure Principle, Group Psychology and Other Works*, 1–64.

Freud, S. (1925) Some Psychical Consequences of the Anatomical Distinction between the Sexes. *The Standard Edition of the Complete Psychological Works of Sigmund Freud, Volume XIX (1923–1925): The Ego and the Id and Other Works*, 241–258.

Frosh, S. (2013) *Hauntings: Psychoanalysis and Ghostly Transmissions*. London: Palgrave Macmillan.

Luckhurst, R. (2008) *The Trauma Question*. London and New York: Routledge.

Nagel, J. (2013) *Melodies of the Mind: Connections Between Psychoanalysis and Music*. London and New York: Routledge.

Roskies, D. (1992) Introduction. In S. An-Sky, *The Dybbuk and Other Writings* (edited by D. Roskies). New York: Schocken.

Safran, G. (2010) *Wandering Soul*. New York: Harvard University Press.

Schwarz, D. (1997) *Listening Subjects: Music, Psychoanalysis, Culture*. Durham: Duke University Press.

Spiegel, S. (1967) *The Last Trial*. Woodstock: Jewish Lights Publishing, 1993.

Steiner, J. (2006). Seeing and Being Seen: Narcissistic Pride and Narcissistic Humiliation. *International Journal of Psychoanalysis*, 87, 939–951.

Wolfe, G. (2010) Love and Desire 'Between Two Deaths': Žižek avec An-Sky. *International Journal of Žižek Studies*, 3, 1–22.

Žižek, S. (2001) *On Belief*. London: Routledge.

Žižek, S. (2005) Neighbours and Other Monsters: A Plea for Ethical Violence. In S. Žižek, E. Santner and K. Reinhard (eds) *The Neighbor: Three Inquiries in Political Theology*. Chicago: University of Chicago Press.

Chapter 8

Process and medium in the practice of filmmaking

The work of Jayne Parker

Carla Ambrósio Garcia

I

'When I think about film I feel it. When I handle film I see it.' This is the beginning of a text piece written by Jayne Parker (2011) that she contributed to a book on the importance of analogue formats in the digital age – the publication that accompanied Tacita Dean's exhibition of *Film* at the Tate Modern in London.[1] They are two short statements on the process of working with the medium of film that, to my mind, generate multiple others, for example: thinking through a physical object; feeling your way through a thought; the feeling of thinking a medium; the physical actions of a thinking process; feeling, when handling an object; the way an action makes you feel; the physicality of the creative process and medium.

Throughout her career as an artist and filmmaker, Jayne Parker's primary medium has been 16mm film, though most of her later work featuring musical performances is, from a 16mm original, transferred to and shown either on Digibeta or DVD for sound quality reasons. In this article I draw on object relations psychoanalysis in order to suggest an understanding of some of her works, as well as the specificity of the process through which they are created, and the specificity of their medium.[2] The various developments that Wilfred Bion makes from Melanie Klein's concept of projective identification will be central to this discussion.

In his contribution to Dean's publication, the artist Matthew Buckingham (2011) asks: 'What *else* can the quality or "voice" of that medium say? What is the content of that form?' His questions seem to propose the idea that a medium might communicate something that is not immediately apparent, something that is difficult or indeed impossible to grasp, and that therefore the content of a form might elude conventional forms of articulation. This could be a similar issue to the one Bion refers to as he reflects on the difficulties of communication in the analytic setting. He writes:

> The impossibility of communication without frustration is so familiar that the nature of the frustration is forgotten. [...] In psycho-analytic work the

problems are more obtrusive than usual because the subject is novel and its difficulties uncharted; difficulties become more marked still when the material to be communicated is pre- or non-verbal. The psycho-analyst can employ silences; he, like the painter or musician, can communicate non-verbal material. Similarly, the painter can communicate material that is non-visual and the musician material that is inaudible.

(Bion, 2007 [1970]: 15)

Non-verbal material, its significance, and the difficulty in communicating it, might thus be articulated in what might be taken at first as non-articulations. Parker's work inspires a way of thinking about the medium of film and the process of working with film that foregrounds the relations between embodied subject and material support, and internal and external worlds, which arguably move beyond more conventional forms of articulation.

In the course of my argument I engage with some of the different views of art and new media theorists on the issue of medium specificity – with particular focus on some of Rosalind Krauss's comments on the work of Richard Serra – but I shall first consider a few important points in Bion's theory of thinking.

II

In an early article entitled 'Attacks on Linking', Bion writes that the denial of the use of projective identification, either on the mother's part or the infant's, 'leads to a destruction of the link between infant and breast and consequently to a severe disorder of the impulse to be curious on which all learning depends' (2007 [1959]: 106–7). This passage in Bion's article begins to give form to what later becomes his model of links, in which curiosity, or the epistemophilic instinct, will be placed alongside Klein's love and hate dyad as an equally important motive force in mental life. In this model Bion postulates the three basic links that an emotional experience can establish: the L (love), H (hate) and K (knowledge) links, and their negatives as no-emotions or defences against emotion (1991 [1962]: 42–3). –K is a defence against or envious hatred of the emotional experience of learning (ibid.: 95–8).

It is also in 'Attacks on Linking' that Bion speaks of an 'internal object which in its origin was an external breast that refused to introject, harbour, and so modify the baneful force of emotion' (2007 [1959]: 108). Here the breast is already conceived of as something that can contain and transform projected emotions. This theory is developed in subsequent work: the infant can project a bad object (a sense impression or emotion that is unassimilated, which Bion names beta-element) onto the mother. When the mother is receptive to the projected bad object and is able to transform it into an emotion that the infant can tolerate, the beta-element is converted into an alpha-element that can be re-introjected in a constructive way to the personality (Bion, 2007 [1961]). In this way the mother's role is vital in containing the unbearable emotions that the infant projects into her and in processing them into a tolerable form.

This formulation of the growth of thinking culminates in the theory of container/contained, which is still derived from Klein's idea of projection of a split-off part of the personality into the breast, but goes further in its recognition of the *communicative* aspect of the mechanism, and its role in learning and growth. The projected part is to be called the contained, and the container is that into which the contained is projected (Bion, 1991 [1962]: 90). This configuration becomes observable in any relationship, such as between the mystic or messianic idea and a group of individuals. In a symbiotic relationship, container and contained are transformed through positive growth; in parasitism the explosiveness of the contained makes the container disintegrate, and/or the rigidity of the container reduces the meaningfulness of the contained. Bion gives the example of how the verbal expression of an idea can constitute a parasitic link between container and contained:

> The more successfully the word and its use can be 'established', the more its precision becomes an obstructive rigidity; the more imprecise it is, the more it is a stumbling-block to comprehension. The new idea 'explodes' the formulation designed to express it.
>
> (Bion, 2007 [1970]: 80)

Before I return to Parker's text, it is important to underline that container and contained perform the function of containing and being contained in relation to each other: a word contains meaning, but the meaning also contains the word through its use.

III

Following the two statements with which I began this article, Parker's text piece lists words, words that sometimes follow each other as lines in a poem might do.[3] The words are divided into groups, preceded by headings variously related to the medium of film and the process of working with film. Many of these words appear as though they were collected from a glossary of film terms, in which definitions have been left out. Under the heading 'MATTER', Parker writes: 'physical / real / actual / it is / what it is' (2011). This extract could perhaps be seen to make a reference to film's indexicality, but it is also an example of how Parker's list seems to be about something that cannot be articulated other than through tautological expression: film is what it is; to make is to materialise; time is duration; space is location; projection, a light beam. 'PROCESS' is:

> contact / printer / optical / printer / freeze frame / reframe / step print / bi-pack / live action / documentation / narration / animation / construction /

deconstruction / building / structuring / dismantling / fragmenting / cutting / drawing / the eye / the hand / the heart

(ibid.)

The heart mentioned in such close proximity to machines that manipulate film establishes a link also suggested by Tacita Dean, when she makes the following comments on the process of editing film on a Steenbeck cutting table: 'I am wedded to the metronome beat of the spool as it turns. I count time in my films from the clicking as the core collects the film' (Dean, 2011: 20).[4] The diction of a list of words also produces a pulse, a rhythm, a machine-like speech. 'The eye' and 'the hand' are repeated in the list, under the headings 'APPARATUS' and 'EDIT', next to words such as camera, aperture, shutter, fade. In Parker's films, the body often appears in relation to an object, an object that can be body-like. Moreover, what is inside these bodies is often spilled out, then swallowed, sometimes in such close exchange as the music that circulates inside and outside the performer's body and the musical instrument. As the writer Ali Smith (2008) has noted, Parker is 'an explorer of the endless negotiation between external and internal'.

In this regard the film *K.* (1989)[5] is a good example. In the first part of the film, which is silent, a woman, standing naked in an empty studio, begins to pull out of her mouth what appears to be her intestine. A long string of the fleshy matter collects on the floor, which is then skilfully woven with her hands and arms. These actions are filmed predominantly using side views, close-ups and medium shots. But the final moment in this first part is a frontal full shot of the woman facing the camera, then raising the woven intestine in front of her, as if to make the relation between the ordered object and herself more explicit. In the second part, which uses diegetic sound, the same woman repeatedly dives into a swimming pool. Again, the action is seen in details, fragments – the hands holding onto the stairs of the pool, the feet standing at its edge – but the final shot is a high-angle view of the pool filling the frame entirely, into which her whole body is seen diving one last time.

The formal development of these two sequences could be seen as a form of the movement between the two positions of the subject in relation to the object that Klein theorised to be operative throughout life, including its pre-verbal stages: the paranoid-schizoid position and the depressive position. The first, in its attempt at ordering the chaos of experience through splitting the object and splitting the ego's relation to it, which results in the splitting of the ego itself, is evoked by the initial fragmented framing of the body; the other position, achieved with a realisation of ambivalence in the relation to the object, which contributes to the integration of objects and self, and their perception as whole, is evoked by the sequences' final images of the performer's body in full view. Yet this idea becomes unsettled when we consider that the final image of the first sequence presents a view of the body from which something internal has been split off; and also that the final image of the second sequence suspends a moment of integration that will not last, as the body cannot breathe, or survive, in the water environment.

When I	angle	foreground	rewind	specimens
think	rotate	background	fast forward	moths
about film	rewind	mid-ground	spool	butterflies
I feel it.	reverse	distance	split spool	bones
When I	superimpose	inside	core	flowers
handle	motor	outside	bobbin	bowls
film I see	clockwork	upside down	the eye	sea creatures
it.	winding	reverse	the hand	piano lid
	claw	scale		open
	registration	size	PROJECTION	closed
	pin gate	life size	light	cavity
	shutter	mid shot	beam	the site
TO MAKE	open/close	close up	sound	of sound
to materialise	the eye	depth of field	24fps	abstract
to touch	the hand	horizon	auditorium	mystery
to feel		infinite	cinema screen	
to notice	FILM		wall	BEAUTY
to see	Celluloid	MOTION	full frame	
to look	emulsion	hand held	transfer	
to find	grain	shake	loss	
to confront	the frame	steady	monitor	
to discover	ratio	locked-off	projector	I am caught in
to recognise	4:3		double headed	the continuum
to realise	16mm	SOUND	back	of the history
	negative	track	projection	of film,
MATTER	positive	magnetic	speaker	between all
physical	b/w	stripe		the films that
real	colour	optical	PROCESS	came before
actual	reversal	silence	contact	and all the
it is	leader	ambient sound	printer	films that
what it is	sprocket	wild sound	optical	will come
	length	wild track	printer	after.
LIGHT	speed	1000 cycles	freeze frame	
daylight	fast	effect	reframe	
light metre	slow	music	step print	
incident	daylight	speech	bi-pack	
reading	tungsten	sync	live action	
reflected	transparent	drop out	documentation	
refraction	scratch	phrase	narration	
filter	dust	pitch	animation	
flare		tone	construction	
silhouette	TIME	resonance	deconstruction	
solarise	duration	vibration	building	
shadow	24fps	breath	structuring	
image	silent speed	the ear	dismantling	
dark	slow motion	(pressure of	fragmenting	
sun	time-lapse	the bow)	cutting	
moon	reverse		drawing	
	instantaneous	EDIT	the eye	
APPARATUS	moment	rushes	the hand	
camera	now	leader	the heart	
Bolex	stop	spacing		
body	freeze	mark	MEANING	
lens	parallel	Chinagraph	subject	
eyepiece	action	pencil	object	
aperture	reel time	cut	prop	
f-stop	real time	splice	things	
focal length		splicer	in the world	
focal plane	SPACE	splicing tape	people	
prime lens	location	camera tape	trees	
extension tube	point of view	gaffer tape	animals	
macro	head on	jump-cut	plants	
magnification	side on	dissolve	musical	
wide angle	reverse angle	fade	instruments	
zoom	establishing	pace	cello	
tripod	shot	phrase	body	
pan	in frame	track lay	strings	
tilt	out of frame	dub	vibration	

Figure 8.1 Jayne Parker in *FILM*: Tacita Dean

Source: Tate Publishing, 2011. © Tate 2011. Reproduced by permission of Tate Trustees

The silence of the first part and the spilling of the internal organ suggest a link between the studio and the internal world; the sound in the second part suggests a move to the external world. At the same time, in the first part the interior is brought out into the open, into view, into the exterior; and the pool could be seen as a protective womb-like space or interior space. In his introductory article to the artist's monograph, A. L. Rees notes that in Parker's films meaning is never predetermined or fixed, it is transformed (2000: 13).

Rees also observes that the empty studios, the swimming pools and the auditoriums that appear in Parker's work can be seen, to a certain extent, to emulate the spaces of the cinema and the gallery in which the films are shown (ibid.: 18). Elsewhere, he relates these spaces to the idea of the interior:

> Parker's films emphasise the idea of the interior in at least three ways. The interiority of the performers is made objective in the form of gesture. All action takes place inside rooms, pools and [...] stage and concert room. Finally, the films are shaped to their necessary conditions of viewing, in the dark of cinemas or galleries. Her films are structured around this taut control of the medium and its viewing space.
>
> (Rees, 1999: 116)

In this connection, and particularly in the case of *K.*, I would introduce a fourth space: the editing room. Parker is the performer in this film, as well as the editor. In one of her statements, she writes that when she began performing in her films, the importance of witnessing herself carrying out these actions emerged (2000: 7). The interior spaces in which, in Parker's words for the synopsis of *K.*, she is making 'an external order out of an internal tangle' (ibid.: 60), resonate through the space in which she is witnessing herself doing this, while performing similar actions on the material of film: cutting, dismantling, structuring, building. This relation of the subject to the material, to space and to process reverberates through to the space in which the film is experienced.

This leads me back to Parker's list of words, which on some levels brings to mind Richard Serra's *Verb List*, written during 1967–68, and that he describes as 'actions to relate to oneself, material, place and process'.[6] The list begins thus:

> to roll / to crease / to fold / to store / to bend / to shorten / to twist / to dapple / to crumple / to shave / to tear / to chip / to split / to cut / to sever / to drop ...

Most of the list is composed of such actions involved in the process of making sculpture, though the material itself is never specified. Still, it can be observed that marble, for example, cannot be crumpled, folded or bent. At that time Serra makes a film entitled *Hand Catching Lead* (1968),[7] in which a hand performs continuously the actions of grasping and dropping pieces of lead that fall from above and outside the frame. Rosalind Krauss contextualises this work within minimalism's strategy of serial composition in which there is no organising hierarchy, and also

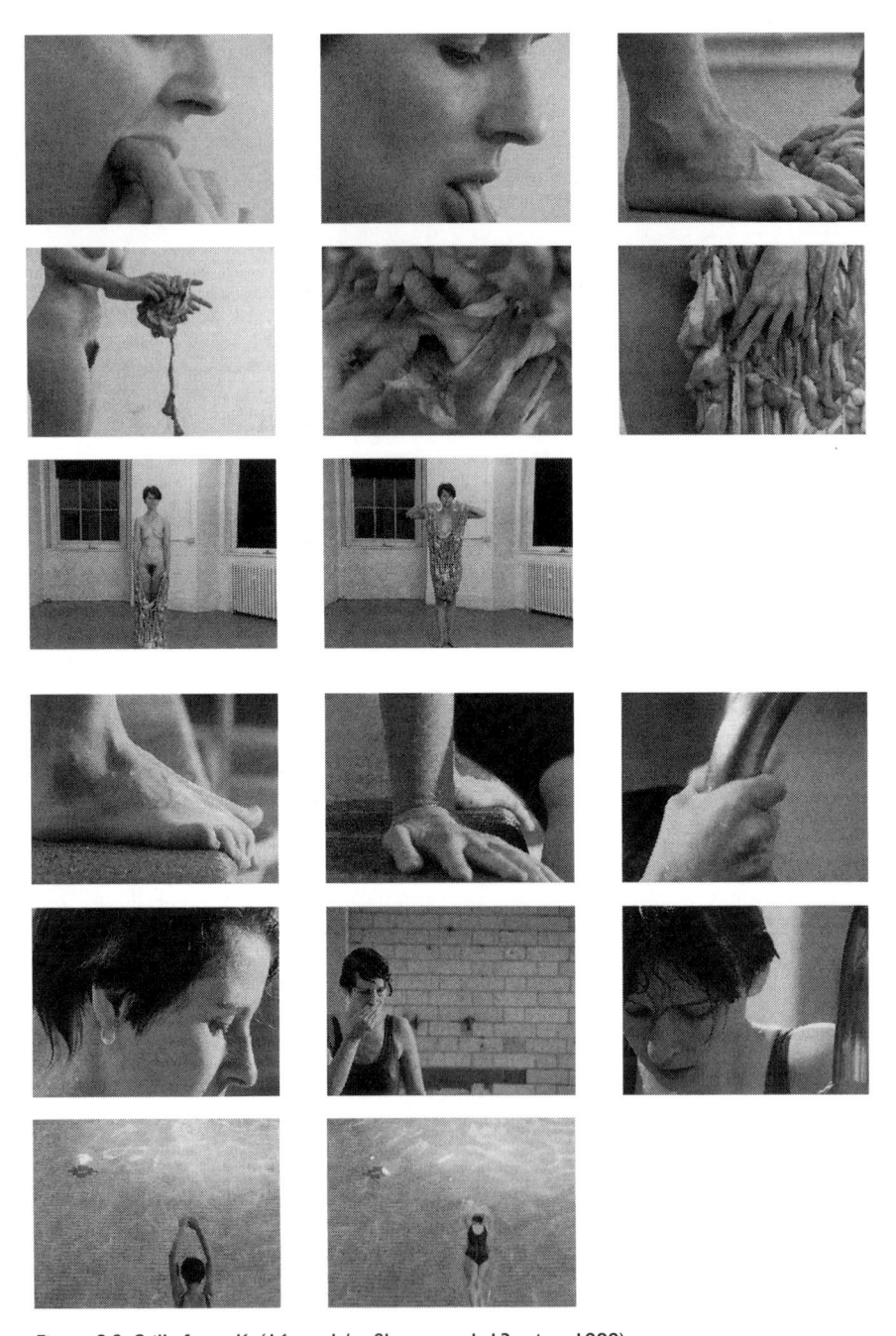

Figure 8.2 Stills from *K.* (16mm b/w film, sound, 13 mins, 1989)
Source: © Jayne Parker. Reproduced by permission of the artist

– because of its (apparent) focus on the action itself – within what was referred to in the late 1960s as 'pure process' (1986: 103–4). But for Krauss the specific material of lead in this film is important in at least two ways: in that its passage through the frame echoes the passage of film through the projector's gate (giving *Hand Catching Lead* a dimension of self-reflexivity typical of modernism) and also in that it is the material support of sculpture. While the film connects with minimalist sculpture's compositional repetitiveness, it also distances itself from the latter's lack of references to the processes and actions that create it. Krauss writes:

> The logic of process that had led Serra to turn to film as a way of manifesting a pure operation on a physical material was also a way of opposing the rigid geometries of minimalist sculpture in which a viewer was presented with an object whose construction was a closed system, secreted away within the interior of the object, invisible and remote. […] 'To catch' is a process conceived within the strategic terms of this critique; but 'to catch lead' represents a decision that what is at stake in this critique is the status of sculpture.
>
> (ibid.: 104)

Sculpture could now be an action on a material, filmed on film. Sculpture was moving beyond its conventional forms of articulation. It became an action to relate to oneself, material, place and process. In her later, seminal text *'A Voyage on the North Sea': Art in the Age of the Post-Medium Condition*, Krauss comes back to the context in which Serra's work developed, considering the influence that Jackson Pollock had in a new understanding of medium. She states that part of the painter's aim in moving his canvases from the easel to the floor was 'to transform the whole project of art from making objects, in their increasingly reified form, to articulating the vectors that connect objects to subjects' (1999: 26). Richard Serra's systematic attempt to find the logic of such events or actions is important to him, Krauss defends, in ways that take his work beyond modernist concerns of what a medium reduced to its physical support might be (ibid.: 26–7).

The argument that Krauss forms in her text is that even modernist approaches to medium specificity have to understand the medium as self-different, in the sense in which Jacques Derrida demonstrates that an interior can never be separated or uncontaminated by an exterior, and thus a medium can never be self-identical or pure (ibid.: 32). A medium aggregates conventions and meanings that cannot be reduced to a mere physical basis, and this is, in Krauss's view, what the structuralist filmmakers failed to see (ibid.: 44–5). Yet the recognition of such a differential condition does not imply that a medium cannot be used in critical and specific ways. A medium's 'differential specificity' only implies the possibility of its critical rearticulation and reinvention (ibid.: 56). Thus, film cannot be reduced to its condition of discrete fragments mechanically set in motion before a frame, though these are meaningful aspects of the medium when considering a film such as *Hand Catching Lead*; similarly, Jayne Parker's *K.* is in consonance with the physicality of film, though this has not always been regarded as the medium's most salient attribute.

There is a further aspect to Krauss's examination of *Hand Catching Lead* within its historical context. She observes that the framing of the disembodied hand frees the notion of the artist's body as a coherent whole, which is seen to be part of a wider aim to de-psychologise the artist/performer (1977: 279). Minimalism's antithetical response to abstract expressionism was a relocation of the work's meaning to the outside, to cultural space, to the surface of the body, rather than to an inner, private, psychological space (ibid.: 270). However, in my view, and considering also more broadly some of the actions that appear on the *Verb List*, these actions do seem to evoke, or even *materialise* operations that take place in the internal world.

In Serra's list can be found the verb 'to split', and later 'to repair', which would perhaps best describe the main psychical operations in each of the aforementioned positions formulated by Klein, namely to split the object in the paranoid-schizoid position, and to repair the attacked object in the depressive position. 'To enclose', 'to surround', 'to encircle', also found in the list, evoke ways of containing the object and being contained by it, as Bion formulated in his later theory of thinking. 'To tie', 'to bind', 'to join', 'to match', could be seen to refer to links between subjects and objects, to objects put in relationships, perhaps those postulated by Bion: the Love, Hate, and Knowledge links. 'To tear', 'to cut', 'to sever', is to attack those links.

It is also interesting to note that following the two opening statements, Parker begins her list precisely with the verbs 'TO MAKE / to materialise'.

New media theorist Lev Manovich investigates what he calls 'operations', a word that he uses to define computer data manipulation techniques such as copy, cut, paste, select or composite. He maintains that these operations are not media-specific, and that in fact they can be found not only in software but also in society's ideologies and imaginaries (2001: 118), as well as its practices. He writes:

> The concept of an operation can also be employed to think about other technologically-based cultural practices. We can connect it to other more familiar terms such as 'procedure', 'practice', and 'method'. At the same time, it would be a mistake to reduce the concept of an operation to a 'tool' or 'medium'.
>
> (ibid.: 121)

Manovich's conceptualization of operations is an integral part of the larger project that he undertakes in the cited book, as he attempts to draw attention to the continuities that exist between new media and older technologies or cultural forms. Still, in his analysis of operations as algorithms that transform computer data, there can be discerned the ways in which these particular operations might be different from other kinds of operations; sometimes a difference is paradoxically discernible in an affirmation that aims to convey a continuity, such as the following: 'What before involved scissors and glue now involves simply clicking on "cut" and "paste"' (ibid.: 130). The intention is to establish that the operations involved in working with different media remain the same, perhaps because they could be described with the same words ('to cut' and 'to paste'); nevertheless, what is also apparent in Manovich's statement is that in the two cases the means employed are very different, to such an extent that it would be plausible to expect different end results. In Bion's terms, we could ask whether this is an instance in which the idea or meaning 'explodes' the verbal expression used to describe it.

Krauss argues that a medium cannot be reduced to the physicality of its support, and Manovich claims that an operation cannot be reduced to a medium. Still, I am interested in considering the way in which, for example, 'to cut film' might differ from 'to cut digital moving images'. Such a distinction raises the question of the significance of the physicality of what could be the 'physical analogue' of a psychical process. Since a psychical process can take place in phantasy, it may be supposed that there is no significance in the physicality of the creative process and medium. But in one of the lectures Bion gave in São Paulo in 1973, there can be found a few observations that suggest otherwise. Bion remarks:

> Melanie Klein's theory is that patients have an omnipotent phantasy; the way one can verbalize that phantasy is that the patient feels that he can split off certain unpleasant and unwanted feelings and can put them into the analyst. I am not sure, from the practice of analysis, that it is only an *omnipotent* phantasy, that is something that the patient cannot *in fact* do. [...] I have felt [...] that when the patient appears to be engaged on a projective identification it can make me feel persecuted, as if the patient can in fact split off certain nasty feelings and shove them into me so that I actually have feelings of persecution or anxiety.
>
> (Bion, 1990 [1973]: 68)

A few years later, in one of another series of talks, Bion comes back to this idea that 'the patient does something to the analyst and the analyst does something to the patient; it is not just an omnipotent phantasy' (1980 [1977]: 14–15). When Bion remarks that X 'does something' to Y, and that this is not simply a phantasy, what is it then that happens? One of the participants asks precisely this question. Interestingly, Bion begins by stating that 'Things which are called material can be regarded as being outside our province because they are facts of physical make-up. *But* [...] I would [...] suppose that thought enters into a phase which I could call primordial' (ibid.: 24) (my emphasis). Bion continues with reflections on the nature of speculative imaginations. And at the end of his response, he offers the following imaginative conjecture:

> I can imagine [...] that the walls of the uterus might be so restricting that there is no alternative but for the mother to evacuate the creature which is

inside, and for the creature which is inside to get out and make an adjustment from life in a watery fluid to life in a gaseous fluid.

(ibid.)

Thus, Bion expands the understanding of a situation that was before conceived of as being an 'omnipotent phantasy' with the example or model of a very physical situation that both mother and infant have to submit to.

Bion is of course well aware that the birth process is also a psychical process, but the beginning of his response to the question shows unmistakably that here he is focusing on its physical aspect. A physical model is being used to rethink thinking and communicating, because something is *done* to the subjects that they can *feel*. Such a physical model can also help to rethink the importance of the physicality of the creative process and medium – in the practice, and experience, of moving images.

In Bion's statement there is a certain attention to the qualities or capacities of container/contained and to the adjustment needed in their transformation: the contained needs to make an adjustment (change its qualities) in order to exist in a container with different qualities, and the container will also change through the agency of the contained. This image evokes the second sequence of *K.*, a repeated attempt to make an adjustment to live, breathe in a different environment. Creativity needs internal conceptions of container/contained, but it is through the creative process and medium that artists/filmmakers attempt to find container/contained in the physical world, so that they can become internal conceptions again in a continuous process of transformation and development of meaning. The (internal) contained makes an adjustment to the (external) container, and this materialised adjustment, resistance, agency of the physical world is at once container *and* contained, external *and* internal, externalised *and* internalised. It cannot be taken to be insignificant, easily substituted with something else. It is through process and medium that artists/filmmakers can be seen to be 'working through', and to do things that can be felt.

'To cut' is not the same as 'to cut film', and 'to cut film' is not the same as 'to cut digital moving images'. And 'to cut film', in its differential specificity, has not always been the same either; to paraphrase Krauss, 'to cut film' at this point in the history of the medium, represents a decision that what is at stake is the status of moving images. At this point in time, 'to cut film' is to create an object whose construction is an open system.

The physicality of the process of working with film and of the film medium is very different from that of the process of working with digital moving images and of digital media. To disregard the difference between film and digital is to contribute to a certain debasement of language. It is to disregard the content of a form. Bion cautions against this problem in relation to the vocabulary used in analysis. He notes:

The language we use is so debased that it is like a coin which has been so rubbed that it is impossible to distinguish its value. 'I'm terribly frightened' says the patient. What about it? Terribly. Frightened. These words are commonplace. But I now become alert when I hear that word 'terribly' because it is so worn. It's terrible weather; it's terrible this; it's terrible that; the word means nothing.

(ibid.: 14)

Bion is alluding to a statement by Immanuel Kant, which he sometimes referred to: 'Thoughts without content are empty, intuitions without concepts are blind' (Kant, 1929 [1787]: 93). Words, thoughts, language, can become empty, devoid of content; and intuitions can become lost if they do not find an appropriate container. Serra, and Krauss, know that it is not only important to consider what the hand is catching in *Hand Catching Lead*, but also to consider what it is that can be done with lead, that is, what vectors can be articulated in the subject's connection to that material. And in order to consider these issues, Serra made, specifically, a film. In Parker's work there can also be found a preoccupation with the vectors that the (embodied) subject can articulate through the physicality of an object and of space.

In Parker's film *Foxfire Eins* (2000),[8] the cellist Anton Lukoszevieze performs a piece composed by Helmut Oehring. The synopsis of the film explains: 'The child of profoundly deaf parents, Oehring's first language was signing. Oehring hears music as gestures – for him music comes out of movement' (Parker, 2000: 61). Gesture is indeed foregrounded in the images of the film, as the performer is against a black background wearing black clothes, which contrast with the brightness of his face and hands; working through the physicality of the cello, both the facial expressions and the movement of the hands convey a sense of effort, rigour, concentration, emotion.

The body of the instrument is visible, but its neck is dark and at the top it dissolves into the abstractness of the background; thus sometimes we cannot see what the hands of the performer are touching. Also, the eyeline of the performer points to something offscreen, which we never see. We cannot see, but his eyes and hands are being held, or contained, by something concrete, and *that* we can see. To my mind, this tension is similar to what the film presents of the process by which it is created, and of the medium in which it is created: similar to a painting that can communicate non-visual material, and to music that can communicate material that is inaudible, process and medium in film is nevertheless always concrete, present, felt.[9]

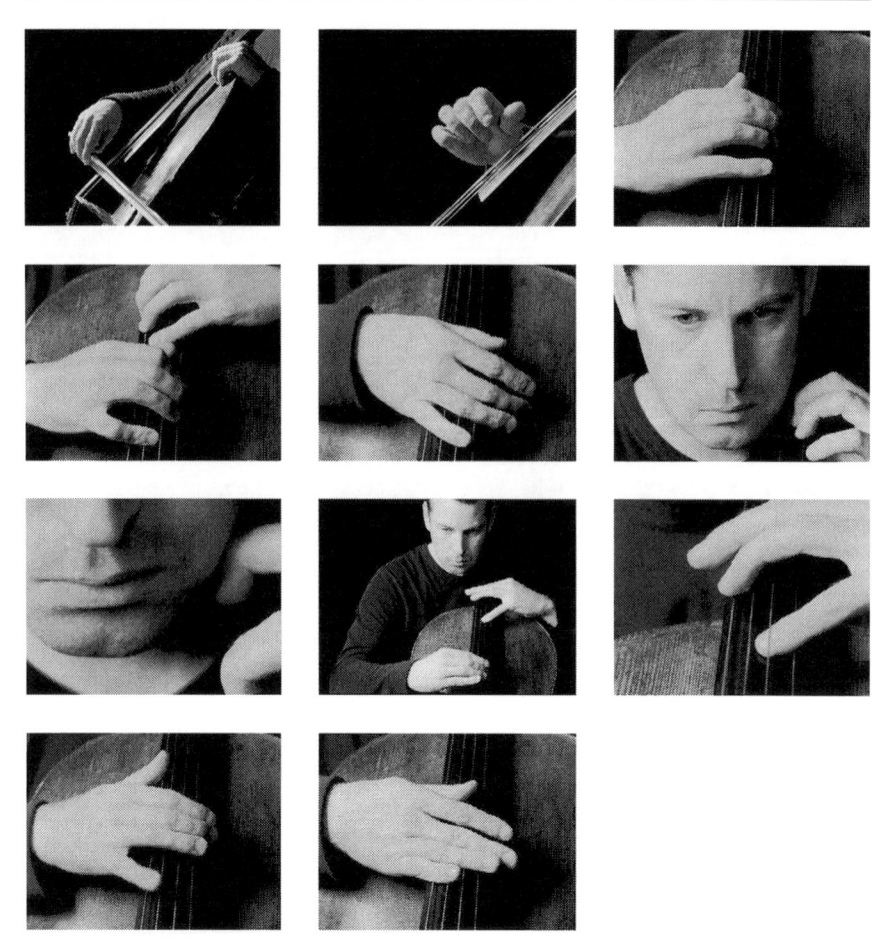

Figure 8.3 Stills from *Foxfire Eins* (16mm film, video, b/w, sound, 10 mins, 2000)

Source: © Jayne Parker. Reproduced by permission of the artist

Notes

1 This exhibition took place between October 2011 and March 2012.
2 For a recent and fascinating collection of articles that approaches the creative process from a Winnicottian perspective see Part 3 of Kuhn, A. (ed.) (2013) *Little Madnesses: Winnicott, Transitional Phenomena and Cultural Experience*. London: I.B. Tauris.
3 Subsequently, Parker produced another text piece and two black and white images that have close affinities with the work under discussion. See Parker, J. (2012) ABC of Music and Film, *Sequence*, no. 3, pp. 4–6.
4 Chris Marker's *La Jetée* (1962) is an interesting example of this connection: the sound of the heartbeat in the film is not originally that of the protagonist, but of the film editor (Jean Ravel). See Cooper, S. (2008) *Chris Marker*. Manchester: Manchester University Press, p. 50.

5   Jayne Parker, *K.* (16mm b/w film, sound, 13 mins, 1989) [on DVD].
6   Richard Serra quoted in Buchloh, B. (1978) Process Sculpture and Film in the Work of Richard Serra, in H. Foster and G. Hughes (eds) (2000) *Richard Serra*. Cambridge, MA: MIT Press, pp. 1–19 (p. 7). For a reproduction of Serra's *Verb List*, see pp. 8–9 of the same article.
7   Richard Serra, *Hand Catching Lead* (16mm b/w film, silent, 3 mins 30 secs, 1968). In this film it is interesting to note the pulse of the action, which again connects with the pulse of reels collecting film, and with the heartbeat.
8   Jayne Parker, *Foxfire Eins* (16mm film, video, b/w, sound, 10 mins, 2000).
9   I am grateful to Sarah Cooper, Patrick ffrench, Vicky Lebeau and Agnieszka Piotrowska for their comments at various stages of working through the ideas in this article; thank you also to Jayne Parker and Vanessa Garden at Tate Publishing, for their kind permission to reproduce the images.

References

Bion, W. R. (2007 [1959]) Attacks on Linking, in *Second Thoughts: Selected Papers on Psycho-Analysis*. London: Karnac, pp. 93–109.
——(2007 [1961] A Theory of Thinking, in *Second Thoughts: Selected Papers on Psycho-Analysis*. London: Karnac, pp. 110–19.
——(1991 [1962]) *Learning from Experience*. London: Karnac.
——(2007 [1970]) *Attention and Interpretation*. London: Karnac.
——(1990 [1973]) *Brazilian Lectures*. London: Karnac.
——(1980 [1977]) *Bion in New York and São Paulo*. Ed. by F. Bion. Perthshire: Clunie Press.
Buchloh, B. (1978) Process Sculpture and Film in the Work of Richard Serra, in H. Foster and G. Hughes (eds) (2000) *Richard Serra*. Cambridge, MA: MIT Press, pp. 1–19.
Buckingham, M. (2011) Matthew Buckingham: Artist, in N. Cullinan (ed.) *Tacita Dean: Film*. London: Tate Publishing, p. 57.
Cooper, S. (2008) *Chris Marker*. Manchester: Manchester University Press.
Dean, T. (2011) Film, in N. Cullinan (ed.) *FILM: Tacita Dean*. London: Tate Publishing, pp. 15–47.
Kant, I. (1929 [1787]) *Immanuel Kant's Critique of Pure Reason*. Trans. by N. K. Smith. London: Macmillan Press.
Krauss, R. (1977) *Passages in Modern Sculpture*. New York: Viking Press.
——(1986) Richard Serra: Sculpture, in H. Foster and G. Hughes (eds) (2000) *Richard Serra*. Cambridge, MA: MIT Press, pp. 99–145.
——(1999) *'A Voyage on the North Sea': Art in the Age of the Post-Medium Condition*. London: Thames & Hudson.
Kuhn, A. (ed.) (2013) *Little Madnesses: Winnicott, Transitional Phenomena and Cultural Experience*. London: I.B. Tauris.
Manovich, L. (2001) *The Language of New Media*. Cambridge, MA: MIT Press.
Parker, J. (2000) Filmography, in *Jayne Parker: Filmworks 79–00*. Exeter: Spacex Gallery, pp. 59–62.
——(2000) Statement, in *Jayne Parker: Filmworks 79–00*. Exeter: Spacex Gallery, p. 7.
——(2011) Jayne Parker: Filmmaker & Artist, in N. Cullinan (ed.) *FILM: Tacita Dean*. London: Tate Publishing, p. 109.
——(2012) ABC of Music and Film, *Sequence*, no. 3, pp. 4–6.

Rees, A. L. (1999) *A History of Experimental Film and Video*. London: British Film Institute.
——(2000) The Artist as Filmmaker: Films by Jayne Parker, 1979–2000, in *Jayne Parker: Filmworks 79–00*. Exeter: Spacex Gallery, pp. 9–30.
Smith, A. (2008) Jayne Parker, in *Jayne Parker: British Artists' Films*. UK, BFI, 1980–2005 [cover essay on DVD].

Chapter 9

Zero Dark Thirty – 'war autism' or a Lacanian ethical act?

Agnieszka Piotrowska

Introduction

Zero Dark Thirty (2012, dir. Kathryn Bigelow) is a controversial film. Most notably, it has been accused both in the popular press and in some scholarly reviewers of justifying torture during the enhanced interrogations scenes of suspected terrorists. In the UK *The Guardian* led the campaign demolishing the film's intellectual credibility, for example in the articles by Glenn Greenwald (2012) and Slavoj Žižek (2013), displaying quite an extraordinary fury in their criticism of Bigelow's film and her main character.

It is my belief that the film did not justify torture but it is not what this essay centres on, although I will touch upon the issue later on. The chapter focuses on the main character, Maya, and her relationship to the events as they unfold. I aim to discuss her ultimate commitment to the project of capturing Osama bin Laden as presented in Kathryn Bigelow's film through the lens of Lacanian notion of the ethical act consisting of 'not giving up on one's desire' and, once the commitment is made, to be able to be faithful to it 'beyond the limit' as Lacan puts it (Lacan [1959–60] 1992: 305) or – 'to the end', in Žižek's words (1989). I will also suggest that Maya's position is also a response to trauma, as, in a way, is that of Antigone, the protagonist under scrutiny in Lacan's (1992) *Seminar VII* on ethics.

In connection with that I will engage, among other writings, with a blog by Dr William Brown[1] and a discussion of the film and Maya's role in it. In his blog, in essence, Brown suggests that Maya's dogged determination to capture Bin Laden as presented in the film, and constructed as such by the director, is a form of autistic behaviour, characterised by a complete lack of empathy. He calls her behaviour and conduct 'war autism'.

I will suggest that far from suffering from any kind of autism, metaphoric or otherwise, the film tracks Maya's metamorphoses from being a victim of the (patriarchal) system to acquiring agency and power of her own, be it within the limits of what she is allowed to choose. I also argue that Maya's position in this situation denotes an interruption and *not* an approval of patriarchal procedural systems that she is a part of.[2] Despite the fact that Maya's 'no' is aimed in the end mostly at shaking the immobilising procedures of the system run by male line managers, it is that 'no' which succeeds in delivering Bin Laden – and possibly restoring some kind of equilibrium in the world, like the act of Antigone, despite the violence inherent in both.

Neither Antigone nor Maya are straightforwardly 'good' in a way that would fit into Christian (or indeed Lévinasian) systems being characterised by loving one's neighbour or by the Infinite Responsibility for the Other in Emmanuel Lévinas (1981). Here, Maya, like Antigone, is indeed 'monstrous', 'inflexible', 'inhuman' – and yet her commitment to the chosen path is also full of dignity and beauty. I will suggest that the reformulation of Lacan's ethics of desire by Alain Badiou ([1993] 2002) offers a helpful theoretical paradigm with which to consider Maya's stance.

'Autistic' or 'not giving up on her desire?'

Brown refers to a number of autistic 'symptoms' as he sees them in the film, namely Maya's alleged inability to form eye contact with the people she encounters, for example, her friend and colleague, Jessica. He suggests 'that Bigelow's film may indeed normalize torture, as well as the mental conditions that allow it (i.e. a lack of empathy), and that this in turn may well influence audiences and their attitudes towards violence'. In order to substantiate his argument, Brown evokes well-known claims by neuroscientists and psychologists, particularly referencing Christian Keysers, who was one of the key figures in the discovery of mirror neurons, and describes his experience with an autistic man, Jerome, as involving Jerome always looking around the room but – significantly – 'never into my eyes' (Keysers, 2011: 18, cited in Brown's blog) and Simon Baron-Cohen, Britain's leading expert on autism. Brown cites the latter's suggestion that there are two stages to empathy: recognition and response. As Baron-Cohen says, 'both are needed, since if you have the former without the latter you haven't empathised at all' (Baron-Cohen, 2011: 12). Brown claims that Maya shows neither. To my mind this is a very problematic trope indeed. Maya's actions do not stem from a lack of empathy but rather, if anything, come directly from it, as I hope to demonstrate. Her determination (no matter what), in Lacanian terms, is an ethical act. In order to discuss it theoretically, I now turn to Lacanian ethics of desire.

The ethics of desire

The issue of ethics versus desire in the work of Jacques Lacan is a complex matter but here I will contain the discussion to *Seminar VII*, given in 1957, entitled *The Ethics of Psychoanalysis*. It is here we find Lacan's notorious and controversial notion: '*ne pas céder sur son désir*',[3] translated as a confusing 'not to give ground relative to one's desire' (Lacan, 1992 [1959–60]: 321). Zupančič (2000) and Žižek (1994 [2005]) translate this instead as simply 'not giving up on one's desire' (Žižek, 1994: 61).

At the heart of this discussion of ethics in *Seminar VII*, there is for Lacan the figure of Antigone (and not Oedipus – although he is mentioned) – the protagonist of Sophocles' play written in 441 BC about the daughter of Oedipus who disobeys the current ruler of her kingdom, Creon, as she insists on performing several times the act of burial of her deceased brother Polyneices, knowing as she does that the act will evoke the fury of Creon and will result in her certain death. In the event, despite the pleas of her family, including her sister Ismene and her fiancé Haemon (who happens to be Creon's son), she carries on with the repeated attempts to bury her brother and, as the punishment, she then is herself buried alive in a cave. When Creon changes his mind too late and breaks the entrance to the cave, Antigone is found already dead, having committed suicide, presumably choosing her agency again over a slow and painful death by starvation. As a direct result of her actions, her fiancé commits suicide too, as does his mother.

When the facts of Sophocles' classic are put this way, it is very clear that the proposition that this is somehow the pinnacle of ethics one should aspire to is hardly attractive to a contemporary reader or spectator. And yet, Antigone, her dazzling beauty in her determination to do the thing she is committed to, has fascinated scholars, poets and writers for centuries. It is far beyond the scope of this essay to offer even the briefest of reviews of literature pertaining to this tragic figure over the centuries. Suffice to say that the play, and Antigone herself, has been a subject of speculations and re-writes by Racine, Hegel, Goethe and many others. She has been appropriated by the feminist icon and the radical thinker Judith Butler (2003). Most recently Bonnie Honig, in her fascinating book *Antigone Interrupted* (2013), offers both a review of the scholarly work to date on Antigone as well as her own interpretations of what she might mean in the history of ideas and defiant stances against male authority. Honig's crucial move is to propose Antigone's act as interrupting a circle of trauma and chaos.

There are very many aspects to the Antigone tale and certainly one could offer a feminist critique demolishing Antigone's power and attractiveness as a role model. After all, here is a woman written by a male writer, who sacrifices herself for another man, her brother, at the hand of yet another man, for no great public cause and to no great effect. Horror and destruction follows. In the end, however, despite the unfashionable nature of somehow noticing the gender divide (the reluctance of course ironically being post-Lacanian),[4] Antigone's '*no!*' vis-à-vis Creon, a 'no' that she is willing to die for, and does, stands for a symbol of a young woman defiantly resisting the masculine narrative that masquerades as a display of power but is revealed as impotent and utterly unable to bring about any kind of resolution. Antigone's act is driven by her *unconscious* desire and love, according to Lacan, which then becomes a conscious decision. Her desire is to bury her brother but also it is a desire to find a closure to the trauma, and to the curse of her land and its people. As such, Lacan claims, anybody's ethical choice will resonate with that of Antigone: 'Even if you are not aware of it, the latent fundamental image of Antigone forms part of your morality' (Lacan, 1992: 284). Let's see what Antigonian traits can be found in Maya.

If the events of 9/11 constitute an unspeakable trauma in which the body of the nation is irrecoverably wounded and altered, Maya's utter commitment to the project of finding and killing Bin Laden could be seen as a forced choice designed to restore some kind of equilibrium in her world. Like the action of Antigone, Maya seeks a final closure to the wars, violence and horror that preceded the sequence of events portrayed in the film. After an initial meek compliance, the quest to find Bin Laden becomes her life mission for which she believes she has been saved. Bigelow thus introduces a notion of destiny in the middle of this very contemporary and un-sentimental film. This is a move that does resonate with the notion of the Greek 'Atë', which I will return to later in this chapter.

As I am evoking Antigone and Lacan's reading of her in a discussion about a film about war, it is important to recall that it is in this seminar that Lacan questions the whole project of 'love thy neighbour' as something to aspire to. If you do anything noble, Lacan warns, there might well be, and usually are, other *unconscious* motives for your actions. It is perhaps just as well to be aware of them, rather than persevere with the idealistic and deceitful proposition of inner virtue.

Lacan sees a notion of polite goodness as unhelpful in defining what an ethical act is. He reminds us that Freud has a problem with the Love Thy Neighbour notion too and quotes from Freud's *Civilisation and its Discontents* (1930) saying that man's innate tendencies lead us to 'evil, aggression, destruction, and thus also to cruelty'. Man, he goes on to say, will use his neighbour: 'to use him sexually without his consent, to appropriate his goods, to humiliate him, to inflict suffering on him, to torture and kill him' (Freud in Lacan [1959–60] 1992: 185).

There is thus a problem, which is both ontological, at the very heart of who we are as so-called civilised people, and the ethical one. If we really follow our instincts, we might end up murdering each other more frequently than we do. But if we *pretend* to be good, this is hopeless too as it leads to further deceptions and lasting corruptions of society through the very notion of charity. Controversially, Lacan criticises philanthropy, giving an example of St Martin as he gives his coat to a beggar. He claims that it is but a gesture that makes no attempt at understanding the heart of the matter here or meeting a real yearning on the part of the beggar:

> We are no doubt touching a primitive requirement in the need to be satisfied there, for the beggar is naked. But perhaps over and above that need to be clothed, he was begging for something else, namely, that Saint Martin either kill him or fuck him. [...] In any encounter there's a big difference in meaning between the response of philanthropy and that of love.
>
> (ibid.: 186)

Lacan suspects any gesture of kindness is often tainted with other unconscious emotions, such as a need to control the Other rather than love him. Lacan comments sarcastically: 'It is a fact of experience that what I want is *the good* of others provided that it remains in the image of my own' (ibid.: 187, my emphasis). In other words, as long as you are the Same and not the Other, I can be good to you. In contrast Lacan proposes a different approach to ethics: if you wilfully betray your readiness to keep discovering what your desire might be, or somehow submit to the demands of 'the service of goods', i.e. societal systems and procedures that destroy meaning, your very *compromise* is unethical. This is what Lacan goes on to say:

> And it is because we know better than those who went before how to recognize the nature of desire, which is at the heart of this experience, that a reconsideration of ethics is possible, that a form of ethical judgment is possible, of a kind that gives this question the force of a Last Judgment: Have you acted in conformity with the desire that is in you? […] Opposed to this pole of desire is traditional ethics.
>
> (Lacan, 1992: 314)

And a few pages later, he repeats again, positioning the psychoanalytic encounter in the same terms:

> I propose then that, from an analytical point of view, the only thing of which *one can be guilty is of having given ground relative to one's desire*. Whether it is admissible or not in a given ethics, that proposition expresses quite well something that we observe in our experience.
>
> (ibid.: 319, my emphasis, noting a different translation of the French as mentioned previously)

In order to be ethical then, one has to discover one's desire first of all and then be able to hold on to it, 'no matter what'.

Antigone and Maya

Lacan ([1959–60] 1992) tells us at the outset that Antigone is beautiful, she

> is made for love rather than hate. In short, she is a really tender and charming little thing, if one is to believe the bidet-water commentary that is typical of the style used by those virtuous writers who write about her.
>
> (ibid.: 262)

However, quite quickly, according to Lacan, Sophocles lets us see Antigone's unfeminine strong mindedness, which frightens the Chorus: in her discussion with Ismene, her sister, she appears quite hostile and stubborn. Lacan points to the Chorus's disdain for Antigone: they cry out a Greek word 'ωμός', which Lacan says one might translate as 'inflexible' (ibid.: 263). But Lacan elaborates that the Greek word ωμός means *more* than just 'inflexible', namely:

> It literally means something uncivilized, something raw. And the word 'raw' comes closest, when it refers to eaters of *raw flesh*. That's the Chorus's point

of view. [...] This is then how the enigma of Antigone is presented to us: she is inhuman.

(ibid.: 263, my emphasis)

A connection therefore exists between the body, 'the raw flesh', the destruction, and Antigone's desire. It is that determination, that 'inhuman' stubbornness performed unexpectedly by a beautiful young woman, that has disturbed the spectators' expectations both vis-à-vis Antigone and indeed Maya.

Maya as Antigone-like figure

Robert Burgoyne (2014, forthcoming) points out rightly that *Zero Dark Thirty* places the body at the centre of its articulation of history, amongst other elements, through Maya being forced to witness the enhanced interrogations carried out by her colleagues on the suspects right at the outset of the movie, following the harrowing audio recordings of those who perished during the horrors of 9/11. These enhanced interrogations were a response to the bodily trauma of 9/11 and the atrocities that followed. On her arrival Maya is immediately subjected to the trauma of witnessing a bodily abuse of the Other, and we as spectators are subjected to that trauma too. Clearly she got a job at the CIA voluntarily, but we do know that when she first arrives at her new posting in Pakistan, it is not her choice ('did you want to come here?' she is asked and she answers – 'no!!'). Far from her being untouched by the tortures she witnesses (as suggested by Brown), Burgoyne points out that Maya's response is immediate, bodily and emotional. It is not that she is incapable of holding the gaze of the Other, it is that she is, to start with, too shocked by what she sees to *want* to look:

> Her hands at times covering her eyes, clutching her jacket, then forcing herself to watch, Maya is foregrounded in the scene's shot patterning: her experience of torture tracks an arc of emotion and performance that progresses from witnessing, to complicity, to coercive agency.
>
> (Burgoyne, 2014, forthcoming)

Burgoyne also focuses on a sequence in which Mayas studies on-screen footage of the endless interrogations in which she observes the torture with a view of learning something that might help the investigation. This is when she discovers the name Abu Ahmed – this is what is repeated over and over again. But in fact it seems that nothing else is discovered through this torture, and it is possible that that name was known before, through more traditional intelligence, as it is put forward to the prisoners. It is not that Bigelow condones torture. She shows us what the institutional procedures have allowed. The noises of disapproval on the parts of the critics vis-à-vis the director rather than the system that produced the procedures are to my mind misplaced. If anything, Bigelow is very careful to show that the actual effectiveness of the technique is at least questionable: the victims do not speak in a coherent way and the torturers, the nice, well-educated American operatives, are so confused and traumatised by the experience that they appear to miss vital information even when it is given.

Brown rightly points to the importance of gaze in the film: the film's narrative is about that which is visible and that which is not. During the tortures, executioners demand speech from those who are tortured; but they ask for more, they want them to *look* at them too. *Zero Dark Thirty* like the play *Antigone* thus continuously links the gaze, the language and *the body*: these happen to stand for Lacan's three registers: the Imaginary, the Symbolic and the Real. It is as early as the seminar I am discussing here, given in 1957, *Seminar VII* (on ethics), that Lacan clearly introduces the importance of *all* three[5] and certainly not just the language alone. We remember that Oedipus in an act of total impotence takes out his eyes so as to vanquish his gaze: this he achieves but the Chorus and the spectators' gaze still torment him despite not seeing the horrors with his eyes. Bigelow makes us see the horrors. To blame her for insisting on the presence of the spectator's gaze is to confuse registers: she makes us look to confront our passive acceptance of the world we live in.

Maya's Atë

Lacan in his discussions of Antigone focuses on the word used in the Sophocles original, namely Atë, which can be translated as 'fate', 'destiny' – and 'human misery'.[6] Lacan interprets Atë as a narrow range within which to operate and within this range it is important to find out what one's desire is and then to follow it to the end. Not everybody must make such a dramatic choice: 'One does or does not approach Ate, and when one approaches it, it is because of something that is linked to a beginning and a chain of events' (ibid.: 264). Antigone's Atë is that she is the daughter of Jocasta and Oedipus, the parents who committed unwillingly murders and incest, and that both of her brothers took part in a war against each other and that they are now both dead. This she cannot undo. But she can decide what to do faced with Creon's unreasonable edict.

What is then Maya's Atë and her destiny in *Zero Dark Thirty*? We know nothing about her background at all, apart that she joined the CIA very young. One could suggest that she shares her Atë with the rest of us post 9/11 – and particularly with those who were born in the United States: a long shadow of that tragedy that has cast darkness over the contemporary history ever since. The film reminds the viewer what the world we live in now entails: wars all over the world in the name of peace, secret areas in which people are tortured in our name, unexpected terrorist attacks and countless deaths.

Maya's initial conversations with the female friend reveal that she has nobody in her life but work. She has no boyfriend, no lover, no friends, no hobby. This is what William Brown sees as further proof of her 'war autism', her lack of empathy. Indeed even at the outset perhaps Maya already begins to appear a little 'inhuman', a little 'inflexible' like Antigone.

In Sophocles' *Antigone,* or rather perhaps Lacan's reading of it, there is a moment when she first of all laments her dead brother and her fate ('atë') weeping 'like a bird', simply a hurt young woman bemoaning her bad fortune. The moment of metamorphosis into the unmovable 'monstrous' comes after it becomes clear that Creon will not shift his position – Antigone's forced choice is a response to the immovability of the male ruler and his procedures, as Shaviro would say. When it comes to it, the forced choice is a simple one: to give in or to continue to the end. In *Zero Dark Thirty* the key moment comes when Jessica, Maya's friend and colleague, also devoted to her work but perhaps in a more ordinary human way, gets blown up by a (male) suicide bomber. It is the moment in which Maya, staring at the blank computer screen, is waiting for a reply that never comes, which marks her turning. It is an absence of either body or the language or indeed the gaze that makes her then more than inflexible: in her pursuit of her goal – she becomes 'monstrous', like Antigone. Maya does not lay down her life for her cause, meaning she does not die in the film, but she has no life outside her mission. There is also no doubt at all that she would have given her life in a literal sense if that was what had been called for. We do witness her car being shot at – she carries on, to the end.

Maya's agency perhaps lacks the glamour of Antigone's undertaking as it mostly consists of her attempts to subvert procedural apathy of the patriarchal organisation she works for. To this end she behaves completely outside the accepted norms of institutional conduct, threatening and even abusing her exclusively male bosses and demanding she is given a freer reign. A female colleague draws her attention to the vital piece of information but when violence is actually carried out, it is always conducted by men in Bigelow's film. Once Maya's dogged determination succeeds and the order is given to instigate the attack on Bin Laden's den, she again is alone with a group of military men to whom she says: 'you will kill Bin Laden for me'. Her apparent bodily fragility and beauty, like that of Antigone, is in Bigelow's film juxtaposed with the physical roughness and strength of the men who are also somehow confused and uncertain as to what they are doing and why, despite having that procedural power still vested in them. The contrast between the (masculine) physical strength and the (feminine) mental strength and intellectual ability is striking in the film.

Before moving to the final section of this paper, it is perhaps worth mentioning that the Lacanian call of not giving up on one's desire can create moral difficulties, which Žižek theorised as a possibility of being ethical but immoral at the same time, as at the diagram below (Figure 9.1) demonstrates. I have cited and discussed this conundrum elsewhere (Piotrowska, 2012, 14) in connection with the documentary film project.

Žižek says that:

> the saint is ethical (he does not compromise his desire) and moral (he considers the Good of others) whereas the scoundrel is immoral (he violates moral norms) and unethical (what he is after is not desire but pleasures and profits, so he lacks any firm principles).

(2005 [1994]: 67)

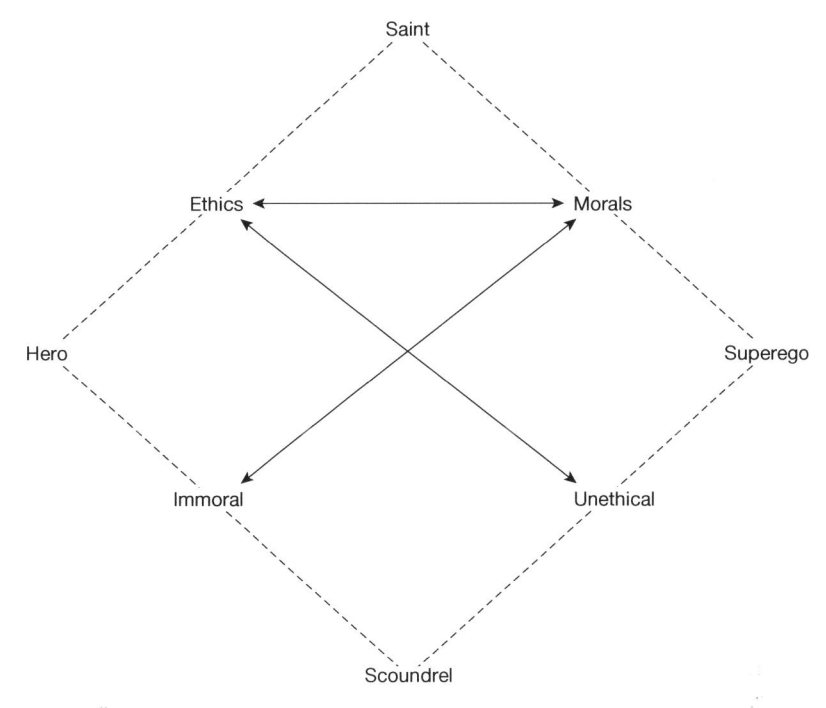

Figure 9.1 Žižek's diagram
Source: Žižek (2005: 67)

It is here that one could wonder again whether Maya's conduct and that indeed of Antigone was moral as well as ethical, given that their monstrous 'inflexibility' does cost innocent lives (in Antigone's case: the fiancé, the sister, her future mother-in-law, etc.).

It is really Alain Badiou in his *Ethics: an Essay on the Understanding of Evil* ([1993] 2002) who presents a different approach, which by his own account draws from Lacan's dictum but is clearer and more exigent. He is very insistent that 'there can be no ethics in general, but only an ethic of singular truths, and thus an ethic relative to a particular situation' (Badiou, [1993] 2002: vi), although he did accept that one has to take into account the network of relationships it sustains. Badiou develops a list of criteria that define an 'event', a moment of revelation for the 'I' when a decision to act is taken. One of these criteria is a universal possibility of joining 'the event' that would differentiate it from a possible 'simulacrum'. So it was St Paul who decided to be the orator for Christianity after his revelation on the road to Damascus – and anybody else could have had this revelation. One could argue that both Maya and Antigone could fulfil Badiou's criterion: there are no *a priori* exclusions in either of their decisions. Badiou's ethic is a helpful and clear development of Lacanian ethics but its further discussion is beyond the scope of this paper.

The beauty versus the horror

But there is something else going on here, both in *Antigone* and in *Zero Dark Thirty*. It is the main protagonist's gender, her youth and, most importantly, her beauty: the monstrous is also beautiful, which confuses and fascinates the cinema spectator in the twenty-first century as well as *Antigone*'s Chorus and no doubt Ancient Greece's audiences. Lacan is very careful *not* to invest Antigone's commitment to her cause with any libidinal undertones, which would have been such an easy move because of her origins. But other scholars have wondered about it. Critchley (2007), in his discussion of Lacan's notion of sublimation in *Seminar VII*, makes two points: the first one is in relation to one's (sexual) desire, which instead of being repressed is sublimated – somehow given an expression other than a sexual one. The second point is to do with beauty, which is inherent in sublimation of desire – at least in *Seminar VII*:

> What is the moral goal of psychoanalysis? 'The moral goal of psychoanalysis consists in putting the subject in relation to its unconscious desire.' This is why the sublimation is so important, for it is the realisation of such desire.
> (Critchley, 2007: 73)

In *Seminar VII* the person who sublimates her trauma through an act, which is both beautiful and ethical, is Antigone. In *Zero Dark Thirty* Maya's energies are sublimated into her project too with no space for anything else. There is no physical sexual love in the lives of either of these protagonists. Instead, they engage with the bodily ugliness and horror of the war waged by men. Susan L. Carruthers (2013) in her *Cineaste* article makes an observation that there is the 'Old Testament zeal' in Maya's work (ibid.: 52). But then, without referencing any theory or psychoanalysis, she makes a point that there is something 'latently sexual about Maya's relentless quest for her man' (ibid.: 52). And when the final moment comes after the hectic heist Carruthers again connects this to Maya's supposed latent sexuality: 'When she tilts her head back, tears trickling, after the body bag's climactic unzipping, the scene is suggestively postcoital: lips apart, hair tangled, chest heaving. All passion spent' (ibid.: 52).

The above is not how I responded to the scene but the point is that Maya's energy, perhaps her libidinal energy, is present in the film and sublimated into her mission. The scene of Maya identifying the body is anticlimactic but meaningful. It is a scene in which Bigelow *manipulates* the gaze through withholding the sight of the body. In the construction of the film that gaze is not ours to hold: it is Maya's.

Robert Burgoyne sees Maya's beauty as disturbing 'the usual operative models' in the genre. For me it also resonates with Honig's notion of a creative interruption. An 'interruption' might carry with it more readily also positive meanings – that of a rupture which disturbs and interrupts the status quo thus bringing about generative effects not least because of subverting the expectations of gender, class, race – and procedures. Its openness, as named by Burgoyne below, I see as precisely such an opportunity. I cite Burgoyne's lengthy quotation on *Zero Dark Thirty* because it could also be applied to *Antigone*, both the play and the character, whose impact on thinkers, writers and our attitude to violence, commitment and ethics has been so immense over the centuries, and so very difficult to quantify. It is this disturbing and interrupting quality of the work and of the female characters, that Burgoyne comments on here:

> The character's youth and sculpted beauty troubles the paradigm of purposive violence; her striking 'whiteness,' for example, creates a disturbing and dramatic contrast of skin tones and textures during the interrogation scenes, producing a visual overtone, an Eisensteinian conflict, that is not easily accommodated by genre codes. At the same time, her beauty challenges the easy notion that violence is deforming and dehumanizing. Instead, the effect of violence on both character and history is left open, unresolved in the film's narrative program.[7]
>
> (Burgoyne, 2014, forthcoming)

Finally there is also the issue of Maya's face, at the very end of the film: a face for me not expressing any 'passion spent' after a sexual encounter but rather a realisation that her success might offer a closure of a kind but has carried with it death and further mourning too. This is reminiscent of Béla Balázs' writings about the importance of the close-ups in feature film:

> The soul of a landscape or indeed any milieu presents itself differently at different points on its surface. In human beings, too, the eyes are more expressive than the neck or shoulders, and a close up of the eyes irradiates more sound than the entire body in long shot. The director's task is to discover the eyes of a landscape. Only in close ups of these details will he grasp the soul of its totality: its mood.
>
> (Balázs, 2010 [1923]: 44)

It is Maya's final close-up, reflective, tired, tearful but defiant, which defines what this film is about: an act that is tragic but ethical.

Final remarks

My point in this chapter has been that Maya's commitment to her cause is not engendered by her alleged lack of empathy but rather her conscious and stubborn commitment, however problematic and controversial it might be, to her chosen path. That commitment could be theorised as her 'not giving up on her desire' in Lacanian terms, thus constituting an ethical act. Maya's desire is fuelled by conscious and unconscious mechanisms, which the film hints at but does not spell out. What a Lacanian psychoanalytical reading can bring into a discussion of this film and others is a reminder of the unknowingness that is also a part of the human condition.[8] There is a lack of reasonableness about Maya, which disturbs and interrupts the viewers' accepted norms, particularly male viewers, and from that stand point alone one could argue that it comes down in a line descending from Antigone, another inflexible stubborn and beautiful woman rejecting the rules and procedures of the patriarchal systems of her time in ways that some might view as immoral.

My very final thought is that it is a mistake to confine psychoanalysis to the particular structuralist readings of it that influenced the film theory post 1968 and that privileged language and identification. Psychoanalysis has always put the body as a crucial focus of its interrogations. What Lacan reminds us of is that the Real, the body, and our desires, conscious or otherwise, come from a complicated mixture of places, including our heritage, our place in history and society, but also out ability to respond to our 'atë'.

Zero Dark Thirty is a decisive gesture; a 'gesture' being a term describing film, that Jennifer Barker deploys in *The Tactile Eye* (2009: 78). Despite its universal quality, what the film gestures to me is different from what it has gestured to William Brown or Susan Carruthers, for example, for a number of reasons, but certainly because we bring into the reading of it not only our scholarly experience, and the experience of watching films, but also our conscious and unconscious knowledge of the world, which includes our bodily position in it, including gender. It is not necessarily identification (Metz) or empathy (Barker) that the film might evoke but rather our transferential relationship to its body, or 'its narrative program', as Burgoyne above suggests, through our bodily response and our unconscious, which will contribute to it.

Notes

1   http://wjrcbrown.wordpress.com (accessed 29 November 2013).
2   For an excellent discussion of these procedures in the film, please see Stephen Shaviro's blog: www.shaviro.com/Blog/?p=1114#comments
3   It appears that Lacan doesn't actually use this kind of invective but instead says: 'La seule chose dont on puisse être coupable, c'est d'avoir cédé sur son désir' [the only thing you can be guilty of is to have given up on your desire – my translation]. See J. Lacan, *Le séminaire livre VII, L'éthique de la psychanalyse*, Seuil, 1986, p. 329.
4   Judith Butler's idea of gender's performativity in *Gender Trouble* has its origins in *Seminar XX* in which Lacan proposes that gender is not biologically determined.
5   Lacan's interest on the body grows until in *Seminar XX* it is his key focus of interrogation (a fact completely ignored during the heyday of post-68 psychoanalytically influenced film theory and today).
6   Atë can also be translated as a delusion that leads to a disaster – this note was kindly given to me by Richard Seaford, Professor of Classic and Ancient History at the University of Exeter, in our discussions on Antigone.
7   See Richard Dyer (1997) for an insightful analysis of how 'whiteness' functions as a complex sign in film.
8   It is perhaps coincidental, and again unfashionable to point out, but the majority of the critics appalled by the film and Maya and cited by Greenwald in his piece mentioned previously are all male: Andrew Sullivan, Adam Sewer, Jay Rosen, Michael Tomasky,

not to mention Slavoj Žižek who somehow has a blind spot for this Antigone-like figure, Lacanian though he is. I also choose to ignore here the very unfortunate use of the notion of rape as both a metaphor and comparison by Brown and Žižek in the works cited.

References

Badiou, A. ([1993] 2002) *Ethics: An Essay on the Understanding of Evil*. Trans. by P. Hallward. London and New York: Verso.
Balázs, B. (2010 [1924]) *Early Film Theory: Visible Man and The Spirit of Film*. Ed. Erica Carter. New York: Berghahn Books.
Barker, J. (2009) *The Tactile Eye*. Berkeley: University of California Press.
Baron-Cohen, S. (2011) *Zero Degrees of Empathy*. London: Penguin.
Burgoyne, R. (forthcoming) in D. LaRocca (ed.), *The Philosophy of War Films*. Lexington: University of Kentucky Press.
Butler, J. (1990) *Gender Trouble*. London & New York: Routledge.
Butler, J. (2003) *Antigone's Claim: Kinship Between Life and Death*. New York: Columbia University Press.
Carruthers, S. L. (2013) 'Zero Dark Thirty'. *Cineaste*, 38 (2 Spring), 50–53.
Critchley, S. (2007) *Infinitely Demanding: Ethics of Commitment, Politics of Resistance*. London & New York: Verso.
Dyer, R. (1997) *White: Essays on Race and Culture*. London and New York: Routledge.
Freud, S. (1915) Observations on Transference-Love (Further Recommendations on the Technique of Psycho-Analysis III) in *Standard Edition of the Complete Psychological Works of Sigmund Freud. Volume XII*. Trans. by J. Strachey. London: Hogarth Press & the Institute of Psychoanalysis, pp. 157–71.
Greenwald, G. (2012) 'Zero Dark Thirty: CIA Hagiography, Pernicious Propaganda'. *The Guardian*, December 14. www.theguardian.com/commentisfree/2012/dec/14/zero-dark-thirty-cia-propaganda
Honig, B. (2013) *Antigone Interrupted*. Cambridge: Cambridge University Press.
Keysers, C. (2011) *The Emphatic Brain*. Munich: Social Brain Press.
Lacan, J. (1992 [1959–60]) *Seminar VII. The Ethics of Psychoanalysis 1959–1960*. Trans. by D. Potter. London and New York: Routledge.
Lacan, J. (1998 [1981]) *Seminar XI. The Four Fundamental Concepts of Psychoanalysis*. Miller, J-A. (ed.) Trans. by A. Sheridan. London & New York: W. W. Norton.
Lévinas, E. (1981) *Otherwise than Being*. Trans. by A. Lingis. The Hague: Martinus Nijhoff Publishers.
Metz, C. (1988 [1982]) *Psychoanalysis and Cinema: The Imaginary Signifier*. Trans. by C. Britton, A. Williams, B. Brewester & A. Guzzetti. London: Macmillan.
Piotrowska, A. (2011) Animating the Real – A Case Study. *Animation: An Interdisciplinary Journal*, 6(3) (November 2011), 335–353.
Piotrowska, A. (2012) 'The Conman and I: A Case Study in Transference in Documentary.' *Studies in Documentary Film*, 6(1), 15–29.
Piotrowska, A. (2014) *Psychoanalysis and Ethics in Documentary Film*. London and New York: Routledge.
Žižek, S. (1989) *The Sublime Object of Ideology*. London: Verso.
Žižek, S. (2005 [1994]) *The Metastases of Enjoyment: Six Essays on Woman and Causality*. New York: Verso.

Žižek, S. (2013). 'Kant and Sade: The Ideal Couple'. Accessed October, 2013. www.egs.edu/faculty/slavoj-zizek/articles/kant-and-sade-the-ideal-couple/

Zupančič, A. (2011 [2000]) *Ethics of the Real: Kant and Lacan*. London and New York: Verso.

Blogs and websites

http://wjrcbrown.wordpress.com/ (last accessed 29 November 2013).

www.shaviro.com/Blog/?p=1114#comments (last accessed 28 November 2013).

www.theguardian.com/commentisfree/2012/dec/14/zero-dark-thirty-cia-propaganda (last accessed 5 December 2013).

www.theguardian.com/commentisfree/2013/jan/25/zero-dark-thirty-normalises-torture-unjustifiable (last accessed 9 December 2013).

Chapter 10

An atheist's guide to feminine jouissance

On *Black Swan* and the other satisfaction

Ben Tyrer

Black Swan (Darren Aronofsky, 2010) is a film clearly concerned with the body and embodied experience: to take even the most superficial examples, before she steps out of bed in the morning, Nina cracks and flexes her feet; after an injury, a physiotherapist plunges her hand deep under Nina's ribs; and so on. As such, the prevailing doxa might suggest that (Lacanian) psychoanalysis would have little to say about *Black Swan*. Indeed, the philosophical turn in Film Studies seemed to be predicated, in part, precisely *on* that claim and the rejection of Lacan. Lacanian film theory has – just as Thomas Leroy says of *Swan Lake* – been *done to death*: every good film-philosopher knows what it involves and why it is fundamentally flawed. This may (or may not) be the case, but theorists such as Joan Copjec, Slavoj Žižek and Todd McGowan have demonstrated that there remains the possibility of a properly Lacanian film-philosophy that engages with the complexities of Lacan's own work and remains sensitive to the exigencies of the cinema: it is to such a project that this chapter aims to contribute by engaging film and theory in a mutually informing relationship.

We are all familiar with the one I might call "the good old Lacan of time immemorial", the Lacan of the *mirror stage* and the *unconscious structured like a language*; but to this, we must add "another Lacan", the Lacan who claims, for example, that "being is the jouissance of the body as such" and who presents new possibilities for embodied encounters in both psychoanalysis and the cinema (1998: 6). We should not, however, treat these two – the *Other Lacan* and the *Good Old Lacan* – as a binary pair between whom there can be no rapport; they exist on the continuum of his theoretical work and its development. But it must also be recognised that the concept of jouissance takes on an increasingly important role in Lacan's thinking and occupies a central position in neo-Lacanian film-philosophy. As such, Néstor Braunstein observes that, in *Encore*, Lacan characterises jouissance as "substance", and it is furthermore – Braunstein notes – "the 'substance' with which we work in psychoanalysis" (2003: 102).[1] And so we could, I suggest, even go a step further to consider "jouissance" as being the very *body* of Lacanian psychoanalysis itself.

With this in mind, *Black Swan* presents an opportunity to explore psychoanalysis and the body, and in doing so I will suggest ways of reading the film and approaching its staging of femininity through different modes of *enjoyment*. Furthermore, considering the film in terms of jouissance allows us – following Kate Ince's exhortation that we "bring bodies back in" to psychoanalytic film criticism (2011) – to *bring Lacan back in* to a discourse on psychoanalysis and embodiment in the cinema. Like Thomas's interpretation of *Swan Lake*, the film *Black Swan* can make Lacanian psychoanalysis *visceral* and *real* by compelling us to recognise the "jouissance of the body" once more. As such, this chapter will explore how the film takes us around the types of enjoyment described by Lacan's Graph of Sexuation: on the masculine side, the dissatisfaction of phallic jouissance in Nina's training regime, the image of a corresponding (infinitely satisfying) Other jouissance that is embodied by Lily and promoted by Thomas, and how this manifests itself as the masturbatory jouissance of Nina's fantasies; and then, on the feminine side, the jouissance immanent to embodied experience, the enjoyment Nina derives from dancing – and thus becoming – the Black Swan.

A libidinal economy of the phallus

My starting point is the contention that *Black Swan* presents Nina as caught within the closed circuit of phallic jouissance in what Lacan describes as masculine structure. The usual proviso should be offered at this point: that these terms pertain to *logical*, rather than biological, categories and so the anatomical "sex" of subjects here is not necessarily what is at stake. Instead, my reading of *Black Swan* engages with the ways that subjects organise their enjoyment in either a "masculine" or a "feminine" way, and – for most of the film – Nina is very clearly the subject of phallic jouissance. She strives and strives, and she is pushed on and on by Thomas and by her peers. Her mother tells her that she is the most dedicated dancer in the company. The film emphasises, over and over, Nina's commitment to her course and to her cause. And this cause is, of course, the Lacanian *objet a*: the object-cause of desire, the gravitational centre of the phallic orbit.

For Lacan, this is the path that characterises phallic jouissance, or the enjoyment of masculine structure. Masculinity, Lacan defines with two logical formulae – "all x Phi x" and "there is one x not Phi x" – that determine "man's" set, and the mathemes that represent "his" jouissance: $\$ \rightarrow a$, the vector of fantasy, and the signifier Φ that supports it.[2] I have elsewhere examined the differing ontologies suggested by a Lacanian theory of sets, so here it will suffice to say that masculinity presents a sort of "closed set" (an All) that is determined by an Exception, which defines it from the outside.[3] What is important here, in relation to my reading of *Black Swan*, is the kind of jouissance provided by such a structure and, crucially, the role of *fantasy*. Man's enjoyment is that which is permitted to him – as a "castrated" subject, alienated in the Symbolic order – by the phallic function. Man is a set where the phallic function is valid ("all x Phi x") and so his jouissance is considered "phallic": it is jouissance in the grip of the primacy of the phallus. However, there is also one for whom the phallic function is *not* valid. The other formula ("there is one x not Phi x") means that there is some x who is not subject to the phallic function, who refuses castration and thus delimits the All. This is the primal father who is able to *enjoy fully* (Lacan 1998: 79). Phallic jouissance is thus sustained by the fantasmatic ideal of a non-castrasted Exception who has access to greater jouissance. Man *qua* castrated is haunted by the sense of another, better satisfaction that insists upon and through his fantasy.

And it is here that we return to Nina. Nina's libidinal economy is organised around this phallic phantasm, this ideal (and *unobtainable*) end.[4] She certainly derives a satisfaction from her work but it is a paltry jouissance – to use Bruce Fink's term – compared with the full jouissance to which she aspires. For example, when she is prevented from finishing her practice dance for Thomas, Nina feels compelled, on returning home, to repeat the routine: to spin round and round, chasing the enjoyment that she thinks she *should* have. When it is denied to her again – as she painfully cracks her toe during the workout – Nina constructs a *fantasy* of reaching completion by lying to Thomas that she finished the routine. She is spurred on by the idea that if she can just achieve a flawless performance, then she can achieve this flawless, exceptional satisfaction that the phallic libidinal economy promises to her. She repeats throughout the film that she aims for *perfection*. She tells Thomas that all she wants is to be perfect: echoing Fink's characterisation of the other jouissance, access to which he describes as 'the fantasy that we could attain such *perfect*, total, (…) spherical, satisfaction' (2004: 157). Nina's striving for perfection is thus a striving for the jouissance that would match her ideal and of which the phallic jouissance of her quotidian experience offers her only a glimpse, a fraction.

The fallibility of phallic jouissance

As Nina practises for her performance as the Swan Queen, she visibly strains every muscle and sinew in her body, pushing herself further and further as if she could touch or embrace this perfect jouissance physically. However, the crucial Lacanian insight here is that such satisfaction is, strictly speaking, impossible. This is because phallic jouissance relates to *objet a*, which keeps the subject in perpetual motion, searching always for what cannot be attained. It is therefore characterised by *failure* because, Lacan insists, 'The object is a failure. The essence of the object is failure' (1998: 58). And so, for Nina here the libidinal economy can function only in a permanent state of (dis)satisfaction. Nina has very clearly given up a certain portion of her enjoyment to the Other, to the phallic regime of the ballet (which is to say, she is subject to *castration*): she leads an ascetic life, focused solely on her dance (and therefore on the promise of a better jouissance). She is reduced to phallic jouissance, which is limited by that remainder which forever escapes her grasp (*objet a*), and for this reason there is no way in which the enjoyment available to her can make up for the sacrifice she has made, no way in which she can overcome the inadequacy of phallic jouissance.

Indeed, following Bruce Fink, we should try to hear "phallic" as "fallible", and thus to recognise the *fallibility of phallic jouissance* as an experience that must necessarily disappoint the subject (2004: 159). Nina scrutinises each gesture and pose of her choreography, giving the sense that she can only be satisfied by *perfectly embodying* every step. Nina's aim, therefore, may well be a flawless jouissance but, enjoying through masculine structure, her object can only ever be *objet a* and so she is consigned continually to miss her target. Phallic jouissance does not measure up to Nina's expectations of enjoyment: this inadequacy is felt in relation to the supposed other jouissance, of *perfection*. Indeed, the gulf between the fallible and this infallible jouissance can be felt in the repeated insistence from Thomas that she go through her routine *again* and *again*. Here, the Lacanian ear should hear the call, "*encore*": the demand to repeat what Jane Gallop calls "the phallic performance" in order to reach *something more* (1982: 35). This excess, this encore, persists as an ideal for Nina that her own performance can lead to *another satisfaction*.

The other jouissance is the jouissance of the other

The other, better satisfaction posited by phallic jouissance finds its body in a figure of the Other. Phallic jouissance is haunted by the persistent sense that there is an Other who *really* enjoys. For Nina, this exceptional "one" is Lily: who lives life with an apparent passion and ease seemingly unavailable to Nina. Therefore, to paraphrase Žižek, what really bothers Nina about Lily is her *enjoyment*.[5] Nina imputes to her an excessive jouissance: she appears like a stain of enjoyment in Nina's world. This is mostly clearly exemplified in the recurring motif of Lily's laughter, which – in Nina's mode – we can interpret as a bodily sign of her special enjoyment. For example, when Thomas introduces Nina at a party as his new prima ballerina, she accepts the applause but cutting through this is *Lily's laughter*. The camera shows Lily from Nina's point of view, her hand on the chest of her companion; she is laughing at his *bon mot*, oblivious to her surroundings. Her voice, her smile, her gesture – all signs of her jouissance – thus impinge on Nina, diminishing *her* satisfaction at what should be the crowning moment of her career.

As Jacques-Alain Miller suggests, jouissance imputed to the Other is the source of antipathy: Nina's resentment of Lily (*qua* Other) is a "hatred of the particular way, of the Other's own way, of experiencing jouissance" (1994: 79). Indeed, this structure is built into the narrative of *Swan Lake* itself: Odette is perpetually haunted by that Other figure, Odile, the one who spoils her enjoyment, and has access to another, *better jouissance*. This schema is, in turn, worked into the narrative of *Black Swan* as the rivalry between Nina and Lily grows. For instance, after Nina oversleeps, she is forced to go through her preparation while watching Lily dance *her* part. Lily glides effortlessly through Nina's own choreography – her enjoyment clear to see – and Thomas responds with praise more enthusiastic than he gives to Nina. Lily's Black Swan seems to perform a jouissance that Nina cannot access, and so her resentment of Lily – *as enjoying Other* – grows. The phallic libidinal economy therefore gives rise to Other jouissance as its *beyond*, and, as is so often the case, *Black Swan* tends to figure this "beyond" as *Woman*.

Woman and God's jouissance

If, for Lacan, "Woman" does not exist, then the image Nina has of Lily constitutes her *as* Woman, *the one who really would exist*. This figure is promoted by Thomas throughout the film. He implores Nina to watch the way Lily moves: effortlessly, imprecisely. As if to emphasise this, Lily – all in black, her hair flowing freely, contrasting to Nina's tightly wound bun – spins too quickly and steps into her partner. They laugh. Nina studies her intently. Thomas thus encourages this perception of Lily as Woman, as enjoying Other and, moreover, pushes Nina to accept the role (as it is clear he has done to Beth – his last prima ballerina – in the past). This position is his *little princess*: the one who can perform satisfaction satisfactorily for him. Indeed, Thomas even goes so far as to describe Beth to Nina as *perfect*: a letter touching Nina's own enjoyment and forcing the circulation of her libidinal economy.

Nina's jouissance is thus related to Thomas and to Beth. Here I will note that, while the usefulness of an outmoded term such as "frigidity" is questionable, my approach in this instance is determined by the film itself, which repeatedly labels Nina as frigid. It is important to recognise, moreover, that it is primarily *for Thomas* that Nina appears "frigid". Crucial therefore to Nina's relationship with him is Lacan's question of how frigidity can be "mobilized" (2007: 616). Geneviève Morel explains that, "any hope of a cure through lovemaking, which would imply that frigidity can be reduced to sexual frustration, would be futile ([what Lacan refers to as] 'the usual failure of the dedicated efforts of the most desired partner'" (2002: 87). Whether Thomas is, in fact, *the most desired partner* (or simply a rapist) is not necessarily clear, but what *is* clear is that his *dedicated efforts* – which is to say, his repeated attempts to push Nina into sexual action – bring about the *usual failure* in overcoming what appears to him as her "frigidity".

This is most apparent when Thomas takes Nina back to his apartment. Here, he quizzes her on her sexual history, and Nina's response is defensive and embarrassed; it seems that she cannot bear even to talk of "jouissance", such is her "frigidity". He pushes her, bullies her, but she persists in silence. This, first of all, resonates with the image of a woman's jouissance as Other jouissance, where Lacan suggests that women experience it, but cannot say anything about it.[6] This is a defining feature of the phallic perspective on the Other (sex): the masculine subject imputes a special enjoyment to the Other and then insists that the Other must tell him all about it! The fact that Nina will not – *cannot* – tell him about spurs him into "therapeutic" action, as he prescribes his most potent "somatic" cure for her "frigidity". He tells her, like some professor of jouissance, that he has "homework" for her: to go away and touch herself. That this "cure" will not work becomes clear through the repeated – *and failed* – attempts Nina makes to touch herself and so to "touch" this enjoyment, *which cannot be awoken simply on command*.

What is most notable about this scene is the sense that the jouissance involved in Thomas's conversation with Nina is *all his*. It is *Thomas* who "gets off" on talking about getting off; the whole scene is articulated around *his* enjoyment and his attempts to paint Nina with it too. And if we consider Thomas as Leroy/*le roi*/ the King, then it is only a small step from here to the figure of *God*. He is the Father as Exception: as Lacan notes, "Christianity naturally ended up inventing a God such that he is the one who gets off (*jouit*)" (1998: 76). Masculine structure is, as Marcus Pound suggests, therefore *ontotheological* (2008: 109). In positing an Other jouissance, phallic jouissance insists upon a theology of being by conceptualising in the beyond a "Supreme Being" who enjoys ("there is one *x* not Phi *x*"). Therefore, it is Thomas that takes a masculine position, here and throughout the film, as the One who enjoys: a position situating him *as God*. But he is a God that awakens only himself, and so it is tempting to recast this apartment scene – *pace* Miller – as "Woman and God's Jouissance".

Thomas thus puts himself in the place where, as Lacan suggests, "there is something we cannot enjoy. Call it the jouissance of God, with the meaning included in that of sexual jouissance" (2005: 61). And, moreover, Thomas attempts to constitute Nina as Woman, a partner to him in this jouissance, in a mode where the sexual relation *would* exist and they would both access full satisfaction together: he and she taking exceptional places as God on one side and Woman on the "other". Thomas thus advocates a sort of *pousse-à-la-femme* for Nina, pushing her towards "Woman". And conversely, it seems that she comes to see him *as* God, the One with whom she must establish a special relationship in order to reach perfect jouissance. This puts us in the realm of the mystic.

The ecstasy of Saint Lily

For Lacan, it is the mystic who has access to a special jouissance. He remarks that materialist philosophers in his audience were surprised that "I situated a certain Other between man and woman that certainly seemed like the good old God of time immemorial" (1998: 68). He explains that, unlike the theologians, *he* cannot do without God *because he deals with the Other*. He informs his audience, "So today, I am going to show you in what sense the good old God exists" (ibid.). The God that exists is, as I have already suggested, the Supreme Being of the masculine ontotheology, and that Lacan discusses in relation to Woman and *jouissance beyond the phallus*. This passage from *Encore* is the source of the most devastating misreading of the theory of sexuation and must therefore – as Lacan himself notes – be approached with great caution.[7] Crucially, he adds, "This Other (...) must have some relationship with what appears of the other sex" (ibid.: 69): the key to understanding Lacan here is to understand that he is discussing *what appears, from the masculine pole, of the other sex as "Other sex"*. That is to say, we must understand Lacan's discussion of the mystic's jouissance – even against some of his own declarations – as a manifestation of *masculine structure*: a conflation of the image of "Woman" with the position of the One. This is the key point for my approach to questions of God, Woman and jouissance through Lacan and *Black Swan*.

The theological dimension of Other jouissance resides in the fact that it persists at the level of *belief*: Nina believes that Beth had it, Lily has it, and that it can be reached through a relationship with "God". It is this dimension that Lacan emphasises when he notes, in relation to mysticism, "you are all going to be convinced that I believe in God", before adding, "I believe in the jouissance of woman insofar as it is extra" (ibid.: 77). Approached in this way, I suggest, we can frame his discussion of the mystic as belief in *Woman*'s enjoyment that exceeds the phallic realm. And it is this belief that Thomas uses to push Nina towards mystical experience. Indeed, *qua* "God", Thomas advocates the kind of mystical jouissance Lacan positions with the Other, and an experience that centres on *Lily*. He explains to Nina that perfection is not just about control, but also letting go, which can lead to *transcendence* (although, he adds, very few are capable). As Thomas's instructions make clear, the ontotheology of masculine structure in *Black Swan* means that we are dealing with the transcendent: *a going beyond*. Indeed, Lacan refers to the father function/God as that "*at least one* who transcends that which takes the phallic function" (2011: 106). And so we can say that "His" partner (Woman) is also one who transcends into Other jouissance. The very few who achieve this transcendence are therefore, in the Lacanian framework, *the mystics*.

Lacan's favoured example of this "Woman" is Teresa of Ávila, whose intensely orgasmic encounter with the Divine is rendered in Bernini's statue of *The Ecstasy of Saint Teresa*. Her enjoyment, he suggests, is the jouissance at "the God face" of the Other (1998: 77): the divine, Other jouissance. The mystical experience therefore suggests an enjoyment that transcends quotidian satisfaction; it points to what Lacan calls a *jouissance beyond the phallus* (and which, I insist, we must recognise as the Other jouissance, total satisfaction). And when we reach Lacan's question – "Doesn't this jouissance one experiences (…) put us on the path of ex-sistence?" (ibid.) – we can see that the *ecstasy* of the mystic's jouissance means that she does not simply stand outside herself in enjoyment, but that her enjoyment – *qua* Other jouissance – makes *her* "stand out", puts her in a position where she ex-sists in relation to the Symbolic: which is to say that – like God – *she insists from the outside*, in an extimate relation to the masculine set. In *Black Swan* this exceptional Woman – who has access to the ecstatic jouissance of the mystic – is embodied by Lily. Indeed, in Nina's delusion-fantasy, where she sees her with Thomas backstage, Lily is quite literally *the one who fucks God*.

Moreover, this image of Lily *as* the mystic (as the one who enjoys with God, in ecstatic jouissance), and the compulsion of Nina towards this image, reaches its highest intensity when the pair visit a bar. Lily's jouissance is plain to see: she bites hungrily into a burger, talks with her mouth full about sex and Thomas, and flirts with those around her. The contrast with Nina here is stark: dressed in light colours against Lily's black, she gently nibbles at her food and refuses to engage in conversation about carnal matters. Lily tells her that she needs to relax and offers her a pill: that this is MDMA is signalled by Lily's reference to the resultant high as *rolling*. Lily then utters the magic words for Nina: echoing Thomas, she tells her it will loosen her up and adding, crucially, that it will let her see the night sky. Lily thus offers Nina the opportunity for *transcendence*: for a chance to reach for the perfect satisfaction of mystical experience. Spurred on by Lily's demonstration of *her* jouissance, Nina eventually acquiesces to Lily's command. MDMA is, of course, better known as *ecstasy*, and the jouissance Lily offers to Nina therefore promises that mystical ex-stasis – that standing out, going beyond – which would make her Woman.

Sexual jouissance does not reach the Other

This point, at which Nina finally comes to enjoy as Lily does, should, moreover, be understood as the point at which Nina comes to enjoy *as she thinks the Other enjoys*. For Lily's part, her jouissance relates to what Žižek calls "permissive biopolitics" (2013): a hedonism that fully submits to the superegoic injunction – uttered by the waiter who brings their food – to "Enjoy!", to consume more and more. As the *encore* here suggests, this is a libidinal economy no less caught in the phallic loop because the subject continually chases greater and greater jouissance. However, for Nina, the image she takes of Lily's hedonism is as a genuine picture of full satisfaction: Lily is the Woman who can teach her to enjoy. That this perspective is a *fantasy* becomes clear as the night develops.

For Lacan, "Jouissance, qua sexual, is phallic – in other words, it is not related to the Other as such" (1998: 9). This means that man, "who can believe he approaches [woman]", in fact approaches nothing but "the cause of his desire (…) designated object *a*" (ibid.: 72). As I have suggested, Lacan renders this on the Graph with the vector $ → *a*: the formula for fantasy. On the masculine side, there is no sexual relationship (i.e. man and woman do not form a complementary *whole*) because, in the sexual encounter, man encounters only the object that phallic jouissance puts in the place of the Other. He therefore misses his partner because all he reaches is the phantasm. Paradoxically, then, sexual jouissance – as phallic jouissance, which is concerned only with object *a* – should be considered an '*a*-sexual' form of enjoyment (ibid.: 127).

There can be no clearer indication of this autistic dimension of phallic jouissance than the sexual encounter between Nina and Lily, during which Lily transforms into Nina herself. When Nina broaches the topic with Lily the next morning and discovers that Lily did not spend the night with her, Nina is struck by the realisation that her enjoyment was a *fantasy*: in which she never dealt with anything other than the object, 'which takes the place of the missing partner' (ibid.: 63). Furthermore, it is for this reason that Lacan refers to phallic jouissance as *masturbation*, which he describes as "the jouissance of the idiot" (ibid.: 81). This is not some moralistic pronouncement on the "solitary vice" but an etymological pun on the root of "idiot" in the Greek, *idios* (as pertaining to the *self*), that constitutes the phallic libidinal economy as a sexual *idios kosmos*. Phallic jouissance is a *solitary* jouissance (but by no means a *vice*) even *with* a "partner", and the sex scene is therefore the most significantly *masturbatory* sequence in

Black Swan overall. Here, the film lays bare the very structure of fantasy: rendered literally, as Nina having sex with herself. That this fantasy is of Lily – as she who has access to greater jouissance – reveals it, furthermore, to be the fundamental masculine fantasy of Woman as Exception, as enjoying Other.[8]

The atheism of feminine jouissance

If my discussion of *Black Swan* and jouissance so far has been fixed within the phallic field, then the question must be asked: What is *feminine jouissance*? Does *Black Swan* provide an answer? To address this question, we must turn, first of all, to feminine structure. As is the case for masculine structure, Lacan posits two formulae – "not-all x Phi x" and "there is not one x not Phi x" – that characterise ~~Woman~~'s set. Beneath these formulae are the mathemes for the jouissance derived from this structure. First, ~~La~~ $\rightarrow \Phi$, which suggests that phallic jouissance is (nonetheless) available to those who situate themselves on feminine side and, therefore, so too is the realm of *fantasy* (as I have already suggested is the case for Nina). And second, crucially, ~~La~~ $\rightarrow$ S(A barred). "~~La~~" corresponds, in English, to ~~Woman~~: written as "barred" to indicate that "she" does not support a universal (the "universal" quantifier is negated: "not-all x"). This is because the feminine set does not situate itself in reference to an Exception ("there is not one x not Phi x") that would ground a universal set of "All". Taken together, these formulae produce instead a "not-all" (*pas-tout*): to be understood as an *open* or *indefinite* set.

While the not-all is one of Lacan's richest theoretical innovations, the key to approaching the Lacanian concept of a properly feminine jouissance is first to address the formula: "there is not one x not Phi x". It can be read as "there is not one x who is *not* subject to the phallic function", meaning that it is a negation of the "father function". This is to say that, as Lacan explains, the "there is not one x" is "is simply an indication of (…) the Signifier of the barred Other [*A barré*]" (2011: 104), and is equivalent to his statement that *there is no Other of the Other*. There is no exceptional One on the feminine side that would determine feminine jouissance or necessitate the creation of another, flawless jouissance because – for ~~Woman~~ – the Other does not have access to some special secret; it is always-already a *failure*.

We can now begin to critique the theism of masculine structure. Recalling Lacan's remarks in *Encore*: when touching upon the Other jouissance, it becomes clear that God is required. Indeed, Lacan suggests that, "It is insofar as her jouissance is radically Other that woman has more of a relationship to God" (1998: 83). According to the terms of *masculine logic*: the Other sex requires God. Woman (*not* ~~Woman~~) as the representative of the Other jouissance is thus situated at the God face of the Other, and so *belief* in Woman's jouissance (as mystical enjoyment) is equivalent to belief in God. As I've suggested, phallic jouissance posits Other jouissance as an ineffable, unknowable beyond. However, what Lacan allows us to see is that what is supposedly "beyond the phallus" – Nina's perfect jouissance, Lily's mystical ecstasy – is nothing but a fantasy projection of masculine structure.

Black Swan posits Lily as the absolute Other beyond the phallus: she embodies this jouissance beyond. However, from a Lacanian perspective, we can say that she serves as a screen for fantasy: she gives body to the fact that *there is nothing beyond*. What Lacan refers to as the "God hypothesis", we can understand therefore as the process by which man posits Woman as the Other sex (ibid.: 45).

However, Lacan states that, "The Woman (*La-femme*) in question is another name of God, and this is why she does not exist" (2005: 14). The universal "Woman" does not exist because "God" does not exist (and thus they remain "partners" on the masculine side). Feminine structure is not compatible with the figure of "God" because there is *no exception*, nothing beyond. Feminine structure is therefore *strictly atheist*: there is simply no place for God on the right hand side of the Graph.⁹ This means that the *jouissance* of feminine structure is also *atheistic*. It does not pertain to the Other (*qua* phallus/God/A) but to a jouissance of the not-all, of the barred Other: *a jouissance of the lack in the Other* J(A barred). To recall my discussion of "frigidity" in *Black Swan*, we can now refer to Lacan's proposed solution: that the goal of analysis is to bring about an "unveiling of the Other" (2007: 616). Morel describes this as encouraging the subject "to glimpse that point 'behind the veil'" (2002: 87), which I suggest we interpret as *an unveiling of the lack in the Other*. Nina's phallic jouissance is based upon the image of the Other as (A): as whole and full of jouissance. For what I want to identify as Nina's *feminine* jouissance, then, what is required is not *God*, but the relationship that W̶o̶m̶a̶n̶ has with (A barred).

The immanent sublime of embodied experience (or becoming a swan)

There is no transcendent guarantor for the feminine side: this structure does not imply a going beyond, or a jouissance "out there". Instead, it depends upon *immanence*: a non-theological, strictly materialist *jouissance* "in here". In order to understand this proposition, we must follow Lacan's advice and "see in what respect the jouissance of the body can serve a purpose here" by turning to *Black Swan* on the one hand, and to a rethinking of sublimity on the other (1998: 71). Tarja Laine has produced a fascinating study of *Black Swan* in terms of what she calls the "uncanny sublime" and the split between body and soul necessitated by the paradoxical demand of ballet to deny the materiality of the body.¹⁰ However, I wish to turn the sublime back towards this very materiality to posit a jouissance of the body in Nina's experience of dancing (and becoming) the Black Swan.

When dealing, in Lacan's terms, with the "not-all, which contains a jouissance other than phallic jouissance, the jouissance properly called feminine", another logic is required (2011: 103–104). If masculine structure leaves the subject trapped in the bad infinity of phallic and Other jouissance (like Achilles forever chasing the tortoise), then feminine structure is – rather than access to a transcendent beyond – an opening up of the immanent possibilities of enjoyment. The picture of this properly feminine jouissance in *Black Swan* clarifies as the film reaches its own climax. As Nina struggles with her double in the dressing room during the first night's performance, "Lily" insists it is "her" turn, pushing Nina to give herself over to the fantasy of the Exception. Instead, Nina "kills" that part of her self that is bound to the phallic libidinal economy, stabbing "her" with a shard of broken mirror. If *Black Swan* is about Nina's struggle with two aspects of herself (as two differing possibilities for jouissance), then, in killing the image of Lily, Nina effectively "traverses the fantasy" of the enjoying Other and comes to identify with her own enjoyment: her sinthome.[11] The particular organisation of Nina's enjoyment – *her sinthome* – is centred on the image of the swan (and a specific understanding of the Black Swan in particular). Nina insists it is *her* turn: asserting an "atheistic" approach – i.e. not based on God and Woman (*or Thomas and Lily*) – which provides a chance for her to experience a jouissance that cannot be reckoned within the phallic logic, but *not*, I should add, one taking her into the beyond. It is an immanent jouissance: a jouissance of embodied experience.

In order to conceive of this non-theological mode of enjoyment, it will be necessary to turn to the *logic of sublimity*. Copjec has convincingly demonstrated that Lacan's formulae of sexuation can be understood in terms of Kant's antinomies, with the masculine a "dynamic" failure of the sexual relationship, subject to an external limitation, and the feminine a "mathematical" failure predicated on an inherent deadlock.[12] What remains is to offer a concomitant reading of *jouissance* in the same terms. Most commentaries – *including Copjec's* – tend to omit the bottom half of the Graph of Sexuation, which pertains specifically to jouissance, and fail to elaborate the connection between the top and bottom of the Graph on the basis of jouissance. This can be achieved with reference to a logic elaborated by Žižek. He describes the dynamic antinomy as that which "announces another dimension, that of the noumenal"; which is to say, something that is *beyond* us (corresponding to the masculine logic of a sublime "out there"). The mathematical antinomy – Žižek suggests – is, conversely, the properly *materialist* dimension of Kant's thought: it suggests the sublime generated as a result of recognising an inherent failure (2000: 38). *This*, I suggest, is the feminine logic of a sublime "in here".

Feminine jouissance persists but cannot be counted within the phallic field; however, the idea that it *exceeds* the phallic would point towards a dynamic sublime in terms of that which is *beyond us*, which would run the risk of returning, once again, to the jouissance *beyond the phallus*. What is required here is the kind of "Hegelian reversal" of Kant that Žižek suggests: we retain *the basic dialectical moment of the Sublime* as the inadequacy of the phenomenality to the Thing, but we must understand, with Hegel, that *there is nothing beyond phenomenality*.

> Crucially, the experience of the Sublime remains the same: all we have to do is subtract its transcendent presupposition – the presupposition that this experience indicates, in a negative way, some transcendent Thing-in-itself persisting in positivity beyond it. In short, we must limit ourselves to what is strictly immanent to this experience.
>
> (Žižek 1989: 206)

Bringing Žižek's logic of sublimity together with Lacan's logic of sexuation, therefore, I suggest that feminine jouissance cannot be conceived of *within* the phallic field, but this does not mean that it is "beyond the phallus". As Claude-Noële Pickmann notes, the not-all is situated not beyond but *at the very heart of the Symbolic* (2002). Therefore, it certainly *does* pertain to the sublime; however – rather than the masculine fantasy of the sublime of a *dynamic* antinomy, forever pushing its own impossibility into the ineffable beyond – feminine jouissance is fully present, as an enjoyment comparable to the sublime of a *mathematical* antinomy: inherent to experience itself as an *immanent, material* jouissance.

Throughout the film, Nina has denied herself enjoyment in the hope that this will lead to better jouissance: to *perfection*. However, Nina conflates the potential for *her own* jouissance with the ideal of *another* jouissance (of Woman). When she finally sheds herself of the illusion of the Other's enjoyment, she is able to embrace the full flood of jouissance that her own body can provide. Until the final dance of the Black Swan, Nina had been utterly horrified by the gradual transformation of her body into that of a swan. She picks at the sore on her back, eventually pulling through her skin the tip of a small black feather, which she contemplates in shock and disgust. However, her attitude changes after stabbing "Lily", which, I have suggested, signals an opening up of new possibilities of enjoyment. Nina then dances the Black Swan Pas de Deux with a power and passion previously unseen, and it is here that I propose Nina *begins* to find a feminine jouissance: she makes small noises of satisfaction as swan-flesh ripples across her body, while the audience applaud and her partner exclaims. What follows is clearly the most significant point of *Black Swan* but, I insist, we must approach it very carefully: even against a straightforward reading suggested by the film itself. As she prepares to perform the incredible turning fouettés of the coda, Nina looks down at her arms as swan-flesh continues to race across them. She acknowledges the change with a satisfied smile. She then takes to the stage once more as feathers begin to sprout from her skin; she spins again and again and with each turn her arms become *wings*, her body is covered with feathers. She strikes her final pose as a fully formed *black swan* before the film cuts to an extreme long shot, showing a human form on stage but casting the shadow of a Nina-Swan on the rear wall.

It would be easy to interpret the transformation here as a metaphor for Nina's transcendence of her body: the mystical ex-stasis that Thomas insists she achieve through her dance. However, this is emphatically *not* what Nina's experience of "becoming a swan" suggests. That this is a *feminine* jouissance is indicated by the very *lack* of transcendence here: Nina's satisfaction as the Black Swan needs no reference to the Other (God, Thomas or Lily). Her turning fouettés do not take her into a dynamic beyond; instead, it is apparent that what Nina is experiencing is the enjoyment of every inch of her body. In this moment, the source of her jouissance is nothing but her own material existence: she is revelling in the embodied experience of the dance itself, palpably deriving jouissance *from* this embodiment. Moreover, Nina's encounter with her own body here recalls Colette Soler's proposition that feminine jouissance can be felt in the radical, corporeal disruption precipitated by extreme physical action (2005: 306). Soler relates this to childbirth, illness and sport (therefore, not reducing the question to *anatomy*), but *Black Swan*'s staging of Nina's body *in extremis* would also insist on adding dance to that list as well.

The feminine jouissance of *Black Swan* is therefore – to repurpose a term from Jean-François Lyotard – an "immanent sublime": jouissance of the experience of the body.[13] However, this unexpectedly *embodied sublime* must be stripped of any connotation of an "unpresentable" beyond; rather this is – as I have stated – a fully *materialist* sublime, based on the mathematical antinomy. It is not feminine structure *itself* that is "unpresentable" but that feminine structure is another way of approaching *the unpresentable as such*. Feminine sexuation does not equate to an entry into the beyond (as purported in the mystical experience); instead, it constitutes a new mode of relation to the Symbolic Order, which recognises (and therefore *enjoys*) the Other as not-all. The formulae for feminine structure insist that the phallic function remains valid but in relation to an open set, which is constituted *without exception*. To recall Žižek's logic of sublimity, everything remains the same; we merely remove the reference to the transcendent One and appreciate what is immanent to the experience. It is an acceptance of the non-theological, material enjoyment available through the body.

Therefore, *pace* Lyotard, it is not simply a question of rendering the sublime as immanent *to* the work of art (although this is certainly *also* the case); it is the question of rendering a literally, paradoxically *immanent sublime*. Nina achieves feminine jouissance in the moment that she accepts her transformation into the Black Swan: it is not that she "loses herself" in the mystical experience, but that she "finds" her own corporeality by fully embracing the sublime satisfaction of her sinthome – the kernel of enjoyment – that takes the body of a swan. Rather than covering over the Real with a veneer of the Imaginary, as is the wont of masculine structure, the Lacanian feminine allows for an opening up and an appreciation of the Real as immanent to the Symbolic and so we can say that *Black Swan* thus stages the *immanent sublime of feminine jouissance*.

Death, psychosis, sinthome

If the film ends, as it is commonly read, with Nina's death, then this death is "necessary" to the extent that she finally reverts *back* to the logic of the phallic libidinal economy (this masculine paradigm signalled visually by her reversion to the White Swan costume) and so persists to the end in her pursuit of Other jouissance. Nina herself, having rearticulated her body within the phallic field, insists on interpreting the experience of feminine jouissance *as* a transcendent, mystical ecstasy. Nina's psychosis – differently from Schreber's, then – involves being turned into "Woman" (*La femme*) by "God" (Thomas).[14] She is constantly pushed towards the image of the Other (sex) by those around her, and her pathology involves total submission to that image. It is not that Nina finds "liberation through madness", but that *this is not where we find Nina's madness*. It is the White Swan – not the Black – that stands for her psychosis. The jouissance she derives from the Black Swan would constitute her sinthome: that which could knot a psychotic structure.[15]

Instead, Nina assumes the position of the Other, and thus finally loses herself. As she lies (presumably) dying backstage, she tells Thomas – with a beatific expression – that *it was perfect*. If we recall the (phallic) image of Achilles pursuing the tortoise, we should note that Lacan observes that, they meet only "at infinity" (1998: 8). The realisation of such a jouissance coincides with the realisation of the impossible-Real Thing. As such, in maintaining her phallic course towards the Other, Nina's path to jouissance is, as Lacan suggests, "the path toward death" (2008: 18). She thus falls into the same trap as those readers of Lacan who would figure feminine jouissance as *absolutely Other*. Rather than accepting the immanent jouissance of the body she experiences as the Black Swan, she denies this feminine logic – and with that her sinthome – and her insistence on transcendence forces her back towards the White Swan: towards the *beyond* and into death.

Apropos of Lyotard – and following Laine to a certain extent, but approaching the question differently – *Black Swan* does not simply point *towards* the sublime but directly contains and presents it to us as spectators, and in this way allows us to experience such sublimity. However, in order to avoid Nina's fate, it must be understood in terms of the logic of *feminine jouissance*: not as an ineffable beyond, but as a fully embodied experience. Indeed, on my first viewing of the film, it was the final Black Swan fouettés that most stood out. My encounter with this moment – Nina's jubilation in the transformation of her body into a swan – provided both the "kernel" of my *own* enjoyment of *Black Swan* and a starting point for my thinking about the film. It led me to consider the different modes of Nina's jouissance, and the sheer materiality of her enjoyment in that moment in particular allows me to suggest that, if we speak of the body in cinema, it seems *Lacan has not yet made his exit*.

Notes

1   Cf. Lacan (1998: 23–24).
2   See Lacan (1998: 78).
3   See Tyrer (2012) and *Out of the Past: Lacan and Film Noir* (forthcoming).
4   As Agnieszka Piotrowska has pointed out to me, the classic Lacanian reading here might refer to a deficiency in the function of the Name of the Father for Nina, which would relate to *psychosis*.
5   Cf. Žižek (1993: 203).
6   Cf. Lacan (1998: 71).
7   Cf. Lacan (1998: 74 & 77).
8   Cf. Žižek (2007: 155).
9   It is for this reason that Claude-Noële Pickmann can state: "the not-all is atheistic in itself" (2004: 25). I am grateful to Claude-Noële for sending me some of her work on feminine structure.

10 I am grateful to Tarja Laine for providing me with a draft version of the chapter on *Black Swan* from her forthcoming book on Aronofsky. My own thinking was partly initiated by a version of her work presented at the *Film-Philosophy* Conference (2012). As such, my analysis of the film should be considered something of an *uncanny psychoanalytic double* of Laine's phenomenological account.
11 Cf. Žižek (1989: 124).
12 See Copjec (1994: 201–236).
13 Cf. Lyotard (1991: 128).
14 The question of Nina's "psychosis" in the film is a crucial one but its further investigation is unfortunately beyond the scope of this chapter.
15 Recalling the classic theory of psychosis, the sinthome is what would compensate for the foreclosure of the Name of the Father (see Lacan 2005).

References

Braunstein, N. (2003) Desire and jouissance in the teachings of Lacan. In J-M Rabaté (ed.), *The Cambridge Companion to Lacan*. Cambridge: Cambridge University Press.

Copjec, J. (1994) *Read My Desire: Lacan Against the Historicists*. Cambridge, MA: MIT Press.

Fink, B. (2004) *Lacan to the Letter: Reading Écrits Closely*. Minneapolis, MN: University of Minneapolis Press.

Gallop, J. (1982) *The Daughter's Seduction: Feminism and Psychoanalysis*. London: Macmillan.

Ince, K. (2011) Bring bodies back in: For a phenomenological and psychoanalytic film criticism of embodied cultural identity. *Film-Philosophy*, 28(1), 1–12.

Lacan, J. (1998) *Encore: The Seminar of Jacques Lacan, Book XX: On Feminine Sexuality, the Limits of Love and Knowledge, 1972–1973*. Ed. J-A. Miller. Trans. B. Fink. New York: Norton.

Lacan, J. (2005) *Le séminaire de Jacques Lacan: Live XXIII, Le sinthome*. Paris: Seuil.

Lacan, J. (2007) *Écrits*. Trans. by B. Fink. New York: Norton.

Lacan, J. (2008) *The Seminar of Jacques Lacan, Book XVII: The Other Side of Psychoanalysis*. Ed. J-A Miller. Tran Russell Grigg. New York: Norton.

Lacan, J. (2011) *Le séminaire de Jacques Lacan: Live XIX, ... ou pire*. Paris: Seuil.

Laine, T. (2012) Sublime Sensation: *Black Swan*. Film-Philosophy Conference 2012. King's College London, London, UK. 14 September.

Lyotard, J-F. (1991) *The Inhuman: Reflections on Time*. Trans. G. Bennington and R. Bowlby. Stanford, CA: Stanford University Press.

Miller, J-A. (1994) *Extimité*. In M. Brachner (ed.), *Lacanian Theory of Discourse*. New York: New York University Press.

Morel, G. (2002) Feminine conditions of jouissance. In S. Barnard and B. Fink (eds), *Reading Seminar XX: Lacan's Major Work on Love, Knowledge and Feminine Sexuality*. Albany, NY: SUNY Press.

Pickmann, C-N. (2002) *Of a Femininity that is Not-all*. Lacanian School of Psychoanalysis, San Francisco, USA. 2 March.

Pickmann, C-N. (2004) Examining a clinic of the not-all. *The Letter: Irish Journal for Lacanian Psychoanalysis*, 30, 19–30.

Pound, M. (2008) *Žižek: A (Very) Critical Introduction*. Grand Rapids, MI: Wm. B. Eerdmans Publishing Co.

Soler, C. (2005) *What Lacan Said about Women: A Psychoanalytic Study*. Trans. John Holland. New York: Other Press.

Tyrer, B. (2012) Film noir doesn't exist: A Lacanian topology. In D. Henderson (ed.), *Psychoanalysis, Culture and Society*. Newcastle: Cambridge Scholars Publishing.

Žižek, S. (1989) *The Sublime Object of Ideology*. London: Verso.

Žižek, S. (1993) *Tarrying with the Negative: Kant, Hegel and the Critique of Ideology*. Durham, NC: Duke University Press.

Žižek, S. (2000) *The Ticklish Subject: The Absent Centre of Political Ontology*. London: Verso.

Žižek, S. (2007) *The Indivisible Remainder: On Schelling and Related Matters*. London: Verso.

Žižek, S. (2013) *Ideology: The Terror of Permissive Biopolitics*. Birkbeck College, London, UK. 27 November.

Filmography

Black Swan (2010) Directed by Darren Aronofsky. USA: Fox Searchlight.

Chapter 11

Documentary and psychoanalysis
Putting the love back in epistephilia*

Michael Renov

"Documentary and Psychoanalysis": until rather recently, that paper title would have struck many as announcing a rather unlikely pairing, along the lines of, say, "documentary and fly-fishing" or "documentary and the art of paper maché." As a cultural practice, documentary filmmaking has been with us for nearly a century: since 1914, if we think of Edward Curtis's proto-ethnographic film, *In the Land of the Headhunter*; 1922, if we take as documentary's genesis Flaherty's *Nanook*; 1926, if our touchstone is Grierson's first deployment of the "D"-word in his review of Flaherty's *Moana*. But if we think of documentary as an object of consistent inquiry, we must skip ahead a half-century or so to the 1970s when film studies emerged as an academic discipline.[1] Yet, in the books of scholars such as Erik Barnouw and Richard Meran Barsam, no thought was given to possible affiliations or alliances between nonfiction film and the "P"-word, psychoanalysis, that still controversial intellectual tradition and psychotherapeutic practice inaugurated by Sigmund Freud at the turn of the twentieth century.

Those first American authors, Barnouw, Barsam, and Lewis Jacobs were of a generation of film scholars that gave little heed to the latest theoretical trends sparking debates, making their way to the U.S. from Paris by way of London – structuralism, semiology, post-structuralism, feminism, postmodernism, deconstruction, and, of course, psychoanalysis. All of these contested areas of study came to be explicated and applied to film studies as an emerging discipline in the 1970s. Psychoanalysis, in particular, took hold and became entrenched. The transition from a staunchly scientific semiology to an approach deeply influenced by Lacanian psychoanalysis by such luminaries as Christian Metz ("The Imaginary Signifier") and Roland Barthes (*Camera Lucida* and its attention to "the impossible science of the unique being") inaugurated a sea change of sorts for Anglo-Saxon film scholarship by the late 1970s. Psychoanalytic theory was mobilized as a way to comprehend the seductiveness of the filmic text, to understand what lay beneath or behind those sounds and images.[2] Cinematic reception was on occasion characterized as "oneiric," "fantasmatic," engaging a psychic register in the spectator associated more with the primary than the secondary process (the realm of desire, the drive, impulses rather than thematics tamed through secondary revision). But these generative accounts of the cinema and its reception were exclusively linked to the feature-length fiction film which was, according to Christian Metz, the "king's highway of filmic expression."[3]

Amidst the flurry of intellectual excitement surrounding psychoanalytic theory as a political weapon for feminists or as a new language for exploring cinema's universal appeal, the study of the documentary film remained the province of a rather stuffy if politically progressive older crowd that skewed old, white, and male. The focus in the 1970s was on compiling the historical record of the nonfiction film as a worldwide phenomenon, sometimes with clarity and elegance (e.g., Barnouw's classic volume, *Documentary: A History of the Non-Fiction Film*). There was not yet a critical mass of intellectual inquiry or writing associated with the documentary tradition that merited the phrase "documentary studies." This domain of research was most assuredly not attracting the scholarly attention of the young, the female, the queer, the ethnically and intellectually diverse as is now the case.

The milestone publication was *Representing Reality* (1991) in which Bill Nichols offered a rigorous analysis of the rhetorical and discursive principles that condition the documentary film as well as the modes of its exposition. At last a book brought to the study of documentary a kind of theoretical ambition missing until that moment.[4] But *Representing Reality* made a case for nonfiction film as serious business, that is to say as fundamentally argument-driven, more aligned with rhetoric or moral suasion than with art or imagination or desire. This was a strategic move (a foundational move in many ways) because it announced the intellectual seriousness of the nonfiction film while positing its political *bona fides*. But for Nichols, in his treatment of the documentary film, subjectivity – that multilayered construction of selfhood imagined, performed and assigned – was principally "a social subjectivity … [a] subjectivity dissociated from any single individuated character."[5] Documentary was first and foremost to be understood in relation to social movements, to media activism and to the promulgation of public policy so that the filmic construction of a self (a monadic unit rather than a cadre within a mass or class) was less crucial than the arguments that nonfiction film could make about a world in need of change. Crudely put, Marx trumped Freud; the Marxian subject of history was preferred, considered more apposite to the study of documentary than the psychoanalytic variant.

For many reasons, that formulation was inadequate to the moment for the late 1980s/early 1990s witnessed an explosion of personal filmmaking that wrestled with subjectivity at the crossroads of the private and the public spheres. In the first-person work of Isaac Julien, Marlon Riggs, Su Friedrich, Gregg Bordowitz, Richard Fung, Rea Tajiri and many others, social crisis was figured as personal *and* political. As I argued in *The Subject of Documentary*, the assertion of "who we are" emerged at that moment as a vital expression of agency and political commitment. These documentary artists were, through their films, *performing resistance* to inadequate state support during the AIDS pandemic or working through the legacies of gendered or racial oppression as well as familial dysfunction. Notions of social subjectivity were ill equipped to capture such an interiorized landscape, the stuff of the psychoanalytic tradition.

In *Representing Reality* Nichols famously posited the very useful notion of epistephilia as the durable underpinning of documentary discourse. "Documentary realism aligns itself with an epistephilia," he wrote, "that marks out a distinctive form of social engagement." He continued: "In igniting our interest, a documentary has a less incendiary effect on our erotic fantasies and sense of sexual identity but a stronger effect on our social imagination and sense of cultural identity. Documentary calls for the elaboration of an epistemology and axiology more than of an erotics."[6]

Without a doubt, Nichols struck a responsive chord among many with this formulation. I would characterize epistephilia as something like a politically engaged version of intellectual curiosity. It was utterly consistent with the proposal – on the very first page of the text – that documentary film was one of the discourses of sobriety, one of the systems (like science or politics or religion) that has instrumental power and entails consequences. This was important as a way to stake a claim for documentary as distinct from the fiction film, more ethically charged (hence axiology), more rhetorically forceful, more consequential as a vehicle of knowledge production. If the feature-length fiction film was the king's highway of filmic expression, documentary was a vital detour to a serious destination. The abnegation of an erotics also freed the documentary scholar from the need to wade through the dense and occasionally obfuscating critical literature that had sprung up around psychoanalytic film theory. Having said all that, I would still argue that Nichols' characterizations of the documentary film in *Representing Reality* were timely and distinctive and not at all wrong. But they were, at the same moment, woefully inadequate.

The word epistephilia in itself was not the problem so much as its partial realization. It is not the turn to the "episteme," that is knowledge (as opposed to "doxa" or belief) that went awry so much as the indifference to the "philia," the love. I would want to argue that an erotics was always at issue for the documentary, but in the broadest sense Freud (and Marcuse after him) intended it, as the motor force behind all human endeavour. Seen from this perspective, documentary is a very special species of sublimation that seeks to work through compelling issues, social contradictions, or private demons.

Again, on a tactical level, I understand why Nichols may have eschewed erotics for documentary. After all, the famous *Cahiers du Cinema* collective texts of the 1970s on *Young Mr. Lincoln* and *Morocco* (translated in the pages of *Screen*) posited that, for the Hollywood model of cultural production, erotics tended to displace politics through a carefully wrought sleight of hand that the *Cahiers* texts deciphered in meticulous detail (à la Barthes' *S/Z*). This meant that a politicized dimension or ideological arena foregrounded in the classical Hollywood film (as in the matter of nation-building in John Ford's *Young Mr. Lincoln*) tended ultimately to be pushed aside by the dramatic elements, often via the construction or troubling of the romantic couple. The distinguishing mark of documentary, then, very rightly seemed to be its preference for arguments and political agendas rather than their textual repression. But what was sacrificed by that stratagem, the denial of erotics? I would argue that, at the precise moment of that formulation (epistemology and axiology over erotics), documentary was estranged from psychoanalysis which, though arguably on the wane at that moment within North American film studies, had been a tremendously fruitful direction of study, indeed an intellectual wellspring for film studies.

Instead the documentary film was to be aligned with discursive seriousness, historiography, public policy. As I've stated, this approach resonated for many audiences. Semioticians, historians, cognitivists and analytical philosophers could find a home for themselves in a documentary world thus formulated. In a lengthy essay in the edited collection, *Post-Theory* (1996), Nöel Carroll devoted much energy to staking a claim for what he deemed the most pertinent formulation of documentary film as veridical discourse in contradistinction to the work of those he dismissed as "postmodernists." The conflict he outlined – between his philosophically informed understanding of the documentary film versus the work of those he deemed radical skeptics – was to be waged "in the trenches of epistemology." Ironically Nichols and I, who by then had taken issue with Nichols' characterizations of documentary as I shall explain shortly, were lumped together with Brian Winston as the postmodernists (this despite the fact that none of us had ever written a word about postmodernism in relation to documentary film). But, if the struggle was indeed to be waged in the trenches of epistemology (and the books of scholars such as Carl Plantinga and Trevor Ponech indeed followed that path), where did that leave a burgeoning field of documentary studies? What ground had been ceded? And where was the love?

I would argue that leaving the "love" out of epistephilia meant setting aside the deepest sources of documentary's appeal. I would call it "the appeal of the real" and I think it helps to explain the ubiquity of reality television as a global phenomenon as well as the consistent critical and popular success of the documentary film in recent years. Plainly put: no notion of epistephilia can hope to suffice without acknowledgement of the unconscious. Because love can never be wholly rationalized or contained, epistephilia must always retain traces of *l'amour fou*. Why are we driven to make and preserve images of history, those of our family, our country, our life world? What is the nature of human perception and how does a camera allow us to interrogate and expand our understanding of the phenomenal world? What accounts for our attraction to a particular image or camera movement, our urge to watch certain documentary sequences again or again? What enlivens our eye and ear as we encounter the semblance of others, those perhaps very like ourselves, or perhaps very unlike, on screens large and small? Such questions certainly inspired our documentary ancestors, among them Joris Ivens, Dziga Vertov and Jean Painlevé.

This is not to say that we are bereft of more rationalist motivations for a turn to the documentary form. Adrift in a rapacious 24-hour news cycle, we're starved for intelligent formulations regarding our social environs and the challenges we face, explanations for why we are who we are. Just as urban America, land of the overfed, is nonetheless rife with what have been called food deserts, today's cultural consumer is pummelled by information yet starved for knowledge.

But beneath our conscious motivations, our intellectual curiosity, our need to know, lurks another perhaps more determinative register. In Elizabeth Cowie's elegant formulation, it's a twofold activity of which we speak – "recording reality, desiring the real" – the rational and programmatic dimension of the documentary enterprise (recording reality) set alongside the elusive perhaps ineffable but no doubt unquenchable domain of desire. Desire, as we know since Freud, is of the order of the drive. It is unceasing, temporarily sated but never quiescent this side of the grave. We may speak of our quest to acquire knowledge – an acquisitive act with an aim and an outcome – but we ignore at our peril an un-nameable itch that accompanies it. What can I possibly mean by this?

Knowledge (the "episteme" portion of epistephilia) is unhinged by desire. In my introduction to *Theorizing Documentary* published some twenty years ago, I turned to Julia Kristeva's formulation of delirium as outlined in her essay "Psychoanalysis and the Polis" in an effort to explain why the documentary film and its certifiable appeal can never be fully contained within the sober precincts of knowledge. To those who espouse notions of an objective reality available for representation, the unspoken presumption of the documentary epistephile, Kristeva issues this caveat:

> Delirium is a discourse which has supposedly strayed from a presumed reality. The speaking subject is presumed to have known an object, a relationship, an experience that he is henceforth incapable of reconstituting accurately. Why? Because the knowing subject is also a *desiring* subject, and the paths of desire ensnarl the paths of knowledge. ... [W]e normally assume the opposite of delirium to be an objective reality, objectively perceptible and objectively knowable, as if the speaking subject were only a simple knowing subject. Yet we must admit that, given the cleavage of the subject (conscious/unconscious) and given that the subject is also a subject of desire, perceptual and knowing apprehension of the original object is only a theoretical, albeit undoubtedly indispensable, hypothesis.[7]

If we accept this idea of the cleavage of the subject – that is, acknowledge the existence and efficacy of the unconscious – and if we entertain Kristeva's claim that "the paths of desire ensnarl the paths of knowledge," then we are bound to enlarge our understanding of epistephilia. In a chapter of *The Subject of Documentary* entitled "Charged Vision: The Place of Desire in Documentary Film Theory," I make reference to the notion of the "lure" as developed in Jacques Lacan's *The Four Fundamental Concepts of Psycho-Analysis*. There Lacan offers an account of the rivalry between Zeuxis and Parrhasios, two painters of antiquity vying for the mantle of artistic supremacy. While Zeuxis paints grapes so ably that even the birds swoop down to peck at them, Parrhasios paints only a veil but a veil so lifelike that Zeuxis asks to know what has been painted behind it. In Lacanian terms, the fable illustrates a triumph of the gaze over the eye, the drive over the object. Likewise, in our encounter with the documentary film, our desire to pierce the veil sustains our attention to the image well beyond either perceptual or knowledge-based demands. What drives our need to know? What lies behind and beyond our intellectual curiosity?

> I think of my films as documentaries. I never fantasize. I have never invented something just for the sake of making an interesting image. I am always struggling to get an equivalent on film to what I actually see.
>
> Stan Brakhage[8]

The late Stan Brakhage is considered by many to have been America's premiere avant-garde filmmaker with a career spanning 50 years and more than 100 films. One of his first films, *The Wonder Ring* (1955), was a short work commissioned by artist Joseph Cornell who wished to have a filmic memento made of New York's Third Avenue El before its destruction. It is a luminous work, silent, filled with shimmering images that play at the edges of abstraction. Some of these dancing images are reflections captured from the imperfect window glass of the moving car, rippling distortions attracting the eye of the filmmaker, neither graphically produced nor optically printed. These images are the product of Brakhage's visual fascination, offered up to the viewer as the equivalent of what he sees. It is what we ourselves might have seen had we been there and had we been so attentive.

Desire is figured as irrepressibly horizontal, fugitive, never in its place. In Lacanian terms, desire can only arise in the subject on account of a fundamental separation between the self and its object: "The subject cannot desire without itself dissolving, and without seeing, because of this very fact, the object escaping it, in a series of infinite displacements."[9] *The Wonder Ring* is perhaps a meditation on the impossibility of capturing and preserving its nominal object, the Third Avenue El. The play of the signifier but even more forcefully the moment of perception – the artist's and our own – become the objects of cathexis. We will never see enough or know enough of that now-vanished train, its sleepy occupants or the apartment buildings whizzing past. Their proper memorialization is doomed to failure. All remain encased in an inaccessible past just beyond our grasp. What we are given to see and can see again and again thanks to the Criterion Collection DVD is, as in the Lacanian fable, an instance of the triumph of the gaze over the object.

Now, by way of conclusion:

Over the past twenty years, something we can now justifiably call documentary studies has forcefully emerged. We know about the lively documentary film festival and film market circuit: IDFA, Sheffield, HotDocs in Toronto, True/False in Columbia, Missouri, It's All True in Latin American, the biannual Australian International Documentary Conference, and the Yamagata International Film Festival in Asia. To that can now be added an equally lively documentary studies conference circuit, principally Visible Evidence now celebrating its twentieth year, but also Documentary Now! held here in the UK. The Visible Evidence book series from the University of Minnesota Press now includes some twenty-eight volumes covering an array of topics developed from diverse disciplinary frameworks. A thousand flowers have bloomed.

On the other hand, documentary's connection to psychoanalysis has not been universally welcomed. My own paper at the inaugural Visible Evidence conference at Duke University in 1993 was entitled "The Distrust of the Visible" by which I hoped to signal that the conference's very name contradicted Freud's frame-breaking insights regarding the unconscious ("by far the greater part of psychic life"). Visible Evidence, a phrase I myself may have suggested, was always intended as a bit tongue in cheek – along the lines of "seeing is believing." In that first presentation I hoped to suggest that documentary was long overdue for the sort of rigorous interrogation that the great nineteenth-century "masters of suspicion" (Paul Ricouer's term for the unholy trinity of Marx, Nietzsche, and Freud) had long ago recommended.

Elizabeth Cowie's contribution to *Collecting Visible Evidence* (1999) on "The Spectacle of Actuality" was an important and historicizing foray into the documentary film's entanglement with regimes of knowledge associated with psychoanalytic theory. From their very introduction into early twentieth-century visual culture, representations of actuality – including footage of shell-shocked World War I soldiers – emerged as both spectacle and knowledge, grounded in history yet rife with paradox, at times erotically charged, offering up the imagination of mastery. As she says in her introduction to *Recording Reality, Desiring the Real*, documentary's "pleasures of spectacle, voice, and identification" were, from the outset, coupled with its project of informing and educating.[10] At last documentary studies has been put more fully into conversation with a tradition of psychoanalytic inquiry that has enriched film studies for half a century.

I also must acknowledge the new and groundbreaking contribution of Agnieszka Piotrowska,[11] whose recent book, *Psychoanalysis and Ethics in Documentary Film* (2014) departs from divining the psychoanalytic underpinnings of documentary spectatorship or textuality, focusing instead on documentary practice. Piotrowska argues for the high stakes entailed in any maker/subject encounter in the documentary field. Lives are being narrated, bodies represented, trust gained and confidences shared. Piotrowska dares to suggest that this scenario and the depths of the soul and psyche it touches are not so far afield from that which obtains in the analytic setting. Here she evokes the Lacanian construct – *le sujet supposé savoir* – the subject supposed to know. The one wielding the camera and commanding the editing bay becomes the one upon whom trust must be bestowed, as might be the case with a parent or analyst, or nothing meaningful can be spoken or revealed. This, Piotrowska reminds us, is the realm of transference, that delicate state of being in which feelings and desires of an earlier formative moment (as toward a parent) are redirected to the analyst. As proposed by Freud, discussed by Lacan and others, through transference a special and quite delicate sort of love affair can take hold. It is Piotrowska's bold claim that such a love may also ensue between the filmmaker and her subject.

Building on Piotrowska's argument, one might well ask why we need limit the transferential condition to the moment of production. I would argue that the successful documentary film is the one that manages to overcome the *resistance* of the viewer. If I cannot trust the filmmaker's deep knowledge and passionate engagement with the subject at hand, her mastery and reinvention of a slice of the world, I will not be able to settle into an acceptance of what I'm shown. If Coleridge once wrote of the necessity of a willing suspension of disbelief for the reader of fiction, something akin to that may occur for the documentary viewer as well. Only in this instance the suspension of disbelief would be rooted in both willing and unconscious domains, the latter spurred by textual effects as well as the residue of personal history. I might make that leap of faith based on several factors: a shared or at least not opposing ideological stance (viz., the split in reception for any Michael Moore film); a confidence that the filmmaker knows more about the topic than I do; an intuition of the filmmaker's emotional honesty; resonances with my own experience. These conditions align with both the knowing and desiring dimensions of documentary reception discussed by Cowie. Only if these conditions are met is the audience member likely to be fully receptive to the film and to the ministerings of the filmmaker who must become for the moment *le sujet supposé savoir*. Without proper transference, the viewer may resist the experience of knowing and desiring that can be transformative.

I conclude on such a speculative note by way of suggesting that we are only now with this new work opening up the field of psychoanalytic documentary studies in a comprehensive way. Much remains to be done. For the remainder of the day and from here on out, please join me in putting the love back in epistephilia.

Notes

* This paper was first delivered at the UCL conference on Psychoanalysis and Documentary in May 2013.
1 Lewis Jacobs' *The Documentary Tradition*, first published in 1971, deserves mention in this context although it does not offer the extensive historical overview found in Barnouw and Barsam.
2 Psychoanalytic theory was also wielded as a political weapon. See in this context Laura Mulvey's canonical text, *Visual Pleasure and Narrative Cinema*, originally published in the pages of *Screen* in 1975 and much anthologized.
3 Christian Metz, *Some Points in the Semiotics of the Cinema, Film Language: A Semiotics of the Cinema*, trans. Michael Taylor (New York: Oxford University Press, 1974), 94.
4 William Guynn's *Cinema of Nonfiction*, published in 1990, offered a serious semiological analysis of the documentary film but in a manner that didn't resonate

with broad audiences or with filmmakers as was the case with Nichols' book the following year.
5 Bill Nichols, *Representing Reality* (Bloomington, IN: Indiana University Press, 1991), 179.
6 Ibid., 178.
7 Cited in Michael Renov, *Theorizing Documentary* (New York: Routledge, 1993), 9–10.
8 Stan Brakhage, "The Independent Filmmaker: Stan Brakhage, Filmmakers on Filmmaking." In *The American Film Institute Seminars on Motion Pictures and Television*, Joseph McBride, ed. (Los Angeles: J.P. Tarcher, Inc., 1983), 203.
9 Jacques Lacan, *The Seminar of Jacques Lacan – Book II*, trans. Sylvana Tomaselli (New York: W.W. Norton, 1988), 177.
10 Elizabeth Cowie, *Recording Reality, Desiring the Real* (Minneapolis: University of Minnesota Press, 2011), 3.
11 Agnieszka Piotrowska, *Psychoanalysis and Ethics in Documentary Film* (London: Routledge, 2014).

Part III

Reflections and destructions, mirrors and transgressions

Chapter 12

Douglas Gordon and Cory Arcangel

Breaking the toy[1]

Robert Burgoyne

Christian Metz writes that cinephilia represents, in part, the impulse to preserve and protect the good object, to save it from obliteration — not the film itself, the celluloid, nor the institution, but rather the social memory embodied in the cinema-object. Two well-known art installations, *The Five Year Drive-By* (1995) by Douglas Gordon and *Super Mario Clouds* (2003) by Cory Arcangel, would seem to make this point explicitly. In both, the impulse to save and protect — the desire to retain the affective inflections of the past — is linked to the artists' childhoods, and thematised in the texts that provide the artists with their source material — *The Searchers* (1956) by John Ford and the video game, *Super Mario Brothers* — both of which have plots that revolve around rescue. The two installations can be read as a way of maintaining these objects in what Metz calls an 'imaginary enclosure of pure love' (1986: 13).

The Five Year Drive-By, a five-year-long projection of *The Searchers* on a drive-in-size movie screen installed, among other places, in the California desert, draws from the artist's memory of the film's powerful effect when he first saw it as a boy. By slowing it down to the point that each frame is held for 45 minutes, it becomes a kind of Deleuzian time-image, a work that is centrally concerned with duration, the passing and arresting of time and self, the near-capture of a moment that is 'frozen in time'. It also suggests the disappearing social memory of the western, a genre that is increasingly fading from cultural memory. The installation in effect amplifies the theme and the plot of the film, which is centred on loss, memory and the 'saving' of a memory of the past.

Cory Arcangel's *Super Mario Clouds* seems to draw from a different cultural encyclopaedia, but the sense of affect surrounding the work is similar. Isolating the moving cloudscape that serves as background to the early video game *Super Mario Brothers*, the artist eliminates the buildings, barriers and the figure of Mario himself to concentrate simply on the clouds drifting by in a serene blue sky. Projected on a large screen in a museum space, the installation suggests the earliest moments of video game culture, the primal scene of an emergent technology linked to the generational memory of the artist. Stripped of the linear forward momentum of the game, the screen becomes an image of transience, of fleeting impermanence, a loop centred on memory, duration and loss. Like *The Searchers*, the goal of the game *Super Mario Brothers* is the rescue of a female figure, in this case the Princess Toadstool, who can be saved only after transiting a game pace filled with hazards. By erasing the quest aspect of the game, however, in order to concentrate on a fragment of mise-en-scene, the artist elicits a distinctive, emotional connection to the past, to childhood and to early game culture.

In this essay, I explore the work of Gordon and Arcangel as a way of rethinking issues circulating around the concept of cinephilia and its relation to memory, creativity, and destruction. Although the gap between classical cinema and video games has been much emphasized in contemporary theory, a shared culture of art practice has emerged around the re-presentation of these two dominant media from two different eras — an art practice that uses the media as a type of 'ready-made'. As one critic has said, contemporary video artists such as Arcangel and Gordon are 'the ideal children of the children of Duchamp'. Reformulating well-known films, video games and television broadcasts, these artists reconfigure the objects of audio-visual culture in a personal way, making explicit, as Metz writes in a different context, the works' 'inaudible murmuring to us of "Love me"' (Metz: 14).

As a resource for creative re-thinking, the cinematic past has served as a cultural ready-made for several generations of avant-garde artists. Beginning, perhaps, with Joseph Cornell's *Rose Hobart* in 1936, and continuing through the 1960s and 1970s to the present day, the visible past of cinema has provided a rich source of imaginative quotation and critique. Earlier avant-garde appropriations, however, often sought explicitly to counteract the fascination of classical film; as Catherine Fowler writes in a recent essay on gallery films: 'artists' film and videomaking has typically operated at a critical distance from the cinema; consequently, any re-use of cinema's past was carried out in a spirit of destruction — of its glamour, its linearity and its illusionism' (Fowler: 27). By contrast, a palpable sense of 'loving the cinema' infuses the work of contemporary gallery artists, an attitude and an approach that is evident in a number of recent installations that take the cinematic past as their subject. In contemporary installations, Fowler writes, artists approach the media past in a spirit of 'collaboration'.

In the work of Gordon and Arcangel, the cinematic and media past provides a new vocabulary for dramatizing the power of media images in subjective and in cultural life. Arcangel has worked in a variety of media, but his most intriguing objects are the repurposed video games, which include a Japanese racing game, stripped of all but an endlessly scrolling road, moving hypnotically from the horizon towards the viewer in an unending loop, an installation he calls *F-1 Racer*, and a new computer program that he wrote for *Super Mario Brothers* called *Mario Movie*, in which Mario floats through obstacles, encounters antagonists drawn from Pac-Man, falls endlessly through video space racing by game objects and game architecture, and winds up alone on a cloud, crying.

Gordon's work also encompasses a wide range of materials and media. His cinematic ready-mades include, in addition to *The Five Year Drive-By*, the earlier *24 Hour Psycho* (1993), a slowing-down of the Hitchcock film to a 24-hour running time; *Through the Looking Glass* (1999), a dual screen projection of the famous 'You lookin' at me?' scene from Martin Scorsese's *Taxi Driver* (1976), in which two images of Travis Bickel face each other as the spectator stands between them; and *Between Darkness and Light (After William Blake)* (1997) in which two films are projected onto the back and the front of a semi-transparent cinema screen so that the images bleed through and are lightly superimposed. The two films, *The Song of Bernadette* (1943) and *The Exorcist* (1973), are both films about possession, sacred and demonic. They are non-synchronized, and thus appear differently, with different combinations of images every time they are viewed. The images of Regan's grotesquely distorted face demonic head superimposed on the images of a praying Bernadette, or of Bernadette's nineteenth-century peasant mother walking out of Regan's suburban mansion, are typical of the combinations created. As J. Hoberman writes:

> However much *The Song of Bernadette* and *The Exorcist* may crash each other's parties, they emerge as essentially the same movie — lit by candles, filled with crosses, endlessly talking about God and faith. Bernadette will never exorcise *The Exorcist*, but united as between darkness and light, they constitute a pageant.
>
> (2006)

The sense of reverie and homage in these works, the cinephilic fascination with the object, amplifies the strange, dreamlike power of media images, reminiscent, perhaps, of Claes Oldenburg's enormous clothespins, buttons, and lipsticks. The media hacks of Arcangel and the cinematic appropriations of Gordon exemplify, in many ways, the collaborative relationship with the past discussed by Fowler. Themes of loss and regret, however, are also evoked in these works. In a few powerful paragraphs in his chapter, 'Loving the Cinema', Metz touches on the emotional cross-currents that characterize cinephilia. Comparing the cinephilia of the film historian and the archivist, the cinephilia of the ardent champion of certain auteurs, and the cinephilia of the theorist, he makes the striking point that all cinephilia comes at a cost: the mystery and fascination of the cinema, in every case, is converted into something else. Depending on the particular form it takes, it can become a kind of fetishism, as in the obsessive drive of the collector or the extreme connoisseur; or it can become a kind of sadistic voyeurism, seen in the discourse of the 'expert' or the theorist who desires nothing more than to 'take the film apart'. As Metz writes: 'To study the cinema: what an odd formula! How can it be done without "breaking" its beneficial image ... by breaking the toy one loses it' (1986: 80).

In 'The Philosophy of Toys', Baudelaire wrote about the child who broke apart his toy and hurled it across the room in an effort to get a response to the question 'where is its soul?' (1853). In many ways, the art installations of Gordon and Arcangel can be seen precisely as 'breaking the toy'. Stripping away the narrative armature of *The Searchers* or the game elements in *Super Mario Brothers*, the works of Arcangel and Gordon hint at a sense of ambivalence. The love of cinema's past, or the past of early video game culture that animates these installations, can be seen as the restaging of loss — the loss of a past relationship to a fictional world and its mechanisms of belief, a loss that is consoled by isolating, freezing, repeating, supplementing, and disarticulating certain bits and pieces of the imaginary plenitude of the film or game (Metz: 80). In *Super Mario Clouds*, for example, Arcangel destroys the childhood toy by erasing Mario himself from the game, along with the game's hazards and challenges, physically removing parts of the code — an act that is followed by a transcendent rebirth and reparation, in which the video game, now distilled to a moving cloudscape, a memory-trace, is elevated to a new life and hung on a gallery wall. Similarly, in *The Five Year Drive-By*, Gordon stills the unfolding narrative momentum of the film, holding it in place in order to penetrate its mysteries and enigmas — a key motive for the work, according to Gordon — a gesture of love that is fused with the gestures of sadism, seizing the film 'against the grain' (Metz: 15) in order to keep it in a kind of uninterrupted dream. Arresting the narrative, the image becomes monumental. As Joe Fyfe writes, 'In the old movies that Gordon likes to use ... the actors are powdered and then polished by light to read like an idealized version of what we look like, which is what traditional figurative sculpture does' (2007).

The complex relation to the cinematic past, the dramatic gesture of seizing film against the grain in order to accentuate its idealized forms, recalls the basis of film in still photography, and brings us back along a forgotten path of film history, reversing the transition from still to moving images that was much emphasized in early film projections. Writing about the astonishment that attended the first film screenings, Tom Gunning (1995) has argued that the audiences' sense of surprise and pleasure was enhanced by the dramatic, *trompe-l'oeil* presentation with which the films were introduced, a presentation that emphasized the moment of transformation from still to moving pictures. The first Lumiere projections, for example, dramatized the instant when the static image burst into lifelike movement, as a still image was first projected onto a screen, held for a while, and then animated by the projector. Rather than a naïve belief in the realism of the moving image, the amazement that greeted the first moving image projections was more an appreciation of the feat of creating lifelike movement in a photographic medium. The 'birth' of cinema in 1895 was understood, Gunning argues, as a style of theatre comparable to prestidigitation, magic theatre and illusionism. And in his view, the key to the dramatic impression created by the first projected films was the showman-like heightening of the passage from static image to moving pictures.

The reverse evolution explored by Gordon, the slowing down and near freezing of the image can be seen then as a form of analysis, an attempt to discover the core sources of fascination alongside or beneath the diegesis, where the fictional world is somehow intermingled with personal, subjective life. Roland Barthes' short essay 'The Third Meaning', is instructive here. He writes:

For a long time, I have been intrigued by the phenomenon of being interested and even fascinated by photos from a film (outside a cinema, in the pages of *Cahiers du cinéma*) and of then losing everything of those photos (not just the captivation but the memory of the image) when once inside the viewing room — a change which can even result in a complete reversal of values.

His fascination with the still image is bound up with its seemingly personal, subjective mode of address:

> The still offers us the *inside* of the fragment ... It is not a specimen chemically extracted from the substance of the film, but rather the trace of a superior *distribution* of traits of which the film as experienced in its animated flow would give no more than one text among others.
>
> (Barthes: 67)

Critics as diverse as Laszlo Moholy-Nagy and Laura Mulvey have also explored this idea, but only in a fragmentary way. Mulvey writes of the advent of DVDs, and the ability to stop, rewind and freeze-frame at will, suggesting that

> this new, freely accessible stillness, extracted from the moving image, is a product of the paradoxical relation between celluloid and new technology. It is primarily the historic cinema of celluloid that can blossom into new significance and beauty when its original stillness ... is revealed in this way. The cinema has always been a medium of revelation.
>
> (Mulvey: 139)

Certain filmmakers take the impressive power of stasis to an extreme, eliminating movement altogether in their films. In two recent essays, Justin Remes summarizes a rich tradition of what he calls 'stasis films' or 'furniture films' — films whose default setting is stasis — focusing in particular on the work of avant-garde artists such as Michael Snow, Andy Warhol, and Hollis Frampton. Remes writes:

> One of the most pivotal components in the furniture aesthetic is radical repetition. When a composition or a film takes some unexpected turn, our attention is piqued — we become interested in what the next development will be. But when a musical phrase or cinematic shot is repeated again and again, *ad infinitum*, the artwork fades into the background and our attention becomes focused elsewhere. In visual art, this repetition often leads to a degradation of signification. This was Warhol's goal: 'The more you look at the same exact thing, the more the meaning goes away, and the better and emptier you feel.'
>
> (in Remes, 2014: 11)

Gordon's installations, especially *24 Hour Psycho* and *The Five Year Drive-By*, expand on the static, frozen tableaux that occur throughout the history of film, exaggerating the stillness, holding and stretching every moment in the films he treats, decelerating the films to the point that narrative disappears, restaging the fundamental opposition of movement and stasis. Rather than a framework in which 'meaning goes away', however, Gordon's work can be seen as a form of analysis: it brings the latent content of the films to the fore. What is *Psycho* (1960), after all, if not a movie about holding on to memory and freezing time? And what is *The Searchers*, if not a movie about the impossibility of moving on, the impossibility of leaving the past behind?

At first glance, the work of Cory Arcangel would appear to be driven by very different questions, and to refer to a very different cultural encyclopaedia. The mediascape of video game culture initially seems quite distant from the iconic, monumental imagery of classic Hollywood. Arcangel's work, however, has surprisingly close affinities to the 'furniture film' projects of the 1960s and 1970s discussed by Remes. Opening the game cartridges in old Nintendo or Atari games, Arcangel first removes the chip installed in them to delete some of the gaming code, and then reformulates the work, soldering the pieces back together in order to produce contemplative, repetitive moving image installations. The hypnotic movement of the endlessly scrolling road in 'F-1 Racer' and the oneiric horizontal drift of the two-dimensional clouds in *Super Mario Clouds* are devoid of narrative event, and draw on the contemplative iconographies long associated with Snow or Warhol. Similarly, his film *Super-slow Tetris* — an eight-hour performance of a radically decelerated Tetris game, moves directly into the rarified zone of non-event associated with *Empire* (1964) or *Sleep* (1963). As Remes writes, in words that could easily be applied to Arcangel,

> Films like *Sleep* and *Empire* are best understood as *furniture films*, works which open up new ways of thinking about cinematic reception by inviting a series of distracted glances rather than a focused and comprehensive gaze ... What is interesting about many of Warhol's films is not the content per se, but the cinematic *experience* that they engender — as well as their conceptual originality
>
> (Remes, 2014: 2)

As part of the installation of *Super Mario Clouds* and *Mario Movie*, Arcangel provides detailed instructions on the technique of deleting code from the Nintendo chip, how to reprogram it, and how to resolder the new program back into the game console, demystifying the video game in order to re-illusion it. Arcangel also describes the complete digital formula for constructing both the original game as well as his own game art. The demystification of the computer code and the inclusion of programming instructions constitute a kind of semiotic analysis, the uncovering and description of the game's codes and subcodes. Rather than being directed to an increasingly esoteric understanding of the game form, however, the impulse behind

Arcangel's gesture seems more in the spirit of open-source software, the democratization of art. The computer games Arcangel treats were created early in the history of the medium, and are thus relatively simple to program and to understand, which allows for a kind of primitive artistic appropriation and manipulation. Here, the hand of the artist returns in a medium that had been defined by digital code. Seemingly as far removed from the hand of the artist as they could possibly be, digital video games, in the work of Arcangel and other game artists, can now be linked with the return of craft-based art forms such as hand-made books, YouTube videos, sculptures made from repurposed materials, and audio remixes.

Arcangel's media hacks and rewrites are extraordinarily various. Beyond the recoding of video games, one of his recent installations stages a kind of assault by computer program on the artifacts of mainstream pop culture — more specifically, the cultural memory embedded in mainstream popular culture. For example, in the installation he calls *Untitled (After Lucier)* (2006), he rebroadcasts in a continuous repeating loop The Beatles' first televised performance on *The Ed Sullivan Show* in 1964, one of the most iconic moments in the history of the television medium. Over time, the video performance slowly decomposes; during the first week or so of its run, the historic video looks normal. As time wears on, however, the pixels shift shape, enlarging into blocks, distorting and making the four Beatles, their guitars and their signature haircuts almost unrecognizable. They become, as one writer says, 'increasingly indistinct and further from memory … an artifact of digital compression and cultural disintegration' (Berwick: 1). As Arcangel says, in what seems like an echo of Warhol, 'The longer it goes on, the better the piece looks, and the less embarrassing it is' (in Berwick: 2).

By intervening in the temporal unfolding and narrative architecture of classic films and video games — subtracting movement from classic films, creating minimalist interpretations of audio-visual artifacts that ordinarily clamor for attention — the artists Gordon and Arcangel draw the focus to the interior life of the work, the concealed codes that constitute what Barthes calls the inarticulable 'third meaning'. In doing so, however, both artists seize an already existing text against the grain, subjecting the film or the game — and the social memory embodied in the film or the game — to a radical disarticulation. In this respect, their work is distinct from that of Warhol and the 'furniture films' Remes analyzes: *The Five Year Drive-By* and *Untitled (After Lucier)* are works that are explicitly engaged in a historical project, literally, engaged in the cinematic rewriting of a deeply patterned historical past. I have suggested that the ambivalence of the artistic gestures I describe here — the loving selection of the text, its destruction, and its restoration to wholeness in museum and gallery settings — can be seen as a kind of Kleinian splitting: an act of violence against the text — a text that is loved, violated, and then remade and transformed, elevated to an object of high cultural value. I would now like to extend this argument in a somewhat different direction by shifting the focus to a broader cultural and historical sphere.

Unfolding over the course of weeks and months, the contemplative works of Arcangel and Gordon resist the pace of spectacle and media culture, dominated by speed, novelty, and distraction. They address the spectator at a level of sensual engagement that forces a change in viewing habits. In early modernism, as David Campany writes, the 'photo-eye and the kino-eye (film-eye) were the driving metaphors for a new and dynamic intimacy between "man" and optical machine' (Campany: 10). The optical machines of contemporary video game culture, however, go well beyond the speed and spectacle of early and mid-century modernist culture, incorporating an accelerated motor component, a heightened interactive merging of the tactile and the optical. For his part, Arcangel works in the opposite direction of the adrenalized thumb culture that has developed around video games: 'I like to take the interactivity out of things actually' (in Berwick: 2). Working against the dominant current, he discovers a quality of slowness in video games, a quality of slowness that reads as resistance to speed, a slowness that responds to the kineticism of media culture with hypnotic and repetitive loop sequences that impose a slow pace upon the viewer.

Victor Burgin describes contemporary visual culture as a 'cinematic heterotopia' a network of overlapping but distinct cinematic interfaces and experiences (Burgin: 198). Drawing from Michel Foucault's description of heterotopias — spaces where several sites that are incompatible in themselves are juxtaposed — Burgin focuses on the crosscurrents of the mediascape and the way they converge in the typical, daily experience of the ordinary person. Television and the internet, CDs and cellphones, mp3s and the cineplex, podcasts, Wii, DVDs and instagram — the extraordinary multiplication of audiovisual forms in contemporary culture has created a world in which we are now 'entertained from cradle to grave whether we like it or not' (MacCabe, 2003: 301).

One of the consequences of this cinematic heterotopia, as Burgin describes it, is that films are now often viewed in fragments, rather than from start to finish. And they are viewed with varying degrees of attentiveness, ranging from indifferent observation to active engagement. The spectrum of media forms universally available in contemporary culture, that cross into the spectators' lives whether they seek out the experience or not, makes the ordinary spectator into an unwitting mimic of one of the great avant-garde experiments of the early twentieth century, what the surrealists Andre Breton and Jacques Vache called the 'derive', the practice of dashing from one cinema to another in order to achieve the disorientation that the surrealists believed could open onto a critique of everyday life. This once radical practice of disorientation has, in effect, become a mainstream activity, a powerful way to customize pleasure. In its passage to the everyday, the fragmentation and decomposition of film has, as Viktor Shklovsky said, 'completed its journey from poetry to prose' (in Burgin, 2007: 198).

A number of recent theorists have expressed pessimism and alarm, however, over the media's power over subjective life. The range and penetration of audiovisual culture has led some writers to argue that the cinematic now 'possesses' the spectator, that the 'society of the spectacle' has now installed itself in the unconscious psychic registers to the point that it is now 'in virtual command of our memories' (Burgin: 204). Society, in this view, has become a homogeneous mass that comes to 'share an increasingly uniform common memory' (Burgin: 205). The philosopher Bernard Steigler uses the term 'prosthetic memory' to describe the global audiovisual industry dedicated to producing a synchronized state of consciousness through the agency of 'temporal objects' — objects, like cinema or television, or a popular melody, that take shape only in relation to the consciousness that apprehends it, and that 'elapse' in synchrony with the spectator's consciousness. Cinema and television are paradigmatic expressions of the production of temporal objects, as masses of people tune in to the same television programmes at the same time, or head to the cinema for the opening weekend of blockbuster films. Rather than community or collectivity, Burgin argues, the uniformity that results creates a 'homogeneous impersonal mass who come to share an increasingly uniform common memory' (Burgin: 206).

The control of subjectivity through orchestrated temporal experiences creates, in this understanding, a kind of 'degraded' subjective environment, much as the biosphere is degraded by capital-intensive industries, and much like society is degraded by exploitation and vast inequality. This view accords with Felix Guattari's description of the contemporary world as defined by three 'ecologies', the environmental, the social and the mental, all of which are subject to what he calls 'integrated world capitalism'. The global audiovisual industry, for Steigler and Guattari, exemplifies the ecology of mind — which comes down to the control of memory and consciousness. As Burgin summarises:

> Renewing Deleuze's vision of a 'society of control' Steigler's prospectus is bleak, it conjures a world in which the global audiovisual industries, now in virtual command of our memories, determine what is visible and invisible, what may be heard and said, and what must remain inaudible and unutterable ... [it] conjures a world in which the spectator is 'possessed' by cinema.
> (Burgin: 206–7)

Metz, for his part, makes a similar statement from a very different analytic stance. As he explains,

> The cinematic institution is not just the cinema industry ... it is also the mental machinery — another industry — which spectators 'accustomed to the cinema' have internalised historically ... The second machine [is] the social regulation of the spectator's metapsychology.
> (Metz: 7)

In my view, the works considered in this essay, and the growing interest in the cinema as a material medium for the artistic exploration of subjectivity, memory, and culture, offer a striking rejoinder to Steigler's gloomy prognosis concerning the 'uniform common memory' of contemporary culture. Charged with personal and cultural affect, the film sequences and video games featured in the work of Gordon and Arcangel may very well speak to a subjectivity and a culture 'possessed by cinema', but their creative response to this possession is artistically innovative and informed, sparking an active process of creative remembering, very different from the prosthetic memory of mass audio-visual control described by Steigler. Indeed, the common cultural memory that has formed around these works, their heightened, iconic status within a culture of images, is a key part of their address to the gallery spectator, who here encounters his or her own vernacular cultural touchstones on unfamiliar terms.

In a recent essay, Fowler describes the evocation of cinematic memory as a key strategy of the 'gallery film' as it has developed since the 1990s, highlighting the fact that an increasing number of museum installations take the past of the cinema, and its relation to the spectator's present perceptions, as their subject. She distinguishes three main forms of engagement with the cinematic past in gallery installations: films in which cinema's past is replayed, as in the work of Gordon, without material changes to the image track itself; films that reenact the cinematic past, as in the restaging of *Rear Window* (1954) in Pierre Huyghe's *Remake* (1998), with different actors 'quoting' the dialogue and gestures; and finally, films in which the cinematic past is remade obliquely, with well-known films serving as the ground on which new films and sequences are constructed. The remaking of the cinematic past is exemplified by Salla Tykka's *Zoo* (2006), a film roughly based on the drowning sequence of *Vertigo* (1958), which serves as its shadow text. A dual image track of spectator memory and emotion is evoked in these films: the spectator's memory of the original film is solicited and reanimated while the new gallery film is unfolding. As Fowler writes: 'the way cinema is "remembered" in gallery films produces an alternative sense of the "visual" and hence of the "image" … is it the visible image itself, or the invisible, imaginative associations it carries that capture us?' (Fowler: 35). In these approaches to cinema's past lives, the interpenetration of cinematic memory and the subjective script of personal memory is foregrounded. 'The act of watching a film', as Maya Deren wrote in 1960, is 'a continuous act of recognition … like a strip of memory unrolling beneath the images of the film itself, to form the invisible underlayer of an implicit double exposure' (in Fowler: 37).

In the work of the artists I have discussed in this essay, however, there is something more elemental taking place, a complicated balancing act between attacking the medium itself — freezing the image, looping an iconic scene so that the film seems to confront its own specularity, forcing the pixels of a TV broadcast to dissolve into entropic blobs — and returning it to a purer condition, where the illusions of movement and narrative event are highlighted and dissolved. The artist Raphael Montanez Ortiz, a leader of the Destructivist movement who is best known for his 'ceremonial' destruction of grand pianos (whose cries and moans he records), describes his acts of destruction in art in shamanistic terms:

> it's a spiritual process; it's a shamanic process. But within the shamanic context there is this alchemy, this transmutiveness when you take a piece of furniture and you release the spirits that are contained within it. But beyond

that, it's returning the materials back to the nature that they've been captured from and have imprisoned in this object.

(Ortiz, 2011: 2)

In many ways, the work of Gordon and Arcangel 'returns the materials back to the nature they've been captured from', releasing the basic materials of film and video — the still image, the scrolling background, the pixelated screen — from the confines of narrative, temporal progression, and dramatic representation. By 'breaking the toy', the artists reveal a deeper level of fascination, one that links to the animistic basis of cinematic illusion, and its intrinsic patterning of creation and destruction.

Note

1   Some of the material from this chapter is reprinted from 'Customizing Pleasure: "Super Mario Clouds" and the John Ford Sky' from *Cinephilia in the Age of Digital Reproduction*, vol. 1, edited by Jason Sperb and Scott Balcerak. Copyright © 2009 Jason Sperb and Scott Balcerak. Reprinted with permission of Columbia University Press.

References

Barthes, Roland (1975) *The Pleasure of the Text*, trans. Richard Miller. New York: Hill and Wang.
——(1977) 'The Third Meaning: Research Notes on Some Eisenstein Stills', in Image Music Text, trans. by Stephen Heath. New York: Hill and Wang.
Baudelaire, Charles (1853) 'The Philosophy of Toys', trans. Paul Keegan. Available at: http//gv.pl/index.php/main/szkola/lalki/pdf/baudelaire.pdf (Accessed 8 September 2012).
Benjamin, Walter (1978 [1928]) 'Surrealism', in Peter Demetz (ed.) *Reflections*. New York: Harcourt Brace Jovanovich, 177–92.
Berwick, Carly (2006) 'Open Source Art?' *DigitAll Magazine*. Online. Available at: www.samsung.com/Features/BrandMagazine/magazinedigital1/2006_winter/feaC02a.htm (Accessed 11 May 2007).
Burgin, Victor (2007 [2006]) 'Possessive, Pensive and Possessed', in David Campany (ed.) *The Cinematic*. Cambridge, MA: The MIT Press, 198–209.
Campany, David (2007) 'Introduction//When to be Fast? When to be Slow?', in *The Cinematic*. Cambridge, MA: The MIT Press, 10–17.
Fowler, Catherine (2012) 'Remembering Cinema "Elsewhere": From Retrospection to Introspection in the Gallery Film', *Cinema Journal*, 51(2), 26–45.
Fyfe, Joe (2007) 'JF Gordon'. Available at: www.artcritical.com/fyfe/JFGordon (Accessed 11 May 2007).
Gunning, Tom (1995) 'An Aesthetic of Astonishment: Early Film and the (In)Credulous Spectator', in Linda Williams (ed.) *Viewing Positions: Ways of Seeing Film*. New Brunswick: Rutgers University Press, 114–33.

Hoberman, J. (2006) 'Twin Peaks: this season's smartest double bill is a match made in heaven and hell', *Village Voice Online*. Available at: www.villagevoice.com/film/0631,hoberman,74039,20.html (Accessed 11 May 2007).

MacCabe, Colin (2003) *Godard: a Portrait of the Artist at 70*. London: Bloomsbury.

Metz, Christian (1986) *The Imaginary Signifier: Psychoanalysis and the Cinema*, trans. Celia Britton, Annwyl Williams, Ben Brewster and Alfred Guzzetti. Bloomington: Indiana University Press.

Mulvey, Laura (2007 [2003]) 'Stillness in the Moving Image', in David Campany (ed.) *The Cinematic*. Cambridge, MA: The MIT Press, 134–9.

Ortiz, Raphael Montanez (2011) 'Interview with Pedro Reyes', in Laser/Disc/Scratch/Destruction: Raphael Montanez Ortiz Catalog, Labor Art Gallery, Colima, Mexico, April 5–May 21, 2011, p. 2.

Remes, Justin (2012) 'Motion(less) Pictures: The Cinema of Stasis', *British Journal of Aesthetics*, 52(3), 257–70.

——(2014) 'Serious Immobilities: Andy Warhol, Erik Satie, and the Furniture Film', *Screen*, 55(4) (forthcoming).

Chapter 13

Mirror images
D.W. Winnicott in the visual field

Vicky Lebeau

'Polemic: devaluing of all other pictures; provocation of the viewer, who sees himself instead of a picture': thus Gerhard Richter, reflecting on the effects of mirrors when placed in the art gallery (Obrist 2002: 99). At least since the construction of *4 Panes of Glass* in 1967, mirrors and glass – installed, sculpted, framed – have become part of Richter's aesthetic idiom, their attempt to make an object 'provocatively perfect' (Godfrey et al. 2011: 23). The recent major retrospective of Richter's work at Tate Modern, London – *Gerhard Richter: Panorama* ran from October 2011 to January 2012 – included *4 Panes of Glass*, *Double Pane of Glass* (1977), *Mirror* (1981), *11 Panes* (2004) and *6 Panes of Glass in a Rack* (2002–11). Reflecting on the chronological trajectory as well as the thematic preoccupations of Richter's oeuvre, the curators of *Panorama* dispersed these works amongst Richter's paintings, photo-paintings and colour charts. *4 Panes of Glass*, for example, was installed in the second room of the exhibition, 'Art after Duchamp', helping to secure the dialogue between Richter's installation and Marcel Duchamp's *The Bride Stripped Bare by Her Bachelors, Even* – also known as *The Large Glass* – produced between 1915 and 1923. *Double Pane of Glass* – two sheets of glass, made opaque by grey paint – was shown alongside the grey paintings and colour charts on which Richter was working from the late 1960s to the mid-1970s; *Mirror* – the work that helped to prompt this article – was hung to reflect a group of abstract colour paintings from the early 1980s, including *Hedge* (1982: hung directly opposite *Mirror*), *Yellow-green* (1982) and *Abstract Painting* (1983).

First shown at Städtische Kunsthalle in Düsseldorf in 1981, *Mirror* is, as Richter explains in interview, a 'piece of bought mirror. Just hung there, without any addition' (Obrist 2002: 272). Not framed, not made, there is nothing to distinguish *Mirror* from any other mirror apart from Richter's decision to hang it on the wall of a gallery; ready-made, then, or to borrow André Breton's description of that scandalous mode of not making art: 'an ordinary object promoted to the dignity of art object simply by way of the artist's choice' (Breton, cited by de Duve 1996: 93). That is, *Mirror* belongs to a tradition of aesthetic endeavour that finds its icon in Duchamp's *Fountain* – the urinal not exhibited at the Grand Central Palace in New York in 1917 – and its cause in the promotion of the autonomy of the art object (art is what an artist calls 'art' – a tautology unpacked, with exhaustive flair, by Thierry de Duve in *Kant After Duchamp*).

Polemic, provocation: Richter knows what he is doing with his *Mirror*, its intervention in the history of making and looking at pictures. On the attack, *Mirror* devalues pictures: painting or photograph, what art can compete with its flawless reproduction of the world in flux? What picture – abstract, realist, still, moving – can rival its continuous, if transient, capture of colour, line, blur, movement? Above all, perhaps, it connives against the conventions of looking at images made to be seen, visible, in the here and now, once and for all (what T.J. Clark has described as the 'fiction of visibility' supporting our ways of thinking and writing about images (Clark 2006: 9)). By contrast, to look at *Mirror* is to look at whatever happens to be caught up in that reflecting surface. Hanging there, it mirrors what comes before it: pictures, people, objects, spaces. 'Even,' Richter acknowledges, 'at the risk of being boring' (Obrist 2002: 272). Propped on the world, it loses – if it ever had – that much-vaunted autonomy of the ready-made. To look at *Mirror* is to change it. It has no identity with itself (what Theodor Adorno describes as the inherent desire of every artwork); nor can it stabilise the images that it reflects back into the world (Adorno 1997: 5). At rest, *Mirror* cannot be seen. Reproduced on the page, for example, *Mirror* is no longer a mirror; it loses its capacity to reflect, becoming a photograph of a mirror and its reflections, made immobile, unchanging. In this sense, it is impossible to 'see' *Mirror*, impossible to stabilise its 'meaning'. As art object, as image, it exists in the flow of time and movement; it is at once immediate and elusive, tedious and vital. 'For surviving this world' is Richter's response when asked, in interview, about the purpose of art: 'like bread, like love,' he continues (Godfrey et al. 2011: 24). An object to live with, then, in a world struck by need and desire: wondrous, everyday, ready-made.

Does *Mirror* matter? What does it matter to the ongoing dialogue between psychoanalysis and studies in the visual field? Putting pressure on our ways of looking at and thinking about pictures, *Mirror* can solicit a form of attention in which interpretation gives way to reflection, object gives place to environment. As such, it can become an object to think with about what appears to be a moment of transition – and, for me, revived potential – in the relation between psychoanalysis and the image: today, on the cusp between psychoanalysis and the visual field, there is a 'turn' towards the writings of D.W. Winnicott and, more broadly, the British Independent Tradition nurtured by both his writings and his practice.[1] Environment, mirror: two of the most significant words in Winnicott's lexicon, used to explore what he calls 'dependence [as] a living fact', with all the consequences of that fact for his intervention in the theory and practice of psychoanalysis (Winnicott 1974: 103). In particular, 'Mirror-role of Mother and Family in Child Development', first published in 1967, is an invitation to revisit the figure of the mirror in terms of the relation between psychoanalysis and the image.[2] Ever since Freud's advice to the would-be analyst in 1912 that he should remain 'opaque to his patients and, like a mirror ... show them nothing but what is shown to him', the mirror has been one of the founding metaphors of psychoanalytic practice: a strange mirror, certainly, the analyst reflecting not the visible but the hidden and removed from the patient's field of vision (Freud's technical innovation in the 1890s that, as Kenneth Wright points out, has left a gap in psychoanalysis where the face should be) (Freud 1912: 118; Wright 1991). But a mirror that – as metaphor, as object – draws psychoanalysis into the long history of human wondering about reflection and perception, image and illusion, visible and invisible (that fascinating world beyond the looking-glass).[3]

It's a history that agitates through the various encounters between psychoanalysis and the visual field: notably, the rapid development of a psychoanalytic film theory, or 'Screen' theory, grounded in the figure of the mirror. 'Thus film is like the mirror': in 1975, Christian Metz's groundbreaking, if wayward, analogy was propped on Jacques Lacan's 'Le Stade du Miroir' and, more broadly, Lacan's concept of the imaginary; however flawed – 'this mirror,' Metz acknowledged, 'returns us everything but ourselves'; it is another 'strange mirror' – it helped to create a body of work poised to engage the 'passion for perceiving' (to borrow Metz's phrase) through the discipline of psychoanalysis (Metz 1982: 45; 49; 58). Or more precisely, through the work of Freud and Lacan. The encounter between psychoanalysis and the visual field has been, and often remains, deeply engaged with the concepts emerging from Freud's analysis of sexuality and sexual difference in the 1920s and 1930s (identification, voyeurism, fetishism, castration, disavowal) and from Lacan's incomparable 'return to Freud' (imaginary, symbolic, real, gaze, suture, objet petit a, sinthome). One way of telling the recent history of psychoanalytic film theory, for example, is to say that, since the 1960s, it has arrived in two 'waves', both of them generated by Lacan (be it the Lacan of identification and the imaginary or the Lacan of the real and the gaze).[4] That the second wave arrives in the mode of a corrective of the first does nothing to disturb the Lacanian edifice; on the contrary, rehearsal of the primal scene of Lacanian film theory, its origins in a supposed misunderstanding of the screen as mirror, may well strengthen its ground. 'Believing itself to be following Lacan, it conceives the screen as mirror; in doing so, however, it operates in ignorance of, and at the expense of, Lacan's more radical insight, whereby the mirror is conceived as a screen': in 1989, Joan Copjec's intervention set the terms for a renewal of Lacanian film theory that, continuing to hold sway, puts Lacan's concept of the gaze, its attention to the domains of the invisible and the absent, at the heart of its project (Copjec 1999: 15–16). At stake is both a reading of Lacan – the concept of the gaze and the break, if that is what it is, introduced by *The Ethics of Psychoanalysis* in 1959–1960 – and the position of Lacan as what, at the beginning of *The Fright of Real Tears*, Slavoj Žižek describes as the 'ultimate background' of psychoanalytic film theory (Žižek 2001: 2).

That this is a form of dogma, brilliant in its very blindspots, is part of its fascination and its provocation. Most provocative, perhaps, in so far as the 'new Lacanianism' (or what Stephen Heath once described as 'Žižek-film') enforces a type of interruption of the psychoanalysis of cinema that came before it (and, possibly, that which comes afterwards) (Heath 1999: 45).[5] Recast as the symptoms of a narrow, and fatally mistaken, reading of Lacan, the idea of the mirror and the imaginary – and, with them, the dialogue between psychoanalysis and cinema as institutions, or apparatuses, with distinctive forms and practices – are relegated to the margins of an erroneous history.[6] Marginalised, too, are those forms of psychoanalytic film theory not identified with the Lacanian cause: in Todd McGowan's recent summary, while there have been works of film theory engaged with, say, Melanie Klein, Winnicott or Carl Jung, they are 'isolated' (McGowan's term: it is an especially freighted word) from the 'primary source' that is Jacques Lacan.[7] 'Paths not taken,' as Lisa Cartwright has recently summarised the (non) relation between film theory and psychoanalysis beyond the Lacanian tradition (Cartwright is especially concerned with Winnicott's object relations theory (Cartwright 2008: 11)).

In other words, the mirror in question in film theory derives from an influential, but only partial, exploration of the vicissitudes of the mirror in psychoanalysis. Whilst Lacan's 'Le Stade du Miroir' became one of the founding texts of psychoanalytic film theory, Winnicott's intervention passed unnoticed, or unused, in writings on cinema and spectatorship.[8] But that Winnicott was not there the first time around is part of the significance of 'Mirror-role of Mother and Family', its capacity to intervene in what we think we know about mirrors and screens – no doubt, Metz's passing comment on the 'subterranean persistence of the exclusive relation to the mother' in his discussion of Lacan's imaginary is agitating through what I'm saying – and to respond to the provocation to thinking about images embodied in Richter's *Mirror* (Metz 1982: 4). From the very beginning of 'Mirror-role of Mother and Family', Winnicott takes the idea of the mirror and gives it back to us differently:

> In individual emotional development the precursor of the mirror is the mother's face. I wish to refer to the normal aspect of this and also to its psychopathology.
>
> Jacques Lacan's paper 'Le Stade du Miroir' (1949) has certainly influenced me. He refers to the use of the mirror in each individual's ego development. However, Lacan does not think of the mirror in terms of the mother's face in the way that I wish to do here.
>
> (Winnicott 1999: 111)

'Mirror-role of Mother and Family' is Winnicott's only explicit, if elusive, response to Lacan's 'Le Stade du Miroir'; as such, it is a tantalising object for those of us exploring the relation between psychoanalysis and the image ('[I]f we are good,' as Winnicott puts it in 1958, 'we are also tantalising. We offer something, but we seem to withhold it' (Winnicott 1958: 425)). To discover Winnicott reading Lacan, or to imagine him discussing the mirror stage with the patient, a woman, central to "Mirror-role of Mother and Family" – 'the patient went on to speak of 'Le Stade du Miroir' because she knows of Lacan's work, but she was not able to make the link that I feel I am able to make between the mirror and the mother's face' – is to be given the opportunity to resist an apparent opposition between the two that, as André Green suggests, has sustained a split within contemporary psychoanalysis (I will come back to this) (Winnicott 1999: 117; Green 2011: 29). The face and the self; looking and seeing; reflecting and recognizing: these are the terms that will govern 'Mirror-role of Mother and Family' as, putting the mother before the mirror, Winnicott forges an extraordinarily subtle account of the origins of a self in the work and the risk of looking and being looked at. In fact, the infant, seeing himself seen by the mother-mirror, becomes the very figure of the emergence of self, mind and creativity:

> What does the baby see when he or she looks at the mother's face? I am suggesting that, ordinarily, what the baby sees is himself or herself. In other words the mother is looking at the baby and what she looks like is related to what she sees there. All this is too easily taken for granted. I am asking that this which is naturally done well by mothers who are caring for their babies shall not be taken for granted. I can make my point by going straight over to the case of the baby whose mother reflects her own mood or, worse still, the rigidity of her own defences. In such a case what does the baby see?
> (Winnicott 1999: 112)

All this, Winnicott tells us, 'belongs to the beginning' and, in attempting to present it, he draws on the words of those patients 'who can verbalize (when they feel they can do so) without insulting the delicacy of what is preverbal, unverbalized, and unverbalizable except perhaps in poetry' (ibid.). Or, perhaps, in the image, be it verbal and visual. The woman with whom Winnicott discusses Lacan is also preoccupied by the paintings of Francis Bacon: she is reading Ronald Alley and John Rothenstein's catalogue to the retrospective of Bacon's work, which opened at the Tate Gallery in May 1962 and draws Winnicott's attention to Bacon's preference for glazing his paintings: 'he likes to have glass over his pictures because then when people look at the picture what they see is not just a picture; they might in fact see themselves' (shades of Richter's *Mirror*) (ibid.: 117). 'Wouldn't it be awful,' she exclaims in the course of her session, 'if a child looked into the mirror and saw nothing!' (ibid.: 116). It's a stark, and unsettling, vision: a child, a mirror, a reflection – of the self, of the world – that, because it is not there, becomes awful; not reflecting, the mirror has become a bizarre object, visible but empty. An object to be looked at, but not into. Like the face of a mother who looks at you but does not make you visible? 'In individual emotional development,' Winnicott insists, 'the precursor of the mirror is the mother's face' (ibid.: 111).

The child who cannot find her reflection; the painter who takes his chance with ours: Winnicott will track the ties between the two back to the earliest responses between mother and baby. Let's recall that elsewhere Winnicott describes the mother who emerges in the very earliest phases of her baby's life as in a state of 'primary maternal preoccupation', 'given over to' her baby in a form of withdrawal from the world (including, to some extent, herself) (Winnicott 1963: 85). Something like a state of fugue, a phase of 'normal illness', the idea of primary maternal preoccupation is essential to Winnicott's exploration of the origins of illusion, imagination and creativity. Nothing less than a reversal of reality takes place via this state in which the mother, identifying with her baby's states of body, need, feeling, mind, creates an environment in which that baby can experience her absolute helplessness – specific prematurity of birth, in Lacan's terms, dependence as a living fact, in Winnicott's – as a form of magical (illusory) omnipotence (Lacan 2002). The wager is extraordinary but, Winnicott insists, profoundly ordinary, too (or, as Green suggests, Winnicott noticed 'what had been escaping everyone's attention' (Green 1996: 287)).

'Mirror-role of Mother and Family' presents Winnicott's most sustained reflection on the significance of the mother's face – her capacity to look at her baby and to see what is there – to that ordinary-extraordinary care. The exchange of looks between two belongs to the environment: the mother's capacity to look at and to give back what she sees in her baby is part of that care; in other words her face, her looking, are forms of holding, handling and object-presenting (the three elements of the environmental function outlined by Winnicott at the beginning of 'Mirror-role of the Mother and Family': on one reading, the mirror could be described as the royal road to the environment for Winnicott). In looking at her baby, the mother's face changes in time (moves, animates) in relation to what she sees in and of her baby: 'the mother is looking at the baby and what she looks like is related to what she sees there'. Brought to bear on a scene at once simple and spectacular, it is worth noting the nuance of Winnicott's words at this point. Not everything is, or can be, caught up in the mother's face, or the gift of her looking back, that, for Winnicott, creates the ground for the 'creative apperception [very schematically, seeing oneself being seen by the mother] ... that makes the individual feel that life is worth living' (Winnicott 1999: 65). (This is also what Winnicott describes, in a few comments on Bacon, as 'creative looking' (ibid.: 114).) The not-seen, the not-reflected – what, in a different context, Juliet Mitchell has inflected as a 'primal nonrecognition' – agitates through Winnicott's discussion of the mother's face be it 'good enough' (alive, reflecting but not-all) or, at the other end of the spectrum, still, paralysed, full of the mother's mood, 'dead' (Mitchell 1998: 124). In such cases, the mother's face – her face, reflecting her moods, her defences – becomes too visible, too perceptible, to the baby, who then loses the potential for self emerging in that precious space between the seen and unseen. The baby looks, Winnicott concludes, but he does not see himself: 'what is seen is the mother's face. The mother's face is not then a mirror' (Winnicott 1999: 113).

To put these points another way: the limits of perception become tangible in that imaginary scene in which a child, standing before the mirror, sees nothing. The phrase may strain our capacity to visualise, but the patient's sense of its terror orients us towards an aspect of the visual field characterised by blankness, emptiness, non-presence. We are some way here from Lacan's fascination with the baby, captivated by the image of his reflection, craning towards the mirror. This is not the domain of mis-recognition, the lure of the image, that psychoanalysis has done so much to explain. By contrast, Winnicott is excavating the maternal dimension of the visual field, its dependence on the structuring function of the mother: as a type of spectacle, the mother's face bears the distinction between movement and stillness, life and death, human and inhuman (think, for example, of the special status accorded to the smile, or what Michael Eigen describes as the 'home base of the human self' (Eigen 1980: 55). '[The baby] learns to distinguish animate objects from inanimate ones,' writes René Spitz in 1945, 'by the spectacle provided by his mother's face' (Spitz 1945: 67). Or, to go back to Winnicott, 'the mother is looking at the baby and what she looks like is related to what she sees there': the baby's experience of being alive, of being seen, comes back to her but relatively, differently. In relation, not reproduction.

Relation, not reproduction: the terms take us back to Richter's *Mirror*. What matters, I think, is that relation in reflection, a reflective relation, coming right to the fore between an artwork and its viewers in *Mirror*. That shift from object to environment, interpretation to reflection is one that runs throughout 'Mirror-role of Mother and Family', sustained by Winnicott's conversations with his patients and their shared uses of Lacan and Francis Bacon, psychoanalysis and visual culture (Bacon, Winnicott insists, is an artist who 'forces his way into any present day discussion of the face and the self'; in Bacon's looking at faces, in his distortion of the human face, there is a painful 'striving towards being seen' (Winnicott 1999: 114)). Crucially, if one of the fascinations of 'Mirror-role of Mother and Family' is its opening wager with Lacan, the other is its remarkable intervention on the limits of interpretation in the practice of psychoanalysis and psychoanalytic psychotherapy. 'Psychotherapy is not making clever and apt interpretations,' Winnicott insists, reflecting on the analyst's task in the light of his discovery of the ties between mirror and mother; 'by and large it is a long-term giving the patient back what the patient brings. It is a complex derivative of the face that reflects what is there to be seen' (Winnicott 1999: 117). Embedded in this statement is the history, and theory, of Winnicott's analytic practice (a practice that is still being understood). There is also a challenge to the predominance of the work of interpretation in our uses of psychoanalysis in visual and cultural studies. What might we do other than or as well as interpret? That is also, I think, the question of Richter's *Mirror* – the ways in which it holds or handles us, the environment it creates.

Postscript

Winnicott and Lacan can seem an unlikely pair. But, reflecting on the perceived opposition, Green has insisted on the convergence between Winnicott and Lacan derived from one of the fundamental questions of psychoanalysis, namely: 'how is it that by means of speech we change something in the structure of the subject, whereas what we change does not belong to the field of speech?' (Clancier and

Kalmanovitch 1987: 121). Emphasising their shared preoccupation with that beyond of the field of speech – what, as we've seen, Winnicott refers to as the unverbalisable – Green points to the importance, as well as the challenge, of bringing Winnicott and Lacan together in the study of the relation between psychoanalysis and the image. Beyond speech, the psychoanalytic method – talking, listening, the 'setting' – refers to or represents something that, while having to find expression in words, exists, and persists, beyond them. How that 'something' is conceived – how or what we think about it – may well depend on our understanding of the psychoanalytic method or model (dream, drive, environment, for example). But that psychoanalysis mediates between language and forms of experience and expression that cannot be caught up into words is part of the wager of its intervention in our ways of thinking about the visual field. Finding the words to say it is certainly one way to describe the process of a psychoanalysis; it could also describe the struggle to forge a language responsive to the difference of our experience of the visual field (what Clark has recently called its precious distance from verbal discourse).[9]

Winnicott, Lacan: the encounter belongs within a very wide theoretical, historical and institutional frame – one that makes the recent turn to Winnicott in visual and cultural studies a remarkably complex undertaking. What Jacqueline Rose once described as 'post-Lacanian orthodoxy' in the humanities may be nowhere more apparent than in psychoanalytic film theory (Rose 1993: 139).[10] No surprise, then, that, as Matt Hills has suggested recently, 'it is tempting to feel that Lacanian orthodoxy has displaced Winnicott's approach' (Kuhn 2013: 103). But to displace Lacan in the name of Winnicott is not only to reproduce a division within psychoanalysis that, as Deborah Luepnitz indicates, is only now beginning to close; it is also to put at risk the analysis of sexuality and representation, image and fantasy, that flourished in film theory through the 1970s and 1980s (Luepnitz 2011: 1–28).[11] Certainly, to think about Winnicott in relation to that flourishing is to discover what is not there – or not perceived to be there – in his work. 'If there were Winnicottians,' as Adam Phillips concludes his brief study of Winnicott's psychoanalysis, 'they would have to recover from Winnicott's flight into infancy, his flight from the erotic' (Phillips 1988: 152). Given its preoccupations, psychoanalytic film theory may well provide one of the settings for such a Winnicottian 'recovery' (this is part of the wider project within which this article sits). Equally, Winnicott may be absent from the founding works of psychoanalytic film theory, but he shares their preoccupation with the topics of perception and illusion, image and identity. To reconsider the figure of the mirror is one way for psychoanalytic film theory to reflect on what it is doing and why; it is also, I think, to begin a conversation in the spaces between Winnicott, Lacan and the provocation of the mirror. A response, in other words, to the question: what happens if you put a mirror in a gallery?

Figure 13.1 Obscure Window 2 by Nicholas Muellner
Source: Reproduced with permission of the artist

Notes

1. Bringing together the work of the Transitional Phenomena and Cultural Experience study group (T-PACE: www.sllf.qmul.ac.uk/filmstudies/t_pace/index.html), the publication of *Little Madnesses: Winnicott, Transitional Phenomena and Cultural Experience* is one example of such a turn. Edited by Annette Kuhn, this volume covers a wide range of cultural objects but there is a marked emphasis on visual experience. Similarly, the recent 'Moving Objects: Film, Relation, Change' conference at Birkbeck, London (January 2014) put object relations theory at the heart of its exploration of psychoanalysis and the moving image.

2. 'Mirror-role of Mother and Family in Child Development' was first published in *The Predicament of the Family: A Psycho-Analytical Symposium*, edited by Peter Lomas, in 1967, and then republished, posthumously, in Winnicott's *Playing and Reality* in 1971 – described by André Green as 'the most important psychoanalytic work since Freud's death' (Green 2011: 43).

3. For a fascinating history of the mirror, see Melchior-Bonnet (2002).

4. Todd McGowan's entry on Psychoanalytic Film Theory for Oxford Bibliographies online exemplifies this mode of telling history: www.oxfordbibliographies.com/view/document/obo-9780199791286/obo-9780199791286-0052.xml (last accessed 6th February 2014). This free online article essentially re-states the Introduction to McGowan (2008).

5. The effect is not unlike that of the repression described by Lacan, in fact, in his seminar on Freud's papers on technique, delivered as part of the training programme of the Société Française de Psychanalyse between 1953 and 1954. Picking up on the phrase 'le mot me manque' – 'the word escapes me' – Lacan draws his audience's attention to the work of repression in the domain of discourse: 'Because, and make a careful note of this,' he exhorts, 'each time that repression takes place … there is always interruption of discourse. The subject says that the word escapes him' (Lacan 1988: 268). A 'repression of discourse' may be one way to describe the occlusion of the mirror and the imaginary taking place in that 'second wave' of Lacanian film theory.

6. His focus is not on the mirror but Stephen Heath makes a similar point: 'it is indicative that Žižek has, in fact, little to say about "institution," "apparatus," and so on, all the concerns of the immediately preceding attempts to think cinema and psychoanalysis (films and novels will thus mostly be referred to without any particular distinction between them as forms)' (1999: 44).

7. See Note 4 for references. Put that way, the task of the film scholar can quickly become that of distinguishing between the thinkers who 'engage with' or 'appropriate' Lacan and those who fully endorse him (the terms are Žižek's who accepts only Copjec and some un-named Slovene colleagues as Lacanians in this strong and somewhat unnerving sense (Žižek 2001: 2)). Or, perhaps, of mounting a defence of the bastions of film theory against encroachment by a reading of Lacan that is not Lacanian enough (not 'good enough', you might say). In a recent critique of Copjec's criticism of the 'first wave' Lacanians, Henry Krips calls for a 'more Lacanian account of the panoptic gaze' to correct her, Copjec's, misreading of Foucault (Krips 2010: 92). The problem with this, as I see it, is that neither defends the need to make theory – a commitment to thinking wedded to de-disciplinisation – nor counters the effects of 'dire mastery' to borrow Routstang's phrase that continue to fuel the criticisms of (psychoanalytic) theory as a dogmatic liability within the humanities (Roustang 1986).

8. To my knowledge, Jacqueline Rose's widely-used introduction to *Feminine Sexuality: Jacques Lacan and the école freudienne*, first published in 1982, was then the only discussion of Lacan's mirror stage to refer to Winnicott's 'Mirror-role of Mother and

Family' (reprinted in Rose 1986: 53). However, it's worth noting that, in 1975, her seminal discussion on 'The Imaginary', presented in response to what Rose described, even then, as the 'fairly loose' uses of that concept in film studies, was silent on Winnicott (Rose 1986: 168).
9 See Clark (2006). *Les Mots Pour Le Dire* is the title of Marie Cardinal's extraordinary account of her analysis, first published in 1975.
10 Rose's concern was that that orthodoxy was then blocking access to the work of Melanie Klein; in light of the 'two waves' of Lacanian film theory, it might well have blocked access to Lacan, too.
11 Certainly, at the one-day conference accompanying the launch of *Little Madnesses*, there was an identifiable theme in the questions from the audience, crudely: 'Where is the unconscious in all this?'

References

Cardinal, M. 1975. *Les Mots Pour Le Dire*. Paris: Le Livre de Poche.
Cartwright, L. 2008. *Moral Spectatorship: Technologies of Voice and Affect in Postwar Representations of the Child*. Durham NC: Duke University Press.
Clancier, A. and Kalmanovitch, J. 1987. *Winnicott and Paradox from Birth to Creation* (includes 'Interview with André Green'). London and New York: Tavistock Publications.
Clark, T.J. 2006. *The Sight of Death: an Experiment in Art Writing*. New Haven and London: Yale University Press.
Copjec. J. 1994. *Read My Desire: Lacan against the Historicists*. Cambridge, MA and London: MIT Press.
de Duve, T. 1996. *Kant After Duchamp*. Cambridge, MA and London: MIT Press.
Eigen, M. 1980. 'The Significance of the Face'. In: Eigen, M. 1993. *The Electrified Tightrope*. Northvale, NJ and London: Jason Aronson Inc.
Freud, S. 1912. 'Recommendations to Physicians Practising Psycho-Analysis'. In: *The Standard Edition of the Complete Psychological Works of Sigmund Freud. Volume XII*. London: The Hogarth Press and the Institute of Psycho-Analysis, pp. 109–120.
Godfrey M. et al. eds. 2011. Gerhard Richter: *Panorama*. London: Tate Publishing.
Green, A. 1997. *On Private Madness*. London: Rebus Press.
—— 2011. 'The bifurcation of contemporary psychoanalysis: Lacan and Winnicott'. In: Kirshner, L.A., ed. *Between Winnicott and Lacan: A Clinical Engagement*. New York and London: Routledge, pp. 29–50.
Heath, S. 1999. 'Cinema and Psychoanalysis: Parallel Histories'. In: Bergstrom, J. ed. *Endless Night: Cinema and Psychoanalysis, Parallel Histories*. Berkeley, CA and London: University of California Press, pp. 25–56.
Krips, H. 2010. 'The Politics of the Gaze: Foucault, Lacan and Žižek'. *Culture Unbound*, 2, 91–102. Hosted by Linköping University Electronic Press: www.cultureunbound. ep.liu.se
Kuhn, A. ed. 2013. *Little Madnesses: Winnicott, Transitional Phenomena and Cultural Experience*. London and New York: I.B. Tauris.
Lacan, J. 1988. *The Seminar of Jacques Lacan. Book I. Freud's Papers on Technique*. Cambridge: Cambridge University Press.
——1992. The Ethics of Psychoanalysis 1959–1960. *The Seminar of Jacques Lacan. Book VII*. London: Tavistock/Routledge.

—— 2002. 'The *Mirror* Stage as Formative of the I Function as Revealed in Psychoanalytic Experience'. In: Lacan, J., *Ecrits*. New York and London: W.W. Norton & Company.

Lomas, P. ed. 1967. *The Predicament of the Family: A Psycho-Analytical Symposium*. London: The Hogarth Press and the Institute of Psycho-Analysis.

Luepnitz, D. A. 2011. 'Thinking in the space between Winnicott and Lacan'. In: Kirshner, L.A., ed. *Between Winnicott and Lacan: A Clinical Engagement*. New York and London: Routledge, pp. 1–28.

McGowan, T. 2008. *The Real Gaze: Film Theory After Lacan*. New York: SUNY.

Melchior-Bonnet, S. 2002. *The Mirror: A History*. London and New York: Routledge.

Metz, C. 1982. *Psychoanalysis and Cinema: The Imaginary Signifier*. London: Macmillan Press.

Mitchell, J. 1998. 'Trauma, recognition and the place of language'. *Diacritics*, 28, 4, 121–133.

Obrist, H-U. ed. 2002 Gerhard Richter. *The Daily Practice of Painting: Writings and Interviews 1962–1993*. London: Thames & Hudson.

Phillips, A. 1988. *Winnicott*. London: Fontana Press.

Rose, J. 1986. *Sexuality in the Field of Vision*. London: Verso.

Roustang, F. 1986. *Dire Mastery: Discipleship from Freud to Lacan*. Arlington, VA: American Psychiatric Press Inc.

Spitz, R. 1945. 'Hospitalism: An Inquiry into the Genesis of Psychiatric Conditions in Early Childhood', *The Psychoanalytic Study of the Child*, I, 53–74.

Winnicott, D.W. 1963 'From Dependence Towards Independence in the Development of the Individual'. In: Winnicott, D.W. 1990. *The Maturational Processes and the Facilitating Environment*. London: Karnac Books.

——1974. 'Fear of Breakdown'. *The International Review of Psycho-Analysis*, 1, 103–107.

——1999. *Playing and Reality*. London and New York: Routledge.

Winnicott, D.W. and Markillie, R. 1958. Review of 'The Doctor, his Patient and the Illness: By Michael Balint London: Pitman Publishing Co. 1957. *International Journal of Psycho-Analysis*, 39, 425–428.

Wright, K. 1991. *Vision and Separation Between Mother and Baby*. London: Free Association Books.

Žižek, S. 2001. *The Fright of Real Tears: Krzystof Kieslowski Between Theory and Post-Theory*. London: BFI Publishing.

Chapter 14

Pinning a tale

The screen, the donkey and the MacGuffin

Carol MacGillivray

In his book, *The Exploits of the Incomparable Mulla Nasrudin*, the Sufi Mystic Idries Shah tells this tale of the varlet Nasrudin: Time and time again Nasrudin passed from Persia to Greece on a donkey. Each time he had two panniers of straw and trudged back without them. Every time the guards turned out his panniers looking for contraband, but they never found any: 'What are you carrying, Nasrudin?' they asked. 'I am a smuggler', he replied. Years later, when prosperous, Nasrudin moved to Egypt and one of the customs officers met him there: 'Tell me, now that you are out of the jurisdiction of Greece and Persia, living here in such luxury, what was it that you were smuggling when we could never catch you?' 'Donkeys', Nasrudin replied (Shah, 1968).

The screen is a paradox in that it can be defined both as a device on which narratives are displayed and also as a screen for something, a concealer. Like the donkey in the story, its function is both to 'show' and to 'hide'. This essay discusses the ontology of the 'screen', first as a framing device for film and its correspondence in psychoanalysis as a boundary between the conscious and the unconscious and second, as 'screen memory', a predominant, psychological mechanism of displacement. Further, this paper looks at what would be the implication of removing the screen by discussing an intra-film experience that does away with it altogether in the form of the *Diasynchronoscope*.

The *Diasynchronoscope* is an emergent new medium in screen-less animation.[1] The system draws on tropes from film, animation, and Gestalt grouping to create replicable, embodied perception of concrete objects moving precisely synchronized with sound – but unmediated by lens or screen. As an embodied medium, it eliminates the screen and all the inherent boundaries that accompany it, using elements of psychoanalysis to create a metaphysical experience. Installations are experienced in a blackout and apparent motion is achieved by animating through attention.

The *Diasynchronoscope* creates a circumstance in which the screen is removed and so the participant is left with her own unconscious memories, fears and fantasies inside the visual experience. By combining psychoanalysis and other theoretical paradigms with case studies of audience experience of artworks made using the *Diasynchronoscope* this essay seeks to explore the ontological status

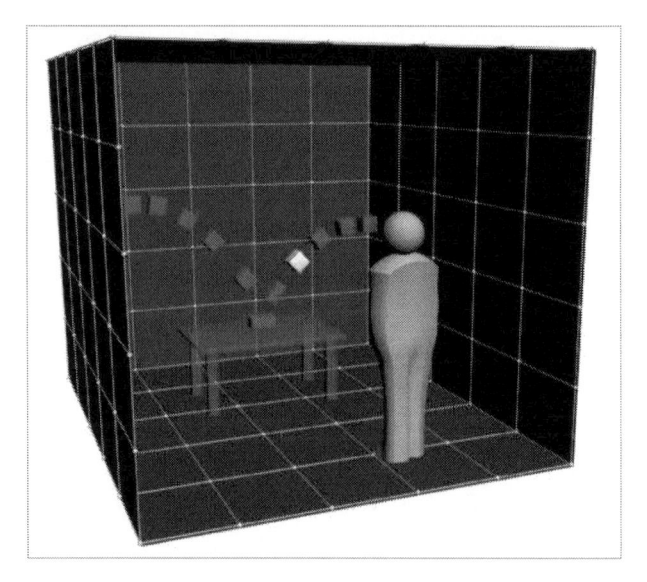

Figure 14.1 A simple visualisation of Diasynchronoscope

given to the screen (and by inference the spectator)[2] and offer a way of solving the paradoxical nature of the screen. Although much has been written about the relationship between the spectator and the screen in film theory based on Foucault's opposition between spectacle and surveillance (Foucault, 1977; Baudry, 1986a; Mayne, 1993), the ontological status of the screen is rarely questioned. Because the *Diasynchronoscope* provides an embodied intra-filmic encounter where the screen is no longer a component and the spectator/viewer becomes participant, it offers a new standpoint for the way the moving image can be perceived.

Two analogies for the screen appear in Shah's tale. First is the 'donkey' of mass media; its ubiquity means that it is hidden in plain sight, it has been smuggled into our world and staged a takeover, and we, as audience have barely noticed because we are too busy looking in the straw, consciously engaging with content. Second, there is an analogy to be found in the story with Freud's writings on screen memory. A screen memory is created from childhood, it marks a traumatic event, but also renders it bearable by replacing it with something less pertinent; it is the screen as 'MacGuffin'[3]. It says 'I am a smuggler' but does not reveal what it is smuggling. Freud wrote, 'Screen memories are like shams ... they are not made of gold themselves but have lain beside something that is made of gold' (Freud, 1899: 307). In Shah's story, the screen memory is the straw; in that it acts as MacGuffin and masker of the truth. In psychoanalytic terms, this masker of trauma is, as psychoanalyst on childhood trauma, Phyllis Greenacre (1949: 77) remarks, one that is 'stubbornly resistant to analysis'. Uncovering the 'sham' is a breakthrough as it reveals the gold that it lies beside, and there is general agreement amongst psychologists that the dissipation of a screen memory is a signal that a patient has entered the closing stages of psychoanalysis (Mahon & Battin, 1981). This essay suggests a new way of reconciling the filmic 'donkey' and the screen memory 'straw' MacGuffin through embodied experience of moving image.

In the *Diasynchronoscope*, the ontological screen is eliminated entirely. There is a commonality to experiencing the *Diasynchronoscope* (as there is with film), but perhaps the first thing to note is that because of its embodied nature, the term 'viewer' with its consequent connotations of passivity is inadequate for someone within the *Diasynchronoscope*. Jonathan Crary (1992: 6) makes a deliberate semantic distinction between 'observer' and 'spectator' taking it back to its Latin roots of: 'observare [which] means "to conform one's action, to comply with", as in observing rules, codes, regulations and practices'. Lev Manovich (2001: 205) also addresses this in a new media context, suggesting renaming 'subjects' first as 'viewers' then as 'users'. The *Diasynchronoscope* challenges the use of passive nouns to describe an audience still further and uses the term 'participant' as a construct to describe the co-authored nature of narratives within the *Diasynchronoscope*. Without having a participant engaged in an audio-visual contract with the artworks and constructing movement using their individual perceptual shortcuts, there is no artwork.

We are very used to perceiving apparent motion on a screen, but apparent motion that eliminates flicker and is veridical, in terms of perspective, focus and parallax is a new sensation. In fact this new sensation creates a considerable sense of wonder, and in part this must be attributed to participants being reflexively aware of sensori-motor feedback that does *not* include optic accommodation for translating a flat image into three dimensions.[4]

The flat screen is a definer of visual space. It is a visual medium with sound added, but acoustic spaces are automatically multi-dimensional. McLuhan probes the distinction between visual space and acoustic space thus:

> [Acoustic space] has no center and no margin, unlike strictly linear space, which is an extension and intensification of the eye. Acoustic space is organic and integral, perceived through the simultaneous interplay of all the senses; whereas 'rational' or pictorial space is uniform, sequential and continuous and creates a closed world.
>
> (McLuhan, 1969)

Although McLuhan formulated the idea of acoustic space to accommodate electronic and digital technologies, acoustic spaces are multi-sensual, and are, by their very nature, somatic (of the body). Such has been the power of the screen as a frame and the notion of the spectator/screen divide that moving image artworks that take on embodiment as a goal for artistic aspiration are rare. The *Diasynchronoscope* was invented with this aspiration.

In the *Diasynchronoscope*, the participant shares an acoustic space with the animation and is able to move freely around the moving image. Static objects are grouped according to Gestalt laws and animation principles to create sequential visual cues that, when lit with projected light, demand selective attention; thus creating the illusion of animated movement. There is no flicker in the light, so the apparent motion is veridical in nature. Many of the artworks deliberately suppress semiotic and symbolic interpretation of objects, by animating platonic solids and eschewing colour, the ambition is to imbue an aesthetic of pure movement. The animation is immersive and sound is also spatialized and synchronous, so that participants perceive a continuous flow of movement that resembles, at a physiological level, interaction with a real-life moving object.

The name comes from combining diachronic (the study of a phenomenon as it changes through time) with synchronous and scope (view). In being so named, it evokes the early animation simulators such as the *phenakistoscope* and the *zoetrope*, regarded as direct ancestors of the project as they too function both as art objects and experimental media.

Feedback from participants brings accounts of being mesmerized, experiencing something 'awesome', 'magic' and outside their previous experience. Many say

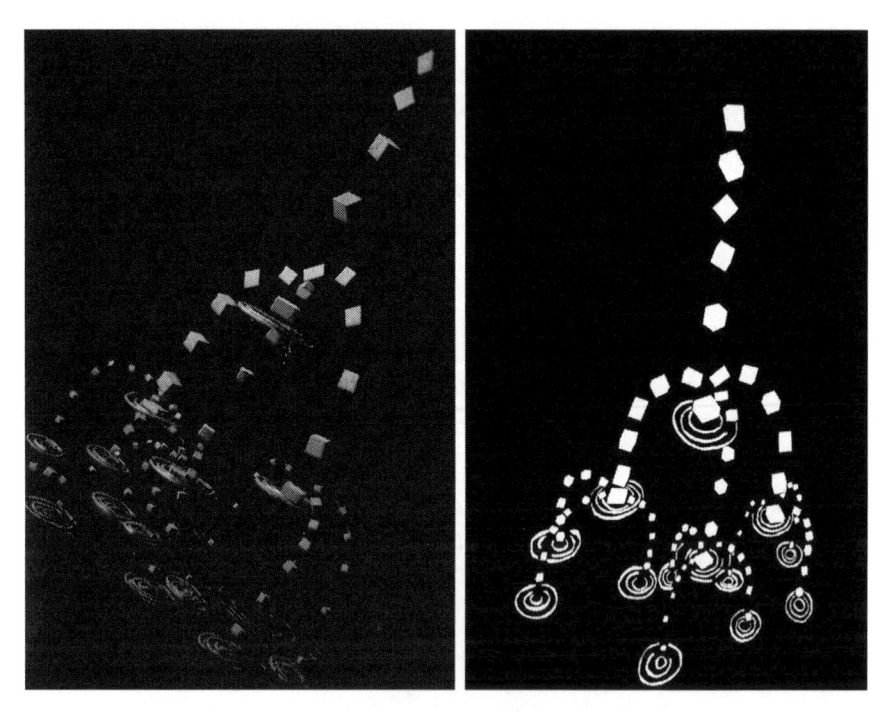

Figure 14.2 The artwork 'One, Two, Three...' (2013). On the left a photograph that shows all the objects lit at once in a holistic representation. On the right is a pure flat graphic with preserved perspective. Although it is impossible to represent a live experience, the difference in these two images goes some way to demonstrating the difference between a flat screen experience and a real time/space experience for the flat page

they could watch it all day, although the looped experiences are no longer than three minutes, and a common sensation is to want to touch the artwork, to connect with it and affirm its concrete nature. In the *Diasynchronoscope*, a sense of wonder is generated by the viewer's perceptions of beholding something new, but without any intervening mediation. Another commonality of experience with the diasynchronic artworks is that they induce a quale of revelation with comments like, 'Wow!', 'Blown away' and 'Alien God object' (MacGillivray & Mathez, 2013). There is a sense that they render the intangible, tangible. This essay argues that this quale of revelation created through embodied art points to a way of reconciling screen memories with the screen as it brings together the conscious with the unconscious.

Freud (1914:146) stated most emphatically how significant screen memories are to psychoanalysis, writing:

> Not only some but all of what is essential in childhood has been retained in these [screen] memories. It is simply a question of knowing how to extract it out of them by analysis. They represent the forgotten years of childhood as adequately as the manifest content of a dream represents the dream-thoughts.

However modern analysis does not share his passion, as Richard Reichbart (2008: 457) points out 'even the particular characteristics of a screen memory, such as its brightness and immediacy, its intactness throughout most of a treatment, and its lengthy imperviousness to analysis, have been lost'.

The Viennese doctor turned psychoanalyst, Otto Fenichel (1953, 1954) emphasized that a screen memory often comes with a command to remember, an 'injunction to note': The individual remembers that at the time of the event represented in the screen memory, she felt an inner injunction, which Fenichel characterized as 'Pay attention! You must remember this scene as long as you live!' Reichbart notes the irony:

> It could equally be stated is that there is an unconscious injunction that is exactly the opposite and of comparable force. It is 'Forget, forget as long as you live' the underlying trauma that the screen memory replaces. This internalized vow is what makes the screen memory so impervious to analysis.
> (Reichbart, 2008: 460)

Thus psychology gives us a paradoxical screen; at once providing both testimony and suppression of a phenomenological event in the conscious and unconscious mind.

There is also a paradoxical element to the film screen. One of the few media analysts who discusses the ontology of the screen *inter alia* is Marshall McLuhan, (1964) whose axiom that the medium is the massage/message, in this case, means that the visual space denoted by the screen both expanded and diminished our horizons – by at once expanding our view and giving us access to global knowledge, and then diminishing it with a border and delivering it via a small rectangle.

As previously stated, this research is not the first to note the parallel between the screen, serving as a boundary from the real world to the unreal, and the boundary between the conscious and unconscious. Philosophers, psychologists and media theorists, when discussing perception of reality or popular screen-based media, are keen to distinguish the differences between conscious and unconscious perception, whether we give something covert or overt attention or, to put it another way, if our perceptions are active or passive. Many cultural theorists such as Paul Virilio (1994) and Sherry Turkle (1997) have noted how the growth of technology serves to separate us directly from the events of real space and real time, and there is much hand-wringing over the invisible framing provided by the insidious mediation of mass media. These theorists want the mediation of the screen to be considered and it cannot be considered unless we are made consciously aware of it. The screen is there, in plain sight, so how can it be that we are not consistently and consciously aware of it? Indeed, if we consider the core ontology of the screen and its parallel nature in relation to the psychological apparatus in Freud's theory of consciousness, we can see that the screen provides stability and constantly displays to its viewer the fact that it is different from 'reality' by virtue of having an edge. In fact as Carter (1990: 73) emphasizes, the screen reifies space, 'enclosing and focusing the viewer's gaze onto the scene which unfolds within its boundaries. Such a device places the frame within the space of the viewer and marks the point where "real space" ends and represented space begins'. This essay contends that this assimilation is present, but by and large unconscious. In terms of Shah's tale; although the donkey is entirely evident, it just does not occur to the guards to consider it as meaningful to their search, because they are distracted by the MacGuffin straw.

In every culture one can observe separate and institutionalized realities that are demarcated from ordinary life. Even the mock fighting of animals demonstrates that the concept of real and unreal can usually be agreed. The indications are that a sane person has little trouble separating the two (Bateson, 1972). There have been comparisons made between the 'frame' of the psychoanalytic setting and the frame of a painting (Milner, 1955) and similarly an analogy between the psychoanalytic process and theatre has been noted by others (Loewald, 1980; McDougal, 1989: 93). Modern psychoanalytic texts make the same point about film (Piotrowska, 2013). The point being that this is quite the normal way of things, to assimilate the boundary between real and unreal, given a non-neurotic viewer[5] and that *the frame is clear*.

When the frame is unclear and there is a blurring of the line between reality and unreality, according to Freud we enter the world of the uncanny: 'an uncanny effect is often and easily produced when the distinction between imagination and reality is effaced, as when something that we have hitherto regarded as imaginary appears before us in reality' (Freud, 1919: 367).

Tropes from the uncanny identified by Freud are: Dismembering, repeating and doubling. Freud (ibid.: 368–9) then enters a long exploration into the linguistic roots of *unheimlich* (literally unhomely), and discovers that the word root 'exhibits one which is identical with its opposite'. On the one hand, *heimlich* refers to 'what is familiar and agreeable, and on the other, what is concealed and kept out of sight'. In the Note for this last statement, Freud also points out that according to the Oxford English Dictionary, a similar occurrence can be noted with the English word canny, 'which may mean not only "cosy", but also "endowed with occult or magical powers". As with *heimlich* and *unheimlich*, uncanny is 'in some way or other a sub-species' of canny. Although both Freud and Jentsch pitched the uncanny as potentially being the stuff of nightmares, both also acknowledge that the uncanny functions differently in artistic works from how it does in everyday life. For Jentsch, this difference is related to art's ability to invoke sensations that 'awake in us a strong feeling for life, without having to accept the consequences of the causes of the unpleasant moods' (Jentsch, 1906: 8).

If we consider the screen as a boundary and demarking barrier between the real and unreal, then the *Diasynchronoscope* removes that boundary and we enter the uncanny – not in the sense of encountering something fearful but in the sense of wondering at the inanimate springing to life. It is indeed at once familiar and new; *heimlich* and *unheimlich*. The tropes of dismemberment, repetition and doubling identified by Freud for the uncanny are entirely present in this medium. Dismembering can be equated to the way the objects often fall, disintegrate then reassemble, the works all use repetition in the shape of looping visuals and audio and the idea of doubling as a *Doppelgänger* motif where attributes of power and autonomy are handed to the one who is in control of the gaze, considered by Freud (1919: 354–6) to be one of the most prominent themes of the uncanny was explored in the Diasynchronic artwork, *Gaffer* 2013, where a single participant is mirrored within the space of the sculpture, then 'gagged' with tape (see Figure 14.3).

That the audience experience is other than seeing screen-based media is tangible in several ways: first, because the works are site-specific, there is a sense of 'authenticity' as defined by Walter Benjamin; of being in the presence of something new, 'real' and immediate. This authentic nature of an original *Diasynchronic* installation in an age replete with reproductive media, is further confirmed by Benjamin's definition of 'aura' over reproduction: 'Even the most perfect reproduction of a work of art is lacking in one element: its presence in time and space, its unique existence at the place where it happens to be' (Benjamin 1936: 215). And his assertion that, 'The presence of the original is the prerequisite to the concept of authenticity' (ibid.: 216).

In German philosopher Martin Heidegger's seminal work in the study of ontology, *Being and Time* (1927*)*, he posits that human beings are characterized by 'inauthenticity'. This inauthenticity results from our innate existence as a 'scene of possibility', which in turn burdens us with 'responsibility and uncertainty' (Bowman, 2003: 68). If we feel ourselves to be unauthentic and we encounter work on screen in the shape of mass media that is clearly unauthentic it is small

Figure 14.3 A captured moment from Gaffer (2012) that creates an uncanny sense of being gagged oneself because of the mirrored reality it invokes

wonder that the uncanny may cause us to feel anxious. However, this anxiety results not from the fact that something becomes animate or springs to life, but because it becomes apparent that it was alive all along. It was hidden in plain view, just as the donkey was in Shah's tale.

If we acknowledge that the implicit screen should be brought to consciousness, then we can see that in order to pass into the conscious realm, the thoughts, impulses, memories and dreams of the unconscious need to undergo some sort of metaphysical, and even physical, conversion. Although Freud's thinking on dreams and the unconscious inspired many art movements, particularly surrealism, Freud viewed modernist artistic activities purporting to bring elements of psychoanalysis to art with a wary eye, as any attempts at 'freeing the unconscious' required heavy mediation and semiotic coding and thus were not 'free', but bounded by the artist.

This has not stopped many artists from exploring how their work might mediate the unconscious (and also how the unconscious might mediate their work). However in rendering an image, the artist cannot avoid creating from a point of view (their own) and providing a semiotic context, however abstract. Although Mitchell (2005) maintains that the ambiguous ontological status of the unconscious is comparable to that of the image, that image is the construct of the artist, imposed on the viewer.

The *Diasynchronoscope* makes concrete the idea of the screen by removing it. It points to the existence of the screen but provides no semiotic context for its absence, just as when the screen memory is removed and reality is unmasked and 'the gold it lies beside' is made manifest, the unmasking reveals that the mask was present. Suddenly the dichotomy between the screen as a display and displayer and the screen as a mask and masker is resolved: while the screen functions as the displayer, in the act of displaying; it is also a type of mask. Strip away the straw and you find the donkey.

The *Diasynchronoscope* is still embryonic as a medium. It is evidently a medium that communicates through moving image as film does and participants who approach it as film feel the difference, saying things such as: 'It invokes a sense of magic, of other worldliness, I have not seen before', 'Awesome, we have got to a dream world' and '[It's] like stepping into another dimension'. They recognize the tropes involved but also know that what they are experiencing is fundamentally and physiologically different from seeing something on a screen. Participants also have to assimilate that although the tropes involved (repetition, changes of speed, dismemberment, reversal of time) come from screen-based media they are combined with recognizable procedures of reality (sensori-motor feedback of parallax, focus and depth perception, combined with freedom to move and embodied comprehension of gravity and scale) (MacGillivray & Mathez, 2012). Hence comments like: 'There is an element of realness to it', 'You know it's showing you, but you don't know what it's showing you' and 'You want to touch it'. These are indicators that the frame that separates reality and unreality has been eradicated. Finally, perhaps the strongest clue to these artworks evoking a profound link in participants between their conscious and unconscious is to be found in typical comments such as: 'I could watch it all day', 'I lost my mind' and 'Like staring at a fire' (ibid.: 2013). Here the *Diasynchronoscope* becomes a tool to enable meditation. It is the contention of this essay that the unconscious needs to be encountered in an embodied way for it to be brought to consciousness; its ambiguous nature needs to be recognized but not necessarily named through text.

This essay explores the idea that the ambiguous ontological status of the "unconscious" is comparable not to something that is framed, but to something that is embodied. It has discussed what happens when the boundary is eliminated entirely and the conscious and unconscious flow freely. It argues that when mediation and narrative are co-authored there is a way for the thoughts, impulses, memories and dreams of the unconscious to begin to pass into the conscious realm without resort to representative and semiotic secondary media. It takes the position that the *Diasynchronoscope* has taken at least a few intuitive next steps towards art unveiling the unconscious.

Notes

1 The *Diasynchronoscope* is an embodied medium and so videos and images do not replicate the experience, however www.trope-design.com/ provides some flavour of the medium through testimony and video (Trope, 2013).
2 This essay is using the term 'ontology' to describe something that is fundamental to all film and thus characterizes the medium in both a concrete and conceptual sense. In support of the latter, according to Stanley Cavell: 'The screen overcomes our fixed distance; it makes displacement appear as our natural condition' (Cavell 1979: 40–41).
3 A MacGuffin can be defined as a meaningless object of everyone's search. It is a plot device. The specific term originated in twentieth-century filmmaking, and was popularized by Alfred Hitchcock in the 1930s.
4 A parallel idea of 'the viewer as exegete' can be found in French psychologist, Kevin O'Regan and US philosopher, Alva Noë's (2001: 943) ideas on sensorimotor perception where they state: 'Visual perception can now be understood as the activity of exploring the environment in ways mediated by knowledge of the relevant sensorimotor contingencies.'
5 Bateson (1972) predicted that in some forms of psychopathology the individual may lack the capacity to accept the paradox of the concurrent existence of that which is within the 'frame' and that which is outside and it has also been noted by O'Regan and Noë (ibid.: 949), in visual experiments with boundaries that we commonly think we see beyond the frame and complete pictures through applying unconscious Gestalt principles.

References

Bateson, G. (1972) (reprinted in 2000) *Steps to an Ecology of Mind: Collected Essays in Anthropology, Psychiatry, Evolution, and Epistemology*. Chicago, IL: University of Chicago Press.

Baudry, J.-L. (1986a) *Ideological effects of the basic cinematographic apparatus*. [1970. Cinéma: effets idéologiques produits par l'appareil de base. Paris: Cinéthique 7–8]. In Rosen, P. (ed.). *Narrative, Apparatus, Ideology*. New York: Columbia University Press: 286–298.

Benjamin, W. (1936) *The Work of Art in the Age of Mechanical Reproduction* (reprinted in 2008, Hannah Arendt, ed.) Illuminations. London: Fontana: 214–218.

Bowman, C. (2003) Heidegger, the uncanny, and Jacques Tourner's horror films. In S.J. Schneider and D. Shaw (eds), *Dark Thoughts: Philosophic Reflections on Cinematic Horror*. Lanham, Maryland, and Oxford: The Scarecrow Press, Inc.: 65–83.

Carter, M. (1990) *Framing Art: Introducing Theory and the Visual Image*. Sydney: Hale & Iremonger.

Cavell, S. (1979) *The World Viewed: Reflections on the Ontology of Film*. Cambridge, MA: Harvard University Press.

Crary, J. (1992) *Techniques of the Observer: On Vision and Modernity in the Nineteenth Century*. London: MIT Press.

Fenichel, O. (1953, 1954) *Economic functions of screen memories*. In *The Collected Papers of Otto Fenichel – Volume I*. New York: W.W. Norton: 113–116.

Foucault, M. (1977) *Discipline and Punish*. Trans. Alan Sheridan. New York, Vintage.

Freud, S. (1899) *Screen Memories*. Standard Edition, 3, London: The Hogarth Press: 301–322.

Freud, S. (1914) *Remembering, repeating and working-through.* In *Vol. XII, The Case of Schreber. Papers on Technique and Other Works. The Standard Edition of the Complete Psychological Works of Sigmund Freud* (1995). The Institute of Psychoanalysis and (London) The Hogarth Press: 145–156.

Freud, S. (1919) *The Uncanny* [*Das Unheimliche*] (reprinted 1990). Art and Literature, Penguin Freud Library Vol. 14. London: Penguin Books.

Greenacre, P. (1949) A contribution to the study of screen memories. *The Psychoanalytic Study of the Child* (3).

Heidegger, M. (1927) *Sein und Zeit.* Translated (1978) as *Being and Time* by John Macquarrie and Edward Robinson, Oxford: Basil Blackwell.

Jentsch, E. (1906) *On the Psychology of the Uncanny*, trans. Roy Sellars, Angelaki 2, no. 1 (1995): 7–16.

Loewald, H.W. (1980) *Papers on Psychoanalysis.* New Haven, CT: Yale University Press.

MacGillivray & Mathez, B. (2012) *Co-authored Narrative Experience: Affective, embodied interaction through combining the diachronic with the synchronistic.* Wellington, NZ: Desform: 62–69.

MacGillivray, C. & Mathez, B. (2013) www.doc.gold.ac.uk/diasynchronoscope/ Website and filmed interviews.

Mahon, E. & Battin, D. (1981) Screen memories and termination. *Journal of American Psychoanalitic Assn.*, 29, 939–942.

Manovich, L. (2001) *The Language of New Media.* Cambridge, MA: MIT Press.

Mayne, J. (1993) *Cinema and Spectatorship.* London and New York: Routledge,

McDougall, J. (1989) *Theatres of the Body: A Psychoanalytic Approach to Psychosomatic Illness.* London: W.W. Norton.

McLuhan, M. (1964) *Understanding Media: The Extensions of Man*, 1st Ed. New York: McGraw Hill (reissued by Gingko Press, 2003).

McLuhan, M. (1969) *The Playboy Interview: Marshall McLuhan* (interviewed by Eric Norden). *Playboy Magazine*, March 1969.

Milner, M. (1955) The role of illusion in symbol-formation. In M. Klein et al. (eds), *New Directions in Psychoanalysis*; republished in Milner (1987): 83–113.

Mitchell, W.T. (2005) *What Do Pictures Want? The Lives and Loves of Images.* Chicago, IL: University of Chicago Press.

O'Regan, J. & Noë, A. (2001) *A sensorimotor account of vision and visual consciousness. Behavoral and Brain Sciences*, 24, 939–1031.

Piotrowska, A. (2013) *Psychoanalysis and Ethics in Documentary Film.* London and New York: Routledge.

Reichbart, R. (2008) Screen memory: Its importance to object relations and transference. *Journal of American Psychoanalytic Assn.*, 56, 455–481.

Shah, I. (1968) *The Exploits of the Incomparable Mulla Nasrudin.* London: Penguin.

Turkle, S. (1997) *Life on the Screen: Identity in the Age of the Internet.* London: Simon and Schuster.

Virilio, P. (1994) *The Vision Machine.* Bloomington, IN: Indiana University Press.

Websites:

www.doc.gold.ac.uk/diasynchronoscope/artworks/stylus/
www.trope-design.com/

Chapter 15

The poetics of maternal loss in Tarkovsky's *The Mirror*

Helena Bassil-Morozow

The Mirror (1975) is a fascinating study of a man's relationship with the mother figure in its various incarnations – as a woman, a symbol, an object, a reflection in the mirror; as unpredictable and terrifying mother nature, as the unconscious that gives birth to male creativity and, finally, as mother Russia – the goddess who devours young men and needs to be protected from enemies. These different mothers are often inseparable from each other as the whole film is an extended metaphor of a search for the ideal parent, for the magical image of a loving and accepting female that has been imprinted in the male hero's mind since he was a baby. In his poetic quest, the protagonist, Aleksei, finds all kinds of mothers, personified in a number of women, but the ideal one, the lost one – remains missing.

Tarkovsky famously claimed to be a poet rather than a filmmaker because 'poetry is an awareness of the world, a particular way of relating to reality'. It is a philosophy rather than a genre (Tarkovsky, 2008: 21). As a result, his narratives tend to be complex and convoluted – they are hymns to narrative non-linearity and abstract symbolism. The plot of *The Mirror* is one of the best examples of this. The film is a beautiful collection of symbols and images, but it is not easy to link them into a coherent narrative. The director himself admits that editing the film was a difficult task – there existed more than twenty variants, which significantly differed from each other structurally:

> At moments it looked as if the film could not be edited, which would have meant that inadmissible lapses had occurred during shooting. The film didn't hold together, it wouldn't stand up, it fell apart as one watched, it had no unity, no necessary inner connection, no logic. And then, one fine day, when we somehow managed to devise one last, desperate rearrangement – there was the film. The material came to life; the parts started to function reciprocally, as if linked by a bloodstream; and as that last, despairing attempt was projected onto the screen, the film was born before our very eyes. For a long time I still couldn't believe the miracle – the film held together.
>
> (2008: 116)

The Mirror switches between three different time frames: before the Second World War (1930s), wartime (1940s), and post-war (1960s). The protagonist Aleksei (who remains behind the scenes for most of the film and is only present in the frame as a disembodied, extradiegetic voice) remembers his childhood before and during the war, his parents, their separation, his mother raising two boys on her own, the spooky country house, the military training, his wife Natalia and son Ignat, and the elderly mother (played by the director's own mother, Maria Vishnyakova). The film starts with a footage of a stuttering youth being hypnotised and then waking up 'healed' from his speech disorder, and ends with the protagonist on his deathbed, holding a birdling in his hand.

This curious but organic combination of Jungian and Freudian imagery can only be understood and analysed from a variety of perspectives. On the surface of it, the film is based on several concepts that are traditionally discussed using the language of Freudian and post-Freudian psychology: the mother, the mirror, the Oedipus complex, the primal scene and the absent father. The mother, Maria (played by Margarita Terekhova) is presented as physically attractive, sexual, flirty, mysterious and warm; the images of the mother from Aleksey's childhood are almost tactile, which renders the idea of the boy's attraction to her.

There exist a number of Freudian and Lacanian interpretations of *The Mirror*, including Gavin (2007), Le Fanu (1987), McGowan (2008), Robinson (2007) and Smith (2004). Predictably, they use the traditional Lacanian arsenal of terms to investigate the mother–son connection: the traumatic gaze, anxieties of speech, lack (*manque*), the *objet petit a* and, of course, the mirror stage. For instance, Alice Gavin, in the article 'The Word of the Father/The Body of the Mother: Dimensions of Gender in Tarkovsky's *Mirror*', concentrates on the opening scene and the female therapist's efforts to lead the subject towards completeness, to unite subject and word (Gavin, 2007: 1). Todd McGowan comments on the merger between fantasy, desire and reality in Tarkovsky's films, including *The Mirror* (McGowan, 2008: 184), and Mark Robinson discusses the tension between lack and desire in the film (Robinson, 2007: 186).

My aim in this article, however, is different. The Freudian and post-Freudian motifs in *The Mirror* are obvious, but to concentrate on the mirror stage would mean to omit a whole layer of Tarkovsky's poetics: his depiction of Motherland and mother nature, his perception of the maternal figure as a symbol and as an archetype, and his vision of the unconscious as an inspiring, brutal creative force. Tarkovsky's symbolism – and particularly his fascination with Russian nature and landscapes – have a particularly Jungian hue. To use solely Lacanian philosophy to analyse Tarkovsky's work would mean to ignore the might, creativity and danger of the maternal figure, all of which the director was keen to emphasise both in his visuals and in his narratives. The maternal figure, Tarkovsky implies, has power – real power, not imaginary power; she is in charge of life and death; she creates and destroys; she moves the world. The mother in *The Mirror* is blatantly Oedipal – and yet, she is also archetypal, eternal, mysterious, dangerous, powerful and unfathomable.

The Freudian mother

The 'Freudian mother' re-emerges all throughout *The Mirror*, and is particularly noticeable in the pre-war scenes of Aleksei's childhood. The impression she gives is that of a dreamy seductress: she is beautiful and knows it, has large grey eyes and often plays with stray strands of her long blonde hair. She is also aware of the power she has over men. Aleksei (as both the child and the grown-up) is consistently used as the focaliser of the narrative, and it is through his eyes that we see the Oedipal female who will remain the obsession of his life.

Importantly, Aleksei does not see her as a human being with a complex character, real suffering and real problems. His vision of her is mediated; he sees her as a dream, as an apparition, as an object, and his early recollections of her are often shown in black and white, and in slow motion. One of the scenes is a version of 'the primal scene': the boy wakes up in the middle of the night, and witnesses the father (Oleg Yankovskiy) helping his wife wash her beautiful long hair in a basin. The mother is hovering over the basin, wet hair hiding her face, and the father is pouring water from a jug to wash away the soap. This symbolic euphemism is both poetic and terrifying, and Tarkovsky ensures that the audience and the protagonist see it as both: terrible and mesmerising. The son halts to observe the moment of intimacy between the two parents, and his shock at what he is witnessing is expressed in the destruction of the house at the end of the scene. Large chips of ceiling start falling down, and water starts flooding through the roof. Shot subjectively, like a dream sequence, in black and white and in slow motion, the scene ends with the destruction of the boy's fantasy of the maternal object belonging to him, for he has just seen that it belonged to another man, and that the two are close. The house – and the psychological safety of the boy's existence – is gone forever with the introduction of the father figure.

In another eerie slow-motion sequence, the mother, wearing a white nightdress that reveals her legs, is levitating over an undone bed. A white bird is visible in the top right-hand corner of the frame. The mother looks both like a witch and a victim, sexualised yet passive, a vaguely remembered and idealised Oedipal object. The image is static. There is a discernible Gothic hue in these two sequences, even though nothing specifically scary happens in them. Their Gothicism comes from the focaliser's perception of the Oedipal dynamic, and from his changing perception of the maternal object. He is experiencing a profound loss – the loss of the paradisiacal state with the idealised female object. The boy has lost the imaginary mother – the one that has always belonged to him and no one else. This mother, the ideal mirror of the boy's psyche, had been a mere fantasy.

In one of the opening scenes (shot in real time and in colour) the child is looking anxiously at a man 'making a pass' at his mother. She is sitting on a fence and smoking. The man (Anatoly Solonitsyn) emerges out nowhere and asks for directions. He is a doctor and he appears to be lost. Yet, as the conversation evolves, its real aim becomes clear: the man guessed that Maria is separated, and decided to try his luck. The sequence renders the focaliser's anxiety at seeing another male approaching 'his' object (now that the main rival, the father, is gone). It is clear that the boy wishes the man to go away; to leave the mother alone. Luckily for the boy, the man embarrasses himself by joining the woman on the flimsy fence (which proceeds to break under his weight), and spectacularly falling down. As the rival retreats, we feel the protagonist's relief at the outcome of the encounter. Thus, he avoids losing her to another man again.

In the post-war scenes, the Oedipal tension is shifted onto Aleksei's former wife, Natalia. Here Tarkovsky made a shockingly curious directorial decision: the wife and the mother are played by the same actress, Margarita Terekhova. The fact that Natalia is an identical copy of the protagonist's mother is deeply Freudian – it emphasises Aleksei's inability to tell the difference between the female objects in his life as well as his inability to see a woman as a real person rather than the ideal lost feminine of his babyhood. The protagonist quarrels with both his mother and his wife, and eventually ends up cutting off both of them. He is also a selfish father – for years he has neglected his son Ignat who is now failing school.

Not surprisingly, Natalia accuses him of being narcissistic, of behaving as if he is above everyone, of being self-obsessed, of never growing up, of emotionally abusing herself and his mother. Natalia naturally associates herself with the mother because the two are playing the same role in the protagonist's life, and both end up being 'not perfect enough' for him. Neither of the two women manage to become the 'good enough mirrors' reflecting his broken self, he rejects them and ends up living on his own. They hysterically try to get through to him, to talk to him, to say something that matters to them as real women, as real people. This does not work. In one of the post-war scenes, the mother complains that one of her friends and work colleagues, Liza, has died. The aged Maria expects comfort and empathy from the son, but gets none. The topic is brushed aside by the protagonist who is too self-absorbed to deal with other people's problems. Significantly, the conversation takes place in an empty room, and both characters are just disembodied voices. This scene epitomises the mother–boy relationship and paradoxically shows their connection as both profound and superficial, existing and non-existent. The mother Aleksei really wants is the mother he lost after witnessing the hair-washing scene – the fantasy mother who had belonged only to him.

The broken mirror

One of the sequences preceding the deathbed scene shows Aleksei as a baby, happily smiling in his cot and enjoying the mother's full attention. She is cooing and proudly showing off her healthy child, the best boy in the world, to a friend. At this stage she is still the perfect mirror of the child's emerging self – the good transitional object, to use Donald Winnicott's term.

Mirroring, as the English paediatrician and psychoanalyst Donald Winnicott notes, goes beyond physical holding and touching – it is also a framework of communication (Wright, 2009: 33). The mother (with her responsive face) becomes a 'transitional object' guiding the child through the phase of uncertainty – brought about by the loss of omnipotence – and through to acceptance of separateness and his limitations of control over the outside world. This transitional stage, Wright notes, cushions the infant against the sudden onset of crude reality, and allows 'the passage into objectivity to be smoothly negotiated' (2009: 33). When it goes successfully, this stage becomes 'an imperceptible phase in the "progress towards independence"' (2009: 33).

Growing out of the paradisiacal state of omnipotence, the child begins to feel insecure and 'separate' from the world. These states of insecurity, anxiety and helplessness, triggered by the feeling of being out of control, are mitigated when the primary carer 'reflects', or mirrors, the infant in all its positive and negative emotional states. By reflecting and precipitating the baby's reactions, and by closely interacting with it, the mother ensures that the baby feels secure and protected – both physically and emotionally.

However, this stage does not mean that the 'mirror' in which the infant sees himself crying, playing and having needs, has to be perfect. The dialogue between the two objects should not be a form of passive reflection, but an active interaction in which both the sides take equal part and receive attention. It is more about participation rather than passive acceptance. Enid Balint writes that the feed-back process, the process 'which starts in the child and acts as a stimulus on the mother, who must accept and recognise that something has happened', presupposes 'an interaction between two active partners', which 'differentiates it from projection and introjection in which one of them is only a passive object' (Balint, 1993: 51).

Mirroring, both as a process and metaphor, is the background of all human development. The nascent self does not emerge out of nowhere: it is shaped by human contact. It is only by linking to and separating from 'the other', from the object that is not 'you', that human beings can gain a better understanding of who they are. It can even be metaphorically seen as a creative process during which a new personality is born out of psychological chaos. Kenneth Wright writes:

> It is central to Winnicott's theory of development that the self has only latent or potential existence until subjectively realized within the responses of another person. Only when self-experience is reflected does the baby adult feel fully alive. His understanding of creativity is bound up with this view: only a subject who is alive in this way can be creative, but equally, being creative enhances the feeling of being alive. It is thus implicit adult creativity involves something analogous to early maternal mirroring, as through the creative person, in the act of creation, performs for himself the activities which the adaptive mother once provided.
>
> (Wright, 2009: 62)

The child's personality is thus created by mirroring and a range of transitional objects – but it is also created by the dynamic between absence and presence of these objects. As he grows up, the child not only gradually learns that he is not omnipotent, and that people in his immediate environment and in the world at large are not objects whose sole duty is to keep him happy and perfectly mirrored – but also that he has a separate personality that is not reliant on mirroring, and that can survive psychologically and physically regardless of the presence of other people in the vicinity.

The mother's task is to successfully guide the baby through the process of separation from the unconscious. Ideally, this should result in the baby's 'maximal psychological maturation' (Winnicott, 1992: 111). The good-enough mother, from Winnicott's view, should astutely sense how to take away the infant's omnipotence without overwhelming him with a feeling of helplessness and despair. Meanwhile, using the mother as a transitional object, the child should be allowed to retain an illusion of control – for the time being: 'The mother's eventual task is gradually to disillusion the infant, but she has no hope of success unless at first she has been able to give sufficient opportunity for illusion' (1992: 11). This view is echoed by Heinz Kohut who argues that optimal frustration is important for the eventual establishment of boundaries and an acceptance of reality and its limits (Kohut, 2009: 123ff).

The protagonist of *The Mirror* clearly sees his mother as having failed to be 'good enough', as being too self-absorbed, as giving too much of herself to the father and neglecting the boy as a result. Interestingly enough, Aleksei's brother is not mentioned beyond the scenes of early childhood – as if the protagonist brushed him away together with the other males competing for the mother's attention.

The mirror is the central symbol of the film, and it is consistently associated with the uncapturable mystery of the feminine. Both Maria and Natalia appear looking at themselves in the mirror in a range of scenes throughout the film. However, even when the physical mirror is not present, they still behave as if they are in front of one – and this invisible mirror, the camera, is, in fact, the focaliser-protagonist. Even when she is accusing Aleksei of being selfish and difficult, Natalia still looks at him seductively (if aggressively), aware of her effect on him, aware of her sexual attractiveness and power. Yet, she is still trying to be visually pleasing, to be the mirror, to reflect his desires and fantasies. She is doing her best to be a passive object, and fails spectacularly in this task, unable to suppress her personality, to become 'the lost ideal'.

Both the mother and the wife are seen by the protagonist as 'imperfect' transitional objects, who could not reflect or support his true self. His mirror is irreparably broken, but he is still looking for the perfect one, for the flawless, all-accepting, all-giving mother who would love him and him alone. Tragically, he is still alone at the end of the film, dying in his room, full of regret at his own inability to relate to real people.

The Jungian mother

Not all mother figures in the film, however, could be explained using Freudian terms. Moreover, Freudian psychology's insistence on the centrality of sexuality in the human psyche is in direct conflict with Tarkovsky's vision of the cinematic image. The imprecise approach to editing in particular and the creative process in general can be explained by the fact that Tarkovsky regards creativity as a pursuit for the truth of vision, and this can only be done if one faithfully reproduces the images born inside, in the unconscious. These images have to be neither precise nor easily digestible. It is not always possible to predict their unfolding in the course of the filmmaking process. They are meant to remain vague and mysterious:

> It is hard to imagine that a concept like *artistic image* could ever be expressed in a precise thesis, easily formulated and understandable. It is not possible, nor would one wish it to be so. I can only say that the image stretches out into infinity, and leads to the absolute. And even what is known as the 'idea' of the image, many dimensional and with many meanings, cannot, in the very nature of things, be put into words. But it does find expression in art. [...] The artist tries to grasp [the principle that makes the image, or a life moment, unique], new each time; and each time he hopes, though in vain, to achieve an exhaustive image of the Truth of human existence. The quality of beauty is in the truth of life, newly assimilated and imparted by the artist, in fidelity to his personal vision.
>
> (2008: 104)

This is where Tarkovsky's philosophy of filmmaking agrees with Jungian psychology. As Steven Walker observes, 'By emphasising the image over the word, Jungian psychology differentiates itself radically from Freudian, Lacanian and other psychologies that stress the task of interpreting the *language* of the unconscious' (Walker, 2002: 3).

Don Fredericksen draws attention to another aspect of the same problem: Freud's 'semiotic' (possibility of exact interpretation) and Jung's 'symbolic' attitude (amplification, or deferred interpretation) to the creative and dream-imagery. Jung does not see the unconscious as being linguistically structured, hence his rejection of semiosis in favour of amplification. Jung writes in *Psychological Types*:

> The concept of symbol should in my view be strictly distinguished from that of sign. Symbolic and semiotic meanings are entirely different things. ... A symbol always presupposes that the chosen expression is the best possible description or formulation of a relatively unknown fact, which is nonetheless known to exist or is postulated as existing. ... Every view which interprets the symbolic expression as an analogue or an abbreviated designation for a known thing is semiotic. [...] The symbol is alive only so long as it is pregnant

with meaning. But once its meaning has been born out of it, once that expression is found that formulated the thing sought, expected, or divined even better than the hitherto accepted symbol, then the symbol is dead, i.e., it possesses only an historical significance. ... An expression that stands for a known thing remains a mere sign and not a symbol. It is, therefore, quite impossible to create a living symbol, i.e., one that is pregnant with meaning, from known associations.

(Jung, 1971: CW6: paras. 814–818)

Thus, a symbol is a relative and 'immediate' thing, rather than a permanent, ready-made set of meanings. In a symbol, the relationship between the signifier and the signified is, indeed, very arbitrary. Drawing upon Jung's democratic position of 'anti-exactness', Don Fredericksen argues:

We must understand that Jung's distinction between sign and symbol ultimately elaborates two distinct modes of apprehending and explaining the psyche and its products – not just two distinct psychologies but two distinct ontologies and philosophies of value.

This point is succinctly illustrated by Jung and Freud's differing explanations of, and attitudes toward, incest fantasy and symbolism. Freud interpreted the incest fantasy concretely. [...] Freud labels the distorted or disguised expressions of the incest wish 'symbols', incorrectly so according to Jung. For the latter, Freud's 'symbols' are in fact signs, standing for the putatively known, albeit repressed, desire of the patient to have physical intimacy with a parent. Their meaning can be completely explained by Freudian analytic procedures that reduce them to their underlying cause.

(Hauke and Alister, 2001: 19)

For Jung, the symbol is always bigger than the sum of the dreamer's (or the author's) biographical details, and significantly deeper than any literal or pre-existed meaning. In contrast to Freud and the post-Freudians, Jung's additional 'layer' of the psyche – the collective unconscious – permitted him to detach the work of art from the Oedipal, sexual or any other personal issues the artist may possess. The work of art grows out of its creator rather like a tree that draws its nourishment from the artist's psyche. It is a force 'that achieves its end either with tyrannical might or with the subtle cunning of the nature herself, quite regardless of the personal fate of the man who is its vehicle' (CW15: para. 114). The work of art is a 'living thing implanted in human psyche' (CW15: para. 114).

Like this, the work of art is born out of its creator against his will, and in response to the current social climate. It may resonate in the author's personal unconscious, of course – or even come out of his personal problems. Yet, when he feels the need to create, the artist only answers the call of the collective unconscious; his issues only naturally grow out from the deepest problems of his society. Through the artist, the unconscious speaks and the collective expresses itself.

For Jung, the urge to create is a living thing, an *autonomous complex*, a split-off portion of the psyche. When activated, it can be so powerful that the artist is barely capable of controlling it. Creative people are mere vehicles for this unstoppable energy that demands to be let out. It is no wonder, then, that artists often forget reality altogether, and become wholly engaged into the process of harvesting the impulse and rescuing it from the depths of the unconscious. The creative person's temporary madness is not subject to his conscious control: 'The divine frenzy of the artist comes perilously close to a pathological state, though the two things are not identical' (CW15: para. 122).

Similarly, Tarkovsky describes the creative process as something springing from the totality of the psyche, but which also involves the artist as a whole person. When one hears its call, one has no other choice but to answer it:

> The artist's inspiration comes into being somewhere in the deepest recesses of his 'I'. It cannot be dictated by external, 'business' considerations. It is bound to be related to his psyche and his conscience; it springs from the totality of the world-view. If it is anything less, then it is doomed from the outset to be artistically void and sterile. It is perfectly possible to be a professional director or a professional writer and not be an artist: merely a sort of executor of other people's ideas.
>
> (Tarkovsky, 2008: 188)

There is a range of mother figures and images in *The Mirror* that are purely symbolic, and are meant to stay mysterious, indecipherable and inexplicable. For instance, mother Nature is unpredictable, diverse, temperamental. Tarkovsky favours long, black and white shots of Russian nature, sometimes in slow motion, which effectively juxtapose the power of nature with the power of Maria as a woman and a mother; as the site of the feminine enigma. Tarkovsky's depictions of nature emphasise the movement of the grass, the force of the storm, the depth and darkness of water in a pond. This is the archetypal mother that is both kind and merciless: the kind mother that gives birth to the boy, and the terrible mother that overwhelms the dying protagonist; mother womb and mother the comforter. The little bird, just born, is his wholesome, unified self; it represents the hope for establishing the lost connection with the mother – and finally finding his lost self – whole and unbroken.

The rebirth actually happens in the final sequence of the film, which follows after the deathbed scene. It depicts the pre-war time frame, and starts with the shot of Maria and the father lying on the grass in the field near the house, and discussing their future baby. Maria is 'aware' of the camera, aware of the presence of the mirror – of the focaliser; she flirts with it and occasionally glimpses at it. It is as if the invisible protagonist wants a confirmation of her presence, a confirmation of her love; and he gets it from her, he gets her attention, which he steals from the handsome father.

The 'happy family' scene is followed by shots of the old Maria, walking in the field with the two boys. In a way, it contains the distilled essence of the film: the mother grew old, but the boy did not grow up. He rejected the idea of maturity, and chose to remain a child forever, locked in the emotional safety of the pre-war world. The focus in this sequence, however, is not on the boys, but on the association of Maria with mother nature: both young and old Marias are shown against the magnificence of the windy fields, the darkened forests, against the distant, milky swirls of fog. The shots of the ageing mother are intercut with close-ups of decaying trees, an abandoned well full of rubbish, the empty house. The birdling that flies off at the end of the deathbed scene is released back into the wild. It represents the protagonist's confined and suffering soul, which is now reborn, resurrected, freed from the stifling influence of the city, from the oppressive grip of life. His soul returns to the parental embrace of nature – the terrible, unfathomable and beautiful mother.

Similarly, Tarkovsky's 'mother Russia' is a powerful goddess. This is a very traditional, archetypal vision of Russia: your country is bigger than you, more important than you; she needs your life, your personal sacrifice. Importantly, she is a woman – she is 'motherland'. In the scenes portraying war time, Aleksei and a group of other boys are shown undergoing military training with a sullen drill sergeant. In freezing conditions, in the snow, the boys learn how to use firearms and to throw grenades. The sergeant is severely displeased with Aleksei who keeps sabotaging the efforts of the group. The instructor sees that the boy does not take the process seriously, that he is too selfish and individualistic, that he questions and mocks the system, that he is incapable of sacrificing himself for his country. In other words, the boy is not yet a man. In the eyes of the sergeant, real men are those who put their motherland above their lives.

This view in confirmed in the newsreel footage to which the military training scene cuts. Tarkovsky admits that he had to look through thousands of metres of film before he found the footage he wanted: the Red Army crossing Lake Sivash in 1943. Tarkovsky was impressed with the camerawork, and deemed the piece unique. What impressed him most, though, was the poignancy of the piece: it was 'an image of heroic sacrifice and the price of this sacrifice; the image of a historical turning point brought about at incalculable cost' (Tarkovsky, 2008: 130). The men knew that they were likely to die soon, yet they kept moving, they kept going on, defying tiredness, defying mud, defying physical pain. Common men became heroes. Tarkovsky continues:

> The film affected you with a piercing, aching poignancy, because in the shots were simply people. People dragging themselves, knee deep in wet mud, through an endless swamp that stretched out beyond the horizon, beneath a whitish, flat sky. Hardly anyone survived. The boundless perspective of these recorded moments created an effect close to catharsis. Later I learned that the army camera-man who had made the film, with such extraordinary penetration into the events taking place around him, had been killed on that same day.
>
> (2008: 130–131)

The director admires the camera man's bravery – and not just his soldier's bravery, or the strength of his spirit. What Tarkovsky admires most is that the man's ability to keep the creative process alive and going in the harshest of conditions, when physical survival rather than creative life should be of paramount importance. This leads us to our last maternal symbol, the principal mother figure in the film, the goddess whose cult Tarkovsky faithfully followed – the mother of creativity. She is the unconscious that gives you voice, she is the powerful Jungian force that makes the artist speak, that gives him freedom, releases his inner self.

This mother is expressed in an effective metaphor. The film opens with the scene (apparently, a TV programme watched by the protagonist) in which a psychologist is hypnotising a young man suffering from a severe form of stuttering. She puts him to sleep, and, upon waking up, he regains the ability to speak without stuttering. The woman is unattractive and somewhat crude; she is very firm and decisive; her voice is loud. Unlike the flimsy boy in her charge, she is confident in what she is doing. Because she manipulates the young man both physically and psychologically, the scene is evidently disturbing. However, this is redeemed by the result we witness at the end of the session – the man is now able to speak, he recognises his own voice, he is not afraid of it, he is able to express himself. The crude female therapist is the mother of creativity who restarts the boy's heart, who renews his life. She is the archetypal mother who is both caring and threatening, dangerous and kind, good and bad, constructive and destructive.

This taps into Tarkovsky's (rather Jungian) vision of creativity as a force that is both powerful and unkind. The archetypal psychologist James Hillman echoes Jung's ideas in that he describes the creative impulse as a wild energy that poses potential psychological dangers for its bearer. Since this energy originates in the collective rather than the personal psyche, it is tricksterish in its nature and may start behaving in a number of uncontrollable ways. It is neutral rather than purely positive. So great is its power over the individual that it might easily overwhelm him – and even make him suicidal. In fact, Hillman argues – the negative feelings and mood fluctuations experienced by the artists under the influence of creativity are normal for someone who is trying to deal with the impulse of this scale. It is not at all surprising that the artist is struggling to keep the impulse in check, to manage it in some way. It is born deep within the psyche, and when it escapes, the delicate human frame is not always capable of holding and stabilising it:

> The creating Gods are the destroying Gods. As Jung said, 'Creation is as much construction as destruction' (CW3: para. 245). The ectopsychic instinctual force, because it comes from beyond the psyche, is more than human and mightier than its possessor. Its possessor is, in fact, always in danger of possession. Working as a compulsion, the force is always 'too much'. One spends one's life trying to slow it, tame it, give it enough time and space, because its haste is the destructive devil within the creative impulse itself. Suicide always remains the fundamental possibility of psychological

creativity, as its reversal, since the destruction of soul is the counterpart of the creation of the soul.

(Hillman, 1998: 36)

Tarkovsky confirms Hillman's view that creativity is neither good nor bad; it should be seen as neutral. The impulse is so powerful that it can overwhelm the creative person – which is a relatively small price to pay for the honour of being a vehicle used by the unconscious for delivering such a precious treasure to the masses. Someone who looks less normal than the rest of the people, and therefore is prepared to sacrifice his life to his art, is a hero:

True artistic inspiration is always a torment for the artist, almost to the point of endangering his life. Its realisation is tantamount to a physical feat. That is the way it has always been, despite the popular misconception that pretty well all we do is tell stories that are as old as the world, appearing in front of the public like old grannies with scarves on our heads and our knitting in our hands to tell them all sorts of tales in order to keep them amused. The tale may be entertaining or enthralling, but will do only one thing for the audience: help them pass the time in idle chatter.

(2008: 188)

The (male) artist, therefore, has to endure a certain amount of inner torment before he can find his voice. His relationship with the creative mother is tempestuous in its painful poeticism. The same is true, however, of all mother–son relationships depicted in *The Mirror*: Tarkovsky's boy, the artist, the brave soldier, the family man is desperately trying to reconnect with the mother; with the powerful feminine who somehow always manages to escape. Like a cunning spirit, she creates the impression of being his mirror, of belonging to him, of flirting with him; but then disappears in the darkened water, dissolves in the wind, melts into the silver fog. He keeps looking for her in vain, and it is the pain of the loss that gives him strength and drives his creative process.

References

Balint, Enid (1993) 'On Being Empty of Oneself', in J. Mitchell and M. Parsons (eds.), *Before I was I. Psychoanalysis and the Imagination,* London: Free Association Books.
Fredericksen, Don (1979) 'Jung/Sign/Symbol/Film', in Christopher Hauke and Ian Alister (2001) (eds.) *Jung and Film: Post-Jungian Takes on the Moving Image*, London: Routledge, pp. 17–55.
Gavin, Alice (2007) 'The Word of the Father/The Body of the Mother: Dimensions of Gender in Tarkovsky's *Mirror*', *UCL Opticon, 1826* (2), pp. 1–6.
Hauke, Christopher and Alister, Ian (eds) (2001) *Jung and Film*, London and New York: Routledge.
Hillman, James (1998) *The Myth of Analysis: Three Essays in Archetypal Psychology*, Evanston: Northwestern University Press.

Jung, C.G. Except where a different publication was used, all references are to the hardback edition of C.G. Jung, *The Collected Works* (CW), edited by Sir Herbert Read, Dr Michael Fordham and Dr Gerhardt Adler, and translated by R.F.C. Hull, London: Routledge.

Kohut, Heinz (1978; 2011) *The Search for the Self*, London: Karnac.

——(1977; 2009) *The Restoration of the Self*, Chicago and London: the University of Chicago Press.

Le Fanu, Mark (1987) *The Cinema of Andrei Tarkovsky*, London: BFI.

McGowan, Todd (2008) *The Real Gaze: Film Theory After Lacan*, Albany, NY: Suny Press.

Robinson, Mark (2007) *The Sacred Cinema of Andrei Tarkovsky*, Maidstone, Kent: Crescent Moon.

Smith, Alexandra (2004) 'Andrei Tarkovsky as Reader of Arsenii Tarkovsky's Poetry in the Film *Mirror*', *Russian Studies in Literature*, 40, 46–63.

Tarkovsky, Andrey (2008; 1984) *Sculpting in Time: Reflections on the Cinema*, Austin, TX: University of Texas Press.

Walker, Stephen F. (2002) *Jung and the Jungians on Myth*, New York and London: Routledge.

Winnicott, Donald (1965) *The Maturational Process and the Facilitating Environment*, London: Hogarth Press.

——(1971; 1992) *Playing and Reality*, London: Routledge.

Wright, Kenneth (2009) *Mirroring and Attunement*, London and New York: Routledge.

Chapter 16

Talking about Kevin
First-, second- and third-person narratives*

Naomi Segal

How can a mass murder committed by an adolescent be understood by his mother? How can that mother be understood by her reader or viewer? This essay will examine the two versions of *We Need to Talk About Kevin* (the novel by Lionel Shriver, 2003; the film directed by Lynne Ramsay, 2011) with particular reference to their different fictional modes: first/second person and third person.

Many studies have been devoted to the question of how psychoanalysis works in relation to literature and many more to putting the relation into practice: implicitly or explicitly they place the author or the reader, the characters or even the text in the position of analyst or analysand.[1] I will not repeat the theories but here is what I see as the baseline. Freudian psychoanalysis is built on two assumptions: first, that everything is an utterance and no utterance is innocent; and second, that our understanding of how a thing is 'done up' (the creation of an artifice, a story, a psyche) can best be based on reversing the way it is undone (analysed).[2]

These two assumptions work, I would argue, broadly the same for the work a psychoanalyst does and for the work a literary critic does. Both are engaged in the task of interpretation; both combine in various proportions a posture of sympathy and suspicion. The most important difference is that psychoanalytic work depends on the material co-presence of two people in the same room – not (for the purist) facing each other or engaging in dialogue, but both in the same time and space, one speaking and the other hearing; whereas literary-critical work is a virtual relationship in which various pairs can be set out in concentric circles. In a first-person text these would be – on one side, moving from the outside in:

- *the 'real author'*: a historical person of flesh and blood, now often dead;
- *the implied author* (see Booth 1961): that is, the figuration of Camus or Shriver that we infer from reading their text/s; and
- *the narrator*: the voice saying 'I' in the text.

And on the other, in parallel, now moving outwards:

- *the narratee*: a person addressed in the text, often another character;

- *the implied reader*: someone the text is implicitly expecting or inviting, but who will often not correspond to the furthest figure; and
- *the actual or 'real reader'*: a person of flesh and blood, but who will be a different person with every different reading.[3]

As for film criticism, the same structures largely apply, subject to the different technical and receptive circumstances: for the purposes of this analysis, for reasons that will hopefully emerge, I shall override these, considering this film as a text that can be consumed by an individual in the form of a DVD.

I want, then, to consider texts as modes of address. Let us assume that you or I are reading a novel by Lionel Shriver or Albert Camus. What difference does it make if that novel is in the first, third or second person?

A third-person fiction has an omniscient narrator who may play an active part in the world they tell us about or may not. But a first-person narrative is always told by a character involved in the story. An extreme case is Camus's *L'Étranger* [*The Outsider*] (1942), in which a first-person narrative makes contradictory demands on the reader: on the one hand we are required to *judge* the narrator who has, after all, committed a murder; on the other we are required to judge him *innocent*. The case for his innocence rests, as the text sets it up, on his refusal to show any emotion he – supposedly – does not feel; in particular, he neither says that he regrets killing the Arab nor that he loved his mother and minded when she died. Yet this same refusal, as Camus himself points out (Camus 1965: 669), could be grounds for judging him pathological and thus guilty. Certainly the court draws this conclusion – if on the feeblest of evidence. The issues are complex and there is no space here to go into them in detail. What I want to focus on is how the narrative itself steers the reader in certain directions.

The first person is a voice, and it may often be a confessing voice. A whole set of short, mainly nineteenth-century French Romantic fictions take the form of a first-person confession, spoken by a youngish man to an older man to whom he tells the sad story of his life, from a stable position of retrospection (see Segal 1988). The story hinges on the death of a beloved woman who has somehow failed him, by loving too much or too little or enigmatically, but who in any case ends up dead, often by his hand. The narratee listens, considers and then, in a closing frame, either absolves the narrator like a kindly priest or condemns him like a judge in a court of law. The reader is invited by implication to share in these possibilities – occasionally both are there together in the voice of a contrasting pair of narratees, as in Chateaubriand's *René* (1802).

In the material, social world the pronouns 'I' and 'you' form a pair, and they are girded about by terms like 'here', 'now' and 'tomorrow', which, like them, locate the speech in a present time and place (Benveniste 1966: 251–57). Third-person pronouns 'he', 'she' or 'they' refer, conversely, to entities that need not be present but are located linguistically, by some preceding noun – the woman I had dinner with, your cousins, Winston Churchill. All entities in a text are virtual, unverifiable, neither here nor now. They may well – in realist writing, they must – invite us to think about them as if they were materially or historically verifiable, and to test them in ways we might try to test people in our everyday lives, but that is no more than a pleasant delusion. Lady Macbeth has breastfed at least one child (see *Macbeth* Act I, scene 7), but we can never know how many children she has.[4] Meursault has killed someone and Kevin has killed several people, but we can never 'know why'. All we can do is talk about them...

What is much more unusual is second-person narrative. Here is what Michel Butor has to say about it. First he observes that 'nous sommes dans une situation d'enseignement' [we are in a pedagogical situation] (Butor 1964: 80) and second, more daringly, that the second person implies a state of interrogation. A magistrate or police inspector may appear to tell the accused his or her own story:

> Si le personnage connaissait entièrement sa propre histoire, s'il n'avait pas d'objection à la raconter ou se la raconter, la première personne s'imposerait : il donnerait son témoignage. Mais [il] s'agit de le lui arracher, soit parce qu'il ment, nous cache ou se cache quelque chose, soit parce qu'il n'a pas tous les éléments, ou même, s'il les a, qu'il est incapable de les relier convenablement.
> (Butor 1964: 81)

> [If the character knew his own story in its entirety, if he had no objection to telling it or telling it to himself, the first person would be used; he would give his statement. But in fact it has to be dragged out of him, either because he is lying, hiding something from us or himself, or because he does not know all the details or even if he does know them he does not know how to link them together properly.]

Whether necessitated by the simplicity or the slyness of the character, the second person suggests their guilt. Butor's own *La Modification* [*Second Thoughts*] (1957), narrated entirely in the 'vous' form, is indeed accusatory, but by implicitly putting the reader into the position of the accused it is more likely to be refused than accepted. Some texts use an internal 'you', addressed to an identified narratee, and here the accusation is more successful.

Here are two brief examples. In a recent article, Keith Reader compares two uses of 'you' in a publication by Régis Debray in 2010 that took the form of a text addressed to Élie Barnavi, *A un ami israélien* [*To an Israeli friend*]. In this text Debray 'addresses Barnavi as "tu" while apostrophising the Israeli state as "vous" and thereby maintains a vital distinction between them' (Reader 2014: 30). Of course English does not allow the distinction common to most other languages (nor does Hebrew, as it happens) between a formal and an informal 'you'. In the case raised here, 'vous' is accusatory and 'tu' conciliatory – though we should not forget that French police officers call the accused 'tu' as a sign of discipline, and once when I leaned too close to the tapestries in the musée Cluny, the attendant said sharply: 'Touche pas!' Here, in either case, the second person is a form of challenge.

It is more precisely accusatory in a short book published in 1952 under the pseudonym François Derais by a young man named François Reymond. The book is called *L'Envers du Journal de Gide* [*The Other Side of Gide's Journal*] and, as the title suggests, it is a riposte to Gide's Journal of the 1940s in which he describes at length, using the pseudonym 'Victor', the behaviour of a 15-year-old boy he had the misfortune to spend six months with during the Second World War in Tunis. In his own book, Reymond takes the unique step of telling his side of the story – the obscure correcting the dominance of the very famous – and he does so in the second person, addressing himself to Gide (dead by the time of publication, but who had been sent it in draft) as 'vous': 'Vous jouiez un peu la comédie du charme; cela se sentait, mais l'on ne s'agaçait pas de vos efforts, on vous en savait plutôt gré. [...] Vous jugiez nécessaire d'être brillant, d'être André Gide' (Derais and Rambaud 1952: 109) [You were play-acting, putting on the charm, that was clear, but no one got irritated, rather the contrary, we were flattered. [...] You felt it necessary to be brilliant, to be André Gide]. His descriptions of Gide's mannerisms, vanity and above all the long-drawn-out battle between them after the 73-year-old failed to seduce him are powerfully drawn through the use of the reviving and challenging 'vous'.

These two examples show how the second-person is intrinsically accusatory. Something slightly similar can happen with a first-person fiction and, I believe, happens in *L'Étranger*: occasionally a 'you'-function is not (or is not only) explicit but may be buried within an 'I'-function. Thus, a coherent reading of this puzzling text, but also a quite painful one, is possible if we find ourselves the implicit *voice* of a 'you' narrative (silent, like the accusation of the Arabs) to which this text is Meursault's response.[5] This means that, as accusers, the text's readers find themselves responsible for causing a crime they cannot countenance, inviting the refusal of a narrator whose narrative they have induced; in short, for conjuring up a text that refuses them. Unlike the self-congratulatory 'homme absurde' [absurd man], they have to concede their implication in the very object that frustrates them. The universal guilt that is the ground out of which the narrative grows must extend to the reader who makes the narrative happen. This is an extreme and disturbing example of the experience of reading in the second person.

With this in mind, I want now to turn to the fictional narrative of Eva Khatchadourian to see how her use of 'you', addressed to the husband she repeatedly asserts she still loves, allows her to do several things at once. Writing two years after what she continues to call 'Thursday', she addresses herself in letters that receive no reply – but this is not unusual for an epistolary novel – to her husband Franklin. She needs to talk. She needs to talk about Kevin, about herself, and about what was there before Kevin was (an element that is almost entirely missing from the 2011 film). As in the nineteenth-century confessional fictions mentioned earlier, this structure allows her to address herself implicitly while and through addressing the other. But, more like a classic psychoanalytic setting, her monologue never turns into a dialogue.

To begin with the startling ending (startling in the book, merely shocking in the film, because there is no second-person structure to contend with) and with apologies for this essential 'spoiler' – it is crucial that we finally understand that, despite many turns of phrase suggesting he is no longer living with her rather than not living at all, we discover in the closing pages that Franklin was, alongside their daughter Celia, Kevin's first victim. So nothing Eva says will reach him. But – as the title stresses – Eva needs to talk to someone. Here are a few of the motives she offers for writing in the form she does: 'it's far less important to me to be liked these days than to be understood (Shriver, 2003: 5); 'this appeal to you' (188); 'this is my account, to whose perspective you have no choice but to submit' (270); and 'Oh my beloved, I may need too badly to tell myself a story...' (453, ellipsis Shriver's). And this, at more length, coming towards the end of the narrative:

> Well, it's another Friday night on which I gird myself for a visit to Chatham [the juvenile prison] tomorrow morning. The halogen bulbs are trembling again, flickering like my stoic resolve to be a good soldier and live out what's left of my life for the sake of some unnameable duty. I've sat here for over an hour, wondering what keeps me going, and more specifically just what it is I want from you. I guess it goes without saying that I want you back; the volume of this correspondence – though it's more of a *respondence*, isn't it? – attests heavily to that. But what else? Do I want you to forgive me? And if so, for what exactly?
>
> (385)

Before I start to examine that last question, it is worth considering what direct forms of dialogue Eva rejects. She does not want to talk to a priest; her mother, despite various problems between them, is actually very understanding, but she does not want to talk to her; she seemingly has no friends; and she certainly does not want to talk to a psychoanalyst: the rare mentions of people in the therapy or medical profession are scathing. She refers for instance (right near the beginning of the narrative, in the first letter) to 'those bullying therapeutic types' (9) – or, discussing a psychiatric diagnosis: 'Dr Rhinestein offered up *postnatal depression* like a present, as if simply being told that you are unhappy is supposed to cheer you up, I did not pay professionals to be plied with the obvious' (101). A page after she reports Franklin's suggestion, following the loss of Celia's eye, that she should see a shrink because 'I'm afraid it's beyond me' (345), she comments 'I didn't want to "talk to somebody", but I'd have given my eye teeth to be able to talk to you' (346).

The whole content of the book is, of course, a study of what it might mean to *talk about* one's child, more particularly about how parents are as often divided as united by their children; but the book's form is steeped in the impossibility of *talking to* another person. My interest here is in the difference between those two prepositional relations. It is not only a question of the intrinsically mediate form of writing rather than speaking – and where film fits in here is an issue I will return to – but more fundamentally to the triangularity so often hidden behind any supposedly dyadic structure. We only need to talk because there is Kevin to talk about, but Kevin has, long ago, since the very mooting of him, murdered speech.

By 'more of a *respondence*' Eva/Shriver is pointing to the lack of replies to her letters (she knows why but we do not, yet), but actually she is saying more. She is suggesting that, like Meursault, her act of narrating is less a challenge than a *response* to a challenge. Or rather, in her case, she is both accused and accusing, accusing and accused.

It is often said that *We Need to Talk About Kevin* is a text about guilt. Herein lies the most obvious parallel with *L'Étranger*: both trace the prehistory of a crime, an attempt to work out 'whose fault it is'. Like many instances of similar excess (we might think of horrific abuses described almost daily in our newspapers, in which – most often gendered this way – the father has committed the crime but the mother is blamed for her passive part), it seems not enough to say that it is the fault of Kevin. Kevin, the argument goes, would not be as he is without the choice of his parents to have him (or someone) and their failures or lack of successes in bringing him up. In particular, his action is the outcome of 'bad mothering'.[6]

Among the commentators, bloggers and critics on the film, there is a passionate debate about 'whose fault it is', whether Kevin is 'born evil' or his mother is to blame, whether the film 'enters her head' or offers us an image of familial-social problems that is more like *The Omen* (dir. Richard Donner, 1976). One brave mother describes her own failure to love her child and her unremitting efforts to keep this hidden. In the DVD commentaries, Ezra Miller (Kevin) considers that 'he wants her to come face to face with the deep dark things that make her a very bad mother', while Tilda Swinton (Eva), who says she fell in love immediately with her newborn twins, nevertheless recognizes the frightening possibility of 'the maternal instinct not kicking in'. She picks up something that is explicit in the book when she identifies what she might have described as the Freudian uncanny: 'the nightmare for her is not that he's violent & horrible in a foreign way but that he's violent & horrible in a really familiar way: it's her horribleness, it's her violence. And that's the nightmare [...] she knows only too well where this is coming from'.

As for the different mode of representation of the film as an adaptation, one critic notes how the director 'breezily dispenses with the structure of the original book' (Collins 2011: n.p.) and another expands: 'Lynne Ramsay, the director of *We Need to Talk About Kevin*, and her co-adaptor, Rory Kinnear, have dropped the epistolary technique. That would have demanded a voiceover narrator and greatly restricted the film's tempo' (French 2011: n.p.). Ramsay herself makes a fascinating, seemingly tangential comment on the figure of Eva when she admiringly observes Swinton's professionalism at eschewing the glamour of her earlier roles, insisting on 'stripping back a lot of the exoticism from her face; she would say herself, "Make me more of an old bag" [...] She's not thinking about how she looks the whole time'. Actually this way of describing women's – especially celebrity women's – conventional compulsion to place all their value in a glamorous appearance is, paradoxically or not, not so much a reversal as an inversion. What a book can do and this one does – what John C. Reilly (Franklin) describes in his commentary as the inside viewpoint of the protagonist that made his part, in the recollection scenes, difficult to play: the idea that 'it's not meant to portray the way it was; it's meant to portray the way it felt to her'[7] – does not, in a film, prevent the whole focus still being on what we see of her, as well as what and how she sees. Thus 'Swinton portrays Eva as a ghost, haunting her past and haunted by it. She is gaunt, hollow-eyed, stunned: her eyes are almost blind, as if she can see only memories (Bradshaw 2011: n.p.). Our gaze is riveted on her ashen face, mouth half-open, eyes glaucous, black hair lank, clothes shapeless and as much too big as Kevin's, out of sheer perversity, were too small. Her isolation, self-laceration and active and passive abuse at the hands of neighbours and workmates, are represented by endless grim headshots, hazy colours with a predominance of raindrops and melodramatic red, in a cityscape of despair. The physical world in which Eva moves is a blur, and she is a blur within it.

What the film can do and the book cannot, then, is combine seeing the protagonist with the protagonist seeing – a very different version of Laura Mulvey's female 'to-be-looked-at-ness' (Mulvey 1975), but a version nonetheless.[8] How this works in relation to the central subject of this essay is that, despite our partial behind-her-eyes position, we are encountering a text that is more third-person than first-person, and there is no second-person perspective left. The lack of letters – in both senses – means that no one, or rather only *everyone*, is addressed. Crucially, the non-existence of Eva's interlocutor does not come as a surprise and does not contribute to any of the ironies of her situation. Nor is the essential question, as it is in the book, who exactly her unresponsive interlocutor is: Franklin, herself or Kevin.

Thus in the film, inevitably, things appear; the screen functions as a closed surface, a third person that does not open up to either sympathy or irony; inevitably, the generic parameters prevent any sense of a narrator confiding. By contrast, the book's first-person narrator has a vivid voice: earnest, lively, harrowed without losing her enquiring mind, and if she is, as Kevin notes, as 'harsh' as he (Shriver, 2003: 321), she is also witty, observant and tirelessly curious. Of course she may – must – be partial, but all texts are partial, in both senses. The question *why* preoccupies her from the start as it never preoccupies anyone else in her family. To trace the answer, she takes us back to her youth, occasionally to her childhood.

Eva Khatchadourian is a successful businesswoman: some years before meeting Franklin she has set up *A Wing and a Prayer*, a forerunner of *Lonely Planet* etc., i.e. a series of guidebooks for seeing the world cheaply and intimately. Scathing about her native USA, she loves travelling, though by the time of her marriage she has begun to notice that, essentially, things aren't as different in other countries as she might wish. Brought up by her widowed, agoraphobic Armenian mother in small-town Wisconsin, she learned to psych herself up as a child running errands to brave the taunts of neighbourhood boys, but something remains: 'if I enjoyed the company of men – I liked their down-to-earth quality, I was prone to mistake aggression for honesty, and I disdained daintiness – I wasn't at all sure about *boys*' (74).

Everyone (including herself) expected Eva to settle down with a wispy, lentil-eating, dope-smoking, poetry-quoting hippy type but 'how lucky we are, when we're spared what we think we want!' (42): instead she meets Franklin Plaskett, a location scout, all-American, Republican-voting, 'a big, broad meat eater with brash blond hair and ruddy skin that burns at the beach. A bundle of appetites. A full, boisterous guffaw; a man who tells knock-knock jokes' (41). If there is a first, fundamental mystery in this book it is what draws Eva to Franklin, or – more subtly – what keeps her loving and needing him long after he has stopped listening to her. But I suggest that this mystery is an essential given which has to explain everything else. Eva tolerates his intolerance because she 'needs to talk' precisely to the contrary personality whose lack of self-consciousness is meant to put a brake on hers. This impulse to dialogue, which is founded on its intrinsic impossibility, is the basis of the book. The story she is telling herself – the accusation against her that she is espousing as well as challenging – only makes sense as a story (an appeal, an exploration, another accusation) that she has intended to be heard by another. The very psychoanalytic choice not to turn monologue into dialogue is the fulcrum on which everything turns – in this case, not a choice but a failure. Kevin is, as he puts it 'the context' (409) of that failure.

The reader is, of course, invited into 'the place of the analyst', the judge, the audience, but most of all, the husband. Franklin's position inside the story is as the object of *direct* encounter (the lover) who becomes, from the moment Kevin is conceived (or earlier?), the *indirect* object of a triangulation. Who is more in a pair with their child becomes an unspoken question – but there are always 'two of us, and one of you' (127).

'*What possessed us?* We were so happy! Why, then, did we take the stake of all we had and place it all on this outrageous gamble of having a child?' (14). Franklin's reason for wanting a baby (a son) is to find the answer to 'the Big Question' (21), to which Eva reacts: 'I did not put my finger on why, but your Big Question left me unmoved. I far preferred my *turn of the page*' (19). The decision to have a child was, then, based on a desire on both their parts for something to change, a new story, 'context' or 'foreign country' – but it was also precipitated by a threatened loss of the pair-bond: one day Franklin's return home is delayed by several hours and Eva, in her terror, vows to create a substitute – that is, another pair... Or is it something rather different? For she also seems to imagine replacement as a kind of extension: 'you made me greedy. Like any addict worth his salt, I wanted more. And I was curious [...] You started it – like someone who gives you a gift of a single carved ebony elephant, and suddenly you get this idea that it might be fun to start a *collection*' (24). The blurring of the numbers and the motives is partly to show us that in every decision, as she puts it elsewhere (of Kevin's act) 'big deeds are a lot of little deeds one after the other' (428). It is also to show us the split in everything, in the individual and, more grievously, in even the happiest couple: 'It is not true that I was "ambivalent" about motherhood. You wanted to have a child. On balance, I did not. Added together, that seemed like ambivalence, but though we were a superlative couple, we were not the same person. I never did get you to like eggplant' (66).

So whose fault is Kevin, and Kevin's act? We only have Eva's story, not least because Kevin only leaves her alive to tell it. Presumably this is mainly so that she remains to see him – 'when you're putting on a show, you don't shoot the audience' (460)[9] – but surely also so that the whole story, the 'context', remains in her keeping. Her narrative is a final attempt to get out of that unwelcome pair-bond – 'I wake up with what he did every morning and I go to bed with it every night. It is my shabby substitute for a husband' (14–15) – by putting herself on trial. We retrace Kevin's life as a screaming baby, a stubborn toddler, unsmiling boy and surly teenager. We observe his studied indifference, his icily tidy room, his mocking articulacy, his choice to get straight Bs, his bizarre dress-sense, his strategic contempt and 'raging' (391) at the world. Unlike his mother (whom of course in so many ways he resembles), he is not 'weird' (377) for he 'applied his intelligence to keeping his head below the parapet' (378). As for Eva's role as 'a bad mother' (81), or rather her 'failure to bond', we see only those events that show him 'on a full-time war footing with his mother' (430) and her almost exclusive, furiously maintained patience. The murders exceed 'even [her] unnatural maternal cynicism' (431). And yet she feels her own guilt alongside his: 'I felt both implicated and irrelevant […] infected, contagious, quarantined' (448).

Like Eva, Kevin does not answer the question why. By the closing pages, he admits: 'I used to think I knew [but] now I'm not so sure' (464). Eva's nearest surmise is that he chose it as a gratuitous act, that is, an act without motive – 'his choice of weapon was meant to ensure to the best of his ability that *Thursday* would mean absolutely nothing' (423). In relation to his collection of computer viruses he comments: 'they're kind of elegant, you know? Almost – pure. Kind of like – charity work, you know? It's *selfless.*' (384). As this shows, the gratuitous or motiveless act may as easily be a good action as an 'evil' one; the key thing is that it should be 'pure' in the sense of unattached, untraceable, that is, impossible to analyse.[10] It speaks to no one while, precisely, being visible to everyone.

Having said this, there is another motive, which brings the question of dialogue and accusation – the 'you-narrative' – back into play. Eva believes that Kevin moved towards the first 'little deed' (428), the first 'teaspoon' (64)-size dig into the hole that buries them all, at the moment he overheard his parents discussing separation. His doting father declares that 'custody is a no-brainer […] And doesn't that say it all' (407), implying that he would have Kevin and Eva Celia. But narrator Eva comments two years later:

> Most children are mortified by the prospect of their parents' divorce, and I don't deny that the conversation he overheard from the hallway sent Kevin into a tailspin. Nevertheless, I was disconcerted. That boy had been trying to split us up for fifteen years. Why wasn't he satisfied? And if I really was such

a horror, why wouldn't he gladly jettison his awful mother? In retrospect, I can only assume that it was bad enough living with a woman who was cold, suspicious, resentful, accusatory, and aloof. Only one eventuality must have seemed worse, and that was living with you, Franklin. Getting stuck with Dad.

Getting stuck with Dad the Dupe.

(410)

Here the third person appears for the only time in Eva's 'talk' to Franklin to refer to him (she has used it a couple of times, self-consciously, to refer to herself), and it is because she is borrowing the voice and thoughts of their son. The triangulation has resolved itself, by the end of the text, into a potential, or is it caricatural, pre-oedipal pair. The endless conflict between her and him is preferable to either of those other apparently loving couples of the post-oedipal contract: Kevin and Franklin or even, perhaps, Eva and Franklin. She never will get to talk about Kevin except – if this is imaginable – to him.

Notes

All translations from French are my own and reference is given to the original texts; unless otherwise noted, all italics in a quotation are the author's. All citations without author-name are from Shriver 2003.

*   Extracts from *We Need to Talk About Kevin* (Serpent's Tail, 2003) appear here by kind permission of Serpent's Tail.

1   For a survey of the use of psychoanalysis in literary criticism, see Wright 1998. A turning-point appeared when, as Shoshana Felman puts it, the common subject–object relation – reader–analyst acts upon text–analysand – is inverted into one where 'the text is viewed by us as a "subject presumed to know"' (Felman 1982 [1977]: 7).

2   These two assumptions, combined and put into practice, are at the root of Freud's psychoanalytic theory and practice as early as the jointly authored *Studien über Hysterie* [Studies on Hysteria] of 1895 and the *Traumdeutung* [Interpretation of Dreams] of 1900.

3   See the work of Iser, Jauss and the Constance School and its development into reader-response theory; for a feminist example see Segal 2010 [1986].

4   The ringing title 'How many children had Lady Macbeth?' was originally used by L. C. Knights in 1933, but it is often attributed to the – in this connection – much maligned A. C. Bradley; see Britton 1961.

5   The gaps and reticences in Meursault's narrative, which create in the reader a sense that we are not being confided in and at the same time that we are prevented from making an 'objective' judgment, are all features that could be expected from an account given in response to unwelcome questions. Meursault tends to placate unwanted enquirers with what he hopes are noncommittal acquiescences; this works on some occasions better than others. Interestingly, Camus himself, alongside the ecstatic definition of his hero as 'un homme pauvre et nu, amoureux du soleil qui ne laisse pas d'ombres' (Camus 1962, p. 1928) [a poor, naked man, in love with the sun that leaves no shadows], also insisted that 'dans tout le [...] livre, il se borne à répondre aux questions' (Camus 1962, p. 1931) [throughout the whole [...] book, he does nothing but answer questions]; or again, 'vous n'avez pas remarqué qu'il se borne

toujours à répondre aux questions, celles de la vie et celles des hommes' (Camus 1962: 1933) [you have not noticed that he does nothing but answer questions, the questions of life or the questions of other people]. This is linked to what Camus describes as a negative aesthetic: 'il n'affirme jamais rien. Et je n'en ai donné qu'un cliché négatif' (Camus 1962: 1933) [he never makes a positive assertion. And I have only given a negative image of this], as well as to the numerous clues that Meursault has an Oedipus-like obsession with universal, matricidal guilt, to which his act is the violent response.

6 This concept, I would argue, permeates all psychoanalysis except feminist psychoanalysis – and even that is not always exempt – and is based on the strange difficulty most people seem to have in viewing mothers through anything but child-shaped lenses. Let us never forget that there is no such thing as the 'good-enough mother': the notion is not a threshold but a tightrope – in Winnicott, it is all too possible for a mother to be 'too good' (see Winnicott 1990: 51). When this essay was first presented as a paper in 2012, to an audience mainly of senior psychoanalysts, the question-time was dominated by angry and anxious accusations against Eva's mothering, made by family psychotherapists who had not read the book on the grounds that it would have been a 'busman's holiday'.

7 Not everyone agrees; for instance, Ben Livant writes: 'I am going to give the book I have not read on which the film is based the benefit of the doubt. I am going to assume that the novel is a compelling read because it successfully provides the psychological interiority of the character of the mother who recalls the story from her first person point of view. It is precisely this inner mentality that the film fails to deliver. Or, maybe the fault does reside with the original source material. Either way, the film never gets inside the head of the mother' (Livant 2012: n.p.).

8 It could, of course, be argued that this term is inappropriate, since Mulvey is describing a male gaze and the director speaking here is female. I'm thinking of how women's concern with their appearance is always implicitly about the demands of a ubiquitous male gaze; we absorb this into everyday self-presentation and Ramsay's terms are strongly reminiscent of that – she seems, in this brief comment, to be marvelling at the heroism of Swinton in choosing to magnetize the implied viewer's gaze to a grim appearance rather than an attractive one – yet I believe it is still the same obsession with being or having to be looked at. Actors and directors can present a woman's body differently from this. The impossibility of direct seeing, as a reader, and the impossibility of not seeing, as a viewer, create two very different versions of address.

9 One comment on the IMDb thread 'The meaning of the movie ending' (accessed 25 August 2012; no longer accessible) raises this issue: 'when Eva asks Kevin why he did it, I got the feeling that she wasn't necessarily asking why he had killed all those people, she has always known that Kevin was evil. But why he had left her alive. She felt that of all the people to die she was the only one who would have deserved to go, because she felt responsible for failing to raise Kevin right, save him from his dark nature'.

10 The 'acte gratuit' [gratuitous act] is most fully represented in the writings of André Gide, especially his *Les Caves du Vatican* [The Vatican Cellars] (1914) and *Les Faux-monnayeurs* [The Counterfeiters] (1925); see Segal 1998, especially chapter 5.

References

Benveniste, Emile (1966), *Problèmes de linguistique générale*, vol I (Paris: Gallimard).
Booth, Wayne C. (1961), *The Rhetoric of Fiction* (Chicago, IL: University of Chicago Press).

Bradshaw, Peter (2011), *The Guardian* (20 Oct 2011): www.guardian.co.uk/film/2011/oct/20/we-need-to-talk-about-kevin-review (accessed 25 August 2012).

Britton, John (1961), 'A. C. Bradley and those children of Lady Macbeth', *Shakespeare Quarterly*, *12*(3) (summer), 349–51.

Butor, Michel (1964), *Essais sur le roman* (Paris : Gallimard).

Camus, Albert (1962), *Théâtre, récits, nouvelles* ed by R. Quilliot and L. Faucon (Paris: Gallimard).

Camus, Albert (1965), *Essais*, ed. by R. Quilliot and L. Faucon (Paris: Gallimard).

Collins, Robbie (2011), *The Telegraph* (20 Oct 2011): www.telegraph.co.uk/culture/film/filmreviews/8839576/We-Need-to-Talk-About-Kevin-review.html (accessed 25 August 2012).

Derais François and Henri Rambaud (1952), *L'Envers du Journal de Gide* (Paris: Le nouveau portique).

Felman, Shoshana (1982 [1977]), *Literature and Psychoanalysis: The Question of Reading: Otherwise* (Baltimore and London: Johns Hopkins University Press).

French, Philip (2011), *The Observer* (23 Oct 2011): www.guardian.co.uk/film/2011/oct/23/need-talk-about-kevin-review (accessed 25 August 2012).

Livant, Ben (2012), *Cinemania*: http://djardine.blogspot.ca/2012/07/we-need-to-talk-about-kevin-uk-2011.html (accessed 25 August 2012).

Mulvey, Laura (1975), 'Visual pleasure and narrative cinema', *Screen*, *16*(3), 6–18.

Ramsay, Lynne (2011), dir., *We Need to Talk About Kevin* (BBC films).

Reader, Keith (2014), 'The *querelle* between Alain Badiou and Éric Marty, contrasted with Régis Debray's *lettre ouverte* to Élie Barnavi and Barnavi's response', *Modern & Contemporary France*, *22*(1), 29–42.

Segal, Naomi (1988), *Narcissus and Echo: Women in the French récit* (Manchester: Manchester University Press).

Segal, Naomi (1998), *André Gide: Pederasty and Pedagogy* (Oxford: Oxford University Press).

Segal, Naomi (2010 [1986]), *The Unintended Reader: Feminism and Manon Lescaut* (Cambridge: Cambridge University Press).

Shriver, Lionel (2003), *We Need to Talk About Kevin* (London: Serpent's Tail).

Winnicott, Donald W. (1990 [1965]), 'The theory of the parent–infant relationship' (1960), in ed. Masud Khan, *The Maturational Processes and the Facilitating Environment* (London and New York: Karnac).

Wright, Elizabeth (1998), *Psychoanalytic Criticism* (Cambridge: Polity, 2nd edn).

Chapter 17

This book has no pictures (a visual documentary of psychoanalysis)

Nicholas Muellner

> A picture: blue couch against birch-paneled wall. Centered above it, a painting. The frame: gold but not gilt. The style: casually post-impressionist, loosely daubed. The sofa is modern, in a gentle late-seventies way: knurled cotton fabric and angled bolster cushions, removable when the patient prefers to lie down. The painting suggests a turtle, bold brushstrokes rendering a shell raked in golden light, from which the green head emerges in profile, marked by a single vermillion eye. It might be titled: sunset with carapace.

I am a photographer. But over the past several years I have been interviewing psychotherapists – from psychoanalysts in private practice to psychiatrists working with mentally ill violent offenders. The practice of psychoanalytic psychotherapy has always embraced the seduction and power of the image, usually as source material for linguistic interpretation. Images become useful for the therapeutic process through translation into language. For reasons both too obvious and still obscure, I want to know, as a dumb photographer, if the creation of visual images can be understood as its own form of analytical response. Do therapists, in other words, make pictures like photographers do?

In these interviews I seek to document the invisible visual content of therapists' work with patients, beginning with the seemingly straightforward question: what do you see in your imagination when patients talk to you? From here, I have accumulated both a catalog of visual descriptions – verbal pictures – from the therapists' imaginaries, and a series of often revealing narratives about the interpretive efficacies, dangers and challenges of these images within therapeutic work. Thus, the material of this visual documentary is, for me, a collection of photographs that aren't pictured: a portrait of a process that is both image-driven and innately immaterial. What follows are some episodes from this still-unfolding fieldwork.

***

> Just this wall, this completely bricked-up wall, that was right behind her, that had no options, that you couldn't climb up or get over, that entirely sealed the room.

The psychiatrist had this image ready for me, because she thought I might ask. She visualized it every time she met with a certain patient: a woman who had done something terrible and irrevocable, and whose anguish was irremediable. The "wall of impossibility" as the psychiatrist called it, was insurmountable: "you couldn't chip it down, you couldn't climb up it, it was just this solid huge thing."

Occasionally, in place of the wall, she visualized the room filled up with insulation foam: "There's nowhere to breathe, there's nothing happening and there's no air, there's no movement."

The patients she worked with had all committed violent crimes, and they arrived to her with not only a history, but one or more "index offenses" around which their life-stories had been reordered. Their lives seemed to open out, forward and back, from these terrible definitive moments.

I asked if she visualizes these dramatic past events. "I imagine them," she said, "as if it's a film."

Interested, I sought to clarify: so you see movement rather than fixed images?

Both, she said, reconsidering. "Probably a lot of it is fixed scenes. In fact, even when I think it's a film, it's probably just a series of fixed scenes. Because there's lots you don't know."

"And they're not necessarily straight-on," she continued. "One patient in particular, when I try to imagine his index offense, it's as if it's happening over to the side. Like a really bad photograph that someone's taken with a snappy camera at a social occasion, where you can see people in it, but they're not facing the camera."

And why, I wondered, do you think you view *that* event in *this* way?

"It's almost as if I don't want to see him doing what he did, as if I'm saying: well, it's not that clear what happened. Part of me wants to understand that he's a very damaged boy. It's partly because of my sympathy that I can't see the whole thing."

Persistently and vividly, this therapist spoke about interiors. If she was interested in a particular case, she explained, she would have not only the patient's figure in her mind, but the layout of a building, or of a room. I asked if these spaces were drawn from research: police narratives, evidence photographs, patient descriptions?

"Mostly," she said, realizing the answer as it came from her mouth, "I invent them."

In one case, her visualization often began with a view of a doorway to the patient's kitchen, with shoes lying around, and part of the breakfast room visible beyond. "I've seen a picture of the outside," she noted. "I've had to imagine the inside." And here she caught herself: "It's interesting that I said 'had to imagine the inside.' I hadn't *had to* imagine the inside at all."

She continued, amazed: "Actually, now that I think about it, I'm always trying to come up with a floor-plan. ... And I've always got exactly the building in my mind; maybe even the trees outside the windows; even the type of kitchen furnishings." She burst out in a sharp laugh of recognition as more detail spilled out:

The bathroom is dated and really the sort of colors that need to be ripped out and replaced – like avocado or light blue, something a bit '70s or '80s. ... In my mind there's a carpet as well, which is old fashioned, isn't it, to have carpet? No one has carpet anymore.

She described another patient's kitchen, which she also knew nothing about: "Country Kitchen effect; pine-fitted, where everything really matches but is really horrible, and you get this very shiny orange pine thing going on when you walk in."

Repeatedly, I ask: why that particular image? Repeatedly she answers: "I don't know!"

I ask if these images develop as the therapy progresses. She replies, architecturally,

I guess you have a basic structure, and the more that you learn, the more you're filling it in, so it becomes more solid. It starts sketchy, and then the detail is added on, like a scaffolding that you're amending or modifying. ... There are always blurred bits as to what has happened, but my mind seems to want to fill it in; to create texture and to create a scene, so that I can understand what happened.

***

In London, I met with a psychiatrist, not as a patient, but to ask him some questions: an interview. Nonetheless, he seated me in the patient's chair and assumed his position in the consulting chair, with the brooding blank length of the psychoanalytic couch laid out between us, gaping and suggestive in unutterable ways.

I asked him to describe what he saw when a patient told him a story – a dream, a memory, a recent event. I clarified: what does the image look like in your imagination, either in a specific case, or in general?

He answered: "I try to avoid seeing images. If I make an image, I am not thinking with my patient."

I asked him if patients ever brought in photographs to show him. "Yes," he said, but he did not like it. "The photograph," he suggested, "is usually a form of resistance – resistance to the analyst seeing or understanding whatever he wants. The image, in other words, obfuscates."

I asked him about the space between what the patient wants to describe, and what he, the therapist, is able to discern.

Sometimes, he said, there is an image present that he cannot see. But his inability to visualize it does not mean it isn't there.

***

A picture: in an otherwise typical Victorian home, the windows of the ground floor are shuttered on the inside. This peculiar architectural inversion is designed as much to prevent looking in as it is to forestall peering out. The slats on these shutters are drawn down and painted shut with an interior eggshell white. But there is one window, cut into an irregular shape by the descending staircase, where sun-faded Marimekko curtains have to do instead. From this slightly elevated vantage, a child could part the fabric and stare down upon the receding heads of his father's patients as they step up the basement stairs and disappear around the bend of a narrow fenced path at the back of the house. While it is equally possible to catch those strangers' arriving faces, even a child of seven knows that to see them fully, frontally, is one transgression too far.

Witnessing those faceless heads – rising like solitary balloons and just as quickly receding – it is impossible not to wonder what those roundish receptacles hold. The child could, perhaps, imagine the pictures they carried of that office's semi-alien terrain: always several degrees cooler and several decades starker than the sentimental jumble above. But the images that unfold from those heads into the father's consciousness, and the pictures that he sends back to the strangers' waiting minds – that parade of shared and shifting tableaux passing just below the floorboards – is undeniable and unimaginable.

***

He began with the flashes: "I don't like to go downstairs and open the door and not know which patient is there. I like to know, because often I have an image right before the hour starts."

What do these images look like, I asked.

"Sometimes" he explained, "it's a scene, or it has a darkness to it. Images like: on a river at dusk." At this moment, as he talked, a peal of church bells began in the distance. "Sometimes it explains to me what's been going on; sometimes it's predictive; not in a mystical way, but because I'm getting something."

Often, he continued, it reflects a mood, "because a mood can be translated into an image. It could be my mood, but most of the time it's the mood that the patient has been in, or is working their way out of or into." Here he talked about light, color, space – the aesthetic vocabulary of visual tone.

This flash, what he calls "having a visual image before an hour" is both "remembering and anticipatory ... remembering what was probably most important, turned into an image ... and anticipating what I should focus on, what I need to remember to keep the framework of the whole process going where it's going."

When asked about his method of responding to patients' narratives in the hour, his answer was emphatic: "The minute I'm hearing anything, I'm seeing things at the same time. I can't help it; it just happens."

"To me," he elaborated, "images are inherently richer than a couple of words. So I certainly consider them equal, if not more valuable." But sometimes, he acknowledged, "they're a counter, a defense, a way of not feeling something painful – something funny, for instance, in place of something that hurts. ... Sometimes the image is a way to understand, but it represents interference with understanding too."

Throughout our conversation, the analyst's vocabulary was infused with optical and chemical processes. "Sometimes," he began, "you may just hear of it like a particular small snap-shot," one that the patient brings up and just as quickly wants to dismiss. "Often," he said, "there is a bit of a struggle to teasing it out." He called this "the push and pull to getting it developed." It was a language that echoed my old experience of the darkroom: "You may work on developing one picture for months," he explained, "or you may do it within 15 minutes. Some pictures take a long time."

He continued: "It's a bit like you're fiddling around with a microscope. You look on low power and high power and you hold it up to the light. You look at it from different angles and you work at it together. You make the image come into existence."

Time, and the tape, were running out, and an impulse pushed me to shift our focus: Why, I asked, do you think a photographer is asking you these questions?

"Photography," he responded, "is always about imagery. How people use it and struggle with it and change it and value it and devalue and are threatened by it. In photography you make images, you don't just click, you do things with them too, and you have to work with yourself about that. The overt aim is different, but underneath, they're cousins."

"Finding ways to produce affect-laden reactions: strong, powerful reactions, things that put people in touch with something about themselves or their lives. That's what I try to do and what you try to do."

***

In London, I met with a psychiatrist, not as a patient, but to ask him some questions: an interview. He bought me coffee; we talked across a table in an empty seminar room.

I asked him about his work with violent offenders, and the relationship between evidence photographs and the patients' descriptions of events.

"The photographs," he noted, "are absolutely static. In the mental images suggested by patients one can feel their movement – they are fluid, not fixed. The photographs are depleted. They never conform to the image that one has because the image is very different: it isn't a photograph."

***

It happened several times in my childhood: my father and I were walking in our neighborhood when he spotted a patient approaching from afar. Each time, he told me, with some urgency, to cross the street and walk on alone. Afterwards, he would catch me up at a trot, his pressed wool slacks flapping around his ankles, and we would continue on. Once I asked if the patient did not know that he had children. My father explained: it was much more important to know how the patients *imagined* his family. If they could see me, they wouldn't have to invent me. To become a good image, I had to remain invisible.

***

In London, I met with a psychiatrist, not as a patient, but to ask her some questions: an interview. Nonetheless, she seated me in the patient's chair and assumed her position in the consulting chair, halfway across the office. I observed her desk, her books, the abstract paintings and landscape posters on the wall.

I asked her to describe her patients' accounts of memories, events and dreams: were they cinematic or photographic; were they narratively or visually seductive?

"Rarely," she said.

What struck her most about her patients' imaginative lives was their unillustrated blankness. Often, the signal fact was the lack of images. She described one patient in particular who almost never generated images that she could visualize or discuss. "The patient," she said, "was almost like a ghost."

"Often," she said, "the patients' images are marked by absence rather than richness, bleakness rather than seduction. But absence," she cautioned, "is itself a kind of image."

***

Unlike the first Lacanian analyst I met with, the second one was not also, secretly, a photographer. But like her predecessor, she started by insisting that the image had no useful place in her clinical practice. This refusal began, subtly, in the email exchange preceding our meeting. She wrote: "I'm not sure if I'll be able to help you but we can talk." And from the moment I followed her through a narrow, elegant doorway into a tastefully appointed office, this point of view became more clear:

> Let me say straight away that it is very mysterious to me, your question, because as a Lacanian psychoanalyst, we work on words, so I don't have images in my mind forming when I speak to patients. I listen to the words. And I try to isolate series of logical terms that are related to each other. And I try to divorce them from the meaning that they think their story has to tell, and to find out what the meaning is that they don't know that their story has.

In her elaboration of this process, the image was, initially, the problem. An image, she insisted, "is a totality. It's constructed as a whole, and you can't interact with it in any way. It's there." Language offers a potential for freedom absent in the image, because a sentence, and even a word, can be taken apart and rearranged.

And this, I asked her, is not possible with an image? "Images," she insisted, "are scenarios; scenarios are screens; screens obfuscate."

And yet, somehow, despite this, and in fact, over and over again, the visual, and visualizations even, kept creeping in. Speaking of the dynamism that childhood memories gain once the psychoanalytic process has taken hold, she enthused:

> It's amazing, because when they're caught up with the experience of the analysis, those scenes take on different meanings and different interpretations, and you see different things at different times, from different perspectives and different angles.

Speaking of a patient: "At the moment I do visualize him putting on the character like an outfit. Because that's what he does; that's what I imagine him doing."

Despite this effusion, she persisted: "Every image is a screen. ... A screen that conceals the truth of your enjoyment ... the beautiful image is concealing a fairly banal and non-glamorous mode of enjoyment. The analyst ..." and here it was impossible not to think of the Wizard of Oz, "... had to take you behind the screen, behind the image."

"But," I too persisted, "this other reality, the hidden and less glamorous one, why is that not also an image?" She paused for a few seconds – what seemed, for her, an eternity without language. "Because it doesn't have a scenario. It's just an enjoyment, of seeing the other reduced to nothingness."

Of what she calls "the fantasmic representation of yourself" she explains, "as an analyst, our job is to break that down and to show what's behind that image."

I wonder, but do not ask: what is a show without an image?

The analyst gave another example of "what an image can conceal" but this one seemed to slip away from her. An artist-patient had talked about a traumatic event for a long time. But it was only once she discovered that she had, without intending to, represented the trauma in an artwork, that she could move on. "What is an image?" the analyst asked herself again. "It's not distinct from words. It exceeds words. It's more than words." Now, in the image, the trauma "was contained and framed, it was in its place" and the patient was free from it. "Some things can't be moved in language," she observed, "they are too heavy. I suppose an image, in that sense, is a way to do that."

Refocusing her eyes on me, she remarked, archly, in the way of people who feel they've been tricked, "well, it appears you have psychoanalyzed me!"

***

We met at seventeen, our first week of college: two teens imagining themselves artists. Decades later, we sit down in her Manhattan office to talk. Behind her head, centered above the psychoanalytic couch, hangs one of my photographs, carefully selected by her many years ago for this position. A dense color landscape image clogged with undergrowth, it deliberately frustrates the urge to focus, foreclosing the illusion of perspective. A picture of impenetrable space.

The interview begins, at first haltingly, and then more freely. Once, she tells me, she caught herself mis-imagining a patient's dream about her, and what she had seen, not heard, was important. As she vividly describes the two different pictures – the patient's and her own – I suddenly notice that the photograph above the couch has started to peel away from its support, the paper lifting free of the permanent adhesive to curl up ever so slightly at one corner. My image, in her office, had begun to come unstuck.

***

Recently, towards the end of an hour, I tell my therapist that I've been wondering about interviewing him.

He asks what I've been *wondering* and what I would want to ask?

Here I am careful to answer professionally, generally, as I always do as an interviewer: I would ask about the images he sees, in his mind, when talking to patients.

But he responds more pointedly: "Do you want to know about *my* images when talking with *you*?"

I freeze, in unanticipated panic, as if I had thought this question could pass undetected. I can feel a threshold being broken: the picture plane that I've imagined sliding out of my control. Finally, automatically, I answer: "I don't believe I want to know."

Suddenly, there is a secret animating the room. He looks right at me, then turns momentarily away. He says nothing. He has seen something, but he cannot find the words. The time is up. As I stand to leave, I cannot help but notice small tears forming at the edges of his eyes.

***

I was thirteen. We were in the middle of a typically fractious family dinner, when, for reasons now forgotten, I referred to the painting of the turtle above the couch in my father's office. A moment of silent confusion was followed by an eruption of laughter. That painting – a turtle? I attempted to explain what was to me so obvious: the red-brown shell, its green head and livid eye. But to the other five people at the table, initially too full of humiliating merriment to respond clearly, my delusion was extraordinary and evident. It was merely a mountainous landscape; the animal's "head" – a patch of green pasture. This truth was undeniable. I could no more reject their mountain than my turtle. The image was a shell and a vista.

***

In London, one psychoanalyst gave me a picture I don't want to shake. He said, the patient and I enter together into the scene, as if going with a child by the hand.

Index

Locators in *italics* refer to figures
Unqualified titles refer to films
Book titles have author name in brackets

A Space Odyssey 71
A Voice and Nothing More (Dolar) 91–2
A Voyage on the North Sea: Art in the Age of the Post-Medium Condition (Krauss) 109
Abstract Painting art installation 171
acousmatic sound: dybbuk myth 93–4, 97–8, 100; *With Jerzy Grotowski, Nienadówka* 38, 40–1, 42–5
acoustic space 185
acting out 25
active apperception 79, 188
actuality, and temporality 42
The Address of the Eye (Sobchack) 4
affective shifts 82, 83. *see also* emotions
Aileen: Life and Death of a Serial Killer 24, *29*, 33
Aileen Wuornos: The Selling of a Serial Killer 24, *29*
ambivalence, maternal 215
analogue formats 102. *see also* medium of film
analysis. *see* psychoanalytic perspectives
Anatomie de l'enfer [*Anatomy of Hell*] 11, 14, 16
anima/animus archetypes 61–6, 70
An-Sky, S. 95–9, 100
Answer to Job 71–2
Antigone (character in Sophocles' play) 118–19, 120–7

Antigone Interrupted (Honig) 119
apparatus 105, *106*
apperception 79, 85, 188
après coup (deferred action/memory) 23, 24–7, 30, 31, 33
Arcangel, Cory 159–69
archetype, mother 195, 203
Aronofsky, Darren 51–8
artistic image 200. *see also* images, cinematic
artistic inspiration 202, 204–5
Aspe, Bernard 63
atë (fate/destiny) 123–5
atheism, of feminine jouissance 139–40
attachments, in documentary film 22–3. *see also* transference love
'Attacks on Linking' (Bion) 103
aural reverberation, dybbuk myth 99
Australian International Documentary Conference 153
autistic behaviour/war autism 117, 118, 123. *see also Zero Dark Thirty*
autonomous complexes 202
awareness of death 94

Bacon, Francis 175–6, *177*
bad objects 103
Badiou, Alain 118, 125
Balázs, Béla 127
Balint, Enid 198

Index

Barker, Jennifer 14, 128
Barnavi, Élie 209
Barnouw, Erik 147, 148
Baron-Cohen, Simon 118
Barsam, Richard Meran 147
Barthes, Roland 44, 147, 162–3
Baudelaire, Charles 161
Baudry, J. L. 22
The Beatles 165
beauty: of nature 66–9; versus horror 126–7
Being and Time (Heideggger) 189
Belloc, Auguste 13
Benjamin, Jessica 51–8
Bergson, Henri 42
Between Darkness and Light (After William Blake) 161
Beyond the Pleasure Principle (Freud) 94
Bigelow, Kathryn 117, 126. *see also Zero Dark Thirty*
Bin Laden, Osama 117–18, 120, 124
binge-eating 85
Bion, Wilfred 103, 111–12, 113
Black Swan 51–8, 131–2, 134, 136–7, 139–45
blank screen approach 78
blog by Dr William Brown 117, 118
body film genre 27. *see also* embodiment
boundaries: crossing 53–4, 56; membranes 11
Bradshaw, Peter 60
Brakhage, Stan 152
Braunstein, Néstor 131
breast: Aileen Wuornos, radio mic placement on 27, 31, 33; infant relation to 103–4
Breillat, Catherine 11–18
'Breillat's Time' (Cooper) 11
Breton, Andre 166
Brin, Ruth 98
British Independent Tradition 172
broken mirror 197–9. *see also The Mirror*
The Bride Stripped Bare by Her Bachelors, Even art installation 171
Broomfield, Nick 24, 26–33, *28, 29*
Brown, Dr William, blog 117, 118
Buckingham, Matthew 102
Buñuel, Luis 16, 38

Burgin, Victor 166, 167
Burgoyne, Robert 122, 126–7
Burnt by the Sun 86–7, 88–9
Butler, Judith 2–3, 37, 119
Butor, Michel 209

Cahiers du Cinéma collective tests 149, 163
Campany, David 166
Camus, Albert 208
capitalism 3, 5, 61, 167
Carnal Thoughts: Embodiment and Moving Image Culture (Sobchack) 1
Carroll, Nöel 150
Carruthers, Susan L. 126
Cartwright, Lisa 174
Caruth, Cathy 31
Casar, Amira 17
case study, psychotherapy 84–90
Catherine Breillat: Indécence et pureté (Clouzot) 11
cellist, Anton Lukoszevieze 113, *114*
Chateaubriand, François-René 208
childhood trauma 23, 24–7, 29, 30, 31, 33
Christianity, *Black Swan* 136–40
cinema: emotional responses 77; intersubjective field 80; and psychotherapy 83–4; and video games 159–69. *see also* film
cinematic: heterotopia 166–7; memory 167, 168
Civilisation and its Discontents (Freud) 120
close ups 127
Clouzot, Claire 11
Collecting Visible Evidence (Cowie) 153
collective unconscious 201
commodification 5, 31
communication, in analytic settings 102–3. *see also* psychoanalysis; therapeutic relationship
compassion 99
complexes 89
conscious perception 188
container/contained 104, 112
control issues, *Black Swan* 53
Cooper, Sarah 11, 12
Cornell, Joseph 160
countertransference 78, 79, 88

Courbet, Gustave (artist) 12–14, 16, 17, 18
Cowie, Elizabeth 151, 153, 154
creative process 202, 204–5
Crouching Tiger 58
cut/cutting film 107, 110, 111, 112

de Certeau, Michel 43, 44
Dean, Tacita 102, 105
death 13; conquering 95; drive 94, 96, 97; jouissance of the body 144; penalty, Aileen Wuornos 28, 29, 33
Death 24x a Second: Stillness and the Moving Image (Mulvey) 15
Debray, Régis (pseudonym) 209
definitions: apperception 79; MacGuffin 192; sinthome 3
democratization of art 165
depressive position 105, 110
Derais, François 210
Derrida, Jacques 37, 40, 44, 109
desire: sublimation 126; unconscious 15; *The Wonder Ring* 152
Destructivism 168–9
Diasynchronoscope 183–92, *184*
diegesis 81, 82
disembodied sound. *see* acousmatic sound
disembodied spectatorship 38–9, 40–1. *see also* embodiment
Documentary: A History of the Non-Fiction Film (Barnouw) 148
documentary film 22–6; Broomfield's films 24, 26–33, *28, 29*; *With Jerzy Grotowski, Nienadówka* 36–48, *46, 47*; and psychoanalysis 147–54. *see also Zero Dark Thirty*
Documentary Now! conference, UK 153
Dolar, Mladen 41, 91–2, 93, 94
donkey analogy, paradox of the screen 183–5, 188, 190
Doppelgänger motif 189
Double Pane of Glass art installation 171
dream images 85, 191
Duchamp, Marcel 171
Duras, Marguerite 12
DVDs 163, 208
The Dybbuk: Between Two Worlds (play by An-Sky) 95–100
dybbuk myth 94–9, 100

ecologies, three 167
Écrits, The Function and Field of Speech and Language in Psychoanalysis (Lacan) 25
The Ed Sullivan Show 165
edit/editing 105, *106*, 107
11 Panes art installation 171
Embodied Encounters symposium 1
embodied encounters with psychoanalyst 25
embodiment, in cinema 2, 3, 4, 5, 81, 82; *Black Swan* 131; documentary film 43, 122, 128; emotional responses 77; Malick's films 60, 72; paradox of the screen 192; touch 5–6. *see also* jouissance of the body; skin
emotions 77; affective shifts 82, 83; documentary film 22; feeling function 61, 62, 64; love/hate/knowledge links 103
empathy 52, 117, 118, 127
Empire 164
Encore (Lacan) 131, 136
energy, psychological (libido) 85, 87–8, 90
environmental ecology 167
epistephilia 149–51, 154
Eros 13
eroticism, in art 6, 12, 13, 14
eternal feminine 13
ethics: of desire 117, 118–21; and morality 124, *125*
Ethics: an Essay on the Understanding of Evil (Badiou) 125
The Ethics of Psychoanalysis (Lacan) 173
Eve 13
execution, Aileen Wuornos 28, 29, 33
exhibition of film, Tate Modern, London 102
The Exorcist 161
exploitation, in documentary film 23
The Exploits of the Incomparable Mulla Nasrudin: (Shah) 183, 184, 188, 190

F-1 Racer (video game) 160, 164
face: and mirror 173, 174–7; and voice/hearing 43
fantasy: apperception 79; *Black Swan* 51, 58, 132–3; incest 201; omnipotence 111, 112, 198–9; other in 52–3, 57

230 Index

feeling function 61, 62, 64. *see also* emotions
feminine jouissance 139–43. *see also* jouissance of the body
feminist: perspectives 2, 3; stereotypes 51. *see also* woman
Fenichel, Otto 187
fetishism 12, 161, 173
film: criticism 208; exhibition 102; festivals 152–3; medium of 102–4, 107, 109–12; moving images 14, 15–16. *see also* cinema
Film Quarterly journal 51
fireball image, *Burnt by the Sun* 86–7, 88, 90
first image 80, 82–3
first-person: in novels 207–13; speech 36–48
Fisher, Tim 51
The Five Year Drive-By art installation 159, 162, 164, 165
Flaherty, Robert 23, 147
flashbacks 100
Foucault, Michel 166, 184
Fountain art installation 171
The Four Fundamental Concepts of Psycho-Analysis (Lacan) 151
4 Panes of Glass art installation 171
Fowler, Catherine 160, 168
Foxfire Eins 113, *114*
Freud, Sigmund/Freudian perspectives 4, 24, 93, 94, 120; *The Mirror* film 195, 196–7, 200; on music 91–2; psychoanalysis 207; on uncanny 94, 188–91
The Fright of Real Tears (Žižek) 173
frigidity 135
Frosh, Stephen 1
Fyfe, Joe 162

Gaffer artwork 189, *190*
gallery films 168
game culture 160. *see also* video games
gaze 41; of other 53; and voice 91–4; *Zero Dark Thirty* 123, 126. *see also* vision
gender: perspectives 2, 3; stereotypes 51. *see also* woman
Gender Trouble (Butler) 3

Gerhard Richter: Panorama 171
Ghost Dance 40
Ghosts 33
Gide, André 210
God, *Black Swan* 136–40
Godmilow, Jill 36–7, 38, 39, 45
goodness, unconscious motives for actions 120
Gordon, Douglas 159–69
grace, way of 66, 67
Grande Odalisque (painting) 12
Graph of Sexuation 141
Green, André 4
Greenacre, Phyllis 184
Greenwald, Glenn 117
Grotowski, Jerzy 36–48, *46*, *47*
Guattari, Felix 167
Gunning, Tom 162
gynaecological metaphors 64

H (hate) links, emotional experience 103
Hand Catching Lead 107, 109, 110, 113
haunting. *see* possession
hearing. *see* voice
Hedge art installation 171
Heffernan, Joanna 13
heimlich and *unheimlich* 189. *see also* uncanny
Hidden Dragon 58
Hillman, James 204
Hills, Matt 178
Hitchcock, Alfred 93–4, 160–1, 164
Hoberman, J. 161
Hockely, Luke 1
Honig, Bonnie 119
horror: movies 27; versus beauty, *Zero Dark Thirty* 126–7
HotDocs film festival, Toronto 152
Huyghe, Pierre 168

identification 51–8, 89
IDFA (International Documentary Film Festival), Sheffield 152
images: artistic 200; cinematic 84, 85, 100; mirror 171–8, *179*; psychoanalytic 86, 87, 88, 219–26
imaginary register 123, 174
immanence 140–3

In the Land of the Headhunter 147
incest fantasy 201
infant development 105. *see also* mother-infant relationship
Ingres, Jean-Auguste-Dominique (artist) 12, 17
inspiration, artistic 202, 204–5
integrated world capitalism 167
integration, and splitting 52
internal objects 103
interpretation: cinematic 80; psychoanalytical 78, 90
intersubjective field 77, 78–81
intrapsychic field 82
Irigaray, Luce 51
It's All True film festival, Latin America 153
Izod, John 1–2

Jacobs, Amber 51
Jacobs, Lewis 147
Janus faced images 84
Jenkins, David 60
Jentsch, E. 189
jouissance of the body 131–2; feminine 139–40; immanence 140–3; other 134; phallic 132–4; sexual 138–9; sinthome 143–4; theological perspectives 136–8; woman 134, 135–6
Joyce, James 3
Jung, C. G./Jungian perspectives 61, 65, 69, 71–3, 79, 81, 87; cinema 84; *The Mirror* film 195, 200–5; therapeutic dyad 77

K. 105–7, *108*, 110
K (knowledge) links, emotional experience 103
Kahana, Jonathan 40
Kant, Immanuel 113
Keesey, Douglas 12
Kennedy, Roger 24
Kevin talking about. *see We Need to Talk About Kevin*
Keysers, Christian 118
Kinnear, Rory 212
kino-eye (film-eye) metaphor 166
Klein, Melanie 102, 105, 110, 111

Krauss, Rosalind 103, 107, 109, 111, 113
Kristeva, Julia 151
Kubrick, Stanley 71

L (love) links, emotional experience 103
La Baigneuse de Valpinçon (painting) 17
La Maladie de la Mort (Duras) 12
La Modifi cation (Butor) 209
La Toilette de la Morte (painting) 13
Lacan, Jacques/Lacanian perspectives 2, 4, 12, 41; documentary film 22, 23; ethics of desire 117–21; four discourses 44, 151; gaze and the voice 91; jouissance of the body 131, 133, 137; language 30; mirror stage 3, 5, 92, 173, 174; *Nachträglichkeit* 23, 24–5, 27; visual documentary of psychoanalysis 224; and Winnicott 173–8. *see also* Seminars
Lacrimosa (music by Preisner) 71
Lagaay, Alice 41
Laine, Tarja 140
Land Without Bread 38
language: Bion 113; Derrida 41; Lacan 2, 25, 30; Yiddish 95
Laplanche, J. 4
The Large Glass art installation 171
Le Sommeil (painting) 13, 17
Lebeau, Vicky 1
Leroy, Thomas 131
L'Étranger (Camus) 208, 212
Lévinas, Emmanuel 118
Lewin, Kurt 78
libidinal economy of the phallus 132–3
libido 85, 87–8, 90
literary critics 207–8
literature, and psychoanalysis 207
logic: of sexuation 142, 143; of sublimity 141–2
L'Origine du monde (painting) 12–14, 16, 18
loss 162; maternal 194–205
love: epistephilia 149–51, 154; identificatory 53, 54, 55; thy neighbour 120
Luckhurst, Roger 100
Luepnitz, Deborah 178
Lukoszevieze, Anton 113, *114*

Macbeth (Shakespeare) 209
MacGuffin 184–5, 188; definition 192
male fantasy of the female 51, 58
Malick, Terrence 60–73
Manet, Édouard 12
Manovich, Lev 110–11
Mario Movie 160
masculine structure, *Black Swan* 132
masturbation, *Black Swan* 51, 54, 132, 138–9
maternal: ambivalence 215; loss 194–205; preoccupation 175–6
matter 104, *106*
McLuhan, Marshall 185, 187
MDMA (ecstasy) 137–8
meaning: cinema 80, 81, 84, 89; psychotherapy 78, 79–80
meditative practice 86, 191
medium of film 102–4, 107, 109–12
membranes, unconscious-conscious 11
memory, prosthetic 167, 168
mental ecology 167
Merleau-Ponty, Maurice 4, 5
metaphor: cinematic 79, 80, 82, 90; gynaecological 64; mirror 172–3, 198; mother 204; photo-eye/kino-eye 166; poisoned water 62
Metz, Christian 22, 147, 148, 161, 167, 173
mid-life transitions 65, 69
Miller, Jacques-Alain 134
Mirror art installation 171–2, 174, 177
mirror: images 171–8, *179*; metaphor 172–3; neurons 118; phase/stage 3, 5, 92, 195
The Mirror 194–5; broken mirror 197–9; Freudian mother 195, 196–7; Jungian mother 200–5
'Mirror-role of Mother and Family in Child Development' (Winnicott) 172
The Mirror Stage (Lacan, Jacques) 3, 5
moments of recognition, *Black Swan* 46
moral goal of psychoanalysis 126
morality, and ethics 124, *125*
mother archetype 195, 203
mother-infant relationship 103–4, 111–12, 174–7, 197–9
mother Russia 194, 203

moving images 14, 15–16, 18
Muellner, Nicholas 6, *179*
Mulvey, Laura 15–16, 18, 22, 163, 213
music: cellist Lukoszevieze 113, *114*; Freud on 91–2; *Parsifal Prelude* by Wagner 62, 69
mutual recognition, *Black Swan* 51–8
mutuality 14, 16
mysticism, *Black Swan* 136–8, 140, 142

Nachträglichkeit (deferred action/memory of trauma 23, 24–7, 30, 31, 33
narcissistic energy 85, 87–8, 90
nature, beauty of 66, 67, 68–9
neuroscientific perspectives 5
New Left Review 3
Nichols, Bill 148–9
Night and Fog 31
9/11 terrorist attack 122
non-rational understanding, films 84–90
non-verbal communication, analytic setting 102–3
not giving up on one's desire 117, 118, 118–21

object relations 102, 103
objectivity, documentary film 22, 40
Obscure Window (photograph) 6, *179*
Oehring, Helmut 113, *114*
Olympia (painting) 12
The Omen 212
omnipotence phantasy 111, 112, 198–9
'One, Two, Three…' artwork *186*
ontotheological perspectives, *Black Swan* 136
open-source software 165
operations 110–11
Ortiz, Raphael Montanez 168–9
other: in fantasy and reality 52–3, 57; jouissance of the body 134, 136–40, 143–4

Panorama: *Gerhard Richter* 171
paradox of the screen 183–92, *184*, *186*, *190*
paranoid-schizoid position 105
Parker, Jayne 102–12, *106*, *108*, *113*
Parsifal Prelude (music by Wagner) 62, 69

passive apperception 79, 188
passivity 17–18. *see also* stillness
penis envy 2
perception 79, 85, 188
persona orientation 65
phallic jouissance, *Black Swan* 132–4, 136, 138–9
phantasy, omnipotence 111, 112, 198–9. *see also* fantasy
phenomenological approach to cinema 4
philanthropy 120
Phillips, Adam 178
'The Philosophy of Toys' (Baudelaire) 161
photo-eye and kino-eye metaphor 166
photography 13, 219, 224; *Obscure Window* 6, *179*
Piotrowska, Agnieszka 2, 153–4
Poem by a Ram to God (Brin) 98
poetics, of maternal loss 194–205
poisoned water metaphor, *To the Wonder* 62
political perspectives 3, 5
Pollock, Jackson 109
Pornocratie (Breillat) 11
pornography film genre 12, 13, 27
possession: cinematic 168; dybbuk myth 94–9, 100; *The Exorcist* 161
post mortem dissection 13
Post-Theory (Carroll) 150
power structures/issues 3, 53
pre-verbal stage, infant development 105
Preisner, Zbigniew 71
primary maternal preoccupation 175–6
process 104–5, *106*, 109
projection 89, 104; other 52
projective identification 102, 103, 111
prosthetic memory 167, 168
proximity senses 92–3
Psycho 93–4, 160–1, 164
psychoanalytic perspectives 77; case study 84–90; and cinema 83–4; documentary film 22–5, 27, 147–54, 219–26; embodied encounters 25; film theory 2, 3, 4, 5, 15, 84–90; intersubjective field 78–9; and literature 207; talking cures 25, 26; third image 77, 79–84
Psychoanalysis, History and Subjectivity (Kennedy) 24

Psychogenic Disturbance of Vision (Freud) 93
psychological: energy (libido) 85, 87–8, 90; field 79
Psychological Types (Jung) 200
psychosis: *Black Swan* 143–4

radio mic, placement on bra of Aileen Wuornos 27, 31, 33
Ramsay, Lynne 212
Rascaroli, Laura 37
real register 123, 128
realism, artistic 13
reality: other in 52–3, 57; and unreality 188–90
Rear Window 168
recognition: moments of 46; mutual 51–8
Recording Reality, Desiring the Real (Cowie) 153
Rees, A. L. 107
Reichbart, Richard 187
Reilly, John C. 213
religion, *Black Swan* 136–40
Remake 168
remodelling 24
René (Chateaubriand) 208
repetition, and deferred effect of trauma 24
Representing Reality (Nichols) 148–9
repression 24, 61, 82, 83
resistance of the viewer 154
response 118
revolution 3
Reymond, François 210
Richter, Gerhard 171–2, 174, 177
Roland Barthes by Roland Barthes 44
Romance 15
Romance X 16, 17
Rose Hobart 160

Safran, Gabriella 95
Savatier, Thierry 13
Scorsese, Martin 161
screen, paradox of 183–92, *184*, *186*, *190*
Screen journal 3
screen memory 183, 184, 185, 187, 191
sculpture 107, 109
The Searchers 159–60, 161
second image 80, 83

second person, in novels 207–13
seduction 85–6
self: and face 175; orientation 65; reflection 68, 79
self-portrait films 36–48
Seminars (Lacan) 43; *VII* 117, 118, 126; *XI* 5; *XX* 2; *XXIII* 3
sensory, meeting with unconscious 11, 12, 14, 16, 17, 30. *see also* embodiment
separation. *see* loss
Serra, Richard 103, 107, 109, 110, 113
sexist stereotypes 51. *see also* gender
sexual desire. *see* desire
sexual jouissance of the body 136, 138–9
Shah, Idries 183, 184, 188, 190
Shakespeare, William 209
shamanism 168–9
Shklovsky, Viktor 166
Shriver, Lionel 207–16
Siffredi, Rocco 16–17
sight. *see* gaze; vision
sign and symbol, Jungian perspectives 200–1
sinthome 3, 141, 143–4
6 Panes of Glass in a Rack art installation 171
skin 11, 15; eroticism 13, 14; touch of fabric 17. *see also* embodiment
Sleep 164
Sobchack, Vivian 1, 4
social ecology 167
The Song of Bernadette 161
Song of Songs, Biblical poem 96
Sophocles 118–19, 123
sound environment, womb 93. *see also* voice
A Space Odyssey 71
speaking in tongues 67
spectatorship 15; *Diasynchronoscope* 185; disembodied 38–9, 40–1; documentary film 22, 24, 32
speech, first-person 36–48, 207–13. *see also* language
splitting 52, 105, 110, 111;
stasis films 163–4. *see also* stillness
Steigler, Bernard 167
Stein, Murray 65
Steiner, John 92

stereotypes, sexist 51. *see also* gender
stillness 15–16 contrast moving image, 17–18, 163; stasis films 163–4
straw analogy, paradox of the screen 183–5, 188, 191
structuralism 109, 128, 147
The Subject of Documentary (Renov) 148, 151
subjectivity, in documentary film 148
sublimation, of sexual desire 126
sublime jouissance of the body 140–3, 144
subliminal qualities, cinema 15, 82
Super Mario Brothers (video game) 159–60, 161
Super Mario Clouds art installation 159, 162, 164
Super-slow Tetris 164
surrealism 166, 191
suture 81
Swan Lake ballet 51, 57, 58, 131, 132
Swinton, Tilda 212–13
symbolic register 123
symbols, Jungian perspectives 200–1
symposium *Embodied Encounters* 1
synchronicity 88

The Tactile Eye (Barker) 14, 128
talking cures 25, 26
Tamkin, David and Alex 97
Tarkovsky, Andrei 194–7, 200, 202–5
Taxi Driver 161
temporality, documentary film 40, 42
Terekhova, Margarita 197
Teresa of Ávila 137
testimonial voice 40
testimony, giving 22
Thanatos 13. *see also* death
Thelma and Louise 58
theological perspectives, *Black Swan* 136–40
therapeutic relationship 77–9, 85
therapy. *see* psychoanalytic perspectives
third: image 77, 81, 83; person, in novels 207–13
'The Third Meaning' (Barthes) 162–3
Through the Looking Glass 161
time: and death 25–6; documentary film 40, 42

tired by the sun 87, 90
To the Wonder 60–7, 69, 73
torture, *Zero Dark Thirty* 118, 122–3, 127
touch 5–6, 14–17. *see also* embodiment; skin
transcendence 137–8, 140
transference 78, 79
transference love: documentary film 23, 153–4; with psychoanalyst 25
transgenerational haunting, dybbuk myth 99
transitional objects 198–9
trauma, childhood 23, 24–7, 29, 30, 31, 33
The Tree of Life 60–1, 63, 65, 68, 69, 70, 71–2, 73
True/False film festival, Columbia, Missouri 152–3
truth, in documentary film 22, 40
24 Hour Psycho 160–1, 164
Tykka, Salla 168

uncanny 5, 15, 42, 188–91; acousmatic sound 40–1, 94, 97–8; blurring of the line between reality and unreality 188–90, *190*
The Uncanny (Freud) 94
unconscious mind 4, 6, 11, 15; collective 201; and conscious perception 188; in documentary film 24; first image 80; integration into consciousness 82; Jungian perspectives 81, 82; neuroscientific perspectives 5; paradox of the screen 191; repression 82, 83; and sensory 11, 12, 14; *To the Wonder* 63; *Zero Dark Thirty* 119, 120, 126, 127–8
unheimlich 189. *see also* uncanny
universe, birth 71
unknowable/unspoken/unspeakable/un-measurable 5
Untitled (After Lucier) art installation 165

Vache, Jacques 166
ventriloquism 40–1, 48, 94
Verb List, Richard Serra 107, 110
Vertigo 168
video games 159–69
viewer-screen relationship 77

violence, *Zero Dark Thirty* 118, 122–3, 127
Visible Evidence conference, Stockholm 153
The Visible and the Invisible (Merleau-Ponty) 5
vision: psychoanalytic focus 91–4, 100; and voice 91–4. *see also* gaze
visual documentary of psychoanalysis 219–26
visual space 185
A Voice and Nothing More (Dolar) 91–2
voice: and gaze/sight 43, 91–4; testimonial 40
voicing 42
A Voyage on the North Sea: Art in the Age of the Post-Medium Condition (Krauss) 109
voyeurism 31. *see also* spectatorship
vulva, representation in film 11, 13, 16

Wagner, Richard 62, 69
Walker, Steven 200
war autism 117, 118, 123. *see also Zero Dark Thirty*
Warhol, Andy 163, 164, 165
way: of grace 66, 67; of nature 66, 67, 68–9
We Need to Talk About Kevin (Shriver) 207–16
whole-body experience, cinema 81. *see also* embodiment
Williams, Linda 27
Wilson, Emma 1
Winnicott, D.W. 52, 171–8, 197–9
With Jerzy Grotowski, Nienadówka 36–48, *46, 47*;
witnessing, dybbuk myth 99
woman: jouissance of the body 134, 135–6, 137, 143; representation in art/film 11, 12, 13, 16. *see also* gender
womb, sound environment 93
The Wonder Ring 152
Wright, Kenneth 173, 198

Yamagata International Film Festival, Asia 153
Yellow-green art installation 171

Yiddish language 95
Young Mr. Lincoln: *Cahiers du Cinema* collective texts 149
YouTube videos 165

Zero Dark Thirty 117–18, 127–8; Antigone and Maya 121–5; atë 123–5; beauty versus horror 126–7; ethics of desire 118–21; war autism 117, 118
Žižek, Slavoj 40, 94, 117, 124, *125*, 134, 138, 141–3, 173
Zoo 168

Printed in Great Britain
by Amazon